studysync®

TEACHER'S EDITION

Suspense!

GRADE 8 | UNIT 1

studysync

studysync.com

Send all inquiries to:
BookheadEd Learning, LLC
610 Daniel Young Drive
Sonoma, CA 95476

2 3 4 5 6 7 QVS 21 20 19 18 17
B

studysync®

GRADE 8 UNITS

Suspense!

UNIT 1

Overview • Pacing Guide • Instructional Path
Extended Writing Project • Research • Full-Text Study

In Time of War

UNIT 2

Overview • Pacing Guide • Instructional Path
Extended Writing Project • Research • Full-Text Study

A Moral Compass

UNIT 3

Overview • Pacing Guide • Instructional Path
Extended Writing Project • Research • Full-Text Study

The Civil War

UNIT 4

Overview • Pacing Guide • Instructional Path
Extended Writing Project • Research • Full-Text Study

Welcome to StudySync

StudySync's comprehensive English Language Arts program for Grades 6–12 is a hybrid print and digital ELA solution. The program leverages cutting edge technology to create an engaging, relevant student and teacher experience. StudySync's multimedia content is available 24/7 from any desktop, tablet, or mobile device. In addition, the program's print resources allow for flexible, blended implementation models that fit the needs of every classroom.

StudySync's Core ELA curriculum was built from the ground up to fully align with the Common Core State Standards for English Language Arts. StudySync provides standards-based instruction that teachers can easily customize, scaffold, and differentiate to ensure all students are ready for college, career, and civic life in the twenty-first century.

STUDYSYNC TEACHER'S EDITION

The StudySync Teacher's Edition is designed to help you understand, pace, plan, and deliver the StudySync Core ELA curriculum to your students. In this **Teacher's Edition** you will find:

1 A list of StudySync Materials available in both your digital teacher account and this print Teacher's Edition.

2 A guide to StudySync's Core ELA Curriculum and additional content.

3 An overview of StudySync Teacher Tools and ideas and inspirations to help you get started today.

4 Resources for each Core ELA Unit in your grade:

Unit Overviews A big picture look at the key texts and skills.

Pacing Guides A day-to-day plan for integrating all Unit content from the Instructional Path, Extended Writing Project, Research, and Full-text Study with hints for reteaching and shortcuts.

Instructional Path Detailed Lesson Plans for each First Read, Skill, Close Read, and Blast.

Extended Writing Project Detailed Lesson Plans for each Extended Writing Project.

Research A teacher's guide to delivering the Research Project.

Full-text Study A Full-text Reading Guide with key passage explications, vocabulary, discussion and close reading questions.

Teacher's Edition

DESIGNED FOR TODAY'S CLASSROOMS

StudySync combines the best of print and digital resources to meet you where you are and take you where you want to be—allowing low-tech and high-tech classrooms to take full advantage of StudySync's **rigor, relevance,** and **flexibility.**

RIGOR AND RELEVANCE

StudySync engages students in a learning experience that reflects the ways they experience the world by providing multiple opportunities for collaboration, social interaction, and exposure to rich media and thousands of classic and contemporary texts.

In addition, StudySync challenges students and helps them meet rigorous academic expectations with:

- Access to diverse characters and points of view with an expansive digital library, searchable by grade level and Lexile®-level.

- Close reading instruction with various levels of text complexity.

- In-depth studies of canonical and contemporary texts, representing all genres including literary and informational.

- Multiple opportunities for developing foundational language and literacy skills, all while building content knowledge and helping students make meaning.

- Practice and application of analytical writing to sources, with prompts and rubrics tied to the CCSS.

FLEXIBILITY

PRINT AND DIGITAL OPTIONS

Whichever format is right for your classroom—digital, print, or a combination of both, StudySync provides a successful learning experience for all students.

In addition to this Teacher's Edition, a *Student Reading and Writing Companion* is also available to allow students to complete assignments on or off line. This consumable student handbook gives students printed access to all readings in a Core ELA Unit's instructional path, including First Reads, text-dependent Think questions, Skills lessons, Close Reads, and writing prompts. The purpose of the student print support is to provide students with close reading opportunities so that they may continue through the course successfully even without daily access to digital. *Please see page xi for a full overview of all StudySync materials available in both print and digital formats.*

MULTIPLE IMPLEMENTATION MODELS

Whether you are using blended instruction, a flipped classroom, or a traditional format, StudySync provides the flexibility to meet your instructional needs. For example, you can:

- Use print options in conjunction with a projector to engage students in a whole-class discussion regarding a text, an assignment, or a StudySync® TV video.

- Have students work in pairs, small groups, or individually to read, annotate, and answer Think Questions. Students can work on a single computer on shared devices; alternatively, they can annotate directly in their student workbooks.

- Schedule time in computer labs for students to bring their Reading & Writing Companions and submit writing online and complete peer reviews.

Specific examples of using StudySync for whole-group, small-group, and individual instruction are provided on page *xxxi* of this guide.

TIPS TO DIFFERENTIATE

Classrooms have a mix of interests, learning styles, and skill levels. Integrating technology makes it easier for teachers to better differentiate and personalize instruction without substantially adding to their workload.

StudySync allows teachers to customize their lessons and to

- Scaffold assignments based on students' interests and reading abilities
- Make assignments and choose texts based on Lexile®-levels
- Access an extensive library of 6–12 content, texts, and excerpts
- Target specific learning objectives, skills, and Common Core Standards
- Tailor instruction to whole-class, small group, or individual needs
- Offer access support—including audio support, closed-captioning, and vocabulary support

CUSTOMIZING YOUR CURRICULUM

With StudySync, you can build the kind of program you've always wanted to teach.
You have the ability to

- Assign a Library text with the existing prompt or write your own
- Modify assignments for differentiated learning levels
- Access Skills Lessons separately from the Units and assign as stand-alone lessons, or pair with another text of your choosing
- Customize assessments by creating your own rubrics and peer review prompts

Leverage StudySync's online platform and peer review system with **your own content** by

- Creating your own writing assignments
- Adding your own Library items to your account, including images and videos

COLLABORATION AMONG TEACHERS

StudySync facilitates collaboration by allowing you to share teacher-created content, rubrics, modified assignments, and new library items with other educators in your subscription. Have a rubric used specifically by your district? Have an assignment that every English teacher in your department will be utilizing? These only need to be created once, helping teachers to save time and to focus on working together.

SUCCESS FOR ALL LEARNERS

StudySync supports students every step of the way. Students experience a seamless online experience for reading and writing, submitting assignments, and writing and receiving reviews with tools that encourage close reading and critical thinking. Students access their assignments and then can view completed work and reviews received in their own online "binder."

Support for All Levels of Learners

- Grade and Lexile®-leveled filters for Digital Library of texts
- Access Path for EL support
- Differentiated learning tools including customizable groups, prompts, and rubrics
- Print materials for work offline

Online Learning Tools

- Collaborative learning platform with online student binders and social learning network
- Online teacher and anonymous peer review platform
- Online test practice similar to PARCC, Smarter Balanced, and other high-stakes test formats

Audio/Visual Resources

- Audio narration of text
- Audio text highlight option
- Online annotation tool
- Closed-Captioning of video resources
- Engaging StudySync® TV & SkillsTV videos

Teacher's Edition

PROFESSIONAL DEVELOPMENT

StudySync's Professional Development is on target and ongoing. Our Professional Development Platform in ConnectED and the Teacher Homepage tab within StudySync provide online learning resources that support classroom implementation and instruction and connect explicitly to the standards. All audiovisual, multimedia, and technology resources include suggestions for appropriate implementation and use.

The **Professional Development course** provides an extensive overview of StudySync as well as support for implementing key instructional strategies in the English Language Arts classroom. The **Teacher Homepage** provides access to digital resources and up-to-date articles on "What's New," with StudySync features and content, plus "Ideas and Inspirations," with tips from featured StudySync users and the StudySync Curriculum team.

Review the Professional Development guides and videos within the StudySync Professional Development Implementation course in your ConnectED account and the content on your Teacher Homepage. Then turn to StudySync's Getting Started Guide to begin!

Teacher's Edition

STUDYSYNC MATERIALS

	Digital Teacher Account	Print Teacher's Edition	Digital Student Account	Student Reading & Writing Companion
Scope and Sequences	●			
Grade Level Overviews	●			
Core ELA Unit Overviews	●	●		
Core ELA Unit Pacing Guides	●	●		
Complete Lesson Plans	●	●		
Core Handouts	●			
Access Handouts	●			
Text Selections and Lessons	●		●	●
Reading Skill Lessons	●		●	
Blast Lessons	●		●	
Extended Writing Project Lessons	●		●	●
Writing Skill Lessons	●		●	●
Research Project Guide	●	●		
Full-text Reading Guide	●	●		
End-of-Unit & End-of-Course Digital Assessments	●		●	
Printable Assessments	●			

Copyright © BookheadEd Learning, LLC

SYNCSTART

SyncStart is a 10-day unit for each grade level that introduces students and teachers to the instructional routines that figure prominently in StudySync. **SyncStart units feature:**

Explicit instruction on annotation, reading comprehension, and vocabulary strategies that students will use on a daily basis in StudySync.

Dedicated time and instruction to help teachers establish a consistent classroom culture of collaborative conversations and peer review.

Extra lesson plan features that help teachers understand how and why StudySync's instructional routines will work in their classroom.

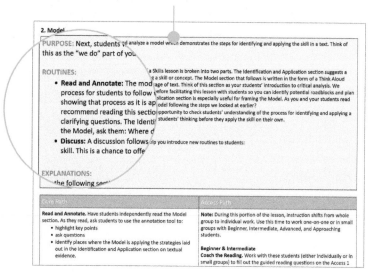

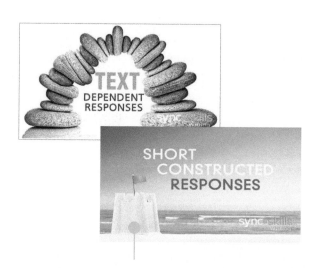

Writing instruction that models the text-dependent and short constructed responses students will regularly compose in the Core ELA program.

Teacher's Edition

CORE ELA UNITS

StudySync's Core ELA curriculum consists of 4 **Core ELA Units** per grade. Each unit covers 45 days of instruction for a total of 180 days of instruction at each grade. A complete **Scope and Sequence** outlines standards coverage for each grade, and **Grade Level Overviews** provide teachers a more in-depth look at the reading and writing instruction in each unit. **Pacing Guides** offer detailed 45-day plans for delivering each unit's content.

Each Core ELA Unit is organized around a unique theme and driving question that challenges students to examine texts through an engaging, challenging lens. Each unit contains five key components:

1. Overview

2. Instructional Path

3. Extended Writing Project

4. Research

5. Full-text Study

OVERVIEW

The Overview of each Core ELA Unit provides a video preview and an introduction to the unit. The Overview also contains lists of readings, key Skills, standards, and other important general information about the unit.

PACING GUIDE

Pacing Guides provide a 45-day plan with day-to-day guidance for implementing each Core ELA Unit. They outline when and how to incorporate instruction from the Instructional Path, Extended Writing Project, Research Project, and Full-text Study. An additional Pacing Guide column helps teachers draw connections between the Full-text Study and the shorter text selections in the Instructional Path.

Pacing Guides also offer ideas for substituting lessons, revisiting difficult concepts, creating multidisciplinary strands of instruction, and designing independent reading programs. These guides show teachers how to bring StudySync's wealth of resources together to create dynamic, engaging learning environments for their students.

DAY	INSTRUCTIONAL PATH	EXTENDED WRITING PROJECT	RESEARCH PROJECT	FULL-TEXT STUDY	CONNECTING FULL-TEXT STUDY TO THEMATIC UNIT INSTRUCTIONAL PATH LESSONS
23	**SKILL** Media			*Harriet Tubman: Conductor on the Underground Railroad* Chapter 5 "Flight" **COMPARE** to *Old Plantation Days*	
24	**CLOSE READ** *Harriet Tubman: Conductor on the Underground Railroad*	**EXTENDED WRITING PROJECT** Literary Analysis		*Harriet Tubman: Conductor on the Underground Railroad* Chapter 6 "The Underground Road"	
25	**FIRST READ:** *The People Could Fly: American Black Folktales*			*Harriet Tubman: Conductor on the Underground Railroad* Chapter 7 "'Shuck this Corn'"	**LINK** to *Harriet Tubman: Conductor on the Underground Railroad* – Ask students to consider the premise of the folktale and discuss why the ability to fly like a bird would be so attractive to African American slaves. In what way does Harriet Tubman help slaves to "fly"?
26	**SKILL** Compare and Contrast	**EXTENDED WRITING PROJECT** Prewrite		*Harriet Tubman: Conductor on the Underground Railroad* Chapter 8 "Mint A Becomes Harriet"	
27	**CLOSE READ** *The People Could Fly: American Black Folktales*	**SKILL** Thesis Statement		*Harriet Tubman: Conductor on the Underground Railroad* Chapter 9 "The Patchwork Quilt"	**LINK** to *Harriet Tubman: Conductor on the Underground Railroad* – How does Harriet Tubman's marriage to John Tubman keep her a "caged bird"? How is this ironic given John's status?

INSTRUCTIONAL PATH

The Instructional Path of each Core ELA Unit contains ten to twelve texts and/or text excerpts from a variety of genres and text types. Program authors, Douglas Fisher, Ph.D., and Timothy Shanahan, Ph.D., developed the instructional routines around these texts to support best practices in reading instruction.

Instruction around texts begins with a First Read lesson. First Read Lesson Plans include think alouds to help teachers model key vocabulary and comprehension skills for students before they read. Students read and annotate texts using either their digital accounts or their print Student Reading and Writing Companions, and First Read lessons conclude with a series of text-dependent Think questions that challenge students to provide textual evidence to support their understanding of the text.

At least three First Reads in every unit also include a StudySync® TV episode, one of the hallmarks of the program. Lessons with StudySync® TV contain additional metacognitive questions in which students reexamine short clips from the video to analyze how students in the model discussion construct meaning and express themselves effectively using academic vocabulary and discussion skills.

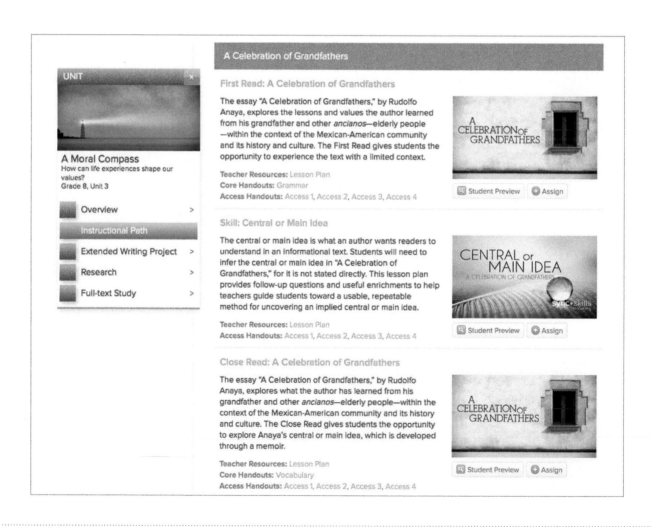

Teacher's Edition

Reading Skill lessons follow First Reads, and apply the Gradual Release of Responsibility Model to deliver explicit instruction that helps students master key skills and reading strategies. Over the course of a unit, students will complete two to three of these lessons each week, offering teachers many opportunities to formatively assess student mastery and growth.

Close Read lessons culminate the instructional reading routine. Close Read lessons begin with an emphasis on vocabulary instruction as students refine or confirm their analyses of vocabulary from the First Read. Close Read lessons then challenge students to apply skills and reading strategies as they reread and annotate the text in preparation for writing their own short-constructed responses.

StudySync Blasts, the fourth lesson type found in the Instructional Path, typify the program's commitment to creating an engaging, twenty-first century context for learning. Each Blast is a short reading and writing lesson with its own research topic and driving question to which students respond in 140 characters or less.

Every assignment in the Instructional Path includes an in-depth Lesson Plan, available to teachers in their digital teacher account and this print Teacher's Edition, with both a Core Path and an Access Path of instruction. The Core Path contains the regular instructional routines that guide students toward mastery. Many lessons also contain Core Handouts—Grammar mini-lessons, Graphic Organizers, Vocabulary quizzes, or Student Writing Models.

The Access Path of each Lesson Plan contains guidance for using the Access Handouts to scaffold and differentiate instruction to insure equity and access for all students. Access Handouts provide a range of important scaffolds for English Learners and Approaching grade-level readers.

Beginner EL → Access 1 Handout
Intermediate EL → Access 2 Handout
Advanced EL → Access 3 Handout
Approaching grade-level → Access 4 Handout

EXTENDED WRITING PROJECT

Writing is an integral part of StudySync's Core ELA curriculum. The curriculum features comprehensive instruction in narrative, informative/explanatory, and argumentative writing forms, and in a wide variety of modes, including full-length essays and narratives, short constructed responses, peer reviews, Blasts, and the digital annotations of texts.

Each unit contains an Extended Writing Project (EWP) that focuses on one of the three primary writing forms and is woven into the instructional fabric of the unit. By the end of the year, each student generates a full-length narrative, informative/explanatory essay, literary analysis (in argumentative form), and an argumentative essay.

Numerous writing Skill lessons in each EWP provide instruction on skills essential to every form. EWP lessons contain Lesson Plans, Core Handouts, and Access Handouts that follow the same conventions as lessons in the Instructional Path.

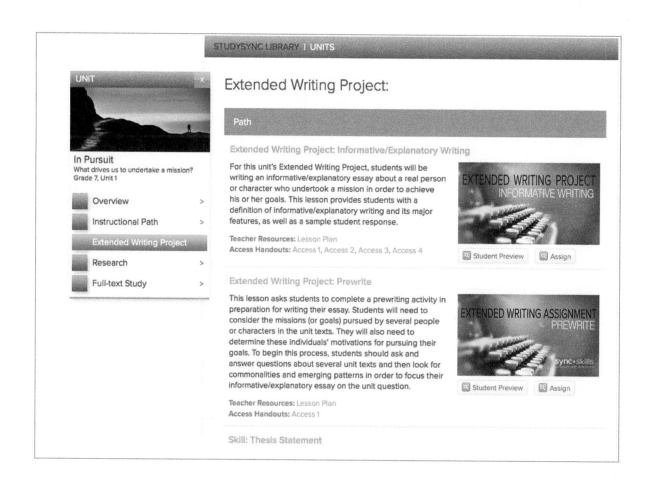

Teacher's Edition

RESEARCH

In addition to the short research students complete in Blast assignments, each Core ELA Unit also contains an in-depth research project in which students explore a new angle of the unit's theme and driving question. This research project is fully integrated into the Pacing Guide, and builds on and complements the unit's key skills. Research projects deepen content knowledge, allow students to read more widely, and offer students the opportunity to present their claims and findings in a variety of formats that address key speaking and listening standards.

CORE ELA | UNITS

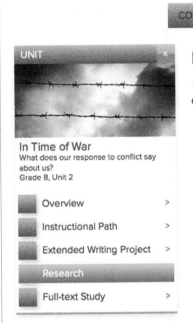

UNIT x

In Time of War
What does our response to conflict say about us?
Grade 8, Unit 2

Overview	>
Instructional Path	>
Extended Writing Project	>
Research	
Full-text Study	>

Research

OBJECTIVES

1. Complete topic-specific group research projects connected to the unit theme and essential question.
2. Participate effectively in a range of conversations and collaborations to express ideas and build upon the ideas of others.
3. Practice and apply research strategies to produce a narrative presentation with multimedia features.
4. Practice, apply, and reinforce the following Grade 8 ELA Common Core Standards for reading literature and informational texts, writing explanatory pieces, conducting research projects, and speaking and listening:

   Reading: Literature - RL.8.1, RL.8.2, RL.8.3, RL.8.4, RL.8.6, RL.8.7, RL.8.10
   Reading Informational Text - RI.8.1, RI.8.2, RI.8.3, RI.8.4, RI.8.5, RI.8.6, RI.8.7, RI.8.8, RI.8.9, RI.8.10
   Writing - W.8.1.A, W.8.1.B, W.8.1.C, W.8.1.D, W.8.1.E, W.8.3.A, W.8.3.B, W.8.3.C, W.8.3.D, W.8.3.E, W.8.4, W.8.5, W.8.6, W.8.7, W.8.8, W.8.9, W.8.10
   Speaking and Listening - SL.8.1, SL.8.2, SL.8.4, SL.8.5, SL.8.6
   Language - L.8.1, L.8.2, L.8.3, L.8.4, L.8.5, L.8.6

TIME
140 minutes (research and presentations)

MATERIALS
Library, online resources, links to topics
StudySync Speaking & Listening Handbook

OVERVIEW
In order to better understand human responses to conflict, students will research a particular person or group of people affected by World War II. Students will explore various mediums, including diaries, letters, speeches, interviews, informational videos, historic articles, contemporary analyses, reference book entries, and images, in order to gather information about the experience of their chosen person or group.

Each Core ELA Unit contains an anchor text. An excerpt of this anchor text is included alongside other literature and informational texts in the Instructional Path. This anchor text is the recommended Full-text Study for the unit and the Pacing Guide for each unit provides teachers a recommended schedule for reading this text alongside the excerpts in the Instructional Path. The Pacing Guide also contains helpful hints to help teachers make direct connections between sections of the anchor text and lessons from the Core ELA Unit.

The Full-text Study Reading Guide supports the close reading of the complete anchor text. Reading guide lessons preview key vocabulary words and include close reading questions. Each Full-text Study Reading Guide section identifies a key passage that will help teachers guide students through an exploration of the essential ideas, events, and character development in the anchor text. This passage will also serve as the jumping off point from which students will engage in their own StudySync® TV-style group discussion.

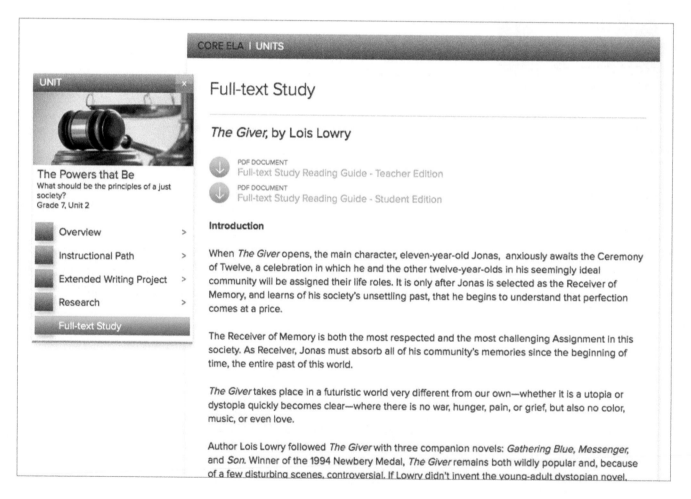

ASSESSMENT

FORMATIVE ASSESSMENT

StudySync supports all forms of assessment. Teachers provide feedback on student writing, using either the ready-made Common Core-aligned rubrics in the program or their own customized rubrics created in StudySync. Lesson plans point teachers toward formative assessment opportunities. Students self-assess and peer-review regularly. First Reads, Skills, Close Reads, and Extended Writing Project process steps offer medium cycle formative assessment opportunities for students and teachers to chart progress toward key learning outcomes.

ANONYMOUS PEER REVIEW

Teachers can use peer review to initiate a cycle of analyzing, writing, and revising that turns students into skilled writers and critical thinkers.

Students learn to
- Respond frequently and meaningfully to the texts they are reading
- Engage in multiple forms of writing, including expository, narrative, and persuasive
- Provide timely, anonymous critiques of other students' writing
- Thoughtfully analyze and revise their work
- Write to an authentic audience they know will be reading their work immediately

StudySync capitalizes on the collective intelligence in a classroom by leveraging the valuable voices of students in the learning process. The anonymous peer review feedback helps students take an active role in supporting each other in the development of their skill sets. Peer review is not anonymous for teachers. They have a window into all student work in order to mediate the process and provide appropriate direction and support.

SUMMATIVE ASSESSMENT

In addition to the formative assessment opportunities embedded throughout StudySync, each Core ELA Unit includes an end-of-unit summative assessment and each grade level includes an end-of-course assessment. These unit and end-of-course tests are located in the Online Assessment tool in the ConnectED account. They can be delivered digitally or in print. They offer robust reporting options, including tracking student proficiency with the Common Core State Standards. This assessment format provides important practice for online standardized tests for students.

ADDITIONAL CONTENT

To go along with the Core ELA curriculum, StudySync continually provides new and additional content that allows teachers to easily customize and differentiate curriculum. The Library, Blasts, Skills, Full-text and other units, and other additional resources provide teachers thousands of extra lessons to go along with the Core ELA curriculum and make StudySync a dynamic, twenty-first century content solution in their classrooms.

LIBRARY

The extensive StudySync digital library consists of more than 1,000 texts and excerpts with supporting digital tools and lesson materials for close reading and critical writing assignments.

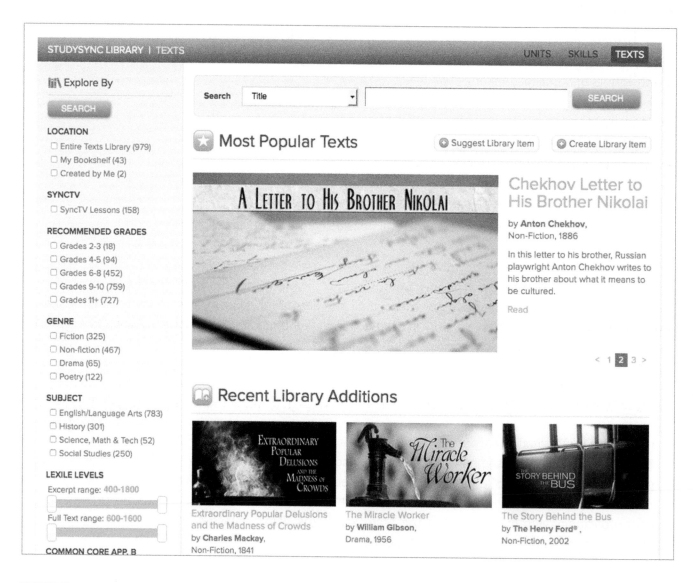

 Teacher's Edition

The StudySync Library is an ever-expanding resource that grows to fit the needs of all teachers. Looking for a passage of Twain's non-fiction to teach alongside *The Adventures of Huckleberry Finn*? Want to provide your students background on the political turmoil in the United States during the 1960s? Need a place to send students as a jumping off point for their own literary explorations? The StudySync Library is your answer.

To facilitate easy searching, in addition to title, author, keyword, topic, and genre searches, all texts in the Library can also be sorted by

- Lexile®-level
- Genre
- Common Core Appendix B exemplars
- StudySync® TV Library items
- Publication date

Every Library selection includes

- Professional audio recordings to support readers of all levels and develop speaking and listening skills
- Online annotation and highlighting
- Common Core-aligned writing prompts

Every Core ELA Library selection includes

- An Audio Text Highlight tool that breaks texts into grammatical and syntactical chunks as students follow along with the authentic audio
- Auto-graded quizzes to formatively assess students' reading comprehension
- Key vocabulary supports
- Text-dependent Think questions

As the StudySync Library continues to grow, these features will expand to selections beyond those included in the Core ELA program to provide teachers even greater flexibility and options for designing their own curriculum.

Texts with StudySync® TV lessons include additional, engaging multimedia lesson supports such as

- Movie trailer-like Previews
- StudySync® TV episodes
- Short-answer Think questions

BLASTS

In addition to the Blasts embedded in the Core ELA Units, StudySync digital teacher accounts house an ever-growing index with hundreds of Blasts that explore contemporary issues and other high-interest topics. StudySync releases new Blasts every school day, staying on top of all the latest news and providing fresh content to help teachers create engaging, relevant classrooms.

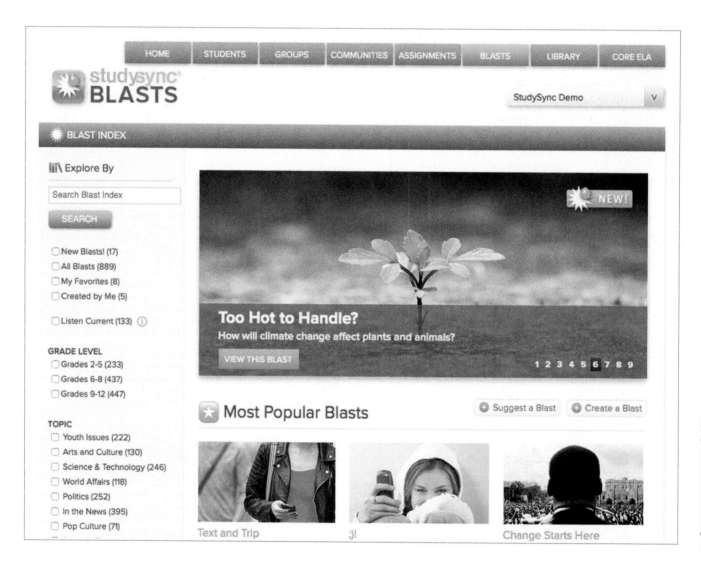

Students respond to the short informational texts and driving questions with 140-character or less Blast responses that allow them to practice clear, concise writing. The peer review platform allows students to read and respond to one another's Blasts, creating a social learning environment that teachers can easily mediate and monitor. Teachers may even elect to join the StudySync National Blast Community, which enables students to read and respond to the Blasts of students from all over the United States.

Teachers can easily differentiate weekly Blasts by choosing to target any of the three Lexile® versions to students. Teachers even have the option to use the StudySync platform to create their own Blasts.

Teachers may also choose to select **Listen Current** Blasts. These weekly Blasts feature a background-building radio story to capture students' attention and help build key listening skills.

SKILLS

StudySync Skill lessons instruct students on the key reading, writing, and language skills and strategies necessary for mastery of the Common Core State Standards. The Skills index in every StudySync digital teacher account allows teachers to search for Skill lessons by grade level, topic, or keyword.

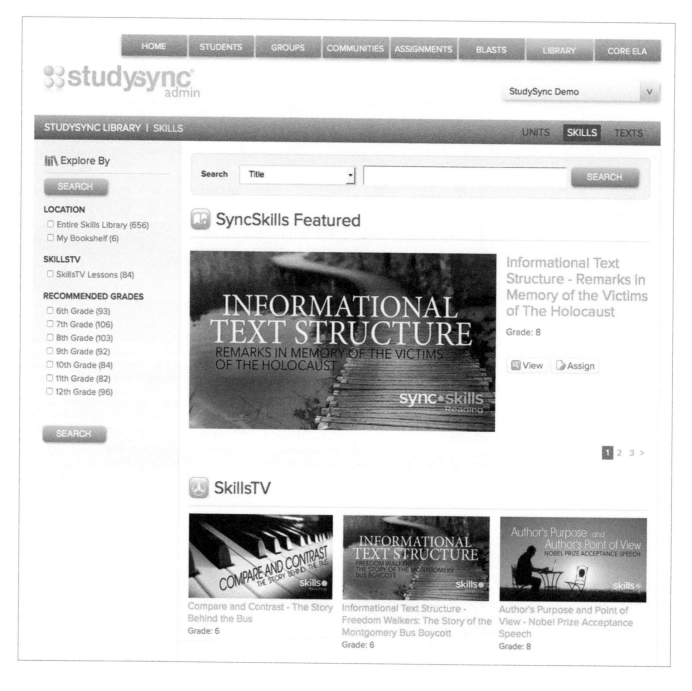

Skill lessons apply the Gradual Release of Responsibility Model. First, students learn the definition of the skill or strategy they'll be applying and watch a Concept Definition video in which students define and break down the key components of a skill or strategy. Next, teachers guide students through a "we do" portion of the lesson, facilitating discussion with follow-up questions from the lesson plan. Many Skill lessons contain SkillsTV videos in which students dramatize the application of a particular skill or strategy.

Lastly, students apply their new knowledge to short questions that ask students to both demonstrate mastery of a standard and provide textual evidence to support their understanding. Teachers receive immediate feedback on these short, formative assessments.

FULL-TEXT UNITS

Each text selected for a Full-text Study in the Core ELA Units also contains a corresponding Full-text Unit. This Full-text Unit provides readings to pair with specific passages of the anchor text and writing lessons that challenge students to compare anchor texts to additional selections.

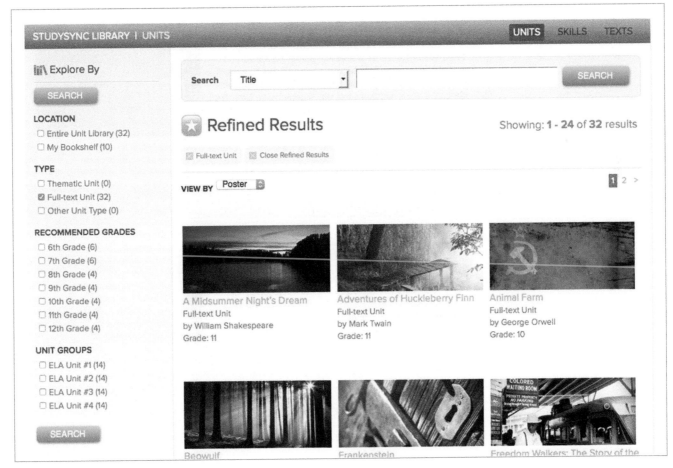

Teacher's Edition

These Full-text Units are not a part of a grade level's 180 days of instruction; however, teachers may wish to draw from them to incorporate materials from other disciplines or develop an alternative, novel-based approach to instruction.

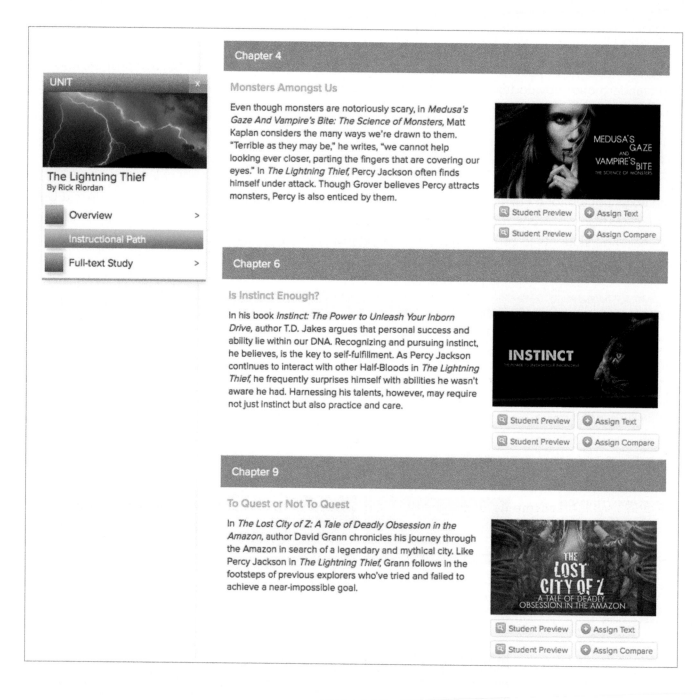

Teacher's Edition

OTHER UNITS

In addition to Core ELA and Full-text Units, StudySync offers teachers a wide range of English Learner, Literature, and Composition Units from which to choose. In the ever-growing Units sections of the Library, teachers will find instructional content that allows them to further customize and differentiate curriculum to suit the unique needs of their students.

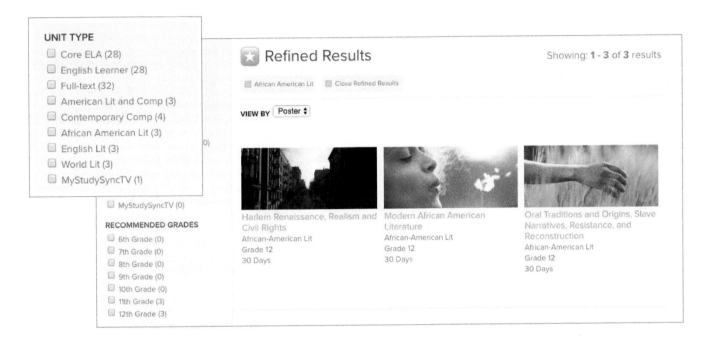

ADDITIONAL RESOURCES

- **Grade Level Assessments** documents contain printable versions of end-of-unit and end-of-course assessments for each grade.

- **Placement and Diagnostic Assessments** aid initial evaluation of student skills to decide on an appropriate instructional level for the student.

- **Foundational Skills** cover phonics, decoding, word recognition, and fluency to help build the skills that lead to students reading independently.

- **Speaking and Listening Handbook** addresses every Common Core ELA standard for speaking and listening and offers usable, repeatable methods and tools for helping students develop and master essential speaking and listening skills.

- **Grammar, Language and Composition Guide** provides additional instruction and practice that can be used for reteaching or preteaching.

- **Vocabulary Workbook** offers students additional opportunities to build and expand their vocabulary.

- **Spelling Workbook** teaches spelling patterns and concepts that apply to various word lists.

- **Standard English Learners Handbook** offers in-depth background information about different instructional routines that can be used with SELs to help them develop their Standard English and understand when it is appropriate to use it.

- **Language Transfers Handbook** provides cross linguistic transfer analysis to help teachers understand the language of students in their classroom.

- **Research-based Alignments** provides a summary of key research findings and recommendations for best practices of instruction in English Language Arts, focused on Reading, Writing, Speaking and Listening, Language, and Media and Technology. Following each section, alignment of the recommendations of the research to specific instruction within StudySync is provided.

- **The Glossary** offers basic summary of essential ELA terminology for each grade level.

Additional Resources

 PDF DOCUMENT
Placement and Diagnostic Assessment

 PDF DOCUMENT
Foundational Skills

 PDF DOCUMENT
Speaking & Listening Handbook

 PDF DOCUMENT
Grammar, Language, and Composition Guide

 PDF DOCUMENT
Vocabulary Workbook

 PDF DOCUMENT
Spelling Workbook

 PDF DOCUMENT
Standard English Learners Handbook

 PDF DOCUMENT
Language Transfers Handbook

 PDF DOCUMENT
Research-base Alignments

 PDF DOCUMENT
Student Glossary

 PDF DOCUMENT
Teacher Glossary

DESIGN YOUR INSTRUCTION

As previously outlined, StudySync provides a rich resource of materials for all ELA students and teachers. Our dynamic, ever-growing curriculum allows for teachers to customize instruction to meet their needs. Whether in a low-tech or high-tech environment, StudySync provides multiple opportunities for whole-group, small-group, and individual instruction. Below are some specific examples of how teachers can integrate StudySync's key features into a variety of classroom contexts.

StudySync Content	Whole group	Small group or pairs	Individuals
Preview and/or Introduction	Project the multimedia Preview and view as a class. Read the Introduction as a class. Follow with a quick discussion about the images and information in the Preview and Introduction.	Have students turn and talk after watching the Preview and reading the Introduction. What images and information stood out? How did their interpretations differ?	Based on the Preview and Introduction, have students jot down predictions, questions, and/or inferences about the text.
First Read	Project a text onto the screen. Model specific skills, including using context clues to determine difficult vocabulary words, and using reading comprehension strategies to parse difficult passages.	Allow students to read and/or listen to the audio reading of the text in pairs or small groups, stopping to discuss thoughts and new vocabulary words as they annotate.	Students read and annotate the text, utilizing the audio or Audio Text Highlight feature as necessary. Alternatively, students can annotate in their print Companion.
StudySync® TV	Project the episode and view as a class. See the corresponding lesson plan for discussion prompts for specific sections of the episode.	Using prompts from the lesson plan, have students hold their own StudySync® TV discussions. Afterwards, briefly share with the whole class ideas that were discussed.	Ask students to jot down ideas from the StudySync® TV episode and their own discussions that might assist with their writing.
Think Questions	Think Questions may be discussed and answered as a class, using the text as support.	Think Questions may be discussed and answered in pairs or small groups before reviewing correct answers with the entire class.	Think Questions may be answered individually, using the text as support.

Skills	Project the Concept Definition video and as a group read the definition of the Skill. If there is a SkillsTV video in the Model sections of the lesson, watch and discuss as a class.	Have students work in pairs or small groups to read through the text in the Model section, stopping throughout to discuss questions and ideas. Work your way around to each group to provide feedback.	Have students individually complete the mini-assessments that conclude Skills lessons. When all students are finished, project the questions and discuss correct answers.
Close Read	Review vocabulary analysis from the First Read. Ask students to compare their context analysis of vocabulary against the actual definitions. Review key skills students will apply in the Close Read.	Close Reads can occur individually or in small groups. If assigning Close Reads for small group work, have students discuss and explain their annotations to one another as they go.	Have students reread and annotate the text in order to complete the Skills Focus questions and prepare themselves for the writing prompt that follows.
Write	Discuss the prompt as a class, making sure students understand the directions and expectations. Display the rubric for the assignment as well.	Allow students time to brainstorm ideas or discuss the prompts with their peers, referring to the text, StudySync® TV episode, and/or previous discussions.	Students individually submit responses to the assigned prompt.
Peer Review	Remind students of your expectations for the peer review process, and inform them of specific directions for this assignment.	In pairs or small groups, have students discuss what they will look for in their peers' responses, based on the directions and rubric. What will an exemplar response include? Report ideas to the whole class.	Students complete peer reviews individually, using the guidelines established.
Blasts	As a class, hold a brief discussion about the prompt. After students read the Background information, discuss the QuikPoll and Number Crunch as a class. Ask students to make predictions on how their peers will answer the QuikPoll, and how the results might differ if answered by another class, age group, etc.	Students should read the Background section in small groups and record notes in their handbooks. Have students discuss questions and ideas that came up as they read. Ask students to split up the Research Links, so that each student researches 2-3 sites and then reports the information back to his or her peers.	Students may read the Background information individually, as well as the information from several Research Links. After discussing the information with their peers, they should craft their 140-character response to the prompt and complete 5 or more peer reviews.

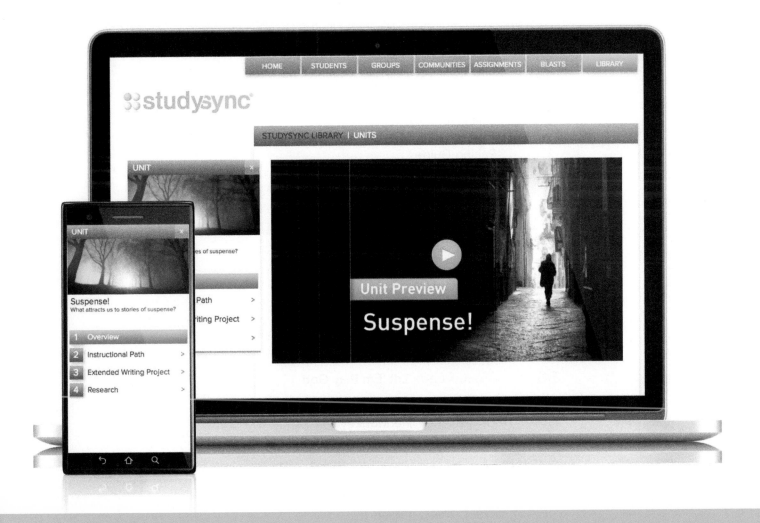

studysync®

Teacher's Edition

What attracts us to stories of suspense?

Suspense!

Suspense!

OVERVIEW MATERIALS

INSTRUCTIONAL PATH

Please note that excerpts and passages in the StudySync® library, workbooks, and PDFs are intended as touchstones to generate interest in an author's work. The excerpts and passages do not substitute for the reading of entire texts, and StudySync® strongly recommends that teachers and students seek out and purchase the whole literary or informational work in order to experience it as the author intended. Links to online resellers are available in our digital library. In addition, complete works may be ordered through an authorized reseller by filling out and returning to StudySync® the order form enclosed in this workbook.

Teacher's Edition   3

EXTENDED WRITING PROJECT

RESEARCH

FULL-TEXT STUDY

Overview Materials

Suspense!

OVERVIEW

UNIT TITLE

Suspense!

UNIT DRIVING QUESTION

What attracts us to stories of suspense?

UNIT OVERVIEW

Hairs rising on the back of your neck? Lips curling up into a wince? Palms a little sweaty? These are tell-tale signs that you are in the grips of suspense.

But what attracts us to suspense? What keeps us from closing the book or changing the channel? What compels us to experience in stories the very things we spend our lives trying to avoid?

Those are the questions your students will explore in this Grade 8 unit.

Alfred Hitchcock. Stephen King. Edgar Allan Poe. The masters of suspense are at work in this unit, and after reading classic thrillers, your students will try their own hands at the genre, applying what they have learned about suspense to their own narrative writing projects. Students will begin this unit as readers, brought to the edge of their seats by hair-raising tales, and they will finish as writers, leading you and their peers through hair-raising stories of their own.

TEXTS

"Let 'Em Play God"	Essay
"The Monkey's Paw"	Short Story
Sorry, Wrong Number	Drama
"Violence in the Movies: Cinematic Craft or Hollywood Gone Too Far?"	Pro-Con/Op-Ed
A Night to Remember	Informational
Cujo	Novel
Lord of the Flies	Novel
Ten Days in a Mad-House	Informational
"The Tell-Tale Heart"	Short Story
"Annabel Lee"	Poem
"The Bells"	Poem

FULL-TEXT STUDY

Lord of the Flies

EXEMPLAR TEXTS

A Night to Remember
Sorry, Wrong Number

ASSIGNMENT TYPES

Blasts: 10
First Reads: 11
Reading Skills: 16
Language Skills: 2
Close Reads: 11
Extended Writing Project Prompts: 5
Writing Skills: 8

STANDARDS FOCUS

RL.8.1, RL.8.2, RL.8.3, RL.8.4
RI.8.5.A, RI.8.6
W.8.3.A, W.8.3.B, W.8.3.C, W.8.3.D, W.8.3.E, W.8.4, W.8.5
SL.8.1.A, SL.8.1.B, SL.8.1.C, SL.8.1.D, SL.8.2, SL.8.3, SL.8.4, SL.8.5, SL.8.6
L.8.1.C, L.8.2.C, L.8.4.A, L.8.4.B, L.8.4.C, L.8.4.D

KEY READING SKILLS

Author's Purpose and Author's Point of View
Theme
Story Elements
Plot
Textual Evidence
Character
Poetic Elements
Word Meaning
Greek and Latin Affixes and Roots

Copyright © BookheadEd Learning, LLC

  Teacher's Edition

KEY GRAMMAR SKILLS

First Read: "Let 'Em Play God" - The Suffixes -ible and -able
First Read: Violence in Movies - Words Often Confused
First Read: "The Tell-Tale Heart" - Verb Moods
Extended Writing Project: Draft - Adjective Suffixes
Extended Writing Project: Revise - More Words Often Confused
Extended Writing Project: Publish - Verb Moods Review

KEY WRITING SKILLS

Organize Narrative Writing
Introductions
Narrative Techniques and Sequencing
Descriptive Details
Writing Dialogue
Audience and Purpose
Conclusions
Transitions

EXTENDED WRITING PROJECT

Reading stories of suspense is one thing; creating them is another entirely. The Extended Writing Project for this unit, however, helps students do exactly that. Skill lessons and clear writing process steps help demystify the narrative writing process and provide students with instruction and practice around all Common Core State Standards addressing narrative writing. In the end, students will have their own tale of suspense to share with their peers and their parents.

Check your digital teacher account to discover new StudySync resources related to this unit.

studysync®

GRADE 8 UNIT 1: SUSPENSE!

PURPOSE

This pacing guide will help you utilize the wealth of resources offered in each StudySync Core ELA unit. The pacing guide weaves lessons from every segment of this Core ELA unit: the Instructional Path, Extended Writing Project, Research Project, and Full-text Study.

The pacing guide presents a suggested plan to cover all content in this unit. You may cover all of these lessons in class, or you may decide to divide the assignments between in-class work and homework. Of course, no one understands your students' needs like you do, and one of the key benefits of StudySync is the ease with which you can adapt, alter, eliminate, or re-organize lessons to best meet the needs of your students. The Shortcuts and Additional Activities section at the end of this pacing guide contains recommendations to help in that regard.

ORGANIZATION

The pacing guide divides the unit into 45 days. Instructional days often have more than a single task. For example, all of the activities on row 1 are suggested to be covered on the first instructional day. Pacing is based on an assumption of 50-minute instructional days, but since schedules vary from school to school you may need to modify the suggested pacing to fit your unique needs.

The column labeled "Full-text Study Connections" often identifies other texts in the StudySync Library that complement the chapter in the Full-text Study students are reading on a particular day. Though these comparative texts are not considered part of the 45 days of Core ELA instruction for this unit, they are listed in the pacing guide in case you would like to include additional texts as part of this unit.

There are no activities or lessons planned for the final two days of the unit, which are dedicated to assessment.

CORE ELA UNIT

DAY	INSTRUCTIONAL PATH	EXTENDED WRITING PROJECT	RESEARCH PROJECT	FULL-TEXT STUDY	FULL-TEXT STUDY CONNECTIONS
1	**UNIT PREVIEW** **BLAST** Suspense!		**SPEAKING & LISTENING HANDBOOK** "Research Using Various Media" **RESEARCH PROJECT PART I** Introduce research project and allow students time to research examples of suspense in different mediums from past to the present – radio stories, articles, films, documentaries.		
2	**FIRST READ** "Let 'Em Play God"		**RESEARCH PROJECT PART II** Ask students to find examples of suspense stories, articles, films and/or documentaries. Have them watch, listen, or read at least 2 suspense stories told in different mediums (e.g. Alfred Hitchcock vs. Edgar Allen Poe) and discuss impact of each medium.		

DAY	INSTRUCTIONAL PATH	EXTENDED WRITING PROJECT	RESEARCH PROJECT	FULL-TEXT STUDY	FULL-TEXT STUDY CONNECTIONS
3	**SKILL** Author's Purpose and Author's Point of View **SKILL** Word Meaning		**RESEARCH PROJECT PART III** Assign groups topics (see list) and begin research (in class and/or online).		
4	**CLOSE READ** "Let 'Em Play God"		**RESEARCH PROJECT PART III CONT.** Students should continue to research.		
5	**FIRST READ** "The Monkey's Paw"		**RESEARCH PROJECT PART III CONT.** Students should continue to research.		
6	**SKILL** Theme		**RESEARCH PROJECT PART IV** Groups should work collaboratively (in class and/or online) on a presentation to present their information to the class.		
7	**SKILL** Story Elements		**RESEARCH PROJECT PART IV CONT.** Students should continue working to create their presentations.		

DAY	INSTRUCTIONAL PATH	EXTENDED WRITING PROJECT	RESEARCH PROJECT	FULL-TEXT STUDY	FULL-TEXT STUDY CONNECTIONS
8	**CLOSE READ** "The Monkey's Paw"		**RESEARCH PROJECT PART IV CONT.** Students should continue working to create their presentations.		
9	**BLAST** Make a Wish		**RESEARCH PROJECT PART IV CONT.** Students should continue working to create their presentations.		
10	**FIRST READ** *Sorry, Wrong Number*		**SPEAKING & LISTENING HANDBOOK** "Presentation Skills" **RESEARCH PROJECT PART V** Allow a couple of groups to present for the class.		
11	**SKILL** Textual Evidence		**RESEARCH PROJECT PART V CONT.** Allow a couple of groups to present for the class.		
12	**SKILL** Plot		**RESEARCH PROJECT PART V CONT.** Allow a couple of groups to present for the class.		
13	**CLOSE READ** *Sorry, Wrong Number*				

DAY	INSTRUCTIONAL PATH	EXTENDED WRITING PROJECT	RESEARCH PROJECT	FULL-TEXT STUDY	FULL-TEXT STUDY CONNECTIONS
14	FIRST READ *Violence in the Movies*		SPEAKING & LISTENING HANDBOOK "Critical Listening"	*Lord of the Flies* Chapter 1 "The Sound of the Shell" COMPARE to *The Coral Island: A Tale of the Pacific Ocean*	LINK to *Lord of the Flies* – Show students the movie trailer for the 1963 version and then the 1990. Compare and contrast the two trailers in terms of their violent content.
15	SKILL Author's Purpose and Author's Point of View				
16	CLOSE READ *Violence in the Movies* BLAST Food For Thought			*Lord of the Flies* Chapter 2 "Fire on the Beach" COMPARE to *The Book of Genesis*	LINK to *Lord of the Flies* – Where is violence (or potential violence) evident in this chapter? How might a film producer bring these moments to life in a film version?
17	FIRST READ *A Night to Remember*		SPEAKING & LISTENING HANDBOOK "Collaborative Discussions"		LINK to *Lord of the Flies* – Compare William Golding's use of sensory details and description to Walter Ford's use of detail and description in the excerpt from a *Night to Remember*. What is the impact of each? How is it similar and/or different?
18	SKILL Author's Purpose and Author's Point of View			*Lord of the Flies* Chapter 3 "Huts on the Beach" COMPARE to *Robinson Crusoe*	LINK to *Lord of the Flies* – Whose point of view is the *Lord of the Flies* told from? What clues in the first chapter reveal the point of view of the narrator?

DAY	INSTRUCTIONAL PATH	EXTENDED WRITING PROJECT	RESEARCH PROJECT	FULL-TEXT STUDY	FULL-TEXT STUDY CONNECTIONS
19	CLOSE READ *A Night to Remember*				
20	BLAST How They Saw It			*Lord of the Flies* Chapter 4 "Painted Faces and Long Hair" COMPARE to *African Genesis*	LINK to *Lord of the Flies* – How did each of the main boys (Ralph, Jack, Piggy and Simon) react to being stranded on the island? What does the reveal about them? Which character's reaction do you identify with most?
21	FIRST READ *Cujo*				
22	SKILL Text Evidence	EXTENDED WRITING PROJECT Narrative Writing		*Lord of the Flies* Chapter 5 "Beast from Water" COMPARE to "Superstition"	LINK to *Lord of the Flies* – While reading Chapter 5 "Beast from Water," make a list of explicit and implicit information (in notes or on the board). Then have students articulate three inferences they made while reading based on the textual evidence.
23	CLOSE READ *Cujo* BLAST Are You a Smart Consumer?	SKILL Organize Narrative Writing			
24	FIRST READ *Lord of the Flies*	EXTENDED WRITING PROJECT Prewrite		*Lord of the Flies* Chapter 6 "Beast from Air" COMPARE to "The Tyger"	LINK to *Lord of the Flies* – While re-reading the excerpt from Chapter 1 in *Lord of the Flies*, ask students to compare and contrast the elements order and chaos in Chapter 1 with those in Chapter 6. What has changed?
25	SKILL Theme				

DAY	INSTRUCTIONAL PATH	EXTENDED WRITING PROJECT	RESEARCH PROJECT	FULL-TEXT STUDY	FULL-TEXT STUDY CONNECTIONS
26	SKILL — Character	SKILL — Introductions		Lord of the Flies Chapter 7 "Shadows and Tall Trees" COMPARE to "If"	LINK to Lord of the Flies – Select another main character other than Piggy and discuss how that character is developed using description, dialogue, and/or situations.
27	CLOSE READ — Lord of the Flies	SKILL — Narrative Techniques and Sequencing			
28	BLAST — Follow the Leader	EXTENDED WRITING PROJECT — Plan		Lord of the Flies Chapter 8 "Gift for the Darkness" COMPARE to The Call of the Wild	LINK to Lord of the Flies – In chapter 8 Jack declares himself chief. The boys split between Ralph and Jack. Who would make the best leader on the island? Why would that boy be the best leader?
29	FIRST READ — Ten Days in a Mad-House	BLAST — Descriptive Details			
30	SKILL — Author's Purpose and Author's Point of View	SKILL — Writing Dialogue		Lord of the Flies Chapter 9 "A View to a Death" COMPARE to "The Song of Hiawatha"	LINK to Lord of the Flies – Imagine how different Chapter 9 would be if it was written from Simon's perspective. How would the chapter change if Simon was narrating it?
31	CLOSE READ — Ten Days in a Mad-House	BLAST — Audience and Purpose			

DAY	INSTRUCTIONAL PATH	EXTENDED WRITING PROJECT	RESEARCH PROJECT	FULL-TEXT STUDY	FULL-TEXT STUDY CONNECTIONS
32	**BLAST** Mental Health, Then and Now	**SKILL** Conclusions		*Lord of the Flies* Chapter 10 "The Shell and the Glasses" **COMPARE** to *Leviathan*	**LINK** to *Lord of the Flies* – Complete a close reading of the conversation between Ralph and Piggy about their role in Simon's death. What does Ralph's reaction reveal about his mental health at this point in the island? How might living on an island in these circumstances impact a person's mental health?
33		**EXTENDED WRITING PROJECT** Draft			
34	**FIRST READ** "The Tell-Tale Heart"	**SKILL** Transitions		*Lord of the Flies* Chapter 11 "Castle Rock"	**LINK** to *Lord of the Flies* – Is the narrator of *Lord of the Flies* reliable? Were there any moments in the novel when you did not trust or believe what the narrator was saying about the boys or what was happening on the island? Explain.
35	**SKILL** Textual Evidence **SKILL** Greek and Latin Affixes and Roots				

DAY	INSTRUCTIONAL PATH	EXTENDED WRITING PROJECT	RESEARCH PROJECT	FULL-TEXT STUDY	FULL-TEXT STUDY CONNECTIONS
36	**CLOSE READ** "The Tell-Tale Heart"	**EXTENDED WRITING PROJECT** Revise		*Lord of the Flies* Chapter 12 "Cry of the Hunters" **COMPARE** to *First Contact— New Guinea's Highlanders Encounter the Outside World* OR *A Long Way Gone: Memoirs of a Boy Soldier*	**LINK** to *Lord of the Flies* — While reading Chapter 12 "Cry of the Hunters," make a list of explicit and implicit information (in notes or on the board). Then have students articulate three inferences they made while reading based on the textual evidence.
37		**EXTENDED WRITING PROJECT** Edit, Proofread, and Publish			
38	**FIRST READ** "Annabel Lee"				
39	**SKILL** Poetic Elements				
40	**CLOSE READ** "Annabel Lee"				
41	**FIRST READ** "The Bells"				
	SKILL Poetic Elements				

DAY	INSTRUCTIONAL PATH	EXTENDED WRITING PROJECT	RESEARCH PROJECT	FULL-TEXT STUDY	FULL-TEXT STUDY CONNECTIONS
42	**CLOSE READ** "The Bells"				
43	**BLAST** When Fear Becomes a Phobia				
44	**ASSESSMENT** StudySync Grade 8 Unit 1 Assessment				
45	**ASSESSMENT** StudySync Grade 8 Unit 1 Assessment				

SHORTCUTS AND ADDITIONAL ACTIVITIES

Shortcuts

In a perfect world, teachers would have time to cover everything, but most teachers feel as though they are in a race against the bell. There is never enough time to cover everything. If you find yourself short on time, there are places where you can trim this unit to ensure you are covering the most important parts. Here are some suggestions for how you can shorten this unit:

1. **Replace the Research Project with a Crowdsourcing Activity:** Instead of a 12-day research project, you can make the research component of this unit an informal exploration using a crowdsourcing activity. To facilitate a crowdsourcing assignment, break students into groups, give each group a question or research topic, and allow them time to research using computers or devices to generate information about their topic. Then allow them to share what they have learned with the class by writing their information on the board or posting it to a shared Padlet Wall (or other online collaborative space).

2. **Eliminate Repeated Author's Purpose and Author's Point of View Skill Lessons:** Each unit focuses on developing specific skills. Some of these skills are repeated throughout the unit to ensure students have plenty of practice with those skills. As the old adage says, "practice makes perfect!" That said, if you are in a rush and looking to cut some of the content in a unit, you can eliminate one or two of these skill lessons and feel confident your students will still be exposed to the information they need about author's purpose and author's point of view.

3. **Content Cuts:** There are several different types of texts presented in a unit — excerpts from novels, nonfiction readings, short stories and poems. If you are running out of time, you may want to eliminate a StudySync selection that focuses on a similar type of text as a previous lesson. For example, in this unit "The Bells" and "Annabel Lee" are both poems written by Edgar Allan Poe. You can opt to teach just one of these poems and use it to discuss poetic elements.

Supportive Materials for Other Disciplines

The Full-text Unit for *Lord of the Flies* contains texts that link the novel to science and history curriculum. *African Genesis*, a book written by Robert Ardrey, finds patterns of behavior in the animal world that are mirrored in the behavior of humans, which can be used to link the anchor text to science and discussions of animal behavior.

Human nature, war and survival are at the heart of *Lord of the Flies* and invite connections to history and social science topics. *Leviathan*, an excerpt from Thomas Hobbes book, explores man's propensity for war exploring the darker side of human nature. The excerpt from the autobiography, *A Long Way Gone: Memoirs of a Boy Soldier*, recounts Ishmael Beah's experiences during the decade long civil war in Sierra Leone. *First Contact: New Guinea's Highlanders Encounter the Outside World*, by Bob Connolly and Robin Anderson, describes what happened when a group of Australian gold prospectors encountered a group of native New Guinean highlanders. Each of these texts links to central themes in the novel providing opportunities for students to make connections to historical events and the human experience.

In addition to the these texts from the Full-text Unit and the Thematic Units for *Lord of the Flies*, there are several StudySync Blasts that can link the text to science and social studies topics. "Creepy. Crawly. Dinner" explores the nutritional value of eating insects; "Group Dynamics" examines the challenges of human interactions; "Follow the Leader" asks the questions "What makes a good leader?"; and "Bullies: The Playground and the Chatroom" delves into the realities of abusive behavior in a variety of contexts. Each Blast assignment includes a "Research Links" section that includes a wide array of resources that provide students with a deeper understanding of the topic.

Suggestions for Further and Independent Reading

Books excerpted in *Lord of the Flies* Full-text Unit provide a springboard for further reading that illuminates the themes of survival, encounters between two civilizations, and children swept up in a culture of violence. The progenitor of many a castaway novel, *Robinson Crusoe* is available in editions catering to all readerships. One of *Crusoe*'s progeny, *The Coral Island*, by R. M. Ballantyne (1857), pits three boys shipwrecked on a Pacific island against cannibals and pirates. William Golding set out to turn this familiar boy's adventure on its ear, conspicuously borrowing the names of two of its characters, Ralph and Jack. Two informational books provide a global perspective on the schoolboys' predicament: *A Long Way Gone: Memoirs of a Boy Soldier* is a first-person account by Ishmael Beah of participating in Sierra Leone's civil war at the age of thirteen. The end of *Lord of the Flies* bears ironic comparison with the mutual discovery of two cultures in *First Contact: New Guinea's Highlanders Discover the Outside World*.

Readings outside the Full-text Unit venture deeper into a young person's heart of darkness, while many also keep contact with adventure and suspense. Books that maintain this balance of darkness and adventure include Robert Louis Stevenson's *Treasure Island* and John Steinbeck's *The Pearl*, both touching on the corrupting influence of greed. John Knowles's *A Separate Peace* and Orson Scott Card's *Ender's Game* examine in subtle and direct ways, conflict between boys set against the backdrop of war; while Suzanne Collins's *Hunger Games* turns child-on-child combat into dystopian entertainment. Readers wanting more William Golding might enjoy his first novel, *The Inheritors*, about the clash between two cultures of prehistoric humans. Finally, Michael Morpurgo's novel, *Kensuke's Kingdom*, traces a conflict between castaways that finds unexpected peaceful resolution.

Difficult Concepts

Although 8th grade students are expected to "cite the textual evidence that most strongly supports an analysis of what the text says explicitly as well as inferences drawn from the text" (RL.8.1), selecting strong textual evidence and making inferences is challenging. These skills require students employ higher-order thinking. Students must read closely to pick up on clues in the text, analyze the explicit and implicit information provided, and draw conclusions based on that information. Students will benefit from explicit instruction on how to make inferences as they read. In addition to providing concrete strategies for making inferences, teachers can return to a Textual Evidence Skill Lesson from the previous unit or grade (e.g. 7th Grade Unit 4 Textual Evidence Skill Lesson for *The Outsiders* or "The Ransom of Red Chief") to allow students the opportunity to practice applying strategies for making inferences with a text they've already read.

Identifying strong textual evidence to support inferences and analysis is also an important yet challenging skill for students at this level. Teachers need to ask text dependent questions that require students back up their statements with strong textual evidence. This skill requires practice. To provide students with more practice, teachers can replace a repeated skill lesson with a First Read assignment for another text or they can spend more time reviewing and discussing the Think Questions from another text in the unit. For example, *Violence in the Movies* and *A Night to Remember* both follow the first Textual Evidence Skill Lesson and can be used to review this skill in depth. Remember that Think Questions 1-3 ask text dependent questions that require students to back up their statements with evidence from the text, so the First Read assignment of any text can be used to support the development of this skill if teachers focus on reviewing the responses to Think Questions 1-3.

Recognizing an author's purpose in a text requires that students analyze and evaluate several elements in the text to discover the reason why the author wrote this text. They must look closely at the title, word choice, and point of view. This requires a close reading of the text with an eye on these specific elements. Students would benefit from examining several different types of texts and discussing each author's purpose in writing his/her text. Teachers can spend extra time reviewing the answers to the Author's Purpose and Author's Point of View Skill Lessons in the unit. In addition, teachers can also provide extra practice with a wide range of texts by searching StudySync Library Skill Index for additional skill lessons that target this concept. Ideally, teachers will want to select skill lessons below the current grade/unit level for additional practice to ensure the texts are accessible.

Read Aloud Selection

Edgar Allan Poe's "The Tell-Tale Heart" is a riveting text told by an unnamed narrator who attempts to convince the reader of his sanity while describing a murder he committed. Long sentences throughout the text are broken by dashes and coupled with sentence fragments to indicate the narrator's anxious, fragmented thinking and deteriorating emotional state. Listening to the story will help students recognize how tools such as inflection, volume, and tone of voice can help them better understand the narrator's character and the events of the story. By reading Poe's story aloud, students have an opportunity to practice using expression, verbal accuracy, intonation, phrasing, punctuation, and pacing to bring the text to life.

Alternate Extended Writing Project Prompts

These alternative prompts provide options for modifying the unit's Extended Writing Project to a different writing form.

1. **Argumentative:** In this unit you have read stories from some of the masters of suspense, including Stephen King and Edgar Allan Poe. Nonfiction texts took readers to a "madhouse" in nineteenth-century New York City, and for a trip on a doomed ocean liner. Of course, not everyone agrees on the elements that make up a suspenseful story. Write an argumentative essay that explains whether you think a fictional story or a nonfiction account of an actual event forms the basis for a better suspense story. To support your ideas include textual evidence from at least two selections in Unit 1 and research from three other print or digital sources.

2. **Informative/Explanatory:** In this unit, you've been reading fiction and nonfiction narratives about characters that are caught up in suspenseful situations. How do authors create suspense, and why do readers keep coming back for more? One way is to develop characters that readers care about and then put them in a dangerous situation. Foreshadowing can also create suspense, by suggesting what may happen without stating it directly. Write an informative/explanatory essay in which you explain how authors in three of the excerpts you have read create suspense. To support your ideas include textual evidence from three selections in Unit 1.

3. **Literary Analysis:** Mr. and Mrs. White and Donna Trenton all have amazing stories to tell as all three of them experience suspenseful, even terrifying situations. Their individual experiences, however, are very different. Write a literary analysis in which you compare and contrast Donna's situation, in which she had no control over the event that took place, and the Whites, who make a decision that creates the suspense. Analyze which work of fiction creates greater suspense for the reader, using examples from each text.

Instructional Path

Suspense!

BLAST:
Suspense!

OVERVIEW

To develop a focus for this unit, students will learn about suspense, consider why people are attracted to it, and make their first attempt at responding to the unit's driving question. Students will explore Research Links to read articles, an interview, and different perspectives about the aspects of suspense.

OBJECTIVES

1. Explore background information about the history of suspense, what creates and attracts people to suspense, and what are the best suspense stories.
2. Analyze a range of literature and informational texts related to the theme of suspense, including essays, opinions, real-life accounts, drama, novel excerpts, short stories, and poetry.
3. Research using hyperlinks to a range of information about suspense, including articles, an interview, and different perspectives.
4. Use technology to produce and publish writing.

ELA Common Core Standards:
Reading: Informational Text - RI.8.1
Writing - W.8.1.A, W.8.1.B, W.8.4, W.8.6, W.8.10
Speaking & Listening - SL.8.1.A, SL.8.1.C, SL.8.1.D
Language - L.8.4.C

RESOURCES

Blast Response - Student Model
Access 1 handout (Beginner)
Access 2 handout (Intermediate)
Access 4 handout (Approaching)

Please note that excerpts and passages in the StudySync® library, workbooks, and PDFs are intended as touchstones to generate interest in an author's work. The excerpts and passages do not substitute for the reading of entire texts, and StudySync® strongly recommends that teachers and students seek out and purchase the whole literary or informational work in order to experience it as the author intended. Links to online resellers are available in our digital library. In addition, complete works may be ordered through an authorized reseller by filling out and returning to StudySync® the order form enclosed in this workbook.

Teacher's Edition   **25**

TITLE/DRIVING QUESTION

Core Path	Access Path
Discuss. As a class read aloud the title and driving question for this Blast. These correspond to the title/driving question for the unit as a whole. Ask students why they like or dislike suspenseful stories. Ask what they already know about how suspense is built. Do they have a favorite suspense story? Remind students that they should not immediately reply to this question. They'll be returning to this question and responding after they've read the Background and some of the Research Links.	**English Learners All Levels & Approaching** **Build Background.** Have students use the Internet or magazines to find pictures that illustrate suspense. Ask them what the pictures tell them about the meaning of suspense. Encourage students to make a concept map as a class to describe suspense and suspenseful elements.
Draft. In their notebooks or on scrap paper, have students draft their initial responses to the driving question. This will provide them with a baseline response that they will be developing as they gain more information about the topic in the Background and Research Links sections of the assignment. You may wish to review with students the Blast Response - Student Model for guidance on how to construct an effective Blast. The Blast review criteria are as follows: 1. Response does not address the driving question or is unclear; language is vague. 2. Response insufficiently addresses the driving question or is mostly unclear; language is mostly vague. 3. Response somewhat addresses the driving question or is somewhat unclear; language is somewhat vague. 4. Response adequately addresses the driving question and is clear; language is mostly precise. 5. Response fully addresses the driving question and is clear; language is precise.	**Beginner & Intermediate** **Draft with Sentence Frame.** When drafting their initial response to the driving question, have students refer to this Blast sentence frame on their Access 1 and 2 handouts: • We love suspense because _____. Point out these two key features of the sentence frame: 1. The introductory clause "We love suspense" borrows language directly from the Blast driving question to provide a response. 2. Ask students to make special note of the conjunction "because" since it asks students to provide evidence for their claims.

Copyright © BookheadEd Learning, LLC

BACKGROUND

Core Path	Access Path
Read. Have students read the Blast Background to provide context for the driving question.	**Beginner & Intermediate** **Read with Support.** Have students read the Blast Background to provide context for the driving question. When they encounter unfamiliar words or phrases, have students refer to the Blast Glossary on their Access 1 and 2 handouts. If there are unfamiliar words that are not included in their glossary, encourage students to check a dictionary or online reference tool, like http://tinyurl.com/6ytby. **Approaching** **Read and Summarize.** Have students read the Blast Background to provide context for the driving question. As they read, ask students to complete the fill-in-the-blank summary of the Background provided on their Access 4 handout. When they encounter unfamiliar words or phrases, have students refer to the glossary on their Access 4 handout.
Discuss. Pair students and have them discuss the following questions: 1. What do some of the best suspense stories have in common? (They make people uncertain, create a sense of mystery, and keep us wondering how it will all turn out.) 2. How does a story like *Dracula* or a character like Sherlock Holmes hold an audience's interest? Explain your inference. (Count Dracula and Sherlock Holmes must not only have interesting plots, but must also be "suspenseful" and keep readers guessing.) 3. How is suspense handled differently in different mediums? (Techniques may be different. In books, the writer relies on words to keep a reader turning pages. In radio, sound effects or a whispered voice to keep listeners involved.)	**Beginner** **Discuss.** Pair Beginning with Advanced (or Beyond) students and have them use the dialogue starter on their Access 1 handout to discuss the topic. Advise them to return to the dialogue and switch roles if they get stuck. **Intermediate** **Discuss.** Pair Intermediate with Advanced (or Beyond) students and have them use the dialogue starter on their Access 2 handout to discuss the topic. Advise them to return to the dialogue and switch roles if they get stuck. If their conversation is progressing smoothly, encourage them to continue the discussion beyond the dialogue starter sheet. They can expand their conversations to discuss other reasons why people love suspense.

Core Path	Access Path
4. What are some of the genres that could include suspense? How do the genres differ? (mystery—often involves solving a crime; horror—often has people wondering how a person might die; spy thriller—often involves adventure)	
5. What do creators of suspense tell us about why suspense remains so exciting even today? (Stephen King thinks those stories help us work through our own bad impulses, whereas Ann Radcliffe thought it gave us a higher degree of life and awareness. It seems that by working on our emotions, suspense helps audiences grow and gain increased awareness of the world.)	

Brainstorm. Remind students about the driving question for this Blast, another version of the driving question for this unit: "Why do we love suspense?"

In their notebooks, ask students to make three columns, one for the Blast Background, one for themselves, and one for someone they know. Start with the Background and have them fill in reasons that the Blast suggests people might love suspense. After they've finished that, have them apply the question to themselves to begin developing a list of reasons why they personally love suspense. Lastly, have them think about someone specific they know and why that person loves suspense. Here's a short of example of how this might look:

Background	Me	Someone I Know
They make the dangerous or terrifying feel real.	I get to imagine how I would react in crazy moments that I hope I'll never really face.	My dad says his regular day is pretty routine and suspenseful TV shows shake that up.

RESEARCH LINKS

Core Path	Access Path
Examine and Explore. Before asking students to explore the Research Links, use these questions to guide their exploration: 1. Look at the Research Links. Why do you think a writer would give a step-by-step process of Alfred Hitchcock's film techniques? (He is considered one of the masters of suspense; studying his techniques can allow others to duplicate his process.) 2. Have students explore the links "Types of Suspense" and "The Top 100 Thrillers." Ask students to find movies they've seen on the list, and to identify the types of suspense presented in those movies. What elements of suspense are found in most of their favorite movies? Why do they enjoy these elements of suspense? Discuss in small groups or as a class, and ask students to identify similarities and differences in their responses.	
	Extend **Research, Discuss, and Present.** Pair or group Beginning and Intermediate students with Advanced students, and assign each pair or group one link to explore. Ask them to discuss the following questions as they explore the link: 1. What are the most interesting ideas? 2. What questions do you have about the information? 3. What did you learn about this "big idea" from reading this link? 4. How did this help you to better understand suspense? Have students briefly share the most important ideas they found in their link with the entire class.

<table>
<tr><td></td><td>

Extend
Tech Infusion
Share. As students explore the links, allow them to create an interactive poster that illustrates the concept of suspense or their favorite suspense story, using an online poster and collage maker, such as Glogster (http://tinyurl.com/ydeyklq). Students can combine text, music, photos, and video before they share them with the class.

</td></tr>
</table>

QUIKPOLL

Core Path	Access Path
Participate. Answer the poll question. Have students discuss their reasons for their answers. Students should refer to evidence from the Background and Research Links to defend their answer.	

NUMBER CRUNCH

Core Path	Access Path
Predict, Discuss, and Click. Before students click on the number, break them into pairs and have them make predictions about what they think the number is related to. After they've clicked the number, ask students if they are surprised by the revealed information.	

CREATE YOUR BLAST

Core Path	Access Path
Blast. Ask students to write their Blast response in 140 characters or less.	**Beginner** **Blast with Support.** Have students refer back to the sentence frame on their Access 1 handout that they used to create their original Blast draft. Ask them to use this frame to write and enter their final Blast. **Intermediate** **Blast with Support.** Have students attempt to draft their Blast without the sentence frame on their Access 2 handout. If students struggle to compose their Blast draft without the sentence frame, remind them to reference it for support. **Beyond** **Write a Claim.** Ask students to use their answer to the poll question to write a strong claim that could be used as the foundation for their Blast. Once students have written their claims, ask them to read their claims to a small group of their peers. This activity will provide them practice writing claims, as well as expose them to claims written by their peers.
Review. After students have completed their own Blasts, ask them to review the Blasts of their peers and provide feedback. To help students respond effectively, read and discuss the Blast review criteria with them before they review one another's Blasts.	**Extend** **Discuss.** As a whole class or in groups, identify a few strong Blasts and discuss what made those responses so powerful. As a group, analyze and discuss what characteristics make a Blast interesting or effective.
	Extend **Revise.** Resend a second version of this Blast assignment to your students and have them submit revised versions of their original Blasts. Do the same responses make the Top 10? How have the answers improved from the first submissions?

FIRST READ:
Let 'Em Play God

OVERVIEW

In this excerpt from "Let 'Em Play God," students look behind the scenes at how a filmmaker makes a suspenseful movie. Alfred Hitchcock explains how allowing the audience to know things the film's characters do not creates a feeling of suspense. The excerpt provides students with an excellent opportunity not only to learn about the elements that make up a suspenseful film, but also to examine a writer's purpose and point of view on a subject.

OBJECTIVES

1. Perform an initial reading of a text and demonstrate comprehension by responding to short analysis and inference questions with textual evidence.
2. Practice defining vocabulary words using context clues and related words, as well as common Latin roots and affixes.
3. Participate effectively in a range of conversations and collaborations to express ideas and build upon the ideas of others.

    ELA Common Core Standards:
    Reading: Informational Text - RI.8.1, RI.8.4, RI.8.10
    Writing - W.8.7, W.8.10
    Speaking & Listening - SL.8.1.A, SL.8.1.B, SL.8.1.C, SL.8.1.D, SL.8.2
    Language -L.8.2.C, L.8.4.A, L.8.4.B, L.8.6

RESOURCES

Grammar handout: The Suffixes -ible and -able
Access 1 handout (Beginner)
Access 2 handout (Intermediate)
Access 3 handout (Advanced)
Access 4 handout (Approaching)

Teacher's Edition

ACCESS COMPLEX TEXT

In "Let 'Em Play God," Alfred Hitchcock analyzes the strategy he uses to create suspense in his films. To begin, he gives an example of a situation that does not evoke suspense. Then he describes his strategy of letting the audience "play God". After a brief discussion that contrasts the puzzling whodunit with the suspenseful thriller, Hitchcock gives a detailed description of how his film *Rope* illustrates this strategy. The complexities of Hitchcock's thinking are reflected in the challenges of the text. To help students understand Hitchcock's theory, use the following ideas to provide scaffolded instruction for an initial reading of the more complex features of this text.

- **Connection of Ideas** - Although Hitchcock discusses abstract ideas such as suspense and letting an audience "play God," he provides concrete examples to explain this thinking. However, because students are likely to be unfamiliar with the example of *Rope,* it may be difficult for them to understand Hitchcock's points. Readers may benefit by viewing an excerpt from the film

- **Specific Vocabulary** - Idiomatic expressions, such as "cry for joy" and work like the devil, may present a challenge for some readers. The expression "work like the devil," is explained for students in the skills lesson.

- **Prior Knowledge** - Students may not be familiar with Alfred Hitchcock and the film and actors cited in the selection. Sir Alfred Joseph Hitchcock (1899–1980) was an English film director and producer. Often nicknamed "The Master of Suspense," Hitchcock pioneered many techniques in both the suspense and psychological thriller genres. After a successful career in England during the silent and early talkie period, Hitchcock moved to Hollywood in 1939 and became a US citizen in 1955. Over a career spanning more than half a century, Hitchcock pioneered the use of a movie camera made to move in a way that mimics a person's gaze, forcing viewers to engage in a form of voyeurism. He framed shots to maximize anxiety, fear, or empathy, and many of his films, such as *Shadow of a Doubt* (1943), *Rope* (1948), and *North by Northwest* (1959), feature fugitives on the run.

1. INTRODUCTION

Core Path	Access Path
Read and Listen. Individually or as a class, read and listen to the Introduction for the excerpt from "Let 'Em Play God." The Introduction provides context for the excerpt and connects it to the big idea in this unit: *What attracts us to stories of suspense?*	**English Learners All Levels & Approaching Read and Define.** Ask students to read the Introduction for "Let 'Em Play God." Have them refer to the Introduction Glossary in the Access 1, 2, 3, and 4 handouts for definitions of key vocabulary terms. **Beginner** **Sentence Frames.** After students read and listen to the Introduction, have them summarize what they learned by completing the sentence frames on the Access 1 handout. Answers are located online.
Build Background. Find out what your students already know about suspense films and stories. To encourage discussion, ask these questions: 1. What are some suspenseful films and stories you've seen or read? 2. What made those films or stories suspenseful? 3. Why do some people like suspense? Why don't they like it? Then have students, either in pairs or small groups, research some of the films that were directed by "the master of suspense" Alfred Hitchcock: • *North by Northwest* • *Foreign Correspondent* • *Notorious* • *Rope* Suggest that each group conduct a short research project to answer the following questions: *When was the film made? Was it an original screenplay, or was it based on a novel, play, or some other source material? What kind of critical response did the film receive when it was released? Did it win or was it nominated for any awards?* Have students include a written plot summary of the film and then discuss their findings. If possible, arrange for students to watch the film they are researching.	**English Learners All Levels & Approaching Complete and Discuss the Chart.** Have these students complete the Imagine exercise in the Access 1, 2, 3, and 4 handouts that asks students to imagine the kind of suspense movie they would create. After students have completed the exercise, have small groups of students discuss their ideas on how they would make a movie suspenseful.

2. READ

Core Path	Access Path
Make Predictions about Vocabulary. There are five bold vocabulary words in the text. As students read the text, ask them to make predictions about what they think each bold vocabulary word means based on the context clues in the sentence. If you are in a low-tech classroom and students are reading from printed copies or a projected text, ask students to record predictions in their notes, so they can be easily referenced in class. If your students have access to technology, they can use the annotation tool to make their predictions.	**Note:** This exercise, which extends vocabulary instruction, should be completed when the class shifts from whole group instruction to individual work during the "Read and Annotate" exercise.

Core Path

It might be helpful to model this for students before they begin reading. Either using the board or projecting the actual text, focus in on the sentence that uses the word "debunking":

- Offhand this may sound like **debunking,** but I do not believe that puzzling the audience is the essence of suspense.

Model for the class how to use the overall structure and meaning of the sentence and the sentences around it, the word's position, and other clues to define the unfamiliar vocabulary word. In this case, point out these context clues:

1. Hitchcock says his films have been described as thrillers, dark mysteries, and chillers, but never whodunits or puzzlers. It seems as if he's going to set the record straight and correct the way his films have been "described" versus what he's really doing.

2. Instead, though, Hitchcock tells us that's not what he's doing. The key phrase here is "this may sound like." He's making sure readers know he's not correcting (or "debunking") the way his films have been "described".

3. The conjunction "but" is also important. Readers may be expecting Hitchcock to correct the perception of his films, but instead of "debunking" that perception he is confirming it. He hasn't made whodunits or puzzlers because he doesn't find those types of films suspenseful. So to "debunk" something must mean "to expose or discredit".

Access Path

Beginner, Intermediate, & Approaching Pair Practice.

1. Pair students with more proficient readers.

2. Give them an additional sentence that contains a new vocabulary word.

3. Ask the less proficient readers to complete a think aloud using the teacher-led Make Predictions about Vocabulary activity as a model, while the more proficient reader actively listens.

4. The less proficient readers should use the context clues in the sentence to try to determine the meaning of the new vocabulary word.

5. After the less proficient readers have completed the think aloud and made a prediction about the word's meaning, allow time for the proficient reader to add his/her own thoughts and clarify any points of confusion.

6. Once they've completed this think aloud, encourage them to use a dictionary to confirm the definition of the new vocabulary word. Have them refer to the Text Glossary on their Access 1, 2, and 4 handouts for definitions of key vocabulary terms in the text. Encourage them to add any additional vocabulary words or idioms they find in the text and look up definitions for those words and idioms online or in a dictionary.

Core Path	Access Path
Model Reading Comprehension Strategy. Before students begin reading, model the reading comprehension strategy of rereading by using this Think Aloud that talks students through the first paragraph of text. First explain to your students that rereading is: *reading an entire passage more than once, or reading certain excerpts multiple times in order to uncover meaning and improve comprehension.* Explain to students how rereading will help them understand the selection and better prepare them to remember and find textual evidence to support their ideas in discussions. • When I read the first paragraph, I see the mention of the word "suspense". I can reread this section to determine why the author thinks this word is important. • Then I read that producers, writers, and actors all strive for suspense. Rereading this part makes me want to learn more about how suspense works for these different creative people. • I read that the author, Alfred Hitchcock, says people often ask him to define suspense. If I reread this paragraph to understand the author's purpose, I can predict that the next paragraphs will be about how to use suspense as a tool in a story.	**Note:** This exercise, which extends instruction around reading comprehension strategies, should be completed when the class shifts from whole group instruction to individual work during the "Read and Annotate" exercise. **Beginner & Approaching** **Model Reading Comprehension Strategy.** Have students work in pairs to practice rereading and think aloud strategies using the Model Reading Comprehension Strategy exercise on the Access 1 and 4 handouts. If needed, distribute the Model Reading Comprehension Strategy exercise to Intermediate and Advanced students as well.
Read and Annotate. Ask students to read and annotate the excerpt. Have students use the annotation tool as they read to: 1. use context clues to analyze and determine the meaning of the bolded vocabulary terms. 2. ask questions about passages of the text that may be unclear or unresolved. 3. identify key concepts, information, and details in the text and make connections between them. 4. note unfamiliar vocabulary. 5. capture their reactions to the ideas in the text.	**Beginner** **Coach the Reading.** While other students read, annotate, and discuss the text independently, work with Beginning students, listening to the audio of the text and pausing periodically or when any student has a question. Coach students in articulating their questions for the group and in highlighting and annotating the text. Have students use the Annotation Guide on the Access 1 handout to support them as they highlight and annotate the text. For further support, ask questions about the text such as:

Core Path	Access Path
	• Is there anything about the excerpt that you don't understand?
	• How does Hitchcock create suspense?
	Intermediate
	Listen to the Audio. Have these students listen to the audio of the text and use the definitions on the Access 2 handout to help them with words or idioms that may be unfamiliar. If students need help with annotating the text, have them use the Annotation Guide on the Access 2 handout.
	Advanced
	Pair with Proficient Peers. Have Advanced students work with English proficient peers to read, annotate, and discuss the text. Have students use the Annotation Guide on the Access 3 handout to support them as they highlight and annotate the text. Encourage them to listen to the audio of the text if needed.
	Approaching
	Use the Annotation Guide. Have students use the Annotation Guide on the Access 1 handout. Encourage students to use the Text Glossary if there are words of idioms they don't understand. After working with the Beginning students, you may wish to check this group's progress and provide support as needed.
Discuss. In small groups or pairs, have students discuss the questions and inferences they made while reading. To help facilitate discussions, refer to Collaborative Discussions in the Speaking and Listening Handbook. Have students follow the rules of collegial discussions and, when warranted, qualify or justify their own views in light of the evidence presented.	**English Learners All Levels & Approaching** **Answer and Discuss.** Use the extra time while on- and beyond- grade-level students are discussing their first reads of the text to work individually and in small groups with English Learners and Approaching readers as outlined above. Should those students complete their first reads quickly, integrate them into the on- and beyond- grade-level discussion groups. Otherwise English Learners and Approaching readers will be given an opportunity to participate in text discussions with their peers later in the lesson.

Core Path	Access Path
1. What does Hitchcock mean by the idea that an audience should "play God"? (He doesn't mean this literally. He means "God" in the sense that the audience watching the movie should know more than the characters know about the events in the plot, as in the idea of God as omniscient, or all-knowing.) 2. According to Hitchcock, how might a viewer react to seeing a movie character get hit if the viewer does not know anything about the character? Why? (Audience reaction depends on whether the character is "a killer or a hero". If the audience doesn't know what sort of person the character is, they don't know how to react.) 3. How might a viewer react differently if he or she knows that the character is a hero? (A viewer would probably be upset if he knew a hero was being hit.) 4. What does it mean to "puzzle" an audience? ("Puzzling" asks the audience to solve a mystery, while creating suspense involves letting the audience knowing something the characters don't know.) 5. What does Alfred Hitchcock, the director and author of this article, want from his audiences? (He wants them to feel deeply while watching the movie, so that they "want to shout" when they realize the hero or heroine is in danger.)	
(G) **Grammar, Usage, and Mechanics.** Distribute the StudySync Grammar handout: The Suffixes -ible and -able. Review with students the use of suffixes as explained in the handout. Then have students complete the practice exercise. (Answers for the practice exercise appear online.) Finally, encourage students to apply what they have learned by analyzing the use of the suffixes *–ible* and *-able* in "Let 'Em Play God." Be sure students have access to a print or online dictionary. Ask students:	**English Learners All Levels & Approaching Mechanics.** Have students pair with more proficient students to complete the activity. Have students use the Access 1, 2, 3, and 4 handouts for further practice with the suffixes *-ible* and *-able*.

Core Path	Access Path
1. In the first sentence of the eleventh paragraph of "Let 'Em Play God," what does the word *plausible* mean? Is it a noun, verb, adjective, or adverb? (*Plausible* means believable; like all words ending in an *-ible* or *-able* suffix, it is an adjective.)	
2. In the last sentence of the eleventh paragraph, what is the root and the suffix of the word *unbelievable*? (*Believe* is the root and *-able* is the suffix; *un-* is a prefix.)	
3. Use your dictionary to look up the Latin-based suffixes *-ible* and *-able*. What are the meanings of these suffixes? (They share the meaning "likely to or capable of".) Look at the word *unbelievable*. How does the suffix *-able* help you determine its meaning? (The suffix *-able* added to *believe* creates an adjective that means "capable of being believed." Additionally, the prefix *un-*, meaning "not," creates a word meaning "not capable of being believed.")	
4. Rewrite Hitchcock's final sentence in the eleventh paragraph without the use of suffixes. Does the meaning of the sentence change? Does it flow as well? (Sample answer: When characters are not to be believed, you never get suspense, only surprise. The meaning of the sentence changes and it's difficult to avoid using passive voice. The use of the suffix *-able* makes this sentence possible.)	
	Extend **Identify and Define.** After reading the text, compile a list of additional vocabulary words. Ask students to reference their annotations and share any vocabulary words that were unfamiliar. 1. As a class, compile a list of unknown words on the board. 2. In small groups, ask students to make predictions about what they think these words mean based on context clues. 3. Each group should work together using dictionaries or devices to define the words and write the definitions in their notebooks.

Core Path	Access Path
	Extend **Analyze and Discuss.** Share this quote from Hitchcock with your class: "There is no terror in the bang, only in the anticipation of it." Use these questions to prompt discussion: 1. What does anticipation mean? (the state of awaiting something) 2. What do you think this quote means? 3. Do you agree with this quote? Why or why not? Give an example to support your answer.

3. THINK

Core Path	Access Path
Answer and Discuss. Have students complete the Think questions and then use the peer review instructions and rubric to complete the peer reviews. Refer to the sample answers online to discuss responses with your students.	**Beginner** **Find the Evidence.** In pairs, have students use the Find the Evidence exercise on the Access 1 handout to help them identify the evidence needed to answer the Think questions. **Intermediate & Advanced** **Sentence Frames.** Have students independently complete the sentence frames exercise on the Access 2 and 3 handouts. Then, in pairs, have students answer the Think questions. **Approaching** **Find the Evidence.** In pairs, have students use the Find the Evidence exercise on the Access 4 handout to help them identify the evidence needed to answer the Think questions.

Core Path	Access Path
	Extend **Debate.** Present students with an issue that can be debated. Allow students to debate the issue as a class or in smaller groups. Debate prompts: 1. Do you agree with Hitchcock that knowing things that the characters don't know creates suspense? Why or why not? 2. Do you think it is important that characters appear to be real in a suspenseful movie? Why or not?
	Extend **Write a Claim.** Ask students to write a strong claim that answers the question: *Which do you think is scarier, a suspenseful movie or a "whodunit" (mystery)?* Once students have written their claims, ask them to read their claims to a small group of their peers. This activity will provide them practice writings claims, as well as expose them to claims written by their peers.

SKILL:
Author's Purpose and
Author's Point of View

OVERVIEW

In this excerpt from "Let 'Em Play God," students look behind the scenes at how a filmmaker makes a suspenseful movie. Alfred Hitchcock explains how allowing the audience to know things the film's characters do not helps to create a feeling of suspense. The excerpt provides students with an excellent opportunity not only to learn about what makes a suspenseful film, but also to examine a writer's purpose and point of view on a subject.

OBJECTIVES

1. Learn the definition of author's purpose and author's point of view.
2. Practice using concrete strategies for identifying and analyzing author's purpose and author's point of view.
3. Participate effectively in a range of conversations and collaborations to express ideas and build upon the ideas of others.

ELA Common Core Standards:

Reading: Informational Text - RI.8.1, RI.8.6
Speaking & Listening - SL.8.1.A, SL.8.1.B, SL.8.1.C, SL.8.1.D, SL.8.2
Language - L.8.6

RESOURCES

Access 1 handout (Beginner)
Access 2 handout (Intermediate)
Access 3 handout (Advanced)
Access 4 handout (Approaching)

1. DEFINE

Core Path	Access Path
Watch. Watch the Concept Definition video on author's purpose and author's point of view with your students. Make sure students understand why it's critical to know an author's purpose or author's point of view when trying to unlock the meaning of a text. Pause the video at these key moments to discuss the information with your students:	**English Learners All Levels & Approaching** **Match.** Have students complete the matching exercise on the Access 1, 2, 3, and 4 handouts as they watch the video. Correct answers are located online.

1. 1:00 - Can you think of any other purpose (or purposes) an author might have? How does genre affect purpose, i.e., how might the purpose of a fiction text differ from that of an informational text? How might it stay the same?

2. 1:18 - Are there any other elements of a text that might offer clues into an author's purpose or author's point of view? What are some additional resources we can use if we are having trouble deciphering the purpose or point of view?

3. 2:03 - Why don't authors of fiction or poetry state their purpose clearly in the same way a politician or an essayist might?

Core Path	Access Path
Read and Discuss. Have students read the definition of author's purpose or author's point of view. Either in small groups or as a whole class, use the questions below to spark discussion among your students about author's purpose and author's point of view.	**Beginner & Approaching** **Fill in the Blanks.** To prepare students to participate in the discussion, have them complete the fill-in-the-blanks activity on the Access 1 and 4 handouts as they read the definition of author's purpose and author's point of view. Correct answers are located online.

1. According to the definition, what are the different purposes a writer might have for writing?

2. Why might an author have more than one purpose for writing?

3. What is the difference between an author's purpose and an author's point of view?

4. How might an author's point of view be related to his or her purpose?

Intermediate & Advanced
Discuss Prompts. To help these students participate in the discussion, prompt them with questions that can be answered with a few words, such as:

- What's usually an author's purpose for writing a story? (to entertain)

Core Path	Access Path
	• When you write an answer to a question about a story, what is your purpose? (to explain) • When you write about an experience that taught you a valuable lesson, what is the point of view? (the point of view is how you felt about it) • What might be your purpose? (to educate or persuade) **Beyond** **Discuss.** Have students discuss author's purpose and author's point of view in books and articles they have read. Compile a list of author's purposes and author's points of views. How does comparing and contrasting books and articles help them better understand author's purpose and the topic?
	Extend **Tech Infusion** **Annotate.** Link to an online article from your class website and ask students to use Diigo (http://tinyurl.com/pbxbxup) to annotate the article highlighting specific words/phrases and make notes about the point of view.
	Extend **Tech Infusion** **Connect.** Using a blogging tool such as Kidblog or Edublog, have students create a post that expresses their point of view on school start times. Are they too early? Too late? Just right? Why? Invite other students to comment by sharing what point of view they think is being expressed and whether they agree or disagree.

2. MODEL

Core Path	Access Path
Watch. Ask students to take notes on the SkillsTV video on author's purpose and author's point of view in "Let 'Em Play God." Remind students to listen for the way the students use academic vocabulary related to the definition of point of view during their discussion. Pause the video at these key moments to discuss the information with your students:	**Beginner, Intermediate & Approaching** **Watch and Answer Questions.** Provide students a second opportunity to watch the video as they answer the SkillsTV Questions on their Access 1, 2, and 4 handouts. The video may be paused at key moments to help them record their responses to the questions.
1. 1:16 - How do words or phrases in the text sometimes exist as a signal for the author's point of view? How did the students use these clues to distinguish this?	**Advanced** **Journals.** Have students note in their journals the strategies the students use in the SkillsTV video to find point of view.
2. 2:16 - What are some strategies the student uses (or could use) to understand Hitchcock's point of view about this subject? How is applying an author's point of view to an outside example (here, other scary movies he's seen) a helpful strategy when thinking critically about a text?	
3. 2:42 - What are some questions to consider when trying to understand an author's purpose? How can you be sure if an inference is correct?	
Read and Annotate. Have students independently read the Model section. As they read, ask students to use the annotation tool to: • highlight key points • ask questions • identify places where the Model applies the strategies laid out in the Identification and Application section on author's purpose and author's point of view	**Note:** During this portion of the lesson, instruction shifts from whole group to individual work. Use this time to work one-on-one or in small groups with Beginning, Intermediate, Advanced, and Approaching students. **Beginner & Intermediate** **Coach the Reading.** Work with these students in pairs to answer the Guided Reading questions on the Access 1 and 2 handouts. Have Beginning students refer to the Model Glossary on the Access 1 handout to help them determine the meaning of difficult words (Note: Provide the Access 1 handout Model Glossary to Intermediate students if necessary). Let students know they'll use these answers to help participate in the discussion about the Model. Sample answers for this exercise are located online.

Please note that excerpts and passages in the StudySync® library, workbooks, and PDFs are intended as touchstones to generate interest in an author's work. The excerpts and passages do not substitute for the reading of entire texts, and StudySync® strongly recommends that teachers and students seek out and purchase the whole literary or informational work in order to experience it as the author intended. Links to online resellers are available in our digital library. In addition, complete works may be ordered through an authorized reseller by filling out and returning to StudySync® the order form enclosed in this workbook.

Teacher's Edition   45

Core Path	Access Path
	Advanced **Identify Evidence.** Provide these students with the same instructions to read and annotate as on- and beyond- grade-level students. In addition, ask Advanced students to complete the Identify Evidence exercise on the Access 3 handout. Let students know that they'll use these answers to help participate in the discussion about the Model. **Approaching** **Guided Reading.** In small groups, have students complete the Guided Reading questions on the Access 4 handout as they read. Let them know that they'll use these answers to help participate in the discussion about the Model. Sample answers for this exercise are located online.
Discuss. After students read the Model text, use the following questions to facilitate a whole group discussion that helps them understand how to identify and evaluate Hitchcock's point of view and purpose for writing in "Let 'Em Play God": 1. What's the first step this Model uses to begin looking for the author's point of view? (The Model notes that writers sometimes use signal words and phrases as a way of telling readers "this is what I think." Hitchcock writes "as far as I'm concerned. . ." This tells readers that the detail that follows is Hitchcock's point of view or opinion.) 2. What idiom does Hitchcock use in this article that explains his attitude toward the audience? What does it mean? (He uses the idiom "work like the devil." Hitchcock maintains that an audience will "work like the devil" for him, or work very hard, if it knows what fate the actors on screen are facing. In other words, the audience will respond and become completely involved with the plot of the movie and what happens to the characters.)	

Core Path	Access Path
3. How does Hitchcock acknowledge and respond to conflicting viewpoints in the article? (In the twelfth paragraph, Hitchcock writes, "Just because there is a touch of murder and an air of mystery about a story, it is not necessary to see transoms opening, clutching fingers, hooded creatures, and asps on the Chinese rug." He then goes back to the plot of the film *Rope*. Rather than show a villain in an obvious way, as some kind of "hooded figure" with "clutching fingers," Hitchcock's villains in *Rope* are "grace and charm itself." Suspense is created through contrast.)	
4. Look back at the excerpt. Are there other examples in the article, besides the second paragraph, where the author specifically states his point of view? (Possible response: In the sixth paragraph Hitchcock writes, "Offhand this may sound like a debunking, but I do not believe that puzzling the audience is the essence of suspense.")	
5. Does the author convince you that his definition of suspense is correct? Why or why not? (Possible response: Yes, because he explains exactly how the audience feels when suspense, as he defines it, is created.)	
	Extend **Tech Infusion** **Mock Interview.** Pair or group students and have them work together to write a mock interview with Alfred Hitchcock. Students should ask questions about suspense and answer them as if they were Hitchcock. They may wish to act out and record their interviews using audio-visual equipment, tablets, or mobile devices.

3. YOUR TURN

Core Path	Access Path
Assess and Explain. Have students answer the comprehension questions to test for understanding. Share the explanations for Parts A and B (located online) with your students.	
	Extend **Share and Discuss.** After students complete the Your Turn section in class, poll students about their responses and, as a class, discuss the different strategies they used to determine the correct answers. Make sure students make connections between the correct answer to Part A (B) and the sentence that supports it in Part B (D). Conduct your poll by asking your students to complete a handout with questions or using Poll Everywhere (http://tinyurl.com/5grl69) or Socrative (http://tinyurl.com/nfz427v).

OVERVIEW

Using context as a clue to the meaning of a word or phrase is crucial for a reader's ability to read complex texts. This lesson plan provides follow-up questions and enrichments to help teachers guide students toward a usable, repeatable method for determining the meanings of unfamiliar words or phrases based on context clues.

OBJECTIVES

1. Learn the definition of word meaning.
2. Practice and apply concrete strategies for using context as a clue to the meaning of a word or phrase.
3. Participate effectively in a range of conversations and collaborations to express ideas and build upon the ideas of others.

ELA Common Core Standards:
Reading: Informational Text - RI.8.1, RI.8.4
Speaking & Listening - SL.8.1.A, SL.8.1.B, SL.8.1.C, SL.8.1.D, SL.8.2
Language - L.8.4.A, L.8.4.C, L.8.4.D, L.8.5.A

RESOURCES

Access 1 handout (Beginner)

Access 2 handout (Intermediate)

Access 3 handout (Advanced)

Access 4 handout (Approaching)

Please note that excerpts and passages in the StudySync® library, workbooks, and PDFs are intended as touchstones to generate interest in an author's work. The excerpts and passages do not substitute for the reading of entire texts, and StudySync® strongly recommends that teachers and students seek out and purchase the whole literary or informational work in order to experience it as the author intended. Links to online resellers are available in our digital library. In addition, complete works may be ordered through an authorized reseller by filling out and returning to StudySync® the order form enclosed in this workbook.

Teacher's Edition   49

1. DEFINE

Core Path	Access Path
Read and Discuss. Have students read the definition of word meaning. Either in small groups or as a whole class, use the following questions to engage students in a discussion about word meaning. 1. For what three purposes do the authors of informational texts use technical terms or words with specialized meanings? What specific examples of words used for each of these purposes come to mind? 2. If a word has more than one meaning, how are readers able to determine which meaning an author intends? What such multiple meaning words come to mind? Should writers be held responsible for building in context clues? 3. For what purpose do the authors of informational texts use figurative language? Do you find such language more helpful or distracting as a reader? 4. What are two context strategies readers can use when they have doubts about unfamiliar words or phrases? Which do you most often use when you encounter unfamiliar words?	**Beginner** **Finish the Sentences.** Have these students complete the sentence frames on the Access 1 handout as they read the definition of word meaning. Have them use the completed sentence frames to help them participate in the discussion. Sample answers for this activity are located online. **Intermediate & Advanced** **Discuss Prompts.** To help these students participate in the discussion, prompt them with questions that can be answered with a few words, such as: • How can a reader determine the meaning for the word "minor" in the following examples: *Even though the team was without Chad for the game, they considered it only a **minor** setback. Since she was still a **minor**, she needed her parents' signature on the loan application.* (By using context clues, a reader can determine which meaning the word is using.) • In what kinds of texts do you find figurative language? (Figurative language is usually found in poetry and fictional texts.) • In what kinds of texts do you find technical language? (Informational texts, reports, encyclopedia articles, and science journals usually have technical language.) **Approaching** **Complete a Chart.** To prepare students to participate in the discussion, have them complete the chart on the Access 4 handout as they read the definition. Correct answers are located online.

Core Path	Access Path
	Beyond **Discuss.** In pairs, provide students with an online news article or print editorial to read. Have students read through the article or editorial, identifying three words they are familiar with but are being used by the writer in an unfamiliar way. Instruct students to work together to form a preliminary definition of each word by using the context clues. After pairs have a preliminary definition for each word they have identified, have them use a print or digital dictionary to confirm their definitions. Remind students that because words can have several meanings, the definition they are looking for may not be the first entry found. Also remind students to be sure to verify that the part of speech for the definition they are looking for matches the part of speech of the word being used in the text.
	Extend **Create Context.** Lead students to brainstorm a list of idiomatic expressions, or figures of speech, and record students' ideas on the board (*get the ball rolling*, *cry over spilled milk*, *root for the underdog*, and so on). Ask each student to select one expression from the class list. Then, ask the student to write a short informational paragraph on any topic that includes the expression and creates a context that explains its meaning. Invite volunteers to read aloud their paragraphs to the class. Lead the class to create a definition for each example expression based on the context of the writing.

2. MODEL

Core Path	Access Path
Read and Annotate. Have students independently read the Model section. As they read, ask students to use the annotation tool to: • highlight key points • ask questions • identify places where the Model applies the strategies laid out in the Identification and Application section • comment on how a word's position or function in the text, as well as the overall meaning of the sentences around it, provide clues about its meaning	**Note:** During this portion of the lesson, instruction shifts from whole group to individual work. Use this time to work one-on-one or in small groups with Beginning, Intermediate, Advanced, and Approaching students. **Beginner, Intermediate & Approaching** **Coach the Reading.** Work with these students (either individually or in small groups) to fill out the Guided Reading questions on the Access 1 and 2 handouts. Have students refer to the Model Glossary on the Access 1 and 2 handouts to help them determine the meaning of difficult words. Let students know they'll use these answers to help participate in the discussion about the Model. Sample answers for this exercise are located online. **Advanced** **Identify Evidence.** Provide these students with the same instructions to read and annotate as on- and beyond- grade-level students. In addition, ask students to complete the Identify Evidence exercise on the Access 3 handout. Let students know that they'll use these answers to help participate in the discussion about the Model. Sample answers for this exercise are located online. **Approaching** **Guided Reading.** Have students complete the Guided Reading questions on the Access 4 handout as they read. Let them know that they'll use these answers to help participate in the discussion about the Model. Sample answers for this exercise are located online.

Core Path	Access Path
Discuss. After students read the Model text, use these questions to facilitate a whole group discussion that helps students understand how to use context as a clue to the meaning of an unfamiliar word or phrase:	

1. How does the Model begin to use context to decipher the meaning of the phrase "on the edge of their seats"? (It identifies the function of the phrase within the sentence.)

2. How does the Model demonstrate how to use a dictionary to gain insight into the meaning of the idiom "on the edge of their seats," even though the expression has a meaning of its own, separate from the meaning of the individual words that form it? (It demonstrates how to use the dictionary to accurately define the word *suspense*, with which the idiom is associated.)

3. How does the Model use the overall meaning of the paragraph to help decipher the meaning of the phrase "on the edge of their seats"? (It identifies the relationship between Hitchcock's discussion of suspense and the use of the phrase.)

4. How might readers, according to the text, confirm the correct meaning of the idiom "on the edge of their seats"? (look it up in a specialized dictionary)

5. What is the effect of Hitchcock's use of the phrase "on the edge of their seats"? (It takes on a double meaning in that it describes the mental state of movie viewers who happen to be sitting in seats.)

6. How does the Model begin to use context to decipher the meaning of the phrase "cry in agony"? (It identifies the function of the phrase in the sentence and verifies the precise meaning of the word *agony* in a dictionary.)

7. How does the Model use the overall meaning of the paragraph to help decipher the meaning of the phrase "cry in agony"? (It identifies the relationship between Hitchcock's discussion of suspense as the goal of writing and the use of the phrase.)

8. What is the word that the phrase "cry in agony" exaggerates? (frustration)

Core Path	Access Path
	Extend **Tech Infusion** **Analyze Context.** Have students write the idiom "on the edge of their seats" in the center of print or digital web diagrams. In the radiating circles, have students describe situations other than watching a suspense film when an audience might be "on the edge of their seats." Ask volunteers for examples. Then lead students to identify the common contextual elements among the examples. You may repeat the activity with the hyperbole "cry in agony."
	Extend **Tech Infusion** **Write.** Ask students to write movie reviews of suspense films or films in other genres by introducing a claim and supporting it with clear reasons and evidence. Provide students with published models of movie reviews and identify and discuss the common elements. Encourage students to incorporate movie-related idioms in their writing and to provide defining context for these idioms: *rolling in the aisles*, *had the audience in stitches*, *glued to their seats*, *state-of-the-art*, and so on. Students may also incorporate multiple meaning words, such as *set* or *shot*, and provide defining context. Students may present excerpts of the reviewed films and their reviews to the class.

3. YOUR TURN

Core Path	Access Path
Assess and Explain. Have students answer the comprehension questions to test for understanding of how to determine word meaning by using context. Share the explanations for Parts A and B (located online) with your students.	
	Extend **Tech Infusion** **Write.** Hitchcock discusses filmmaking as if there is a recipe for success. Form small student groups and have each group use a recipe format or digital template to write a recipe for a "Whodunit" or a "Hitchcock 'Edge-of-the-Seat' Suspense Film" based on ideas from the text as well as students' own ideas. Encourage students to include idioms, hyperboles, multiple-meaning words, and other figures of speech in their recipes and to provide a defining context for each usage. Publish students' recipes in a *How-To-Make-a-Movie* book.

CLOSE READ:
Let 'Em Play God

OVERVIEW

In this excerpt from "Let 'Em Play God," students look behind the scenes at how a filmmaker makes a suspenseful movie. Alfred Hitchcock explains that letting the audience know things that the film's characters do not know creates a feeling of suspense for viewers. The excerpt provides students with an excellent opportunity not only to learn about what makes a scary, suspenseful film, but also to see how a writer expresses his point of view on a subject. The Close Read gives students the opportunity to analyze more deeply Hitchcock's point of view and its effect on the reader's interpretation.

OBJECTIVES

1. Complete a close reading of a passage of informational text.
2. Practice and apply concrete strategies for identifying author's purpose and author's point of view.
3. Participate effectively in a range of conversations and collaborations to express ideas and build upon the ideas of others.
4. Prewrite, plan, and produce clear and coherent writing in response to a prompt.

ELA Common Core Standards:
Reading: Informational Text - RI.8.1, RI.8.4, RI.8.6
Writing - W.8.4, W.8.5, W.8.6, W.8.10
Speaking & Listening - SL.8.1.A, SL.8.1.C, SL.8.6
Language - L.8.2.C, L.8.4.A, L.8.4.C, L.8.4.D, L.8.6

RESOURCES

"Let 'Em Play God" Vocabulary handout
Student Model
Access 1 handout (Beginner)
Access 2 handout (Intermediate)
Access 3 handout (Advanced)
Access 4 handout (Approaching)

1. INTRODUCTION

Core Path	Access Path
Define and Compare. Project the vocabulary words and definitions onto the board or provide students with a handout, so they can copy the vocabulary into their notebooks. Suggest that students consult general and specialized reference materials, both print and digital, to compare the precise meaning of a specific word with their initial vocabulary predictions from the First Read. Review words that students defined incorrectly to understand why they were unable to use context clues to develop usable definitions.	**Beginner, Intermediate, & Approaching Review.** Have students complete the vocabulary sentence frames on the Access 1, 2, and 4 handouts using the vocabulary words. Correct answers are located online.
Review. Have students complete the fill-in-the-blank vocabulary handout for this selection. Answers for the handout are listed online.	**Extend** **Tech Infusion** **Create.** Have students study the vocabulary words and expand their vocabulary by finding related words. Use Snappy Words (http://tinyurl.com/ygysonn) to create word webs using the vocabulary words from the text.

2. READ

Core Path	Access Path
Model Close Reading. Project the text onto the board and model a close reading of the first five paragraphs using the following annotation strategies. While modeling annotation strategies, make notes that tie the text to the focus skill and demonstrate what students are looking for as they read. Here is some guidance for you as you annotate for your students: • As the Skills lesson that precedes this text makes clear, Alfred Hitchcock states his point of view right up front in the second paragraph of the text. The signal words "As far as I'm concerned" are a strong clue to students that what will follow is Hitchcock's point of view.	

Please note that excerpts and passages in the StudySync® library, workbooks, and PDFs are intended as touchstones to generate interest in an author's work. The excerpts and passages do not substitute for the reading of entire texts, and StudySync® strongly recommends that teachers and students seek out and purchase the whole literary or informational work in order to experience it as the author intended. Links to online resellers are available in our digital library. In addition, complete works may be ordered through an authorized reseller by filling out and returning to StudySync® the order form enclosed in this workbook.

Teacher's Edition   57

Core Path	Access Path
• In the next several paragraphs, Hitchcock works to explain his metaphor about the audience playing God. He does this by using an example about a theoretical mystery film.	
• Let's take a closer look at the example that Hitchcock provides. We have six characters involved in a mystery. A man has been murdered and all six are possible suspects but no one is sure including the audience. One of the suspects is knocked unconscious. Hitchcock maintains that unless the audience knows whether this suspect is a hero or a killer, they do not know whether to cheer or weep.	
• So according to Hitchcock, without context, and without understanding more than the characters on the screen, an audience doesn't have a clue about the type of emotional response a scene is meant to elicit.	
• Now let's reread the fifth paragraph in the essay. In what way does this paragraph serve as a good definition for "playing God" as Hitchcock uses the phrase? (Hitchcock writes that if the audience has been told all the secrets that the characters do not know, they'll "work like the devil" for you because they know what fate is facing the poor actors. This is playing God in the sense that, like an omniscient or all-seeing being, the audience knows more than the characters, yet they cannot change their fate on-screen. This creates suspense.)	

Core Path	Access Path
Read and Annotate. Read the Skills Focus questions as a class, so your students know what they should pay close attention to as they read. Then have students read and annotate the excerpt. Ask students to use the annotation tool as they read to: 1. respond to the Skills Focus section 2. ask questions about the author's purpose and point of view 3. make connections between the author's point of view and plot elements in the film *Rope* 4. identify key information, examples, and details 5. note unfamiliar vocabulary and use context as a clue to the meaning of a word or phrase 6. capture their reaction to the ideas Alfred Hitchcock presents in the text As they reread the text, remind students to use the comprehension strategy of Rereading that they learned in the First Read.	**Note:** While on- grade-level students are reading and annotating, work one-on-one or in small groups with Beginning, Intermediate, Advanced, and Approaching students to support them as they read and annotate the text. **Beginner & Approaching** **Read and Annotate.** If these students find the Skills Focus questions difficult, have them use the Annotation Guide on the Access 1 and 4 handouts. The questions in the Annotation Guide correspond to the Skills Focus questions but provide more support.
Discuss. After students have read the text, use the sample responses to the Skills Focus questions online to discuss the reading and the process of searching for the author's purpose and author's point of view.	**Beginner & Intermediate** **Pair and Share.** In small groups or pairs, ask students to share and discuss their annotations with a focus on point of view. You can provide students with questions to guide their discussion: 1. What is the author's opinion about suspense? Cite specific textual evidence to support your statements. (It is so important that producers cry for it, writers cry in agony to get it, and actors cry for joy when they get it.) 2. How does the author show the difference between puzzling the audience and suspense? Cite specific textual evidence to support your statements. (He says he does not make puzzlers, and then provides an example of how he creates suspense instead.)

Core Path	Access Path
	3. What is the author's opinion about "puzzlers" versus suspense films? Cite specific textual evidence to support your answer. (He does not respect puzzlers as much. He does not define what a puzzler is, but asserts that he has never made one, and then goes on to provide an example of his own work creating suspense.)
	Extend **Tech Infusion** **Analyze a Film Excerpt.** Screen the first few scenes of *Rope*, the film Hitchcock references in his essay. Does Hitchcock adhere to his own principles about the audience "playing God"? Does he deviate from this at any point? Are these first few scenes suspenseful? Why or why not? (Note: The first scene from the film, which is curiously similar to Hitchcock's description of a theoretical film in paragraphs 3-5 and possibly a contradiction to his theory, can be found on YouTube: http://tinyurl.com/phgh97j.)

3. WRITE

Core Path	Access Path
Prewrite and Plan. Read the prompt as a class and ask students to brainstorm their reactions to Alfred Hitchcock's point of view in "Let 'Em Play God," and their thoughts about whether the plot of the movie *Rope* that Hitchcock describes in the article is a good example of letting the audience "play God." Students can brainstorm together either as a class or in small groups to begin planning their responses. Remind students to look at the excerpt and their annotations to find textual evidence to support their ideas. You may wish to review with students the Short Constructed Response - Informative/Explanatory Student Model for guidance on how to construct an effective response to the writing prompt.	**English Learners All Levels & Approaching** **Prewrite and Plan.** Have students who are having difficulty organizing their ideas use the Prewrite activity on the Access 1, 2, 3, and 4 handouts to plan their response to the prompt.

Core Path	Access Path
Discuss. Project these instructions for the peer review onto the board and review them with your class, so they know what they are looking for when they begin to provide their classmates with feedback: • Has the writer identified and explained the use of the metaphor "letting the audience play God"? • What sort of evidence did the writer use from the text to support his or her writing? • How well does the writer explain how that evidence supports his or her arguments? • Are the writer's ideas presented in a clear and logical way? • Does the writer write using standard grammar and punctuation? Are there any weak spots? • Has the writer checked for and corrected all spelling errors? • What specific suggestions can you make to help the writer improve the essay? • What thing(s) does this paper do especially well? • Be sure to tell the writer what he or she did well and what he or she needs to work on. Remember that your comments are most useful when they are constructive. After you've looked at the peer review instructions, review the rubric with students before they begin writing. Allow time for students to briefly raise and discuss questions they may have about the peer review instructions and the rubric. Tell students how many peer reviews they will need to complete once they submit their writing.	
Write. Ask students to complete the writing assignment using textual evidence to support their answers. If possible, have students use technology to produce and publish their writing. Once they have completed their writing, they should click "Submit."	
Review. Once students complete their writing assignment, they should submit substantive feedback to two peers. If possible, have students use technology to interact and collaborate with others.	

OVERVIEW

The short story "The Monkey's Paw" by W.W. Jacobs is a famous horror story about a Victorian family that comes into possession of a cursed item that grants wishes. The First Read gives students the opportunity to experience the text with a limited context.

OBJECTIVES

1. Perform an initial reading of a text and demonstrate comprehension by responding to short analysis and inference questions with textual evidence.
2. Practice defining vocabulary words using context clues, and follow up by verifying the preliminary determinations of word meanings.
3. Participate effectively in a range of conversations and collaborations to express ideas and build upon the ideas of others.

ELA Common Core Standards:

Reading: Literature - RL.8.1, RL.8.4, RL.8.10
Writing - W.8.10
Speaking & Listening - SL.8.1.A, SL.8.1.B, SL.8.1.C, SL.8.1.D, SL.8.2, SL.8.6
Language - L.8.4.A, L.8.4.C, L.8.4.D, L.8.6

RESOURCES

Access 1 handout (Beginner)

Access 2 handout (Intermediate)

Access 3 handout (Advanced)

Access 4 handout (Approaching)

ACCESS COMPLEX TEXT

"The Monkey's Paw" is set in Victorian England. Since the story requires some prior knowledge of the culture, a brief summary may be helpful for some readers. The story opens with the White family spending a contented evening together at home. They are visited by Sergeant-Major Morris, who tells stories of his world travels and gives the family a mummified monkey's paw that is said to grant wishes. W.W. Jacobs creates suspense as readers begin to suspect, through foreshadowing, mood, and dialogue, that the consequences of such wishes are terrible. The author continues to build tension and suspense as readers learn the tragic effects of Mr. White's first two wishes. Mr. White uses the third wish just in time to avert further disaster. The elements of the genre are reflected in the challenges of the text. To help students understand the story's theme, use the following ideas to provide scaffolded instruction for an initial reading of the more complex features of this text.

- **Genre** - Literary elements such as suspense, foreshadowing, and mood may require support to help students identify examples and purpose. In addition, students may need help linking story details to determine the theme. Initially, Mr. White says that he doesn't know what to wish for: "I've got all I want." Nonetheless, Mr. White ignores the Sergeant's warning that the monkey's paw is cursed by a holy man who wants "to show that fate ruled people's lives, and that those who interfered with it did so to their sorrow."

- **Specific Vocabulary** - Difficult vocabulary, such as "presumptuous" and "doggedly," may challenge some readers. Remind students to use context clues while reading, and also to use a dictionary to define unfamiliar words.

- **Prior Knowledge** - Students may be unfamiliar with Indian cultural references to "old temples and fakirs and jugglers." Point out that India was a colony of the British Empire during the time the story is set.

1. INTRODUCTION

Core Path	Access Path
Watch. As a class, watch the video preview of "The Monkey's Paw." Have students share their ideas about the story to come based on the preview.	**English Learners All Levels** **Fill in the Blanks.** Ask students to use their Access 1, 2, and 3 handouts to fill in the blanks of the transcript for the preview's voiceover as they watch the preview along with their classmates. Answers are located online.

Please note that excerpts and passages in the StudySync® library, workbooks, and PDFs are intended as touchstones to generate interest in an author's work. The excerpts and passages do not substitute for the reading of entire texts, and StudySync® strongly recommends that teachers and students seek out and purchase the whole literary or informational work in order to experience it as the author intended. Links to online resellers are available in our digital library. In addition, complete works may be ordered through an authorized reseller by filling out and returning to StudySync® the order form enclosed in this workbook.

Teacher's Edition   **63**

Core Path	Access Path
Read and Listen. Individually or as a class, read and listen to the Introduction for "The Monkey's Paw." The Introduction provides context for the short story.	**English Learners All Levels & Approaching** **Read and Listen.** Ask students to read and listen to the Introduction for "The Monkey's Paw." Have them refer to the Introduction Glossary on their Access 1, 2, 3, and 4 handouts for definitions of key vocabulary terms. If there are unfamiliar words that are not included in their glossary, encourage students to check a dictionary or online reference tool, like http://tinyurl.com/pye34kb.
Access Prior Knowledge. Find out what your students already know about superstition. 1. Explain that while this story by W.W. Jacobs may be set long ago in England, the fears created by superstitions have been part of cultures all over the world for centuries. 2. Find out what your students already know about superstitions. First, have students look up the meaning of the word *superstition*, including its roots. As a class or in small groups, generate a list (on the board or on paper) of any information or ideas your students have about superstitions. 3. After compiling a list, ask students to share where their previous knowledge came from. For example, did their ideas come from a movie, friend, television show, book, or family member? 4. Where have students encountered superstitions in their reading? Discuss as a class how writers include superstitions in their works of fiction.	**Beginner & Intermediate** **List Differences.** In pairs, have students use the List Differences activity on their Access 1 and 2 handouts to search the sentences taken from the text for differences between the story's setting and today's world. If students need additional support, have pairs ask each other questions such as: • What do the characters do for entertainment at home? • What do they use for heat and light? • What music do they listen to? • How do they travel from place to place? • What do they wear? **Advanced** **List Differences.** In pairs, have students complete the List Differences exercise in the Access 3 handout that asks students to consider what other differences they can infer from the text that aren't mentioned (lack of TV, flashlights, etc.). Have the pairs generate ideas, discuss the chart, and complete it together.

Core Path	Access Path
	Approaching **List Differences.** In pairs, have students use the List Differences activity on their Access 4 handout to search the sentences taken from the text for differences between the story's setting and today's world. If students need additional support, have pairs ask each other questions such as: • What do the characters do for entertainment at home? • What do they use for heat and light? • What music do they listen to? • How do they travel from place to place? • What do they wear?
	Extend **Make Predictions**. Based on the Introduction, ask students to make predictions about the story elements they would expect to find, and how these elements might contribute to the story's theme.
	Extend **Analyze and Discuss an Adage.** Ask students to analyze the saying, "Be careful what you wish for" (anonymous). Pose questions such as: 1. What do you think this adage means? 2. Do you agree with this adage? Why or why not? 3. If you could add a sentence onto this adage, what would it be?

Teacher's Edition

2. READ

Core Path	Access Path
Make Predictions about Vocabulary. There are five bold vocabulary words in the text. As students read the text, ask them to make predictions about what they think each bold vocabulary word means based on the context clues in the sentence. Have students use the annotation tool to make their predictions. If you are in a low tech classroom and students are reading from printed copies or a projected text, ask students to record predictions in their notes, so they can be easily referenced in class.	**Note:** This exercise, which extends vocabulary instruction, should be completed when the class shifts from whole group instruction to individual work during the "Read and Annotate" exercise.

Make Predictions about Vocabulary. There are five bold vocabulary words in the text. As students read the text, ask them to make predictions about what they think each bold vocabulary word means based on the context clues in the sentence. Have students use the annotation tool to make their predictions. If you are in a low tech classroom and students are reading from printed copies or a projected text, ask students to record predictions in their notes, so they can be easily referenced in class.

It might be helpful to model this for students before they begin reading. Either using the board or projecting the actual text, focus in on the sentence that uses the word "proffered":

- The sergeant-major shook hands, and taking the **proffered** seat by the fire, watched contentedly while his host got out whiskey and tumblers and stood a small copper kettle on the fire.

Model for the class how to use the overall structure and meaning of the sentence and the sentences around it, the word's position, and other clues to define the unfamiliar vocabulary word. In this case, point out these context keys:

1. Look at the structure of the sentence. What is the subject (sergeant-major) and what are the first verbs? (shook / taking) The conjunction "and" lets us know that the sergeant-major was the one who "shook" and who was the one "taking." We also know that the thing he took was the chair, and since the word "proffered" comes before it, we know that it's describing the chair.

2. We can also see that the sergeant-major sits "contentedly" while his host gets out tumblers and whiskey, so we can infer that the "proffered chair" is not something that would upset him.

Note: This exercise, which extends vocabulary instruction, should be completed when the class shifts from whole group instruction to individual work during the "Read and Annotate" exercise.

Beginner, Intermediate, & Approaching Pair Practice.

1. Pair Approaching, Beginning, and Intermediate readers with more proficient readers.

2. Give them an additional sentence that contains a new vocabulary word.

3. Ask the Approaching, Beginning, and Intermediate readers to complete a Think Aloud using the teacher-led Make Predictions about Vocabulary activity as a model, while the more proficient reader actively listens.

4. The student should use the context clues in the sentence to try to determine the meaning of the new vocabulary word.

5. After the Approaching, Beginning, and Intermediate reader has completed the Think Aloud and made a prediction about the word's meaning, allow time for the more proficient reader to add his/her own thoughts and clarify any points of confusion.

6. Once they've completed this Think Aloud, encourage them to use a dictionary to confirm the definition of the new vocabulary word. Have them refer to the Text Glossary on their Access 1, 2, and 4 handouts for definitions of key vocabulary terms in the text. Encourage them to add any additional vocabulary words or idioms they find in the text and look up definitions for those words and idioms online or in a dictionary.

Core Path	Access Path
3. We can also see that the host's actions are what we would consider polite behavior: shaking hands, getting out glasses and drinks, seating the guest by the fire. So, we can also infer that the "proffered chair" is also something polite, like offering a guest a place to sit. Therefore, we can determine that "proffered" is a synonym for "offered." Remind students that they can also verify word meanings using a dictionary or other resource.	

Model Reading Comprehension Strategy. Before students begin reading, model the reading comprehension strategy of ask and answer questions by using this Think Aloud that talk students through the first six paragraphs of text. First explain to your students that asking and answering questions is: *the process of asking yourself questions before, during, and after you read a passage, and then answering the questions and forming new ones as they continue to read.* Remind students that successful reading is not just the mechanical process of decoding text. Rather, it is a process of active inquiry. Good readers approach a text with questions and develop new questions as they read. For example, when reading fiction, students might ask and answer the following questions: • What is this story about? The title is "The Monkey's Paw," so I know the story will have something to do with a monkey's paw. The first six paragraphs don't tell about the monkey's paw, so I will keep on reading. • What problem does the main character have? The problem is not explained yet, but I can infer that it has something to do with the guest that Mr. White is expecting. • How does the setting affect the events of the plot? So far, the setting seems warm by the fire, but also a little threatening, with the dark, cold, rainy night and remote location of the Whites' house.	**Note:** This exercise, which extends vocabulary instruction, should be completed when the class shifts from whole group instruction to individual work during the "Read and Annotate" exercise. **Beginner, Intermediate, & Approaching** **Apply Reading Comprehension Strategy.** Have students listen to the audio version of the excerpt from "The Monkey's Paw." After they listen to the audio recording, ask them discuss the text in small groups. Pose questions, such as: • Do you feel as if you are there in the house with the family? • How does the author get you to want to keep reading? • Give students time to discuss. Call on groups to explain their thoughts to the class.

Please note that excerpts and passages in the StudySync® library, workbooks, and PDFs are intended as touchstones to generate interest in an author's work. The excerpts and passages do not substitute for the reading of entire texts, and StudySync® strongly recommends that teachers and students seek out and purchase the whole literary or informational work in order to experience it as the author intended. Links to online resellers are available in our digital library. In addition, complete works may be ordered through an authorized reseller by filling out and returning to StudySync® the order form enclosed in this workbook.

Teacher's Edition   67

Core Path	Access Path
Point out that as students read further, they can ask themselves additional questions, such as: • What steps is the main character taking to solve the problem? • How do the other characters affect the plot? • How do the events change the characters? Remind students that questions that come up may be answered as they continue reading. However, if students cannot learn answers to their questions by the selection's end, they may need to go back and reread or else make inferences.	
Read and Annotate. Read and annotate the excerpt. Ask students to use the annotation tool as they read to: 1. use context clues to analyze and determine the meaning of bolded vocabulary terms 2. ask questions about passages of text that may be unclear or unresolved 3. identify key information, events, and characters 4. make connections between events and characters' decisions 5. note unfamiliar vocabulary 6. capture their reactions to the events in the text	**Beginner** **Coach the Reading.** While other students read, annotate, and discuss the text independently, work with Beginning students, listening to the audio of the text and pausing periodically or when any student has a question. Coach students in articulating their questions for the group and in highlighting and annotating the text. Have students use the Annotation Guide in the Access 1 handout to support them as they highlight and annotate the text.
	Intermediate **Listen to the Audio.** Have these students listen to the audio of the text and use the definitions in the Access 2 handout to help them with words or idioms that may be unfamiliar. If students need help with annotating the text, have them use the Annotation Guide in the Access 2 handout. After working with the Beginning students, you may wish to check this group's progress and provide support as needed. **Advanced** **Pair with Proficient Peers.** Have Advanced students work with English proficient peers to read, annotate, and discuss the text. Have students use the Annotation Guide in the Access 3 handout to support them as they highlight and annotate the text. Encourage them to listen to the audio of the text if needed.

Core Path	Access Path
	Approaching **Use the Annotation Guide.** Have students use the Annotation Guide in the Access 4 handout to support them as they highlight and annotate the text.
Discuss. In small groups or pairs, have students discuss the questions and inferences they made while reading. Have them also note any new vocabulary. Make sures students follow the rules for collegial discussions. Refer to Collaborative Discussions in the Speaking & Listening Handbook. 1. Where does the monkey's paw come from? (Sergeant-Major Morris got it from a "fakir" in India. He got the paw when the previous owner died.) 2. What information does Morris have about the monkey's paw that he does not completely share with Mr. White? (Morris indicates that the paw might bring bad luck, although he only hints at this.) 3. What is Mr. White's first wish? (He wishes for two hundred pounds.) 4. How is his wish fulfilled? (His son dies in an accident at work. The company gives Mr. and Mrs. White two hundred pounds as compensation.) 5. What is Mr. White's second wish? Why does he make this wish? (At his wife's insistence, he wishes that their son were alive again.) 6. What other questions can you ask and answer? (I can ask what happens after Mr. White makes the second wish. Then I can answer that he and his wife hear a knock at the door. She believes it is their son.)	**English Learners All Levels & Approaching** Use the extra time while on- and beyond- grade-level students are discussing their first reads of the text to work individually and in small groups with English Learners and Approaching readers as previously outlined. Should those students complete their first reads quickly, integrate them into the on- and beyond- grade-level discussion groups. Otherwise English Learners and Approaching readers will be given an opportunity to participate in text discussions with their peers later in the lesson.
	Extend **Identify and Define.** After reading the text, compile a list of additional vocabulary words. Ask students to reference their annotations and share any vocabulary words that were unfamiliar.

Core Path	Access Path
	1. As a class, compile a list of unknown words on the board.
	2. In small groups, ask students to make predictions about they think these words mean based on how they are used in the sentence. (Note: They will need access to StudySync to read the words in context and make predictions.)
	3. Each group should work together using dictionaries or devices to define the words and write the definitions in their notebooks.
	Extend **Make an Inference.** In the second to last paragraph it says that Mr. White makes "his third and last wish," but it doesn't say exactly what he wished. Based on the events in the story, what inference can be made about Mr. White's third wish? Why did he make that wish? Did his third wish come true?

3. SYNCTV

Core Path	Access Path
Watch. As a class, watch the SyncTV video on "The Monkey's Paw". Pause the video at these key moments to discuss the information with your students: 1. 1:38 - How do the students use textual evidence to determine the setting of "The Monkey's Paw"? 2. 2:50 - Amanda and Andrew agree that Mr. White is being "greedy." What textual evidence supports this characterization? How does this bring the group closer to identifying the theme? 3. 3:45 - How does the group build on Amanda's first idea of the theme "be careful what you wish for"? What evidence do they use to narrow the focus of their theme?	**Beginner & Intermediate** **Analyze the Discussion.** Have students use the "Analyze the Discussion" guide on the Access 1 and 2 handouts to identify key points in the discussion and the evidence the students use to determine those points. Sample answers are located online. **Advanced** **Identify the Theme.** Have students discuss and complete the "Central Theme" chart on the Access 3 handout, referring back to the SyncTV video as needed to clarify their answers. Sample answers appear online.

Core Path	Access Path
	Approaching **Analyze the Discussion.** Have students complete the chart on the Access 4 handout by listing textual evidence cited by the students in the video. Sample answers are located online.

4. THINK

Core Path	Access Path
Answer and Discuss. Have students complete the Think questions and then use the peer review instructions and rubric to complete the peer reviews. Refer to the sample answers online to discuss responses with your students.	**Beginner & Intermediate** **Sentence Frames.** Have students complete the sentence frames exercise in the Access 1 and 2 handouts to support their responses to the Think questions. If necessary, distribute sentence frames to Advanced students as well. **Approaching** **Find the Evidence.** Have students use Find the Evidence exercise in the Access 4 handout to help them identify the evidence needed to answer the Think questions.
SyncTV-Style Discussion. Put students into heterogeneous small groups and give them a prompt to discuss. Remind them to model their discussions after the SyncTV episodes they have seen. Stress the importance of citing textual evidence in their conversations to support their ideas. Discussion prompt options: 1. Why do you think Mr. White decided to keep the monkey's paw, even after all his friend's warnings and pleas? Would you have kept it? 2. What do you think was Mr. White's third wish? Why do you think the author leaves it up to the reader's imagination?	**Beginner & Intermediate** **Use Sentence Frames.** Have these students use the sentence frames on Access 1 and 2 handouts to help them participate in the discussion. **Approaching** **Use Think Questions.** Remind these students to refer back to their answers to the Think questions to help them participate in the group discussion.

Core Path	Access Path
	Extend **Debate.** Present students with an issue from the text that can be debated. Allow students to debate the issue as a class or in smaller groups. Debate prompts: 1. Do you think Mr. White's second wish came true? Why or why not? 2. Should Mr. White have used the monkey's paw to make wishes at all? Why or why not?
	Extend **Write a Set of Rules.** 1. Ask students to work in pairs to write a set of rules for using a monkey's paw or another talisman they have learned about or made up. 2. Once pairs have written their rules, ask them to read them to another pair of students. 3. Repeat the process several times. This activity will provide them practice writing instructions as well as expose them to instructions written by their peers.

OVERVIEW

Determining the theme of a text is challenging for many students. This lesson provides follow-up questions and useful enrichments to help teachers guide students toward a usable, repeatable method for identifying the theme.

OBJECTIVES

1. Learn the definition of theme.
2. Practice using concrete strategies for identifying theme.
3. Participate effectively in a range of conversations and collaborations to express ideas and build upon the ideas of others.

ELA Common Core Standards:

Reading: Literature - RL.8.1, RL.8.2
Speaking & Listening - SL.8.1.A, SL.8.1.B, SL.8.1.C, SL.8.1.D, SL.8.2
Language - L.8.6

RESOURCES

Access 1 handout (Beginner)

Access 2 handout (Intermediate)

Access 3 handout (Advanced)

Access 4 handout (Approaching)

Please note that excerpts and passages in the StudySync® library, workbooks, and PDFs are intended as touchstones to generate interest in an author's work. The excerpts and passages do not substitute for the reading of entire texts, and StudySync® strongly recommends that teachers and students seek out and purchase the whole literary or informational work in order to experience it as the author intended. Links to online resellers are available in our digital library. In addition, complete works may be ordered through an authorized reseller by filling out and returning to StudySync® the order form enclosed in this workbook.

Teacher's Edition   73

1. DEFINE

Core Path	Access Path
Watch. Watch the Concept Definition video on theme with your students. Make sure your students are familiar with all the different elements shared in the video-including details, events, people and ideas-as well as how these elements may interact over the course of a text. Pause the video at these key moments to discuss the information with your students:	**English Learners All Levels & Approaching Fill-in-the-Blank Summary.** Have students complete the fill-in-the-blank exercise on the Access 1, 2, 3, and 4 handouts as they watch the video. Answers are located online.

1. 1:00 - Why would authors choose to have readers infer storie's themes? Why don't all authors just come out and state the theme like they do in fables?

2. 1:25 - Why would thinking about a character in a story, and what he or she learns as the plot unfolds, help a reader uncover the theme?

3. 2:37 - Can you think of any evidence that might help a reader identify theme that the students in the video don't mention? Are some pieces of evidence more important for determining theme?

Core Path	Access Path
Read and Discuss. After watching the Concept Definition video, have students read the definition of theme. Either in small groups or as a whole class, use the questions below to engage students in a discussion about theme.	**Beginner** **Complete the Sentences.** Have these students complete the sentences by filling in the blanks on the Access 1 handout as they read the definition of theme. Have them use the completed sentences to help them participate in the discussion. Sample answers for this exercise are located online.

1. Can a theme change throughout a story? Why or why not? (Yes. This is why it is important to analyze the theme over the course of a text as you read.)

2. What are the themes of some books you have read recently? (Answers will vary. Students should differentiate between themes and topics.)

3. Describe a time you have used one of the strategies described in the video to determine the theme of a story or movie. (Answers will vary.)

Intermediate & Advanced
Discuss Prompts. To help these students participate in the discussion, prompt them with questions that can be answered with a few words, such as:

- What is the theme of a text? (the central or most important idea)

- Why is theme sometimes hard to identify for a story? (It isn't always directly stated; it has to be inferred.)

Core Path	Access Path
	• What are you doing when you figure out a theme that isn't stated directly, by using evidence in the story? (inferring)
	• What type of story's theme is usually the easiest to figure out? (fable) Why? (It's usually stated in the text.)
	Approaching **Complete the Sentences.** To prepare students to participate in the discussion, have them complete the sentences on the Access 4 handout as they read the definition of theme. Correct answers are located online.
	Extend **Tech Infusion** **Brainstorm.** After watching the video with students, discuss the themes of movies or books series that are currently popular. Record the examples on an interactive whiteboard or Padlet (http://tinyurl.com/ n7l7cyy). Discuss why they enjoy reading books or watching movies with these themes.
	Extend **Tech Infusion** **Blast.** Create a Blast and ask students to "blast out" the name of a favorite book followed by a hashtag that states the theme.

2. MODEL

Core Path	Access Path
Watch. Ask students to take notes on the SkillsTV video on theme in "The Monkey's Paw" as you watch together. Remind students to listen for the way the students use academic vocabulary related to the definition of theme during their discussion. Pause the video at the key moments to discuss the information with your students.	**Beginner, Intermediate, & Approaching** **Analyze the Discussion.** Have students watch the video again. In pairs, have students complete the chart on the Access 1, 2, and 4 handouts as they watch the video. Sample answers for this exercise are located online.

Please note that excerpts and passages in the StudySync® library, workbooks, and PDFs are intended as touchstones to generate interest in an author's work. The excerpts and passages do not substitute for the reading of entire texts, and StudySync® strongly recommends that teachers and students seek out and purchase the whole literary or informational work in order to experience it as the author intended. Links to online resellers are available in our digital library. In addition, complete works may be ordered through an authorized reseller by filling out and returning to StudySync® the order form enclosed in this workbook.

Teacher's Edition   75

Core Path	Access Path
1. 0:40 - Is there any way to know which of these elements will be integral to the theme of the story? Do all of them play an equal role? Discuss. 2. 1:23 - How do the students know that this passage is important? What makes it stand out, and what reading strategies do the students use to understand its relevance to the theme? 3. 2:10 - Discuss why this is or isn't a solid inference about the story's theme. What are some other possible story elements that can be used to infer theme?	**Advanced** **Journals.** Have students note in their journals the evidence the students in the SkillsTV video cite to support their opinions on: • The passages that are important for figuring out theme • Their inferences about what the theme might be
Read and Annotate. Have students independently read the Model section. As they read, ask students to use the annotation tool to: • highlight key points • ask questions • identify places where the Model applies the strategies laid out in the Identification and Application section on theme	**Note:** During this portion of the lesson, instruction shifts from whole group to individual work. Use this time to work one-on-one or in small groups with Beginning, Intermediate, Advanced, and Approaching students. **Beginner & Intermediate** **Guided Reading.** Work with these students (either individually or in small groups) to answer the Guided Reading questions on the Access 1 and 2 handouts. Have Beginning students refer to the Model Glossary on the Access 1 handout to help them determine the meaning of difficult words. (Note: Provide the Access 1 handout glossary to Intermediate students if necessary.) Let students know they'll use these notes to help them participate in the discussion about the Model. **Advanced** **Identify Evidence.** Provide these students with the same instructions to read and annotate as on-and beyond- grade-level students. In addition, ask Advanced students to complete the Identify Evidence exercise on the Access 3 handout. Let students know that they'll use these answers to help participate in the discussion about the Model. Sample answers for this exercise are located online. **Approaching** **Guided Reading.** Have students complete the Guided Reading activity on the Access 4 handout as they read. Let them know that they'll use these notes to help them participate in the discussion about the Model. Students may want to work in pairs and discuss their answers to prepare them for the class discussion. Sample answers for this exercise are located online.

Core Path	Access Path
Discuss. As students read the Model text, use the questions below to facilitate a whole group discussion that helps them understand how to identify theme in a work of fiction.	**English Learners All Levels & Approaching** Use the extra time while on- and beyond- grade-level students are discussing the Model text to work individually and in small groups with Approaching readers and English Learners as previously outlined. Should those students complete their reading and annotation of the Model text quickly, integrate them into the on- and beyond- grade-level discussion groups.

1. What's the first step this Model uses to begin looking for the theme of this short story? (The Model points out that readers must first analyze the story, look at what motivates the characters, and see what happens as a result of their actions.)

2. What do readers learn about Mr. White in the first paragraph of the story? How might this be related to the theme? (Readers learn that while playing chess, Mr. White puts his king into "sharp and unnecessary perils." This reveals one of his character traits, which may be a clue to the theme in the story.)

3. The Model gives an example of using cause-and-effect relationships to determine the theme. What cause-and-effect relationship in the story suggests that the monkey's paw will grant Mr. White his wish? (Mr. White cries out in disgust when the monkey's paw twists in his hand like a snake after he makes a wish. This suggests that the monkey's paw may be evil and more powerful than the Whites thought.)

4. Look back at the passage. Cite another example in the dialogue between Mr. White and Sergeant Morris that suggests clues to the story's theme. (Possible response: "I threw it on the fire," the sergeant tells Mr. White. "If you keep it, don't blame me for what happens. Pitch it on the fire again like a sensible man.")

5. From the bulleted points under Identification and Application, beneath the definition, which strategy for determining the theme in this story do you think is most helpful? Why? (Possible response: Paying attention to the characters' words, thoughts, and actions. They show the negative effects of wishing on the monkey's paw.)

Core Path	Access Path
	Extend **Pair and Share.** Pair or group students and assign each group in the class a different strategy for analyzing a text to determine theme than the ones used in the Model (characters' words, thoughts, and actions; cause-and-effect relationships). Have each group apply that strategy and explain how it helped them determine the theme. Here are the other strategies: • details about the setting • the point of view of the narrator • events in the story's plot • titles and chapter headings If possible, have students create a blog post about finding the theme using a blog application such as Blogger (http://tinyurl.com/yw6z4v) or Kidblog (http://tinyurl.com/y8vgw36). Invite other students to comment on the posts.

3. YOUR TURN

Core Path	Access Path
Assess and Explain. Have students answer the comprehension questions to test for understanding. Share the explanations for Parts A and B (located online) with your students.	
	Extend **Share and Discuss.** Have students complete the Your Turn section in class. Poll students about their responses and, as a class, discuss the different strategies they used to determine the correct answers. Make sure students make the connection between the correct answer to Part A (D) and the concept of universal truths discussed in the Model. Conduct your poll by asking your students to complete a handout with questions or using Poll Everywhere (http://tinyurl.com/5grl69) or Socrative (http://tinyurl.com/nfz427v).

Copyright © BookheadEd Learning, LLC

Core Path	Access Path
	Extend **Compile.** As a class compile a list of "Test Taking Tips" throughout the year. They can keep this list in their notebooks or the class can save a master list as a Google document or TitanPad (http://tinyurl.com/27vdh73) to edit throughout the school year.

OVERVIEW

While identifying story elements may be easy for most students, analyzing how the story elements contribute to the theme may be more challenging. This lesson plan provides follow-up questions and useful enrichments to help teachers guide students toward a usable, repeatable method for analyzing how individual story elements contribute to the theme.

OBJECTIVES

1. Learn the definition of story elements.
2. Practice using concrete strategies for identifying story elements.
3. Participate effectively in a range of conversations and collaborations to express ideas and build upon the ideas of others.

ELA Common Core Standards:
Reading: Literature - RL.8.1, RL.8.2, RL.8.3
Speaking & Listening - SL.8.1.A, SL.8.1.B, SL.8.1.C, SL.8.1.D, SL.8.2
Language - L.8.6

RESOURCES

Access 1 handout (Beginner)

Access 2 handout (Intermediate)

Access 3 handout (Advanced)

Access 4 handout (Approaching)

1. DEFINE

Core Path	Access Path
Watch. Watch the Concept Definition video on story elements with your students. Make sure your students know all three elements of a story—plot, character, and setting—as well as how the three elements are interrelated. Pause the video at these key moments to discuss the information with your students:	**English Learners All Levels & Approaching** **Match.** Have students complete the matching exercise on the Access 1, 2, 3, and 4 handouts as they watch the video. Answers are located online.

Core Path

1. 0:30 - What typically occurs over the course of a story's plot? How does the action move forward, from beginning to middle to end? What changes or evolves? Discuss.
2. 0:47 - Who are some of your favorite characters from the stories you've read? What makes these characters interesting or likable? Why?
3. 1:20 - How might changing a story's setting affect both its plot and characters? What are some things an author might consider before deciding on the right setting for a particular story?

Read and Discuss. After watching the Concept Definition video, have students read the definition of story elements. Either in small groups or as a whole class, use these questions to spur discussion among your students about story elements, making sure they follow the rules for collegial discussions, use academic terms correctly, and respond to others' questions and comments with relevant evidence, observations, and ideas:

1. Think of another story you know. Who are the characters? What is the setting? What are some of the main events in the story? (Answers will vary.)
2. How might particular lines of dialogue or incidents in a story propel or influence the action, reveal aspects of a character, or provoke a character to make a decision? (Possible answer: Characters reveal their thoughts and feelings to other characters through dialogue. A decision made by a character in a story can influence another character, which can provoke a decision and influence the events of the plot.)

Access Path

Beginner
Finish the Sentences. Have these students complete the sentence frames on the Access 1 handout as they read the definition of story elements. Have them use the completed sentence frames to help them participate in the discussion. Sample answers for this exercise are located online.

Intermediate & Advanced
Discuss Prompts. To help these students participate in the discussion, prompt them with questions that can be answered with a few words, such as:

- What is a story element? (something that contributes to a story)
- What are three important story elements? (characters, plot, and setting)
- How does setting affect character and plot? (This depends on the story. Answers will vary.)

Please note that excerpts and passages in the StudySync® library, workbooks, and PDFs are intended as touchstones to generate interest in an author's work. The excerpts and passages do not substitute for the reading of entire texts, and StudySync® strongly recommends that teachers and students seek out and purchase the whole literary or informational work in order to experience it as the author intended. Links to online resellers are available in our digital library. In addition, complete works may be ordered through an authorized reseller by filling out and returning to StudySync® the order form enclosed in this workbook.

Teacher's Edition   81

Core Path	Access Path
3. Why is the setting of a story important to the story's theme? Think of a familiar story with a definite setting. How might the theme change with a different setting? (Possible answer: The setting can influence what happens to the characters in a story. It might help or hinder them when trying to solve a conflict in the plot. For this reason, a change in setting can affect both the characters in a story, the outcome, and the theme.) 4. Can you think of a time when you used one of the strategies described to help you identify story elements in a book, TV show, or movie? How did you use the story elements to help figure out the theme? (Answers will vary.)	**Approaching** **Complete a Chart.** To prepare students to participate in the discussion, have them complete the chart on the Access 4 handout as they read the definition. Answers are located online. **Beyond** **Discuss.** Have students select a book they've read and describe its story elements. Compile a list of elements. Have students discuss how story elements helped them to infer the theme. How else did story elements help them understand the story?
	Extend **Tech Infusion** **Brainstorm.** After watching the video, ask students to select a book they've read or a TV show or movie they have seen and make a list of the characters, setting, and main events. Compile this list of examples as a class using a whiteboard or a Padlet Wall (http://tinyurl.com/n7l7cyy). Ask students how these various story elements contribute to the theme. Would they make any changes to the story elements that might better contribute to the theme?

2. MODEL

Core Path	Access Path
Read and Annotate. Have students independently read the Model section. As they read, ask students to use the annotation tool to: • identify characters, setting, and important events in the plot • ask questions • analyze how particular lines of dialogue or incidents in the story propel the action and reveal aspects or traits of various characters • identify places where the Model applies the strategies laid out in the Identification and Application section on story elements	**Note:** During this portion of the lesson, instruction shifts from whole group to individual work. Use this time to work one-on-one or in small groups with Beginning, Intermediate, Advanced, and Approaching students.

Teacher's Edition

Copyright © BookheadEd Learning, LLC

Core Path	Access Path
	Beginner & Intermediate **Coach the Reading.** Work with these students (either individually or in small groups) to fill out the Guided Reading questions on the Access 1 and 2 handouts. Have Beginning students refer to the Model Glossary on the Access 1 handout to help them determine the meaning of difficult words. (Note: Provide the Access 1 handout Model Glossary to Intermediate students if necessary.) Let students know they'll use these answers to help participate in the discussion about the Model. Sample answers for this exercise are located online. **Advanced** **Identify Evidence.** Provide these students with the same instructions to read and annotate as on- and beyond- grade-level students. In addition, ask Advanced students to complete the Identify Evidence exercise on the Access 3 handout. Let students know that they'll use these answers to help participate in the discussion about the Model. Sample answers for this exercise are located online. **Approaching** **Guided Reading.** Have students complete the Guided Reading questions on the Access 4 handout as they read. Let them know that they'll use these answers to help participate in the discussion about the Model. Sample answers for this exercise are located online.
Discuss. After students read the Model text, use the following questions to facilitate a whole group discussion that helps them understand how to identify story elements and analyze how they contribute to the theme of the short story. 1. What's the first step this Model uses to begin looking for story elements? (The text in the Model pays particular attention to the setting. It notes that the story takes place in an isolated villa, on the familiar "dark and stormy night.")	**English Learners All Levels & Approaching** Use the extra time while on-and beyond- grade-level students are discussing the Model text to work individually and in small groups with Approaching readers and English Learners as outlined above. Should those students complete their reading and annotation of the Model text quickly, integrate them into the on- and beyond- grade-level discussion groups.

Core Path	Access Path
2. Why does the Model start by looking for story elements instead of making inferences about the theme? (Because before beginning to determine how the characters and setting contribute to the story's theme, it's important to determine exactly who the characters are, what they're like, and how the setting might influence the characters and events of the plot.) 3. Why is it important to identify the important events that take place at the beginning of the story? (It is important because the action builds, so the events at the beginning help the reader predict what might happen next; they also serve as clues to what the theme might be.) 4. Why is setting such an important element in this story? How does it change after Mr. White makes a wish, and what does this change suggest? (After Mr. White makes a wish, the atmosphere in the house becomes depressing and even menacing. Where the fire had burned brightly in the fireplace at the beginning of the story, it is now described as "dying." Outside, the wind is "higher than ever," and Mr. White is startled at the sound of a door banging upstairs. The change in setting seems to foreshadow that something awful will happen as a result of Mr. White's wish.)	
	Extend **Tech Infusion** **Pair and Share.** Pair or group students and assign each group in the class a different section of the short story and use the steps in the Model to identify the story elements. Have each group record its findings. Students should look for: • characters' actions • characters' dialogue • descriptions of characters' thoughts

Core Path	Access Path
	• events in the story's plot • details about the setting Ask the groups to share their findings with the class. Then discuss how these story elements contribute to the theme of the short story. If possible, have students capture pair shares on video using their mobile devices so they can watch their conversations and critique the content.
	Extend **Analyze a Quote.** Write these sentences on the board: "The first man had his three wishes. Yes," was the reply; "I don't know what the first two were, but the third was for death. That's how I got the paw." Have students identify the story elements in these sentences. Who says the dialogue? How do Sergeant-Major Morris's statements foreshadow events in the plot? How do they contribute to the theme?

3. YOUR TURN

Core Path	Access Path
Assess and Explain. Have students answer the comprehension questions to test for understanding. Share the explanations for Parts A and B (located online) with your students.	
	Extend **Share and Discuss.** Have students complete the Your Turn section in class. Poll students about their responses and as a class discuss the different strategies they used to determine the correct answers. Review the theme and the story elements and make sure they understand how the story elements contribute to the theme. Ask the following questions:

Please note that excerpts and passages in the StudySync® library, workbooks, and PDFs are intended as touchstones to generate interest in an author's work. The excerpts and passages do not substitute for the reading of entire texts, and StudySync® strongly recommends that teachers and students seek out and purchase the whole literary or informational work in order to experience it as the author intended. Links to online resellers are available in our digital library. In addition, complete works may be ordered through an authorized reseller by filling out and returning to StudySync® the order form enclosed in this workbook.

Teacher's Edition   **85**

Core Path	Access Path
	• Which character is most responsible for setting the plot moving? (Possible answer: Sergeant-Major Morris sets the plot moving by bringing the monkey's paw to the White home.) • How do Morris's actions contribute to the theme? (Possible answer: Morris throws the monkey's paw in the fire to attempt to destroy it. This suggests that the monkey paw is not worth the trouble it causes.)
	Extend **Tech Infusion** **Mnemonic or Rap.** As a class, write a mnemonic device or a rap to help students identify story elements in a text. They can record their mnemonic or rap and post it on the class website.

Copyright © BookheadEd Learning, LLC

The Monkey's Paw

OVERVIEW

The short story "The Monkey's Paw" by W.W. Jacobs is a cautionary tale about the power of wishes and the high price that sometimes comes with them. The Close Read gives students the opportunity to investigate more deeply the relationship between the story elements and the theme.

OBJECTIVES

1. Complete a close reading of a short story.
2. Practice and apply concrete strategies for identifying the story elements and analyzing the theme of a short story.
3. Participate effectively in a range of conversations and collaborations to express ideas and build upon the ideas of others.
4. Prewrite, plan, and produce clear and coherent writing in response to a prompt.

ELA Common Core Standards:
Reading: Literature - RL.8.1, RL.8.2, RL.8.3, RL.8.4
Writing - W.8.4, W.8.5, W.8.6, W.8.10
Speaking & Listening - SL.8.1.A, SL.8.1.C, SL.8.6
Language - L.8.2.C, L.8.4.A, L.8.4.C, L.8.4.D, L.8.6

RESOURCES

"The Monkey's Paw" Vocabulary handout

Access 1 handout (Beginner)

Access 2 handout (Intermediate)

Access 3 handout (Advanced)

Access 4 handout (Approaching)

Please note that excerpts and passages in the StudySync® library, workbooks, and PDFs are intended as touchstones to generate interest in an author's work. The excerpts and passages do not substitute for the reading of entire texts, and StudySync® strongly recommends that teachers and students seek out and purchase the whole literary or informational work in order to experience it as the author intended. Links to online resellers are available in our digital library. In addition, complete works may be ordered through an authorized reseller by filling out and returning to StudySync® the order form enclosed in this workbook.

Teacher's Edition  **87**

1. INTRODUCTION

Core Path	Access Path
Define and Compare. Project the vocabulary words and definitions onto the board or provide students with a handout, so they can copy the vocabulary into their notebooks. Ask students to compare their initial vocabulary analysis from the First Read with the actual definitions. Review words that students defined incorrectly to understand why they were unable to use context clues or other tools to develop usable definitions.	**Beginner & Intermediate** **Complete the Sentences.** Have students complete the sentence frames on the Access 1 and 2 handouts using the vocabulary words. Correct answers are located online. **Advanced & Beyond** **Write in Journals.** Have students write a journal entry using all of the vocabulary words. Remind them to write sentences that communicate the meaning of the words they are using. **Approaching** **Graphic Organizer.** To support students in comparing their predictions with the correct meanings, have them complete the Graphic Organizer on the Access 4 handout to record the vocabulary words, their initial analysis, and the definitions. Then have them write sentences using the words.
Review. Have students complete the fill-in-the-blank vocabulary handout for this selection. Answers for the handout are listed online.	
	Extend **Charades.** Break students into small groups. Write each vocabulary word on a piece of paper. Have students choose one word at a time and act out the word for the group. The other students in the group should guess the word.
	Extend **Tech Infusion** **Create.** Create online flashcards for the vocabulary using Quizlet (http://tinyurl.com/4gj6tz) or StudyBlue (http://tinyurl.com/6aqluw7).

2. READ

Core Path	Access Path
Model Close Reading. Project the text onto the board and model a close reading of the first five paragraphs using the following annotation strategies. While modeling annotation strategies, make notes that tie the text to the focus skills and demonstrate what students are looking for as they read. Here is some guidance for you as you annotate for your students:	

- As the Skills lesson that precedes this text makes clear, stories have three elements: characters, plot, and setting. In the first few paragraphs, we meet three of our main characters: Mr. White, Mrs. White, and their son, Herbert. We learn the most about Mr. White—that he is willing to put his chess pieces in peril, and that he tries to distract his son from noticing when he makes a wrong move. He does it "amiably," however, so we know he's not a villain.

- We don't know exactly where their home, Laburnam Villa, is located, but we know that it's a cold, wet, and very windy night. The author tells us this directly, so we don't have much to infer there, but we should keep these details in mind as we read the rest of the story, because they could be important to the theme. In what way is this setting typical of a classic horror or suspense tale? (Possible answer: It is the "dark and stormy night" that is a cliche of this genre.)

- We don't know much about the plot here, but since the author puts so much detail into the characters at this point (especially Mr. White), we can assume that his character will be important to what happens in the story. After Sergeant-Major Morris arrives, the chess game ends and Morris entertains his hosts with stories of his travels. Soon he tells them the tale of the monkey's paw.

Core Path	Access Path
• Sergeant-Major Morris tells the Whites that an Indian fakir put a spell on the paw to show that fate ruled people's lives, and that those who interfered with it did so to their sorrow. He advises Mr. White to throw it away, and pitches it into the fire, but Mr. White saves the paw from the flames. • We already know that Mr. White takes chances, having observed him playing chess with his son. He says to Morris, "if you don't want it, give it to me." We can easily predict that Mr. White will make a wish on the paw, and when he does so, he winds up losing his son as a result. He did not take the sergeant-major's warning seriously: "If you keep it, don't blame me for what happens." How could we paraphrase what Morris told the Whites about the paw as the story's theme? (Possible answer: Fate rules people's lives, and those who attempt to interfere with it, or change it, do so to their sorrow.)	
Read and Annotate. Read the Skills Focus questions as a class, so your students know what they should pay close attention to as they read. Then have students read and annotate the excerpt. Ask students to use the annotation tool as they read to: 1. respond to the Skills Focus section 2. ask questions 3. make connections 4. identify key information, examples, and themes 5. note unfamiliar vocabulary 6. capture their reaction to the ideas and examples in the text As they reread the text, remind students to use the Ask and Answer Questions comprehension strategy that they learned in the First Read.	**Note:** While on- grade-level students are reading and annotating, work one-on-one or in small groups with Beginning, Intermediate, Advanced, and Approaching students to support them as they read and annotate the text. **Beginner & Intermediate** **Summarize and Analyze the Text.** Work with these students to complete the Summarize and Analyze the Text exercise in the Access 1 and 2 handouts. They will then use the completed sentence frames to help them analyze and annotate the text so as to complete the Skills Focus questions. Refer to the sample Skills Focus answers online to help them complete the sentence frames and annotate the text.

Core Path	Access Path
	Advanced **Work in Pairs.** Pair these students with more proficient English speakers to work together on analyzing and annotating the text to complete the Skills Focus questions. If these students need more support, have them use the Summarize and Analyze the Text exercise in the Access 3 handout as they work with their more proficient peers. **Approaching** **Summarize the Text.** Have these students discuss and complete the Summarize the Text exercise in the Access 4 handout and use their summary to help them analyze and annotate the text so as to complete the Skills Focus questions. Correct answers for the summary are online. Also refer to the sample Skills Focus answers to aid students with their annotations.
Discuss. After students have read the text, use the sample responses to the Skills Focus questions online to discuss the reading and the process of identifying the story's theme and how the story elements of character and setting contribute to it. Make sure that students have acquired and accurately use academic-specific words and phrases related to the skill, and demonstrate a command of formal English appropriate to the discussion.	**Extend** **Pair and Share.** In small groups or pairs, ask students to share and discuss their annotations with a focus on the point of view. You can provide students with questions to guide their discussion: 1. How do Herbert's comments about the monkey's paw influence his father's decision about using it? (His teasing makes his father feel silly about taking it seriously, and so he makes the first wish as if it can't hurt.) What does the dialogue about the monkey's paw between Herbert and his father reveal about each character? Cite specific textual evidence to support your statements. (Mr. White is a careful, thoughtful man: "Mr. White took the paw from his pocket and eyed it dubiously.'I don't know what to wish for, and that's a fact,' he said, slowly.'It seems to me I've got all I want.'" Herbert is more lighthearted but cares about his parents a great deal: "'If you only cleared the house, you'd be quite happy, wouldn't you?' said Herbert, with his hand on his shoulder...." and "his son, with a solemn face, somewhat marred by a wink at his mother, sat down at the piano and struck a few impressive chords.")

Teacher's Edition

Core Path	Access Path
	2. What is the role of Mrs. White in the story? How do her thoughts and actions influence the plot? How do they contribute to the theme? Cite specific textual evidence to support your statements. (Mrs. White starts to influence the plot more after the first wish is granted. She convinces her husband to make the second wish: "'Wish!' she cried, in a strong voice. 'It is foolish and wicked,' he faltered.'Wish!' repeated his wife." Her actions contribute to the theme by showing that a reckless desire to get what you want no matter the consequences is dangerous.)
	3. How does the author, W.W. Jacobs, use the story elements of setting, character, and plot to support the theme of the story? Cite specific textual evidence to support your statements. (The author uses the setting "weather and darkness"to create a mood of foreboding and tension at times: "Without, the night was cold and wet" and "He went down in the darkness, and felt his way to the parlour...and he caught his breath as he found that he had lost the direction of the door." He uses the character's dialogue and actions to show conflict and tension: "'Good God, you are mad!' he cried, aghast. 'Get it,' she panted; 'get it quickly, and wish—Oh, my boy, my boy!'" These all help to foreshadow negative consequences of the characters' choices.)
	Extend
	Compare and Contrast. Ask students to compare and contrast the three male characters' thoughts and feelings about the monkey's paw. They can record their responses on a three-column chart.

Core Path	Access Path
	Beyond **Create a Dialogue.** The story ends when the knocking at the door stops. The author does not tell the reader what was on the other side of the door, or what happened next between Mr. and Mrs. White. Have students work in pairs to write additional dialogue that tells what Mr. and Mrs. White each thinks was on the other side of the door and how they feel about the last wish. Have students use at least two vocabulary words in their dialogue. Have each pair read their dialogue to the class. Invite students to discuss the dialogue, offering constructive feedback.

3. WRITE

Core Path	Access Path
Prewrite and Plan. Read the prompt as a class and ask students to brainstorm their reactions to W.W. Jacobs's "The Monkey's Paw," and their thoughts about how the combination of story elements—character, setting, and plot—contribute to the theme. Students can brainstorm together either as a class or in small groups to begin planning their responses. Remind students to look at the story and their annotations to find textual evidence to support their ideas.	**Beginner & Intermediate** **Answer and Discuss.** Have students complete the prewriting questions in the Access 1 and 2 handouts and then explain their answers to a partner before they write. Explain to students that when they answer a question—such as "What is one main conflict between the characters in "The Monkey's Paw?"—they need to include a detail, example or quote from the text that supports the statement. For example, students could include the lines, "If you keep it, don't blame me for what happens. Pitch it on the fire again like a sensible man," which reveals that Morris feels strongly that it is a bad idea for Mr. White to take the talisman, and Mr. White still intends to take it despite his warnings. **Approaching** **Answer Prewriting Questions.** Have students complete the prewriting questions in the Access 4 handout to summarize their thoughts before they write.

Copyright © BookheadEd Learning, LLC

Core Path	Access Path
	Extend **Tech Infusion** **Map.** Students can create concept maps online using http://tinyurl.com/5u2koto. Google drawing can also be used to design a concept map.

Discuss. Project these instructions for the peer review onto the board and review them with your class, so they know what they are looking for when they begin to provide their classmates with feedback:

- Has the writer explained how these story elements contribute to the theme of the story?

- Has the writer used his or her understanding of theme to correctly identify the story's theme?

- Has the writer used evidence from the text to support his or her writing?

- What sort of evidence from the text did the writer use to support his or her writing?

- How well does the writer explain how that evidence supports his or her arguments?

- Is the paper organized so that ideas flow from one to the next?

- Is it easy for the reader to follow the writer's train of thought?

- Does the writer use standard grammar and punctuation? Are there any weak spots?

- Which words are especially effective in supporting the writer's argument?

- Are there any words you would change? What are they, and why would you change them? What words would you suggest as replacements?

- What suggestions can you make to help the writer improve the response?

- What thing(s) does this paper do especially well?

- Be sure to tell the writer what he or she did well and what he or she needs to work on. Remember that your comments are most useful when they are constructive.

Teacher's Edition

Core Path	Access Path
After you've looked at the peer review instructions, review the rubric with students before they begin writing. Allow time for students briefly to raise and discuss questions they may have about the peer review instructions and the rubric. Tell students how many peer reviews they will need to complete once they submit their writing. **Write.** Ask students to complete the writing assignment using textual evidence to support their answers. Once they have completed their writing, they should click "Submit."	
	Extend **Critique**. Project a writing sample on the board and ask the class to identify the elements of writing that are strong, as well as those that are weak or in need of improvement. Alternatively, you can put students in small groups and give them photo copies of a writing sample to collaboratively evaluate. After students have had an opportunity to evaluate each others' samples, ask each student to identify an example of strong writing they reviewed in a classmate's writing sample. Together, make a list of traits of strong writing on the board.
Review. Once students complete their writing assignment, they should submit substantive feedback to two peers. If possible, have students use technology to interact and collaborate with others.	

OVERVIEW

The driving question for this unit is "What attracts us to stories of suspense?" To understand more about one of the key features of the suspenseful story, "The Monkey's Paw," students will explore the uses of various lucky charms and traditions. They will learn about the history of these items and practices involving them, as well as how and why people use them now.

OBJECTIVES

1. Explore background information about the use of lucky charms and traditions to make a wish.
2. Research using hyperlinks to a range of information about the history and practice of making wishes and using lucky charms.

   ELA Common Core Standards:
   Reading: Informational Text - RI.8.1, RI.8.6
   Writing - W.8.1.A, W.8.2.A, W.8.2.B, W.8.5, W.8.6
   Speaking & Listening - SL.8.1.A, SL.8.1.C, SL.8.1.D

RESOURCES

Blast Response - Student Model

Access 1 handout (Beginner)

Access 2 handout (Intermediate)

Access 4 handout (Approaching)

TITLE/DRIVING QUESTION

Core Path	Access Path
Discuss. As a class, read aloud the title and driving question for this Blast. Ask students what they know about lucky charms and wishing traditions already. Do they ever use lucky charms or make wishes? Why or why not? Remind students that they should not immediately reply to this question. They'll be returning to this question and responding after they've read the Background and some of the Research Links.	**English Learners All Levels & Approaching** **Discuss a Visual.** Have students view wishing-related images, such as someone blowing out birthday candles, or throwing a coin in a fountain. Discuss how a picture can make us think of words associated with what it shows. As they look at each image, ask: • What words does this photo make you think of? • What is this picture "about"? How would you describe it to a friend? • What other objects or actions do you associate with wishing?
	Beginner, Intermediate, & Approaching **Create a List.** After this discussion, have students complete the Create a List exercise in their Access 1, 2, and 4 handouts.
Draft. In their notebooks or on scrap paper, have students draft their initial responses to the driving question. This will provide them with a baseline response that they will be altering as they gain more information about the topic in the Background and Research Links sections of the assignment. You may wish to review with students the Blast Response - Student Model for guidance on how to construct an effective Blast.	**Beginner & Intermediate** **Draft with Sentence Frame.** When drafting their initial response to the driving question, have students refer to this Blast sentence frame on their Access 1 and 2 handouts: • The lucky charm or tradition I use to make a wish is _____, because _____ _____. Point out these two key features of the sentence frame: 1. The introductory clause "The lucky charm or tradition I use to make a wish is" borrows language directly from the Blast driving question to provide a response. 2. Ask students to make special note of the two blanks. Students should write in the first one the lucky charm or tradition they use to make wishes. Students should provide supporting evidence after the word "because" since it asks students to explain their reasoning.

Please note that excerpts and passages in the StudySync® library, workbooks, and PDFs are intended as touchstones to generate interest in an author's work. The excerpts and passages do not substitute for the reading of entire texts, and StudySync® strongly recommends that teachers and students seek out and purchase the whole literary or informational work in order to experience it as the author intended. Links to online resellers are available in our digital library. In addition, complete works may be ordered through an authorized reseller by filling out and returning to StudySync® the order form enclosed in this workbook.

Teacher's Edition   97

BACKGROUND

Core Path	Access Path
Read. Have students read the Blast Background to provide context for the driving question.	**Beginner & Intermediate** **Read with Support.** Have students read the Blast Background to provide context for the driving question. When they encounter unfamiliar words or phrases, have students refer to the Blast Glossary on their Access 1 and 2 handouts. If there are unfamiliar words that are not included in their glossary, encourage students to check a dictionary or online reference tool, such as http://tinyurl.com/6ytby. **Approaching** **Read and Summarize.** Have students read the Blast Background to provide context for the driving question. As they read, ask students to complete the Background summary provided in their Access 4 handout. When they encounter unfamiliar words or phrases, have students refer to the Blast Glossary on their Access 4 handout.
Discuss. Pair students and have them discuss the following questions: 1. Why do people use lucky charms? (to keep away evil or bring good luck) 2. How did some of these traditions about wishes evolve? (Early people used them to make sense of their environment. When the practices seemed to work, they were used even more.) 3. What are some traditions that you or your family members use to make wishes? (Answers will vary, but should include specific examples to explain their ideas.) 4. If you use a lucky charm, what is it? What object might you like to use as a lucky charm? (Answers will vary, but should include specific examples to explain their ideas.)	**Beginner** **Discuss.** Pair Beginning students with more proficient readers and have them use the dialogue starter on their Access 1 handout to discuss the topic. Advise them to return to the dialogue and switch roles if they get stuck. **Intermediate** **Discuss.** Pair Intermediate students with more proficient readers and have them use the dialogue starter on their Access handout 2 to discuss the topic. Advise them to return to the dialogue and switch roles if they get stuck. If their conversation is progressing smoothly, encourage them to continue the discussion beyond the dialogue starter sheet. They can expand their conversations to discuss other examples of good luck charms or wishing traditions in their own or other cultures.

Core Path	Access Path

Brainstorm. Remind students about the driving question for this Blast: "What lucky charm or tradition do you use to make a wish?"

In their notebooks ask students to make three columns. In the first column, have them list their own personal traditions or superstitions. In the second column, have them explain the origins of that tradition. For the third column, provide students time to research any larger cultural origins they might find for this tradition/superstition. Here's an example:

Tradition	Personal Origin	Other Origins
Throwing water on the car windows of family members who are leaving on a trip.	We first started doing this when my brother left for college for the first time. We were all really sad and then my dad threw his water on the car and it made everyone laugh.	In Baltic countries, some families scatter water on the doorstep after a family member departs to insure them a safe journey home.

RESEARCH LINKS

Core Path	Access Path

Examine and Explore. Before asking students to explore the Research Links, use these questions to guide their exploration:

1. Ask students to look at the "Making Wishes" article. Are any of these superstitions familiar to them? Do they work? Is there any harm in carrying out these superstitions? (Answers will vary, but should include specific examples and reasons.)

Extend
Research, Discuss and Present.

1. Assign each group one link to explore in depth.
2. Ask them to discuss the information:

    a. What are the key points?
    b. What inferences did you make as you read?
    c. What did you learn about this "big idea" from reading this research?

Core Path	Access Path
2. Based on the titles, which Research Link(s) might provide the most complete source on charms and similar objects? ("Amulets, Talismans, and Charms") According to the summary, what can you expect to find out about at this link? (This article explains the differences among these objects and how they are used even today.)	d. How did this help you to better understand the topic? e. What questions does your group have after exploring this link? 3. Allow students time to informally present what they learned.
3. Have students read the article "Why Do We Blow Out Birthday Candles?" Remind students that *facts* can be proven with evidence, and *opinions* may or may not have evidence to back them up. In addition, explain that a *conjecture* is a guess or opinion formed with incomplete information or evidence. As a class discuss the distinction between fact and conjecture in the article. What does the author seem to know? What is he guessing about? How can they distinguish? (The author's claims about the Greeks and Germans are presented as facts. He cites the name of the Greek moon goddess and has more detailed descriptions of these rites. In the fifth paragraph, words like "may have" and "probably" should clue readers to the fact that the author is making an educated guess at the meanings behind these superstitions.)	
	Extend **Tech Infusion** **Share.** As students explore the links, allow them to crowdsource their findings using a backchannel tool like TodaysMeet (http://tinyurl.com/psef72j). Students can post the research they find individually or in groups to share with the class.

NUMBER CRUNCH

Core Path	Access Path
Predict, Discuss, and Click. Before students click on the number, break them into pairs and have them make predictions about what they think the number is related to. After they've clicked the number, ask students if they are surprised by the revealed information.	

QUIKPOLL

Core Path	Access Path
Participate. Answer the poll question. Have students discuss the reasons for their answers. Students should refer to evidence from the Background and Research Links to defend their answers.	
Discuss. Once students have posted their response to the poll, ask them to discuss the results in small groups or as a class. Are they surprised by the outcome?	
	Extend **Take Another Poll.** Have students ask the QuikPoll questions to another group of students, or to friends and family members. Have them compare the results of the two polls and explain any similarities or differences.

CREATE YOUR BLAST

Core Path	Access Path
Blast. Ask students to write their Blast response in 140 characters or less	**Beginner** **Blast with Support.** Have students refer back to the sentence frame on their Access 1 handout that they used to create their original Blast draft. Ask them to use this frame to write and enter their final Blast. **Intermediate** **Blast with Support.** Have students attempt to draft their Blast without the sentence frame on their Access 2 handout. If students struggle to compose their Blast draft without the sentence frame, remind them to reference it for support. **Beyond** **Write a Claim.** Ask students to use their answer to the poll question to write a strong claim that could be used as the foundation for a piece of argumentative writing. Once students have written their claims, ask them to read the claims to a small group of their peers. This activity will provide them practice writing claims, as well as expose them to claims written by their peers.
Review. After students have completed their own Blasts, ask them to review the Blasts of their peers and provide feedback. If possible, have students use technology to present information and ideas efficiently as well as to interact and collaborate with others.	**Extend** **Discuss.** As a whole class or in groups, identify a few strong Blasts and discuss what made those responses so powerful. As a group, analyze and discuss what characteristics make a Blast interesting or effective.
	Extend **Revise.** Resend a second version of this Blast assignment to your students and have them submit revised versions of their original Blasts. Do the same responses make the Top 10? How have the answers improved from the first submissions?

FIRST READ:
Sorry, Wrong Number

OVERVIEW

The drama *Sorry, Wrong Number* by Lucille Fletcher explores the neurotic character of Mrs. Stevenson as she is afraid and alone in her New York City apartment. The First Read gives students the opportunity to experience the text with a limited context.

OBJECTIVES

1. Perform an initial reading of a text and demonstrate comprehension by responding to short analysis and inference questions with textual evidence.
2. Practice defining vocabulary words using context, as well as Greek prefixes.
3. Participate effectively in a range of conversations and collaborations to express ideas and build upon the ideas of others.

ELA Common Core Standards:

Reading: Literature - RL.8.1, RL.8.4, RL.8.10
Writing - W.8.7, W.8.10
Speaking & Listening - SL.8.1.A, SL.8.1.B, SL.8.1.C, SL.8.1.D, SL.8.2, SL.8.6
Language - L.8.4.A, L.8.4.B, L.8.4.C, L.8.4.D, L.8.6

RESOURCES

Access 1 handout (Beginner)

Access 2 handout (Intermediate)

Access 3 handout (Advanced)

Access 4 handout (Approaching)

ACCESS COMPLEX TEXT

Sorry, Wrong Number is a text that is meant to be performed. It has been performed on stage and on the radio, and was also made into a famous film. In order to read the excerpt of the play, students will need to understand the basic conventions of a drama. Stage directions, theatrical terms, character names, dialogue, and situations of the time period in which the play is set may present challenges for students. Use the following ideas to provide scaffolded instruction for an initial reading of the more complex features of this text.

- **Genre** - Note that the author of a play is called a playwright. Explain that playwrights include stage directions to demonstrate how the action of the play should look in performance, including who is on stage, where they are, and any cues, such as for sounds, lights, or character entrances and exits. Remind them that these directions are meant to be performed and not read aloud. However, these directions are read aloud in class for the purposes of helping readers picture the action.

- **Organization** - Point out that a play is divided into acts and scenes rather than chapters. Note that playwrights organize the events using stage directions and dialogue. Stage directions are usually placed in brackets, and in italicized font. Explain that dialogue is indicated first by character names, which are often written in all caps, followed by a colon. The dialogue spoken by a character follows the colon. Readers may also notice that character actions or descriptions, in brackets, are interspersed in the dialogue.

- **Specific Vocabulary** - In order to better picture what is happening on the stage, review terms such as "the curtain rises," "stage set," and "spotlight." Specifically, the playwright explains that the set in this case consists of "three flats," *a flat being* a term for a set piece that forms a wall. Note that part of Mrs. Stevenson's character description is that she is a "neurotic." Because the actions of the play, including its suspense, are linked to that trait, make sure that students understand the meaning of this word and how this trait contributes to Mrs. Stevenson's reactions during the scene. In the phone number, "Murray Hill" is used, which was a convention of phone numbers at the time. Murray Hill is a neighborhood on the east side of New York City.

- **Prior Knowledge** - Students will most likely be unfamiliar with telephone communication as it was practiced in the time the play is set. Explain that all phones were landlines. In addition, point out that most people could not afford a totally private line, but instead had to share using a "party line". This is a telephone service line shared by more than one person. A majority of people in the mid-20th century in the United States and Canada were serviced by party lines, which carried a billing discount over individual service; during wartime shortages, these were often the only available lines. Remind students that the play is set three years after the end of World War II. This information and the role of a telephone operator and switchboard is essential for understanding the play's plot.

1. INTRODUCTION

Core Path	Access Path
Read and Listen. Individually or as a class, read and listen to the Introduction for *Sorry, Wrong Number.* The Introduction provides context for the excerpts students will read.	**English Learners All Levels & Approaching** **Fill in the Blanks.** Ask students to use their Access 1, 2, 3, and 4 handouts to fill in the blanks of the transcript for the preview's voiceover as they watch the preview along with their classmates. Correct answers are located online.
Research. To build background, have your students investigate how telephone systems worked in the 1940s (when the play was written), since they might not understand why Mrs. Stevenson needs the operator to connect her, or how she got connected to the wrong number. 1. Divide the students into two groups. Have one group capture their information in a flowchart that shows the steps of placing a phone call in that time. Have a second group create a Venn diagram comparing communication then and now. 2. Next, have the groups share their research and graphic displays with the class. 3. Check that the students understand the basic system, and remind them that they can refer to the charts as needed to understand the events in the opening scene of the play.	**English Learners All Levels & Approaching** **Build Background.** As a class, view images of switchboard operators from the 1940s and 1950s, such as: http://tinyurl.com/nvl5dkt or http://tinyurl.com/q4a92nv. Ask students to describe what they see in the images. Explain to students how switchboard operators were needed to connect parties. Ask students why switchboard operators are no longer needed today. If time allows, watch a short video that portrays a Day in the Life of a Switchboard Operator: http://tinyurl.com/osbox7g.
	Extend **Tech Infusion** **Create.** Have students work individually or in groups to create an infographic that details the steps and technology needed to place a phone call in the 1940's or one that displays the differences between communication in the 1940's and now. The websites http://tinyurl.com/7eg83c8 or http://tinyurl.com/6vmqltf both have infographic templates so students can add their own text and images.

Core Path	Access Path
	Extend **Discuss the Introduction.** After reading the Introduction, use the information provided to facilitate a pre-reading discussion to get students thinking about the excerpt in *Sorry, Wrong Number*. 1. Why do you think sound effects are important in a drama, as a way to build tension or suspense? 2. What are some important things an author must consider when writing a drama for the radio? 3. How do you think a "neurotic" person might behave?

2. READ

Core Path	Access Path
Make Predictions about Vocabulary. There are five bold vocabulary words in the text. As students read the text, ask them to make predictions about what they think each bold vocabulary word means based on the context clues in the sentence. If you are in a low tech classroom and students are reading from printed copies or a projected text, ask students to record predictions in their notes, so they can be easily referenced in class. If your students have access to technology, they can use the annotation tool to make their predictions. It might be helpful to model this for students before they begin reading. Either using the board or projecting the actual text, focus in on the sentence that uses the word "peripheral": • A spotlight, left of side flat, picks up out of **peripheral** darkness, figure of 1st OPERATOR, sitting with headphones at small table. Model for the class how to use overall structure and meaning of the sentence and the sentences around it, the word's position, and other clues to define the unfamiliar vocabulary word. In this case, point out these context keys:	**Note:** This exercise, which extends vocabulary instruction, should be completed when the class shifts from whole group instruction to individual work during the "Read and Annotate" exercise. **Beginner, Intermediate & Approaching Pair Practice.** 1. Pair these students with more proficient readers. 2. Give them an additional sentence that contains a new vocabulary word. 3. Ask the less proficient students to complete a Think Aloud using the teacher-led Make Predictions about Vocabulary activity as a model, while the more proficient reader actively listens. 4. The students should use the context clues in the sentence to try to determine the meaning of the new vocabulary word. 5. After the students have completed the Think Aloud and made a prediction about the word's meaning, allow time for the more proficient reader to add his/her own thoughts and clarify any points of confusion.

Core Path	Access Path
1. Look at the structure of the sentence. What is the subject (spotlight) and what is the first verb (picks up)? Even though the syntax of this sentence might not be exactly what we're used to reading, we can still understand that a spotlight has been turned on, and it allows us to see (it "picks up") the operator. 2. Because "peripheral" comes before the word "darkness," we know that it's an adjective, so it's describing the darkness. We can also tell from the stage directions at the very beginning that this part of the stage wasn't lit when the scene began, because it says clearly that "only the center part is lighted." So we know that the operator was sitting in darkness when the scene began. 3. We also need to remember that the stage is described as "divided," and so if only the center section is lighted, and the operator is sitting in the darkness, she must be on one side of the stage. Since this darkness is described as "peripheral," we can determine that *peripheral* has to do with things that are on the sides or edges of what's important, or not the main part of something. 4. To verify the preliminary determination of the meaning of the *peripheral,* I can also check the inferred meaning in a dictionary.	6. Once they've completed this Think Aloud, encourage them to use a dictionary to confirm the definition of the new vocabulary word. Have them refer to the Text Glossary on their Access handouts 1, 2, and 4 for definitions of key vocabulary terms in the text. Encourage them to add any additional vocabulary words or idioms they find in the text and look up definitions for those words and idioms online or in a dictionary.
Model Reading Comprehension Strategy. Before students begin reading, model the reading comprehension strategy of making, confirming, and revising predictions by using this Think Aloud that talks students through the first paragraph of text. First explain to your students what the skill means: *When we make a prediction, we make an educated guess about what might happen in the story. As we read further, we can confirm if a prediction was correct, or we can revise a prediction based on how the story is unfolding.* Explain to students how making, confirming, and revising predictions will help them better comprehend the selection and help drive their discussions.	**Note:** This exercise, which extends vocabulary instruction, should be completed when the class shifts from whole group instruction to individual work during the "Read and Annotate" exercise. **Beginner & Approaching** **Apply Reading Comprehension Strategy.** In small groups, have students read the first three paragraphs of the reading selection. Ask groups to make predictions based on what the read. Have students record their predictions in the Access 1 and 4 handouts. After rereading the same three paragraphs, have groups revise their predictions. Circle around and work with groups to elaborate on why they made these predictions. Pose questions, such as:

Core Path	Access Path
• When I read the scene description of the "fussy furnishings" and the bed jacket and details in the room, I can tell that Mrs. Stevenson is a rich woman. • Based on her first actions of being irritated on the phone and taking pills, I can predict that something is wrong. • When I see later that there is a robbery being planned, I can see that my prediction is correct, but I can revise my prediction to tell that the robbers may be headed to Mrs. Stevenson's apartment. I can continue reading to confirm or revise the prediction further.	• What led you to make this prediction? • What evidence from the text makes you think this way?
Read and Annotate. Read and annotate the excerpt. Ask students to use the annotation tool as they read to: 1. ask questions about characters and events 2. make connections 3. identify key details, events, characters and ideas 4. use context clues, such as the position of a word or its function in a sentence, to figure out the meaning of a word or phrase 5. note unfamiliar vocabulary 6. capture reactions to the events in the drama	**Beginner** **Coach the Reading.** While other students read, annotate, and discuss the text independently, work with Beginning students, listening to the audio of the text and pausing periodically or when any student has a question. Coach students in articulating their questions for the group and in highlighting and annotating the text. Have students use the Annotation Guide in the Access 1 handout to support them as they highlight and annotate the text. For further support, ask questions about the text such as: • Is there anything about the play that you don't understand? • What do you think will happen to Mrs. Stevenson? **Intermediate** **Listen to the Audio.** Have these students listen to the audio of the text and use the definitions on the Access 2 handout to help them with words or idioms that may be unfamiliar. If students need help with annotating the text, have them use the Annotation Guide on the Access 2 handout. After working with the Beginning students, you may wish to check this group's progress and provide support as needed.

Teacher's Edition

Core Path	Access Path
	Advanced **Pair with Proficient Peers.** Have Advanced students work with English proficient peers to read, annotate, and discuss the text. Have students use the Annotation Guide in the Access 3 handout to support them as they highlight and annotate the text. Encourage them to listen to the audio of the text if needed. **Approaching** **Use the Annotation Guide.** Have students use the Annotation Guide in the Access 4 handout to support them as they highlight and annotate the text.

Discuss. In small groups or pairs, have students discuss the questions and inferences they made while reading. To help facilitate discussions, refer to Collaborative Discussions in the Speaking and Listening Handbook.

1. Why does Mrs. Stevenson dial the operator? (She can't get through to her husband's office.)

2. What does the pill bottle suggest about Mrs. Stevenson? (Her anxiety may not be a one-time thing; it may be an ongoing issue.)

3. What information does Mrs. Stevenson reveal to the operator about herself? (She has been nervous all day, she's in poor health, and she's all alone tonight.)

4. Why is Mrs. Stevenson even more nervous after hearing the phone conversation? (She knows there is a murder being planned.)

5. How can you explain the fact that Mrs. Stevenson is hearing the men's conversation? (The operator must have put her through to the wrong number.)

English Learners All Levels & Approaching

Use the extra time while on- and beyond- grade-level students are discussing their first reads of the text to work individually and in small groups with English Learners and Approaching readers as previously outlined. Should those students complete their first reads quickly, integrate them into the on- and beyond- grade-level discussion groups. Otherwise English Learners and Approaching readers will be given an opportunity to participate in text discussions with their peers later in the lesson.

Core Path	Access Path
	Extend **Identify and Define.** After reading the text, compile a list of additional vocabulary words. Ask students to reference their annotations and share any vocabulary words that were unfamiliar. 1. As a class, compile a list of unknown words on the board. 2. In small groups, ask students to make predictions about they think these words mean based on how they are used in the sentence. Note: They will need access to StudySync to read the words in context and make predictions. 3. Each group should work together using dictionaries or devices to define the words and write the definitions in their notebooks. **Extend** **Characterization.** After reading the text, have students work in small groups to discuss what the characters are doing and how they respond to each situation. Ask students how they would have felt if they were in Mrs. Stevenson's shoes when she overheard the men's conversation. Ask students why their reactions might differ from Mrs. Stevenson's.

3. SYNCTV

Core Path	Access Path
Watch. As a class, watch the SyncTV video on *Sorry, Wrong Number.* Pause the video at these key moments to discuss the information with your students: 1. 0:39- One student says, "That word, tension. That's exactly what I'm feeling when I'm reading this." What ways do you see Fletcher building tension throughout this excerpt of the play?	**Beginner & Intermediate** **Analyze the Discussion.** Have students use the Analyze the Discussion guide in the Access 1 and 2 handouts to identify key points in the discussion and the evidence the students use to determine those points. Sample answers are online.

Core Path	Access Path
2. 2:05- One student says, "Also, look at the very first setting detail: *expensive rather fussy furnishings*. She's rich". What other setting details do you notice? What do they tell you about Mrs. Stevenson and her husband? 3. 3:50 - One student says, "One of the scarier parts of this scene, is when they can't hear her . . . to me, that does feel like a nightmare." The students use the word *nightmare* multiple times throughout their discussion. What creates the scariness and tension? Use specific examples from the scene in your answer.	
	Extend **Tech Infusion** **Record.** Remind students that *Sorry, Wrong Number* was originally meant to be a radio play. Ask one student in each group to record the audio of their conversation. They can upload their audio to Google Drive or email them to you for review. Ask them to play back the audio and think about what's different about just hearing something, rather than seeing it, too.

4. THINK

Core Path	Access Path
Answer and Discuss. Have students complete the Think questions and then use the peer review instructions and rubric to complete two peer reviews. Refer to the sample answers online to discuss responses with your students.	**Beginner & Intermediate** **Sentence Frames.** Have students use the sentence frames on the Access 1 and 2 handouts to support their responses to the Think questions. If necessary, distribute sentence frames to Advanced students as well.

Core Path	Access Path
	Approaching **Find the Evidence.** Have students use Find the Evidence on the Access 4 handout to help them identify the evidence needed to answer the questions.
SyncTV-Style Discussion. Put students into small groups and give them a prompt to discuss. Remind them to model their discussions after the SyncTV episodes they have seen, and to demonstrate command of formal English as appropriate for an academic discussion. Stress the importance of citing textual evidence in their conversations to support their ideas. To help students prepare for, strategize, and evaluate their discussions, refer to the Collaborative Discussions section of the Speaking and Listening Handbook. Discussion prompt: 1. How does the set and stage direction add to the suspense in this scene? 2. What do you think is going on in this scene? Do you think Mrs. Stevenson is making a big deal out of nothing? Do you think she's mentally unwell or just physically? Do you think Mrs. Stevenson is going to be murdered? Give evidence from the text to back up your ideas.	**Beginner & Intermediate** **Use Sentence Frames.** Have these students use the sentence frames on Access handouts 1 and 2 to help them participate in the discussion. **Approaching** **Use Think Questions.** Remind these students to refer back to their answers to the Think questions to help them participate in the group discussion.
	Extend **Debate.** Present students with an issue from the text that can be debated. Allow students to debate the issue as a class or in smaller groups. Debate prompts: 1. Do you think Mrs. Stevenson is right to feel anxious after hearing the phone conversation? Why or why not? 2. What do you think Mrs. Stevenson should do next? Why do you think so?

SKILL:
Textual Evidence

OVERVIEW

Students may find it challenging to move beyond what is directly stated in a text to make inferences. This lesson provides follow-up questions and useful enrichments to help teachers guide students toward making inferences and citing textual evidence to support them.

OBJECTIVES

1. Learn the definition of textual evidence.
2. Practice using concrete strategies for identifying textual evidence.
3. Participate effectively in a range of conversations and collaborations to express ideas and build upon the ideas of others.

   ELA Common Core Standards:
   Reading: Literature - RL.8.1
   Speaking & Listening - SL.8.1.A, SL.8.1.B, SL.8.1.C, SL.8.1.D, SL.8.2
   Language - L.8.6

RESOURCES

Access 1 handout (Beginner)

Access 2 handout (Intermediate)

Access 3 handout (Advanced)

Access 4 handout (Approaching)

1. DEFINE

Core Path	Access Path
Watch. Watch the Concept Definition video on textual evidence with your students. Make sure students understand the purpose of finding textual evidence in an informational or literary text, as well as the difference between explicit and inferred evidence. Pause the video at these key moments to discuss the information with your students, making sure they follow the rules for collegial discussions:	**English Learners All Levels & Approaching** **Match.** Have students complete the Match activity on the Access 1, 2, 3, and 4 handouts as they watch the video. Correct answers are located online.
1. 0:50 - Why aren't authors always as explicit as possible in stating their meaning or purpose? Why do you think they often leave evidence to be inferred?	
2. 1:11 - How can readers be sure if an inference is valid? Think of a few ways to test the validity of an inference, in addition to the examples given in the video.	
3. 1:49 - Why is inference an important skill when reading both informational and literary works? How can this skill help us deepen our understanding of works in both genres?	
Read and Discuss. After watching the Concept Definition video, have students read the definition of textual evidence. Either in small groups or as a whole class, use these questions to spur discussion among your students about finding textual evidence to make inferences, making sure they follow the rules for collegial discussions, use academic language correctly, and respond to others' questions and comments with relevant evidence, observations, and ideas:	**Beginner & Approaching** **Finish the Sentences.** Have these students work in groups to complete the sentence frames on the Access 1 and 4 handouts as they read the definition. Have them use the completed sentence frames to help them participate in the discussion. Sample answers for this exercise are located online.
1. Why do readers sometimes need to make inferences? (Authors do not always state directly in a text everything they want readers to know.)	**Intermediate & Advanced** **Discuss Prompts.** To help these students participate in the discussion, prompt them with questions that can be answered with a few words, such as:
2. How can using what you know help you make an inference or a reasonable guess? (Using what you already know, or your own prior knowledge, can help you make an inference about a situation or event. For example, if you know that characters are in a big city, and the author refers to a	• What is explicit evidence? (evidence stated directly in the text)
	• How can inferred evidence help readers? (It can deepen their understanding.)
	• What can inferences help readers understand? (intent, meaning, and context)

Teacher's Edition

Core Path	Access Path
"towering stone giant 110 stories tall," you might infer that the author is referring to a tall building because you know tall buildings are often made of stone and are located in big cities.) 3. Why is locating textual evidence important when making an inference? (Textual evidence is used to support any inferences a reader makes. When analyzing and interpreting a text, being able to support inferences by citing text evidence is an important part of a literary analysis.) 4. Describe a time you made an inference, either when reading or watching a movie or TV show. Explain how you made it. (Answers will vary.)	**Beyond** **Discuss.** Have students select a book, poem, or article they have read, and describe inferred evidence they discovered while reading. Have students discuss how they made inferences while reading, and how these inferences deepened their understanding of the text.
	Extend **Discuss a Visual.** Have students look at an illustrated scene from a classic myth, or, alternatively, have them watch a scene from a television show or movie with the volume off. Ask them to make inferences about what they think is happening. Discuss the clues they used to make inferences. Point out that they can apply these same strategies when they read.
	Extend **Blast.** Create a Blast and ask students to "blast out" the definition of making inferences in their own words. Use the poll question to ask students why they think that authors don't always state everything directly.

2. MODEL

Core Path	Access Path
Watch. Ask students to take notes on the SkillsTV video on Textual Evidence in *Sorry, Wrong Number* as you watch together. Remind students to listen for the way the students use academic vocabulary related to the definition of textual evidence during their discussion. Pause the video at the key moments to discuss the information with your students.	**Beginner, Intermediate, & Approaching** **Analyze the Discussion.** Have students complete the Analyze the Discussion chart on the Access 1, 2 and 4 handouts as they watch the video. Sample answers for this exercise are located online.

Core Path	Access Path
Make sure students have come to the discussion prepared, having read the material discussed in the video, and that they refer to evidence in the text during the discussion. In addition, make sure they follow the rules for collegial discussions.	**Advanced** **Journals.** Have students note in their journals the evidence the students in the SkillsTV video cite to support their opinions on:
1. 0:32 - Can you think of some other elements of a text that can be used to make inferences? How can you also use your own knowledge or experiences to make inferences?	• which passages require inference to understand meaning; and
2. 1:38 - Why is understanding the connotations of words an important reading strategy? How is this strategy utilized here to support an inference?	• their inferences about what the meaning might be in each passage.
3. 2:38 - How can the tone of a story help readers make inferences? How does it affect how readers understand what's implied and anticipate what's coming next?	

Core Path	Access Path
Read and Annotate. Have students independently read the Model section. As they read, ask students to use the annotation tool to:	**Note:** During this portion of the lesson, instruction shifts from whole group to individual work. Use this time to work one-on-one or in small groups with Beginning, Intermediate, Advanced, and Approaching students.
• Highlight key points	**Beginner & Intermediate**
• Ask questions	**Coach the Reading.** Work with these students (either individually or in small groups) to fill out the Guided Reading questions on the Access 1 and 2 handouts. Have Beginning students refer to the Model Glossary on the Access 1 handout to help them determine the meaning of difficult words. (Note: Provide the Access 1 handout Model Glossary to Intermediate students if necessary.)
• Identify places where the Model is applying the strategies laid out in the Identification and Application section on textual evidence.	
	Let students know that they'll use these answers to help participate in the discussion about the Model. Sample answers for this exercise are located online.
	Advanced **Identify Evidence.** Provide these students with the same instructions to read and annotate as on- and beyond- grade-level students. In addition, ask Advanced students to complete the Identify Evidence exercise on the Access 3 handout. Let students know that they'll use these answers to help participate in the discussion about the Model.

Copyright © BookheadEd Learning, LLC

Core Path	Access Path
	Approaching **Guided Reading.** Have students complete the Guided Reading questions on the Access 4 handout as they read. Let them know that they'll use these answers to help participate in the discussion about the Model. Sample answers for this exercise are located online.

Discuss. After students read the Model text, use these questions to facilitate a whole group discussion that helps students understand how to make inferences and find textual evidence to support them in the excerpt. Remind students to follow rules for collegial discussions and to use academic vocabulary correctly. In addition, make sure students have read the selection and draw on that preparation by referring to evidence from the text during the discussion.

1. *Sorry, Wrong Number* is a drama. What must readers use to make inferences? (Readers must use clues from the stage directions and the characters' dialogue to make inferences about what is taking place.)

2. What inferences about the main character, Mrs. Stevenson, does the Model text make? (Mrs. Stevenson is fussy, wealthy, and hard to please. She is also most likely ill or in bad health.) What textual evidence does the Model use to support these inferences? (Textual evidence is provided by the author's description of the setting as the curtain rises. The bedroom set contains "expensive, fussy" furnishings. Mrs. Stevenson is in bed, and pill bottles can be seen on a nearby night table.)

3. What else does the Model discuss as a way for readers to make inferences about the characters and events in the play? (the characters' dialogue

4. Look back at the excerpt. How does the characters' dialogue relate to the setting and help readers make inferences? (Possible response: Parts of the dialogue specifically refer to details about the setting. For example, the two men mention that "At eleven fifteen a subway

Please note that excerpts and passages in the StudySync® library, workbooks, and PDFs are intended as touchstones to generate interest in an author's work. The excerpts and passages do not substitute for the reading of entire texts, and StudySync® strongly recommends that teachers and students seek out and purchase the whole literary or informational work in order to experience it as the author intended. Links to online resellers are available in our digital library. In addition, complete works may be ordered through an authorized reseller by filling out and returning to StudySync® the order form enclosed in this workbook.

Teacher's Edition   **117**

Core Path	Access Path
train crosses the bridge. It makes a noise in case her window is open and she should scream." Earlier, the author notes that, as Mrs. Stevenson hangs up the phone, the sound of a train can be heard in the distance. Connecting the setting with the dialogue helps readers make inferences about the characters and events.)	

3. YOUR TURN

Core Path	Access Path
Assess and Explain. Have students answer the comprehension questions to test for understanding. Share the explanations for Parts A and B (located online) with your students.	
	Extend **Share and Discuss.** Have students complete the Your Turn section in class. Poll students about their responses and, as a class, discuss the different strategies they used to determine the correct answers. Make sure students understand that the plan is for the criminals to murder the woman quickly with a knife and then make it look like a simple robbery. Conduct your poll by asking your students to complete a handout with questions or using Poll Everywhere (http://tinyurl.com/5grl69) or Socrative (http://tinyurl.com/nfz427v).
	Extend **Apply.** Put students into small groups of 3 or 4 to design a silent skit. They will need to act out a scene without talking. The class will watch each skit then make inferences about what they thought was happening in the scene based on the details of the performance. After each skit, allow the other groups time to talk about the scene and what they thought was happening. Each group in the audience can share their inferences with the class, and then the group that acted out the scene can tell the class which group(s) made the best inferences.

SKILL:
Plot

OVERVIEW

Students may need help identifying how a plot develops and the elements that contribute to its development. This lesson plan provides follow-up questions and useful enrichments to help teachers guide students toward a usable, repeatable method for uncovering plot in a work of fiction.

OBJECTIVES

1. Learn the definition of plot.
2. Practice using concrete strategies for identifying elements of plot.
3. Participate effectively in a range of conversations and collaborations to express ideas and build upon the ideas of others.

ELA Common Core Standards:

Reading: Literature - RL.8.1, RL.8.3
Speaking & Listening - SL.8.1.A, SL.8.1.B, SL.8.1.C, SL.8.1.D, SL.8.2
Language - L.8.6

RESOURCES

Access 1 handout (Beginner)
Access 2 handout (Intermediate)
Access 3 handout (Advanced)
Access 4 handout (Approaching)

Please note that excerpts and passages in the StudySync® library, workbooks, and PDFs are intended as touchstones to generate interest in an author's work. The excerpts and passages do not substitute for the reading of entire texts, and StudySync® strongly recommends that teachers and students seek out and purchase the whole literary or informational work in order to experience it as the author intended. Links to online resellers are available in our digital library. In addition, complete works may be ordered through an authorized reseller by filling out and returning to StudySync® the order form enclosed in this workbook.

Teacher's Edition   119

1. DEFINE

Core Path	Access Path
Watch. Watch the Concept Definition video on plot with your students. Make sure your students write down the definition of plot and understand its basic components: beginning, middle, and end. Also make sure that they note which story elements interact to shape the plot, including characters, dialogue, setting and events. (For further understanding, ask students to think of another story or fable and analyze its plot elements.) Pause the video at these key moments to discuss the information with your students:	**English Learners All Levels & Approaching** **Match.** Have students complete the matching exercise on the Access 1, 2, 3, and 4 handouts as they watch the video. Answers are located online.

1. 1:00 - Besides dialogue, what other elements can a story use to reveal actions, character and decisions? What if a story contains little or no dialogue?

2. 1:46 - Does plot shape character, or does character shape plot? Or both? Discuss.

3. 2:04 - Must all stories contain a resolution? Why or why not? Is there a difference between a "resolution" and a "happy ending?

Core Path	Access Path
Read and Discuss. After watching the Concept Definition video, have students read the definition of plot. Either in small groups or as a whole class, use the following questions to engage students in a discussion about plot.	**Beginner & Approaching** **Sentence Frames.** Have these students complete the sentence frames exercise on the Access 1 and 4 handouts as they read the definition of plot. Have them use the completed sentence frames to help them participate in the discussion. Sample answers for this exercise are located online.

1. What are the parts of a plot? (exposition, rising action, climax, falling action, resolution)

2. What often happens to a main character after story events lead to the solution of the character's problem, and the conclusion of the plot? (The character has usually changed in some way, and learned from his or her experience.)

3. What kind of order or sequencing do you feel is most helpful to create a suspenseful plot? Are falling action or resolution necessary for a suspenseful plot? (Answers may vary.)

Intermediate & Advanced
Discuss Prompts. To help these students participate in the discussion, prompt them with questions that can be answered with a few words, such as:

- What is the plot of a text? (episodes and events that make up the story)

- What do plot events expose in a story? (Problems that need to be resolved in the course of the story.)

Core Path	Access Path
4. Think of a classic story that we all know well, such as *Cinderella*. What is the plot of that story in a sentence or two? (After her father dies, Cinderella is treated unfairly by her stepmother and stepsisters. She gets help from a magical being to go to a ball and meets a prince there. The prince marries Cinderella, and she is finally free of her stepmother.)	• What does dialogue reveal in a story? (action, and characters' decisions) • What often happens to characters in the course of a story? (They respond and change to solve problems and resolve the plot.) **Beyond** **Discuss.** Have students select a book they've read and describe its plot. Compile a list of examples. Have students discuss how the plot of each work affects what the reader learns about the characters and setting. How might a switch in plot affect not only what the reader learns, but how much he or she enjoys the story?
	Extend **Tech Infusion** **Brainstorm.** Ask students to imagine that they are playwrights and must write their own drama. Have them brainstorm ideas about how they would introduce the setting and characters through stage directions in dramatic literature. Compile this list of examples as a class using a whiteboard or a Padlet Wall (http://tinyurl.com/n7l7cyy).
	Extend **Graphic Organizer.** Have students make a graphic organizer that lists each of the five parts of a plot. Have them fill out what they know so far about the plot of *Sorry, Wrong Number*. Ask them to save the organizer and use it to fill in other parts of the chart as they discuss the rest of the excerpt.

2. MODEL

Core Path	Access Path
Read and Annotate. Have students independently read the Model section. As they read, ask students to use the annotation tool to: • highlight key points • ask questions	**Note:** During this portion of the lesson, instruction shifts from whole group to individual work. Use this time to work one-on-one or in small groups with Beginning, Intermediate, Advanced, and Approaching students.

Core Path	Access Path
• Identify places where the Model applies the strategies laid out in the Identification and Application section on plot	**Beginner & Intermediate** **Coach the Reading.** Work with these students (either individually or in small groups) to fill out the guided reading questions on the Access 1 and 2 handouts. Have Beginning students refer to the glossary on the Access 1 handout to help them determine the meaning of difficult words. (Note: Provide the Access 1 handout glossary to Intermediate students if necessary.) Let students know they'll use these answers to help participate in the discussion about the Model. Sample answers for this exercise are located online. **Advanced** **Identify Evidence.** Provide these students with the same instructions to read and annotate as on- and beyond- grade-level students. In addition, ask Advanced students to complete the Identify Evidence exercise on the Access 3 handout. Let students know that they'll use these answers to help participate in the discussion about the Model. Sample answers for this exercise are located online. **Approaching** **Guided Reading.** Have students complete the guided reading questions on the Access 4 handout as they read. Let them know that they'll use these answers to help participate in the discussion about the Model. Sample answers for this exercise are located online.

Discuss. After students read the Model text, use these questions to facilitate a whole group discussion that helps students understand parts of the drama's plot.

1. According to the Model, what do readers learn during the exposition part of the plot? (The start, or exposition, is where the characters and setting are established. During this part of a story or play the conflict or main problem is also introduced.)

2. How can the description of Mrs. Stevenson be considered to be part of the story's exposition? (It describes who she is, where she lives, and what she is doing. This establishes one or more of the problems the character faces.)

Core Path	Access Path
3. How would the exposition of the plot in this drama be different if it were written as a novel? (The author might include the character's inner thoughts, revealing information about why she is in bed and why she is trying to reach her husband.) 4. How is this exposition similar to other stories or plays you have read? How is it different? (Students should choose a story they are familiar with and compare the style and events of that introduction with the exposition of *Sorry, Wrong Number.*)	
	Extend **Tech Infusion** **Pair and Share.** Ask students to work in groups to act out the excerpt, including the part that is used for the Model. Have them assign a student to each character, as well as to the narrator. When they are finished, have them point out specific places where they saw the plot changing and developing. Encourage them to record their work and post it on a class website.

3. YOUR TURN

Core Path	Access Path
Assess and Explain. Have students answer the comprehension questions to test for understanding. Share the explanations for Parts A and B (located online) with your students.	
	Extend **Share and Discuss.** Have students complete the Your Turn section in class. Poll students about their responses and as a class discuss the different strategies they used to determine the correct answers. Ask students questions to reinforce their understanding of Plot. • How does the author tell the story? (through dialogue) • Where does the rising action begin to take place? (when Mrs. Stevenson is connected to her call)

OVERVIEW

The drama *Sorry, Wrong Number* by Lucille Fletcher, examines the experiences of Mrs. Stevenson, a neurotic woman alone in her New York City apartment who overhears something that would strike fear into anyone. The Close Read gives students the opportunity to experience the text in a more analytical way.

OBJECTIVES

1. Complete a close reading of an excerpt from a work of literature.
2. Practice and apply concrete strategies for identifying textual evidence to use in analysis and to explain the development of plot in a drama.
3. Participate effectively in a range of conversations and collaborations to express ideas and build upon the ideas of others.
4. Prewrite, plan, and produce clear and coherent writing in response to a prompt.

ELA Common Core Standards:
Reading: Literature - RL.8.1, RL.8.3, RL.8.4
Writing - W.8.4, W.8.5, W.8.6, W.8.10
Speaking & Listening - SL.8.1.A, SL.8.1.C, SL.8.6
Language - L.8.2.C, L.8.4.A, L.8.4.C, L.8.4.D, L.8.6

RESOURCES

Sorry, Wrong Number Vocabulary handout
Access 1 handout (Beginner)
Access 2 handout (Intermediate)
Access 3 handout (Advanced)
Access 4 handout (Approaching)

1. INTRODUCTION

Core Path	Access Path
Define and Compare. Project the vocabulary words and definitions onto the board or provide students with a handout, so they can copy the vocabulary into their notebooks. Suggest that students consult general and specialized reference materials, both print and digital, to compare the precise meaning of a specific word with their initial vocabulary predictions from the First Read. Review words that students defined incorrectly to understand why they were unable to use context clues to develop usable definitions.	**Beginner & Intermediate** **Complete the Sentences.** Have students complete the sentence frames on the Access 1 and 2 handouts using the vocabulary words. Correct answers are located online. **Advanced & Beyond** **Write in Journals.** Have students write a journal entry using all of their vocabulary words. Remind them to write sentences that communicate the meaning of the words they are using. **Approaching** **Graphic Organizer.** To support students in comparing their predictions with the correct meanings, have them complete the graphic organizer on the Access 4 handout to record the vocabulary words, their initial analsys, and the definitions. Then have them write sentences using the words.
Review. Have students complete the fill-in-the-blank vocabulary handout for this selection. Answers for the handout are listed online.	
	Extend **Skit.** Break students into small groups, assign each group a vocabulary word, and ask them to design a short skit to demonstrate the meaning of the word for their peers.
	Extend **Crazy Connections.** Write the vocabulary words on index cards. Pick one at a time and ask students to write a sentence that connects the two in as likely or unlikely a way as they find interesting. For example, *neurotic* is connected to *imperious* because an imperious lawmaker may be driven to make odd decisions based on his neurotic nature.

2. READ

Core Path	Access Path
Model Close Reading. Project the text onto the board and model a close reading using the following annotation strategies. While modeling annotation strategies, make notes that tie the text to the focus skill and demonstrate what students are looking for as they read. Here is some guidance for you as you annotate for your students:	

- As the Skills lesson that precedes this text makes clear, the start, or exposition, is where the characters and setting are established in a plot. During this part of the story or play, the conflict or main problem is also introduced. What textual evidence can we cite that gives us some clues about the character of Mrs. Stevenson? (Possible answer: The author of the play describes Mrs. Stevenson as a "querulous, self-centered neurotic.")

- Mrs. Stevenson's initial problem in the play is the fact that she can't reach her husband on the phone. In the second paragraph of the stage directions we read that Mrs. Stevenson slams down her phone in irritation, which tells us that there's some problem with the phone call she's making. She asks the operator to place the call for her, and then begins telling the operator about her situation. How is this text evidence that supports the playwright's description of Mrs. Stevenson's character? (Possible answer: Mrs. Stevenson begins telling the operator all about her circumstances, including the fact that she's ill and has been nervous all day. She assumes in a self-centered way that a complete stranger is going to be interested in her problems.)

Core Path	Access Path
• Once the operator places the call, Mrs. Stevenson finds herself overhearing a private conversation. The two men on the line cannot hear her, but she can hear them. This specific incident in the play propels the action forward. What new problem does this present for Mrs. Stevenson, and why might this incident be a turning point in the plot? (Possible answer: Mrs. Stevenson overhears what may be a murder plot. Since readers already know she is neurotic, this may be a turning point depending on what she decides to do with this information. She doesn't know who the victim might be.)	

Read and Annotate. Read the Skills Focus questions as a class, so your students know what they should pay close attention to as they read. Then have students read and annotate the excerpt. Ask students to use the annotation tool as they read to:

1. respond to the Skills Focus section

2. ask questions

3. make connections between particular lines of dialogue and incidents that propel the action of the drama and reveal aspects of a character

4. identify key information, character traits, and themes, and how the character's traits might influence the events of the plot

5. note unfamiliar vocabulary

6. capture their reaction to the events in the play and how the author goes about building suspense

As students reread the text, remind them to use the comprehension strategy of making, confirming, and revising predictions that they learned in the First Read.

Note: While on- grade-level students are reading and annotating, work one-on-one or in small groups with Beginning, Intermediate, Advanced, and Approaching students to support them as they read and annotate the text.

Beginner & Intermediate
Summarize and Analyze the Text. Work with these students to complete the Summarize and Analyze the Text exercise in the Access 1 and 2 handouts. (Note: The sentence frames for Intermediate students on the Access 2 handout contain fewer scaffolds.) They will then use the completed sentence frames to help them analyze and annotate the text by completing the Skills Focus questions. Refer to the sample Skills Focus answers online to help them complete the sentence frames and annotate the text.

Advanced
Work in Pairs. Pair these students with more proficient English speakers to work together on analyzing and annotating the text to complete the Skills Focus questions. If these students need more support, have them use the Summarize and Analyze the Text exercise in the Access 3 handout as they work with their more proficient peers.

Please note that excerpts and passages in the StudySync® library, workbooks, and PDFs are intended as touchstones to generate interest in an author's work. The excerpts and passages do not substitute for the reading of entire texts, and StudySync® strongly recommends that teachers and students seek out and purchase the whole literary or informational work in order to experience it as the author intended. Links to online resellers are available in our digital library. In addition, complete works may be ordered through an authorized reseller by filling out and returning to StudySync® the order form enclosed in this workbook.

Teacher's Edition   127

Core Path	Access Path
	Approaching **Summarize the Text.** Have these students discuss and complete the Summarize the Text exercise in the Access 4 handout and use their summary to help them analyze and annotate the text so as to complete the Skills Focus questions. Correct answers for the summary are online. Also refer to the sample Skills Focus answers to aid students with their annotations.
Discuss. After students have read the text, use the sample responses to the Skills Focus questions online to discuss the reading and the process of analyzing elements of the plot using textual evidence. Make sure that students have acquired and accurately use academic-specific words and phrases related to the skill, and demonstrate a command of formal English appropriate to the discussion.	**Extend** **Pair and Share.** In small, heterogeneous groups or pairs, ask students to share and discuss their annotations with a focus on the point of view presented in the selection. You can provide students with these questions to guide their discussion: 1. Besides the dialogue, what else gives us information as we read this text? (We also get information [like a description of the setting, and clues to Mrs. Stevenson's personality] from the exposition, or stage directions.) 2. What Mrs. Stevenson's mood before she overhears the two men talking? (Nervous, then also impatient and annoyed because she can't get in touch with her husband.) 3. How does her mood change by the end of the excerpt? (She has gone from annoyance to shock and then horror at what she hears.) 4. What causes the change? (She hears the men planning some violent act against an unknown [to her, so far] woman.)
	Extend **Act.** Break the class into smaller groups. Assign parts to each student to perform, including the stage directions. After a read through of the script, have each group discuss and respond to the following questions: • What does the exposition tell us about Mrs. Stevenson? • What is the significance of the pill bottle?

Core Path	Access Path
	• How might Mrs. Stevenson's anxious nature affect events going forward?
	• Have each group present its findings to the class.

3. WRITE

Core Path	Access Path
Prewrite and Plan. Read the prompt as a class and ask students to brainstorm their reactions to the plot of Lucille Fletcher's *Sorry, Wrong Number*. Students can brainstorm together either as a class or in small groups to begin planning their responses, analyzing the ways in which fear and suspense is introduced and maintained during the play's developing plot. Remind students to look at the excerpt and their annotations to find textual evidence to support their ideas.	**Beginner & Intermediate** **Answer and Discuss.** Have students complete the prewriting questions in the Access 2 and 3 handouts and then explain their answers to a partner before they write. Explain to students that when they answer a question such as *"What is the rising action in this excerpt from* Sorry, Wrong Number?" they need to include a detail, example or quote from the text that supports the statement. For example, students could include the lines:

[FIRST MAN]: At eleven fifteen a subway train crosses the bridge. It makes a noise in case her window is open and she should scream.
MRS. STEVENSON [*shocked*]: "Oh, *hello!* What number is this, please?
GEORGE: Okay. I understand.
These lines show that Mrs. Stevenson is getting more and more detailed information about a crime to be committed in the near future. It also shows that she can hear the men, but no one can hear her, which helps build up a mood of suspense and fear.

Approaching **Answer Prewriting Questions.** Have students complete the prewriting questions in the Access 4 handout to summarize their thoughts before they write. |

Copyright © BookheadEd Learning, LLC

Core Path	Access Path
	Extend **Analyze the Prompt.** Explain that the prompt in this case asks students to consider elements from the play and how they introduce and maintain a sense of fear. Suggest that students copy down each of the suggested elements and write one example next to each. (sound effects: the buzzing signal before Mrs. Stevenson hangs up the phone; line structure: abrupt pauses and exclamations as Mrs. Stevenson overhears the conversation; tone of voice: Mrs. Stevenson raising her voice to the phone to ask who she is calling)

Discuss. Project these instructions for the peer review onto the board and review them with your class, so they know what they are looking for when they begin to provide their classmates with feedback:

- Has the writer written a response that explains how fear and suspense are introduced and maintained in the opening of the play?

- Has the writer discussed how the sound effects, structure of lines, and the sound of characters' voices may have contributed to the development of fear?

- Did the writer address how suspense makes the reader make predictions about the story?

- Did the writer use his or her understanding of plot development to write their response?

- Has the writer used evidence from the text to support his or her writing?

- Has the writer used vocabulary words from the lesson?

Be sure to tell the writer what he or she did well and what he or she needs to work on. Remember that your comments are most useful when they are constructive.

After you've looked at the peer review instructions, review the rubric with students before they begin writing. Allow time for students to briefly raise and discuss questions they may have about the peer review instructions and the rubric. Tell students how many peer reviews they will need to complete once they submit their writing.

Core Path	Access Path
Write. Ask students to complete the writing assignment using textual evidence to support their answers. If possible, have students use technology to produce and publish their writing. Once they have completed their writing, they should click "Submit."	
Review. Once students complete their writing assignment, they should submit substantive feedback to two peers. If possible, have students use technology to interact and collaborate with others.	

FIRST READ:
Violence in the Movies

OVERVIEW

In "Violence in the Movies: Cinematic Craft or Hollywood Gone Too Far?" two authors argue for or against the use of violence in the movies and debate whether or not violent media has an effect on children. Both authors support their conflicting viewpoints with evidence. The First Read gives students the opportunity to begin to explore point of view.

OBJECTIVES

1. Perform an initial reading of a text and demonstrate comprehension by responding to short analysis and inference questions with textual evidence.
2. Practice defining vocabulary words using context.
3. Participate effectively in a range of conversations and collaborations to express ideas and build upon the ideas of others

ELA Common Core Standards:
Reading: Informational Text - RI.8.1, RI.8.4, RI.8.10
Writing - W.8.10
Speaking & Listening - SL.8.1.A, SL.8.1.B, SL.8.1.C, SL.8.1.D, SL.8.2, SL.8.6
Language - L.8.2.C, L.8.4.A, L.8.4.B, L.8.4.C, L.8.6

RESOURCES

Grammar handout: Words Often Confused

Access 1 handout (Beginner)

Access 2 handout (Intermediate)

Access 3 handout (Advanced)

Access 4 handout (Approaching)

ACCESS COMPLEX TEXT

These texts illustrate two distinctly different cause-and-effect viewpoints supported by researched evidence on the societal effects of violence in the movies. In both cases, much of the evidence is academic, derived from published studies and statistical analyses. The alternating viewpoints and their source materials may be challenging for some students. To help students evaluate the credibility of each argument, use the following ideas to provide scaffolded instruction for an initial reading of the more complex features of these texts.

- **Purpose** - Although each author writes to persuade readers to agree with his or her position, the points of view are opposing. To evaluate credibility, readers will need to examine each piece of evidence to determine its type and its source as well as whether each author provides all needed information and addresses valid counter-arguments effectively.

- **Organization** - Each author makes claims regarding the causes of violence in society. Readers will need to identify these cause-and-effect relationships and evaluate the logic of each.

- **Specific Vocabulary** - Psychological or media terminology, such as "desensitization" or "propaganda," may challenge some readers.

1. INTRODUCTION

Core Path	Access Path
Read and Listen. Individually or as a class, read and discuss the Introduction for "Violence in the Movies." The Introduction provides context for the two articles that take positions on opposite sides of an issue.	**English Learners All Levels & Approaching** **Read and Listen.** Ask students to read and listen to the Introduction for "Violence in the Movies." Have them refer to the Introduction Glossary on their Access 1, 2, 3, and 4 handouts for definitions of key vocabulary terms. If there are unfamiliar words that are not included in their glossary, encourage students to check a dictionary or online reference tool, such as http://tinyurl.com/6ytby.

Please note that excerpts and passages in the StudySync® library, workbooks, and PDFs are intended as touchstones to generate interest in an author's work. The excerpts and passages do not substitute for the reading of entire texts, and StudySync® strongly recommends that teachers and students seek out and purchase the whole literary or informational work in order to experience it as the author intended. Links to online resellers are available in our digital library. In addition, complete works may be ordered through an authorized reseller by filling out and returning to StudySync® the order form enclosed in this workbook.

Teacher's Edition   **133**

Core Path	Access Path
Access Prior Knowledge. Find out what your students already think about violence in the movies and other media.	**English Learners All Levels & Approaching** **Access Prior Knowledge.** In small groups, have students create a Venn Diagram to compare violence in movies and violence in the news. After they have completed their diagrams, ask groups to discuss. Then, hold a classwide debate on the topic.

Core Path

Access Prior Knowledge. Find out what your students already think about violence in the movies and other media.

1. Ask students what kinds of things they consider to be "violent" when watching television news, entertainment programs, computer games, movies, theater, or other public media experiences. As a class, compile a list of responses.

2. As a class or in small groups, ask them to discuss their exposure to violence. How many television shows, video games, or movies that they have been exposed to do they consider to have violent content?

3. Take a poll: Do they think that exposure to violent acts or images in the media has had an effect on them? Were they personally more or less likely to act violently after exposure to such media?

4. As a class, compile a list of ways in which young people are exposed to violence. Discuss whether or not students think this is an important issue, and why or why not.

Extend

Discuss the Introduction. After reading the Introduction, use the information provided to facilitate a pre-reading discussion to get students thinking about the points of view in "Violence in the Movies."

1. Do you think that violence in movies can cause people to act aggressively?

2. Do you think filmmakers can create entertaining movies without including violence?

3. Who do you think is responsible for protecting children against media violence?

Copyright © BookheadEd Learning, LLC

Core Path	Access Path
	Extend **Analyze and Discuss a Quote.** "I object to violence because when it appears to do good, the good is only temporary; the evil it does is permanent." (Mahatma Gandhi) 1. What do you think Gandhi means by violence doing "temporary" good? 2. Do you agree with this quote? Why or why not? 3. Do you think violence can be used for good?

2. READ

Core Path	Access Path
Make Predictions about Vocabulary. There are five bold vocabulary words in the text. As students read the text, ask them to make predictions about what they think each bold vocabulary word means based on the context clues in the sentence. If you are in a low tech classroom and students are reading from printed copies or a projected text, ask students to record predictions in their notes, so they can be easily referenced in class. If your students have access to technology, they can use the annotation tool to make their predictions. It might be helpful to model this for students before they begin reading. Either using the board or projecting the actual text, focus in on the sentence that uses the word "aggressive": • Because watching violent movies provides those who might otherwise engage in violent behaviors with an alternative, nonviolent activity, it turns out to be a beneficial activity to those with **aggressive** tendencies. Model for the class how to use the overall structure and meaning of the sentence and the sentences around it, the word's position, and other clues to define the unfamiliar vocabulary word. In this case, point out these context keys:	**Note:** This exercise, which extends vocabulary instruction, should be completed when the class shifts from whole group instruction to individual work during the "Read and Annotate" exercise. **Beginner, Intermediate, & Approaching Pair Practice.** 1. Pair students with more proficient readers. 2. Give them an additional sentence that contains a new vocabulary word. 3. Ask the students to complete a Think Aloud using the teacher-led Make Predictions about Vocabulary activity as a model, while the more proficient reader actively listens. 4. The students should use the context clues in the sentence to try to determine the meaning of the new vocabulary word. 5. After the students has completed the Think Aloud and made a prediction about the word's meaning, allow time for the more proficient reader to add his/her own thoughts and clarify any points of confusion.

Copyright © BookheadEd Learning, LLC

Core Path	Access Path
1. Look at the structure of the sentence. What is the subject (watching movies) and what is the first verb (provides)? From this, we can see that the act of watching movies provides the watcher with something.	4. Once they've completed this Think Aloud, encourage them to use a dictionary to confirm the definition of the new vocabulary word. Have them refer to the Text Glossary on their Access handouts 1, 2, and 4 for definitions of key vocabulary terms in the text. Encourage them to add any additional vocabulary words or idioms they find in the text and look up definitions for those words and idioms online or in a dictionary.
2. From the rest of the sentence, we see that the movie watcher, especially one who "might otherwise engage in violent behaviors" is provided with an "alternative, nonviolent activity."	
3. Finally, in the last part of the sentence, we learn that the act of watching movies is "beneficial" and the pronoun "those" tells us that the people who benefit are the same ones who might have "aggressive tendencies." "The word "aggressive" is an adjective describing *tendencies,* or behaviors; in this case violent behaviors. We also see that those same people are described as "aggressive" in this part of the sentence, and so we can infer that "aggressive" people are violent, and perhaps eager to fight.	

Model Reading Comprehension Strategy. Before students begin reading, model the reading comprehension strategy of asking and answering questions by using this Think Aloud that talks students through the first paragraph of text. First explain to your students that asking and answering questions is:

a process skillful readers use to ask themselves questions about anything that is unclear before, during, and after they read to aid their comprehension. After asking the questions, readers look for ways to answer the questions using the text.

Explain to students how asking and answering questions will help them better comprehend the selection and help drive their discussions.

- When I read the first paragraph, I notice the author is comparing movies in the past with those of today. As I read, I ask myself, "What is this article going to be about?"

Note: This exercise, which extends vocabulary instruction, should be completed when the class shifts from whole group instruction to individual work during the "Read and Annotate" exercise.

Beginner, Intermediate, & Approaching
Apply Reading Comprehension Strategy.

1. In pairs, have students read the first three paragraphs of the Point and Counterpoint articles. Have students write down questions they have in the margins next to the text.

2. Have pairs ask each other their questions. Encourage students to write down the answers next to their questions. Allow students time to practice the reading comprehension strategy of asking and answering questions.

3. Circle around to pairs to check their understanding of the strategy. Encourage students to explain how asking and answering questions helps to better understand a text.

Core Path	Access Path
• The topic sentence of the very next paragraph answers my first question-it is about increasing violence in movies. Reading on, I want to know, "Why is this a cause for concern?" • The remainder of the second paragraph cites statistics about children's exposure to violence in movies and television and I wonder, "Why is this important?" The next paragraph provides an answer about a link between exposure and behavior.	

Core Path	Access Path
Read and Annotate. Read and annotate the Point/Counterpoint essays. Ask students to use the annotation tool as they read to: 1. use context clues to analyze and determine the meaning of the bolded vocabulary terms 2. ask questions about passages of the text that may be unclear 3. make connections between ideas in texts that offer differing viewpoints 4. identify key information used to support each author's points and determine its source and credibility 5. note unfamiliar vocabulary 6. capture their reactions to the information in the text	**Beginner** **Coach the Reading.** While other students read, annotate, and discuss the text independently, work with Beginning students, listening to the audio of the text and pausing periodically or when any student has a question. Coach students in articulating their questions for the group and in highlighting and annotating the text. Have students use the Annotation Guide in the Access 1 handout to support them as they highlight and annotate the text. For further support, ask questions about the text such as: • What evidence does the author who is against violence in movies use? • What evidence does the author who thinks violence in movies does not lead to violence in real life? • Which author provides sound reasoning and relevant evidence? **Intermediate** **Listen to the Audio.** Have these students listen to the audio of the text and use the definitions on the Access 2 handout to help them with words or idioms that may be unfamiliar. If students need help with annotating the text, have them use the Annotation Guide on the Access 2 handout. After working with the Beginning students, you may wish to check this group's progress and provide support as needed.

Core Path	Access Path
	Advanced **Pair with Proficient Peers.** Have Advanced students work with English proficient peers to read, annotate, and discuss the text. Have students use the Annotation Guide in the Access 3 handout to support them as they highlight and annotate the text. Encourage them to listen to the audio of the text if needed. **Approaching** **Use the Annotation Guide.** Have students use the Annotation Guide in the Access 4 handout to support them as they highlight and annotate the text.

Core Path	Access Path
Discuss. In small groups or pairs, have students discuss the questions and inferences they made while reading the Point and Counterpoint essays. 1. How does the first author feel about Hollywood filmmakers? (They use violence instead of good storytelling techniques to entertain audiences.) 2. What is the second author's opinion about parents? (They must teach their children that movie violence is fantasy, not reality.) 3. What is the first author's concern about movie heroes using violence to defeat an enemy? (Children will learn that it's okay to use violence to solve problems.) 4. What does the second author reveal about his own experience with violence in movies? (He watches violent movies and does not act violently.) 5. What does the first author state about the country's top researchers? (They have proven a link between media violence and violent behavior in children.) 6. What does the second author state about the CDC's research in paragraph 13? (Exposure to movie violence is not a risk factor for youth violence.)	**English Learners All Levels & Approaching** Use the extra time while on-and beyond- grade-level students are discussing their first reads of the text to work individually and in small groups with English Learners and Approaching readers as previously outlined. Should those students complete their first reads quickly, integrate them into the on- and beyond- grade-level discussion groups. Otherwise, English Learners and Approaching readers will be given an opportunity to participate in text discussions with their peers later in the lesson.

Core Path	Access Path
7. What types of sources do these authors use for evidence to support their views? What are some examples? (Both writers use scientific research, statistics, or opinions to support their views. The U.S. Bureau of Justice, the CDC, and the MPAA are examples of sources.)	
	Extend **Tech Infusion** **Brainstorm.** Use a virtual post it note canvas such as Padlet (http://tinyurl.com/n7l7cyy) to allow students to brainstorm pros and cons of violence in the movies.
(G) **Grammar, Usage, and Mechanics.** Distribute the StudySync Grammar handout: Words Often Confused. Review with students the use of words often confused as explained in the handout. Then have students complete the practice exercise. (Correct answers for the practice exercise appear online.) Finally, encourage students to apply what they have learned by analyzing the use of the often-confused words in "Violence in the Movies." Be sure students have access to a print or online dictionary. Ask students: 1. In the last paragraph of "Violence in the Movies," the writer discusses "epic literature." What is the definition of *epic*? Can you think of a word is it commonly confused with? (*Epic* as it is used in "Violence in the Movies" means "long tales of heroic deeds"; it is commonly confused with *epoch*, which refers to an era, or a part of history.) 2. In the last paragraph what is the definition of *aid*, as it is used here? What word is it commonly confused with? (The word *aid* is a noun that means "something that helps or assists," such as a learning aid; it is commonly confused with *aide*, which specifically refers to a person whose job it is to help or assist, such as a live-in aide for the elderly.)	**Beginner & Intermediate** **Work with the Teacher.** Remind these students that certain words are often misspelled because they are confused with other words. Write the following statement on the board: *It was there baseball on the ground.* Ask: *Which word is misspelled? How do I fix it?* (The word there *is misspelled here. The word should be spelled* **their** *to be correct here.*) *Spell the three often-confused words that should be in the sentences.* (I went _____ the store so I could buy _____ peppers. I stopped at the post office, _____.) Allow time for students to share their complete sentences. Then have these students participate in the short lesson above with Approaching students. Then work with them to complete the StudySync Grammar handout.

Core Path	Access Path

Core Path

3. Can you find any other often-confused words in "Violence in the Movies"? Give the definition of the word and the word with which it is commonly confused. (Sample answer: The word "affected" as it is used in paragraph 7 of the first essay means "influenced." It is commonly confused with the word "effected" which means, "caused" or "brought about.")

4. What is the effect of precise spelling of often confused words in this and other written works? (Precise spelling of often confused words helps avoid reader confusion and serves to clarify meaning in a written work. In addition, misspellings can cause readers to doubt the accuracy of other parts of a writer's work, too.)

Access Path

Advanced & Beyond

Extend the Search. Challenge these students to work in pairs or small groups to find other often-confused words in "Violence in the Movies." If time allows, have students find often-confused words in articles with the same topic.

Approaching

Analyze an Example. If students need more support on spelling words often confused, call their attention to these words in paragraph 4 under the counterpoint: . . . *low parental involvement, association with delinquent peers, low IQ, poor academic performance...*

Ask: *Which word is commonly confused with a word that sounds just like it? What does the word in the paragraph mean? What does the word it is often confused with mean?* (*Peers* as it is used in "Violence in the Movies" means "a person of the same age," and it is commonly confused with *piers*, which refer to solid supports.) Then have students complete the StudySync Grammar handout.

Extend

Vocabulary Connections. Use the Audio Text Highlight tool to help students identify words and phrases in the text used to evoke emotion in readers.

1. Ask students to read the first paragraph of each article and label the different types of speech for each identified word (noun, verb, adjective).

2. As a class or in small groups, discuss:
   a. What is the author's purpose for choosing these words?
   b. What kind of emotional reaction do you have to these words and phrases?
   c. What words might you substitute to change a reader's emotional response?
   d. Do you notice a pattern in types of speech used to evoke emotion?

Remind students that as they read using the Audio Text Highlight tool, they can pause, repeat, or slow down the audio at any time.

3. THINK

Core Path	Access Path
Answer and Discuss. Have students complete the Think questions and then use the peer review instructions and rubric to complete the peer reviews. Refer to the sample answers online to discuss responses with your students.	**Beginner & Intermediate** **Sentence Frames.** Have students use the sentence frames on the Access 1 and 2 handouts to support their responses to the Think questions. If necessary, distribute sentence frames to Advanced students as well. **Approaching** **Find the Evidence.** Have students use Find the Evidence on the Access 4 handout to help them identify the evidence needed to answer the questions.
	Extend **Debate.** Present students with an issue from the text that can be debated. Allow students to debate the issue as a class or in smaller groups. Debate prompts: 1. Do you think that violence in the movies puts people at risk for violent behaviors? Why or why not? 2. Do you think that filmmakers should be restricted from including violence in movies? Why or why not?
	Extend **Write a Claim.** Ask students to write a strong claim that clearly states their position in relation to the topic they debated. Once students have written their claims, ask them to read their claims to a small group of their peers. This activity will provide them practice writings claims, as well as expose them to claims written by their peers.

Author's Purpose and Author's Point of View

OVERVIEW

Determining the point of view helps readers better understand how an author's beliefs and attitudes can influence what he or she is writing. It also helps them become critical readers and develop their own point of view. This lesson provides follow-up questions and useful enrichments to help teachers guide students toward identifying and analyzing an author's point of view and purpose for writing.

OBJECTIVES

1. Learn the definition of author's purpose and author's point of view.
2. Practice using concrete strategies for identifying author's purpose and author's point of view.
3. Participate effectively in a range of conversations and collaborations to express ideas and build upon the ideas of others.

ELA Common Core Standards:
Reading: Informational Text - RI.8.1, RI.8.6
Speaking & Listening - SL.8.1.A, SL.8.1.C, SL.8.1.D, SL.8.2

RESOURCES

Access 1 handout (Beginner)
Access 2 handout (Intermediate)
Access 3 handout (Advanced)
Access 4 handout (Approaching)

1. DEFINE

Core Path	Access Path
Watch. Watch the Concept Definition video on author's purpose and author's point of view with your students. Make sure students understand the different components of point of view, and how to determine the author's purpose. Pause the video at these key moments to discuss the information with your students:	**English Learners All Levels & Approaching** **Match.** Have students complete the matching exercise on the Access 1, 2, 3, and 4 handouts as they watch the video. Correct answers are located online.

Core Path

1. 1:00-Can you think of any other purpose (or purposes) an author might have? How does genre affect purpose i.e., how might the purpose of a fiction text differ from that of an informational text? How might it stay the same?

2. 1:18-Are there any other elements of a text that might offer clues into an author's purpose or author's point of view? What are some additional resources we can use if we're having trouble deciphering the purpose or point of view?

3. 2:03-Why don't authors of fiction or poetry state their purpose clearly in the same way a politician or an essayist might?

Read and Discuss. After watching the Concept Definition video, have students read the definition of author's purpose and author's point of view. Either in small groups or as a whole class, use the following questions to engage students in a discussion about author's purpose and author's point of view. Make sure students follow the rules for collegial discussions and respond to others' questions and comments with relevant evidence, observations, and ideas.

1. What are the different purposes a writer might have for writing? (An author may write to entertain, persuade, inform, or for a combination of these reasons.)

2. What is the difference between an author's purpose and an author's point of view? (Author's purpose refers to the intention of the author, the reason he or she writes. Author's point of view is the author's perspective on the topic.)

Access Path

Beginner & Approaching
Complete a Chart. To prepare students to participate in the discussion, have them complete the chart on the Access 1 and 4 handouts as they read the definition. Correct answers are located online.

Intermediate & Advanced
Discuss Prompts. To help these students participate in the discussion, prompt them with questions that can be answered with a few words, such as:

- How can you tell what an author's purpose is? (by identifying the central idea; by looking at the word choice or language used; and, sometimes you can tell the purpose by who the audience is)

- What are common purposes for writing? (to entertain, to persuade, to educate, to move)

Core Path	Access Path
3. How might an author's point of view be related to his or her purpose? (The author's point of view can influence or affect an author's purpose, or the reason he or she writes something.) 4. When might an author want to use emotional or descriptive language, or include facts and statistics in his or her writing? (An author might use descriptive or emotional language to stress an idea or an opinion. He or she might support that opinion with facts and statistics as well.)	**Beyond** **Discuss.** Have students discuss author's purpose and author's point of view in books and articles they have read. Compile a list of author's purposes and author's points of view. How does comparing and contrasting books and articles help them better understand author's purpose and the topic?
	Extend **Tech Infusion** **Evaluate.** After watching the video, ask students to read an online speech, such as Patrick Henry "Give Me Liberty or Give Me Death" speech. Ask students to use Diigo (http://tinyurl.com/pbxbxup) to annotate the article, highlighting clue words and phrases and making notes about the author's point of view.
	Extend **Tech Infusion** **Blog.** Discuss the idea that bloggers consistently express point of view in their blogs. Using a blogging tool such as Blogger (http://tinyurl.com/e67d), have students gather in small groups to choose a topic and create a short (150 words) blog expressing a collective point of view on "A Change We'd Like to See at School."Remind students to include elements from the Concept Definition video on point of view. Invite groups to share their blogs with the class.

2. MODEL

Core Path	Access Path
Read and Annotate. As students read the Model text, ask them to use the annotation tool to: • highlight key points • ask questions	**Note:** During this portion of the lesson, instruction shifts from whole group to individual work. Use this time to work one-on-one or in small groups with Beginning, Intermediate, Advanced, and Approaching students.

Core Path	Access Path
• identify places where the Model applies the strategies laid out in the Identification and Application section on point of view	**Beginner & Intermediate** **Coach the Reading.** Work with these students in pairs to fill out the Guided Reading questions on the Access 1 and 2 handouts. Let students know they'll use these answers to help participate in the discussion about the Model. Sample answers for this exercise are located online. **Advanced** **Identify Evidence.** Provide these students with the same instructions to read and annotate as on- and beyond- grade-level students. In addition, ask Advanced students to complete the identifying evidence exercise on the Access 3 handout. Let students know that they'll use these answers to help participate in the discussion about the Model. Correct answers for this exercise are online. **Approaching** **Guided Reading.** In small groups, have students complete the Guided Reading questions on the Access 4 handout as they read. Let them know that they'll use these answers to help participate in the discussion about the Model. Sample answers for this exercise are located online.
Discuss. After students read the Model text, use these questions to help students understand how to identify and evaluate the point of view of the articles. Make sure students follow the rules for collegial discussions. 1. What's the first step this Model uses to begin looking for the author's point of view? (The Model notes the title of the essay. The title "Violence in the Movies: Cinematic Craft or Hollywood Gone Too Far?" immediately alerts readers that the two articles that make up this selection will present two different points of view about a specific topic, and that the authors will try and persuade readers to accept their individual points of view.)	

Core Path	Access Path
2. The Model discusses how authors use specific word choices with the reader in mind. For what purposes might an author choose specific language? (to convey an opinion or belief; to clarify a point of view; to heighten a reader's emotional response) What words does the author use in the "Point" essay to try and draw an emotional response from readers? (The author uses adjectives and descriptive words —"action-packed," "brutal," and "mass destruction" — to heighten the emotional response readers might have to his point of view. Murders are not only committed on-screen, but they are often "brutal." Destruction takes place on a massive scale.) 3. According to the Model, the author of the Counterpoint article does not make use of emotional or figurative language. How does he persuade readers to accept his point of view? Explain. (He supports his opinions with facts and statistics. For example, quotes a professor of psychology as well as the U.S. Bureau of Justice Statistics.) 4. How does the author of the Counterpoint article acknowledge and respond to conflicting evidence or viewpoints? (The author introduces an idea that takes an opposing point of view—the idea that exposure to violence in movies is *not* a risk factor for violent behavior—and uses an example many people can relate to in order to show why this opposing viewpoint should be considered incorrect. He states that just because he has always ridden a bicycle without a helmet, and has never had a head injury, doesn't mean there is no link between not wearing a bicycle helmet and increasing your risk of getting a head injury.)	**Extend** **Tech Infusion** **Demonstrate Supporting Ideas.** Use a virtual post-it note board such as Padlet (http://tinyurl.com/nv79c7y) to create "building blocks" that represent the central idea and supporting ideas of each article.

Core Path	Access Path
	• Starting with the first article, ask students to pull the central idea and supporting ideas from the text.
	• Record each idea on a note (a "block") and place supporting ideas beneath the central idea, to demonstrate physical support and structure.
	• Move select supporting ideas off to the side to show that the central idea becomes unbalanced without sufficient support.
	• Ask students to determine which supporting ideas are strongest. Remove the weaker ideas and rebuild the structure.
	• Repeat the activity with the second article.
	Extend **Tech Infusion** **Poll.** Use Poll Everywhere (http://tinyurl.com/5grl69) to allow students to vote on the following question: "Which author did a better job in convincing you that their point of view is correct?" Have students choose Article 1 or Article 2. Students can respond using cell phones, tablets, or laptops. Share the poll results with the class. Ask students to share reasons they voted for one or the other.

3. YOUR TURN

Core Path	Access Path
Assess and Explain. Have students answer the comprehension questions to test for understanding. Share the explanations for Parts A and B (located online) with your students.	

Please note that excerpts and passages in the StudySync® library, workbooks, and PDFs are intended as touchstones to generate interest in an author's work. The excerpts and passages do not substitute for the reading of entire texts, and StudySync® strongly recommends that teachers and students seek out and purchase the whole literary or informational work in order to experience it as the author intended. Links to online resellers are available in our digital library. In addition, complete works may be ordered through an authorized reseller by filling out and returning to StudySync® the order form enclosed in this workbook.

Teacher's Edition   **147**

CLOSE READ:
Violence in the Movies

OVERVIEW

In "Violence in the Movies: Cinematic Craft or Hollywood Gone Too Far?" two authors argue for or against the use of violence in the movies and debate whether or not violent media has an effect on children. Both authors support their conflicting viewpoints with evidence. The Close Read gives students the opportunity to focus on how the author reveals point of view.

OBJECTIVES

1. Complete a close reading of an informational text.
2. Practice and apply concrete strategies for identifying author's purpose and author's point of view in Point/Counterpoint texts.
3. Participate effectively in a range of conversations and collaborations to express ideas and build upon the ideas of others.
4. Prewrite, plan, and produce clear and coherent writing in response to a prompt.

ELA Common Core Standards:
Reading: Informational Text - RI.8.1, RI.8.4, RI.8.6
Writing - W.8.4, W.8.5, W.8.6, W.8.10
Speaking & Listening - SL.8.1.A, SL.8.1.C, SL.8.6
Language - L.8.2.C, L.8.4.A, L.8.4.C, L.8.4.D, L.8.6

RESOURCES

"Violence in the Movies" Vocabulary handout
Close Read - Student Model
Graphic Organizer: Venn Diagram
Access 1 handout (Beginner)
Access 2 handout (Intermediate)
Access 3 handout (Advanced)
Access 4 handout (Approaching)

1. INTRODUCTION

Core Path	Access Path
Define and Compare. Project the vocabulary words and definitions onto the board or provide students with a handout, so they can copy the vocabulary into their notebooks. Suggest that students consult general and specialized reference materials, both print and digital, to compare the precise meaning of a specific word with their initial vocabulary predictions from the First Read. Review words that students defined incorrectly to understand why they were unable to use context clues to develop usable definitions.	**Beginner & Intermediate** **Complete the Sentences.** Have students complete the sentence frames on the Access 1 and 2 handouts using the vocabulary words. Point out that some of the words are in the questions and some will be in the answers. Correct answers are located online. **Advanced & Beyond** **Write in Journals.** Have students write a journal entry using all of their vocabulary words. Remind them to write sentences that communicate the meaning of the words they are using. **Approaching** **Graphic Organizer.** To support students in comparing their predictions with the correct meanings, have them complete the graphic organizer on the Access 4 handout to record the vocabulary words, their initial analysis, and the definitions. Then have them write sentences using the words.
Review. Have students complete the fill-in-the-blank vocabulary handout for this selection. Answers for the handout are listed online.	
	Extend **Tech Infusion** **Review.** Create a vocabulary review quiz using Socrative (http://tinyurl.com/3k2ucy3). Design multiple-choice questions that require students to apply their understanding of the vocabulary.

2. READ

Core Path	Access Path
Model Close Reading. Project the text onto the board and model a close reading of the first seven paragraphs using the following annotation strategies. While modeling annotation strategies, make notes that tie the text to the focus skill and demonstrate what students are looking for as they read. Here is some guidance for you as you annotate for your students:	

- As the Skills lesson that precedes this text makes clear, an author's purpose for writing might be to inform, persuade, or entertain. The title of this article is phrased as a question, so it becomes immediately clear that the author will try to answer the question, or present different points of view in response to the question. This is our first clue that this article might be written to persuade readers.

- In the first sentence, the author's use of "our" to refer to society and youth reveals the author's point of view—one that he or she assumes is shared by readers. This shared point of view helps draw the audience into the author's point of view, and reveals to us that his or her purpose is to persuade.

- Now let's look at the author's word choice in the first paragraph. The author writes that today's film industry promotes, not just murder, but "brutal murders," and not just destruction, but "mass destruction." These adjectives and descriptive words heighten the emotional response that readers might have to the author's point of view, persuading them to agree with it.

- When we read further, we can see that in paragraphs 2–5 the author cites a number of facts and statistics to support his point of view that violence in motion pictures harms children. What are some of the facts and statistics the author cites in the article? (Possible answers: A recent study by researchers at the Annenberg Public Policy Center (APPC) of the University of Pennsylvania; studies conducted by researchers from six leading

Copyright © BookheadEd Learning, LLC

Teacher's Edition

Core Path	Access Path
professional medical organizations, including the American Medical Association and the American Psychiatric Association.)	

Core Path

- Let's scroll down further and reread the seventh paragraph in the article. Now that we have determined that the author is trying to persuade readers that violence in movies harms children, how does the author respond to conflicting evidence or viewpoints? What example does he give in the seventh paragraph? (The author writes, "Some people do not believe that exposure to violence in movies is a risk factor for violent behavior because they themselves have not been affected by the exposure. However, no one would reasonably argue, 'I've always ridden my bicycle without a helmet, and I have never incurred a head injury. Therefore, there is no link between not wearing a bicycle helmet and increasing your risk of getting a head injury.' Why apply such flawed reasoning when it comes to violence in Hollywood movies?")

Read and Annotate. Read the Skills Focus questions as a class, so your students know what they should pay close attention to as they read. Then have students read and annotate the excerpt. Ask students to use the annotation tool as they read to:

1. respond to the Skills Focus section
2. ask questions about the author's purpose and author's point of view
3. make connections
4. identify key information, examples, details, facts, and statistics, as well as figurative language and descriptive words the writer uses to persuade readers
5. note unfamiliar vocabulary
6. capture their reaction to the ideas and positions in the text

As they reread the text, remind students to use the comprehension strategy of Asking and Answering Questions that they learned in the First Read.

Access Path

Note: While on- grade-level students are reading and annotating, work one-on-one or in small groups with Beginning, Intermediate, Advanced, and Approaching students to support them as they read and annotate the text.

Beginner & Intermediate
Summarize and Analyze the Text. Work with these students to complete the Summarize and Analyze the Text exercise on the Access 1 and 2 handouts. They will then use the completed sentence frames to help them analyze and annotate the text by completing the Skills Focus questions. Refer to the sample Skills Focus answers online to help them complete the sentence frames and annotate the text.

Core Path	Access Path
	Advanced **Work in Pairs.** Pair these students with more proficient English speakers to work together on analyzing and annotating the text to complete the Skills Focus questions. If these students need more support, have them use the Summarize and Analyze the Text exercise on the Access 3 handout as they work with their more proficient peers. **Approaching** **Summarize the Text.** Have these students discuss and complete the text summary on the Access 4 handout. Encourage students to use their summary to help them analyze and annotate the text by completing the Skills Focus questions. Correct answers for the summary are online. Also refer to the sample Skills Focus answers to aid students with their annotations.
Discuss. After students have read the text, use the sample responses to the Skills Focus questions online to discuss the reading and the process of searching for the author's purpose and author's point of view. Make sure that students have acquired and accurately use academic-specific words and phrases related to the skill, and demonstrate a command of formal English appropriate to the discussion.	**Extend** **Pair and Share.** In small groups or pairs, ask students to share and discuss their annotations with a focus on the point of view. You can provide students with questions to guide their discussion: 1. Given your deeper understanding of point of view on a second reading of the text, what do you think the point of view of the first author is? What does the second author believe? Cite specific textual evidence to support your statements. (I think the first author feels strongly against violence in entertainment because she feels that scenes of violence lead to violent behaviors. The second author believes that violence in entertainment doesn't necessarily result in a cause-effect relationship. For example, the second author states "Violent behavior is an extremely complex issue that cannot be reduced to a simple cause-effect relationship.")

Core Path	Access Path
	2. Read the concluding paragraphs of each article. Does each author restate his or her point of view in the article's conclusion? Cite specific textual evidence to support your statements. (The first author does restate her point of view in the concluding paragraph: "Movies should present scenarios in which conflict is resolved through nonviolent behaviors, without weapons. It's time to hold filmmakers accountable for the violent messages they are sending out to society and to our children." The second author also restates his point of view in his concluding paragraph: "The violence we see in movies does not dictate how we act toward one another in real life...We must leave filmmakers to their artistry and allow them to contribute to our culture without censoring their craft.")
	3. How does each author reveal point of view from the first paragraph of the article to the last? Cite specific textual evidence to support your statements. (Both authors clearly state their points of view from the central ideas they present, the language they use, and the word choice. Citing of textual evidence will vary.)
	4. How does each author use language to reveal point of view and evoke a response from the reader? Cite specific textual evidence to support your statements. (The first author uses negative language such as "brutal" and "mass destruction" to describe the violence seen in entertainment. The second author uses moral judgement and calls violence a "storytelling tool" similar to the tools used for suspense and humor. Citing of textual evidence will vary.)
	Extend **Debate.** Split the class into two sides and assign each a Pro or Con stance on violence in the movies. Conduct a debate, in which students will argue and rebut citing information from the articles.

Copyright © BookheadEd Learning, LLC

Core Path	Access Path
	Extend **Tech Infusion** **Record.** Record the debate and post it to your class YouTube Channel, so they can be reviewed.

3. WRITE

Core Path	Access Path
Prewrite and Plan. Read the prompt as a class and ask students to brainstorm their reactions to these articles that present different points of view as to whether or not violence in Hollywood movies has a negative effect on society, particularly children. Students can brainstorm together either as a class or in small groups to begin planning their responses. Remind students to look at both the "Point" and "Counterpoint" articles and their annotations to find textual evidence to support their ideas and answer the questions, *Which author is more convincing? Which author best supports his or her points with strong evidence?* You may wish to review with students the Short Constructed Response - Argumentative Student Model for guidance on how to construct an effective response to the writing prompt. **Discuss.** Project these instructions for the peer review onto the board and review them with your class, so they know what they are looking for when they begin to provide their classmates with feedback: • How has this essay helped you understand each author's point of view? • Has the writer indicated which author is more convincing? • Has the writer stated which author best supports their points with strong evidence? • Did the writer use his or her understanding of point of view and supporting evidence to defend one of the two claims?	**Beginner & Intermediate** **Answer and Discuss.** Have students complete the prewriting questions on the Access 1 and 2 handouts and then explain their answers to a partner before they write. Explain to students that when they answer a question—such as *What kind of language does the first author use?* —they need to include a detail, example, or quote from the text that supports the statement. For example, the first author states that Hollywood portrays "brutal murders" and "mass destruction" in their movies, which is very negative language. **Approaching** **Answer Prewriting Questions.** Have students complete the prewriting questions on the Access 4 handout to summarize their thoughts before they write.

Core Path	Access Path
<ul><li>Has the writer used evidence from the text to support his or her writing?</li><li>Did the writer include additional media evidence support?</li><li>Does the writer use standard grammar and punctuation? Are there any weak spots?</li><li>What specific suggestions can you make to help the writer improve the response?</li><li>What thing(s) does this paper do especially well?</li><li>Be sure to tell the writer what he or she did well and what he or she needs to work on. Remember that your comments are most useful when they are constructive.</li></ul>After you've looked at the peer review instructions, review the rubric with students before they begin writing. Allow time for students to pose and discuss any questions they may have about the peer review and rubric. Tell students how many peer reviews they will need to complete once they submit their writing.	
	Extend **Organize.** Ask students to complete the Venn Diagram comparing and contrasting the use of violence in the movies and its effect on children (see online) to organize their ideas before they type their responses.
Write. Ask students to complete the writing assignment using textual evidence to support their answers. If possible, have students use technology to produce and publish their writing. Once they have completed their writing, they should click "Submit."	
Review. Once students complete their writing assignment, they should submit substantive feedback to two peers. If possible, have students use technology to interact and collaborate with others.	

BLAST:
Food for Thought

OVERVIEW

The Blast Background explores nutrition facts charts, where these charts can be found, the information presented, and how to use them. To develop a better understanding of how knowledge of charts and text features can help students become more informed consumers, students will study an actual nutrition facts chart and practice reading it.

OBJECTIVES

1. Explore background information about nutrition facts charts and how to read them.
2. Research using a hyperlink to an actual nutrition facts chart and instructions on how to use it.

ELA Common Core Standards:
Reading: Informational Text - RI.8.1, RI.8.5
Writing - W.8.1.A, W.8.1.B, W.8.5, W.8.6, W.8.10
Speaking & Listening - SL.8.1.A, SL.8.1.C, SL.8.1.D
Language - L.8.4.C

RESOURCES

Blast Response - Student Model
Access 1 handout (Beginner)
Access 2 handout (Intermediate)
Access 4 handout (Approaching)

TITLE/DRIVING QUESTION

Core Path	Access Path
Discuss. As a class read aloud the title and driving question for this Blast. Ask students what they know about text features. As a class, list different types of text features, such as headings, charts, sidebars, or boldface font, for example. Next, point out that text features are designed to help people read information quickly. For example, one chart that consumers see all the time is a nutrition label. Do they have a sense of how nutrition facts charts work? Remind students that they should not immediately reply to this question. They'll be returning to this question and responding after they've read the Background and some of the Research Links.	**English Learners All Levels & Approaching Discuss a Visual.** Have students view the photograph of a woman shopping in a grocery store with her child. You can find this photo at the following web site: http://tinyurl.com/pyxlmho. Discuss what the mother and child are looking at in the photograph. Prompt students with the following questions: • What do you first notice about the woman and child in the photograph? • What are the mother and child reviewing on the product? • What do you notice about the isle in the photo? What about the shelves? • With so many products, why might it be useful, even necessary, to include some form of labeling on a product?
Draft. In their notebooks or on scrap paper, have students draft their initial responses to the driving question. This will provide them with a baseline response that they will be altering as they gain more information about the topic in the Background and Research Links sections of the assignment. You may wish to review with students the Blast Response - Student Model for guidance on how to construct an effective Blast.	**Beginner & Intermediate Draft with Sentence Frame.** When drafting their initial response to the driving question, have students refer to this Blast sentence frame on their Access 1 and 2 handouts: • Analyzing text features help us to interpret and understand consumer materials because_____ _____ _____. Point out these two key features of the sentence frame: 1. The introductory clause "Analyzing text features help us to interpret and understand consumer materials" borrows language directly from the Blast driving question to provide a response. 2. Ask students to make special note of the conjunction "because" since it requires students to provide reasons and evidence for their claim.

BACKGROUND

Core Path	Access Path
Read. Have students read the Blast Background to provide context for the driving question.	**Beginner & Intermediate** **Read with Support.** Have students read the Blast Background to provide context for the driving question. When they encounter unfamiliar words or phrases, have students refer to the Blast Glossary on their Access 1 and 2 handouts. If there are unfamiliar words that are not included in their glossary, encourage students to check a dictionary or online reference tool, such as http://tinyurl.com/3qe7. **Approaching** **Read and Summarize.** Have students read the Blast Background to provide context for the driving question. As they read, ask students to complete the fill-in-the-blank summary of the Background provided on their Access 4 handout. When they encounter unfamiliar words or phrases, have students refer to the Blast Glossary on their Access 4 handout.
Discuss. Pair students and have them answer the following questions: 1. When did nutrition facts begin appearing on all food packages? (1992) 2. What information appears closest to the top of nutrition facts charts? (calories and cholesterol) 3. Why do those things appear closest to the top of the chart? (because they are the most important information about food to a lot of people) 4. What is the difference between saturated and unsaturated fat? How is labeling these separately, using text features, helpful for consumers? (Saturated fat can raise your cholesterol; unsaturated fat is good for your heart. Consumers can quickly check the label for this key information if they need it.)	**Beginner** **Discuss.** Pair Beginning with Advanced (or Beyond) students and have them use the dialogue starter on their Access 1 handout to discuss the topic. Advise them to return to the dialogue and switch roles if they get stuck. **Intermediate** **Discuss.** Pair Intermediate with Advanced (or Beyond) students and have them use the dialogue starter on their Access 2 handout to discuss the topic. Advise them to return to the dialogue and switch roles if they get stuck. If their conversation is progressing smoothly, encourage them to continue the discussion beyond the dialogue starter sheet. They can expand their conversations to discuss examples of how analyzing text features can help people interpret and understand other consumer materials.

Core Path	Access Path
Brainstorm. Remind students about the driving question for this Blast: "How can analyzing text features help us to interpret and understand consumer materials?"	

In their notebooks, have students make two columns. In the first column, have students list ways text features help them understand how to better use food labels. In the second column, students will list ways text features on labels and packaging can help them make informed decisions about appliances (i.e., refrigerators, toasters, lamps, etc). Here's an example of how the chart might look:

Food Labels	Appliance Labels
- Can help you calculate how much of something to eat in order to get enough vitamins - Makes you aware of serving and portion sizes, according to food companies - Shows you amounts of fat, protein, and the number of calories	- Tells you what it is, what it does, and what kind of power source it needs - Can help you tell whether it will fit in the space you have - Can help you tell how much power it will use - Gives information about safety

RESEARCH LINKS

Core Path	Access Path
Examine and Explore. Use these questions to guide students' exploration of the Research Link: 1. What is the name of this website? What is its purpose, and what text features tell you this? (The top "CONCI, " stands for Central Ohio Nutrition Center, Inc. The title, "How to Read Food Labels for Weight Loss" tells me the purpose of this page is to help people use label information to choose foods that will help them lose weight.)	

Please note that excerpts and passages in the StudySync® library, workbooks, and PDFs are intended as touchstones to generate interest in an author's work. The excerpts and passages do not substitute for the reading of entire texts, and StudySync® strongly recommends that teachers and students seek out and purchase the whole literary or informational work in order to experience it as the author intended. Links to online resellers are available in our digital library. In addition, complete works may be ordered through an authorized reseller by filling out and returning to StudySync® the order form enclosed in this workbook.

Teacher's Edition   159

Core Path	Access Path
2. What are the four recommendations? What text feature helps you find them easily? (Using numbered headings in a font that is darker than the text makes it easy to find the page's basic recommendations. They are: 1) Determine the serving size; 2) Calculate the calories consumed; 3) Evaluate fat, cholesterol, and sodium; 4) Evaluate fiber, vitamins, calcium, and iron.) 3. If you wanted to read more posts on this site, where would you look? (On the right hand side is a list called "Recent Posts," with titles of other posts on the same subject.)	

	Extend
	Research, Discuss, and Present.
	
	1. Assign each group one link to explore in depth.
	2. Ask them to discuss the information:
	   a. What are the key points in this resource?
	   b. What inferences did you make as you read?
	   c. What did you learn about this topic from reading this research?
	   d. How did this help you to better understand the topic?
	   e. What questions does your group have after exploring this link?
	3. Allow students time to informally present what they learned.

	Extend **Tech Infusion** **Share.** As students explore the link, allow them to crowdsource their findings using a backchannel tool, like TodaysMeet (http://tinyurl.com/nogqjow). Students can post the research they find individually or in groups to share with the class.

QUIKPOLL

Core Path	Access Path
Participate. Answer the poll question. Have students discuss the reasons for their answers. Students should refer to evidence from the Background and Research Link to defend their answer.	

NUMBER CRUNCH

Core Path	Access Path
Predict, Discuss, and Click. Before students click on the number, break them into pairs and have them make predictions about what they think the number is related to. After they've clicked the number, ask students if they are surprised by the revealed information.	

CREATE YOUR BLAST

Core Path	Access Path
Blast. Ask students to write their Blast response in 140 characters or less.	**Beginner** **Blast with Support.** Have students refer back to the sentence frame on their Access 1 handout that they used to create their original Blast draft. Ask them to use this frame to write and enter their final Blast. **Intermediate** **Blast with Support.** Have students attempt to draft their Blast without the sentence frame on their Access 2 handout. If students struggle to compose their Blast draft without the sentence frame, remind them to reference it for support.

BLAST: Food for Thought

Core Path	Access Path
	Beyond **Write a Claim.** Ask students to use their answer to the poll question to write a strong claim that could be used as the foundation for a piece of argumentative writing. Once students have written their claims, ask them to read the claims to a small group of their peers. This activity will provide them practice writing claims, as well as expose them to claims written by their peers
Review. After students have completed their own Blasts, ask them to review the Blasts of their peers and provide feedback. If possible, have students use technology to present information and ideas efficiently as well as to interact and collaborate with others.	**Extend** **Discuss.** As a whole class or in groups, identify a few strong Blasts and discuss what made those responses so powerful. As a group, analyze and discuss what characteristics make a Blast interesting or effective.
	Extend **Revise.** Resend a second version of this Blast assignment to your students and have them submit revised versions of their original Blasts. Do the same responses make the Top 10? How have the answers improved from the first submissions?

OVERVIEW

A Night to Remember by Walter Lord takes the reader step-by-step through one of the most devastating disasters of the 20th century, the wreck of the *Titanic*. The author uses interviews with survivors to paint a picture of the final, tragic night of the great, "unsinkable" ship.

OBJECTIVES

1. Perform an initial reading of a text and demonstrate comprehension by responding to short analysis and inference questions with textual evidence.
2. Practice defining vocabulary words using context clues, and follow up by consulting reference materials to clarify precise meanings.
3. Participate effectively in a range of conversations and collaborations to express ideas and build upon the ideas of others.

ELA Common Core Standards:
Reading: Informational Text - RI.8.1, RI.8.4, RI.8.10
Writing - W.8.10
Speaking & Listening - SL.8.1.A, SL.8.1.B, SL.8.1.C, SL.8.1.D, SL.8.2, SL.8.6
Language - L.8.2.C, L.8.4.A, L.8.4.C, L.8.6

RESOURCES

Access 1 handout (Beginner)
Access 2 handout (Intermediate)
Access 3 handout (Advanced)
Access 4 handout (Approaching)

Please note that excerpts and passages in the StudySync® library, workbooks, and PDFs are intended as touchstones to generate interest in an author's work. The excerpts and passages do not substitute for the reading of entire texts, and StudySync® strongly recommends that teachers and students seek out and purchase the whole literary or informational work in order to experience it as the author intended. Links to online resellers are available in our digital library. In addition, complete works may be ordered through an authorized reseller by filling out and returning to StudySync® the order form enclosed in this workbook.

Teacher's Edition   163

ACCESS COMPLEX TEXT

A Night to Remember gives an account of the history-making voyage of the Titanic and its tragic end on the night of April 14, 1912, when it strikes an iceberg and sinks. The author provides readers with various passengers' and crew members' points of view as he explains the beginning of the disaster in a suspenseful, chronological order. To help students understand the idea that history is an accumulation of viewpoints, use the following ideas to provide scaffolded instruction for an initial reading of the more complex features of this text.

- **Organization** - The author moves from one passenger or crew member's point of view to another. This complicated organization may present difficulties for some readers. It may help readers to use web diagrams to understand the idea that one event may be described from many different viewpoints.

- **Specific Vocabulary** - Nautical terminology, such as quartermaster and knots, may present a challenge to some readers. In the British Royal Navy, the quartermaster is the person who steers the ship. Titanic had six quartermasters on board, all of whom took turns. A knot is a unit of speed equal to one nautical mile (1.852 km) per hour, approximately 1.151 mph.

- **Prior Knowledge** - Although most readers may have heard of the ship *Titanic,* some readers will not be familiar with the passengers and their backgrounds. Some knowledge of the culture created on *Titanic* will inform readers' understanding of the tragedy. Some of the richest people in the world were traveling on *Titanic* for her maiden voyage which started in Belfast, in Northern Ireland, and was to end in New York City. This included prominent members of the upper class that included politicians, businessmen and women, bankers, professional athletes, and industrialists. Most people in first class were traveling with an entourage that might include a nurse for the children, a maid, valet, cook, and chauffeur. Many first class passengers also had their pets with them on the voyage. A first class ticket ranged anywhere from thirty pounds to 870 pounds, a huge amount in 1912. In today's money you could expect to pay up to a top price of $50,000 for a first class ticket. The more expensive rooms were a parlor suite and usually had a private deck.

  Students who have seen James Cameron's 1997 film *Titanic* will be familiar with the Grand Staircase and the glass dome that rose above it, but the ship had many other amenities. These included electricity and the new wireless Marconi system. Other amenities found on the First Class deck included a Parisian Café, tea gardens, a heated swimming pool, gymnasium, library, squash court, barber shop, kennel, elevators, and enclosed promenade decks to walk and sit on.

1. INTRODUCTION

Core Path	Access Path
Read and Listen. Individually or as a class, read and listen to the Introduction for *A Night to Remember*. The Introduction provides context for the excerpted chapter.	**English Learners All Levels & Approaching Read and Listen.** Ask students to read and listen to the Introduction for *A Night to Remember*. Have students refer to the Introduction Glossary on their Access 1, 2, 3, and 4 handouts for definitions of key vocabulary terms. If there are unfamiliar words that are not included in their glossary, encourage students to check a dictionary or online reference tool like http://tinyurl.com/6ytby.
Access Prior Knowledge. Find out what your students already know about the *Titanic* disaster. Remind students to listen to the contributions of others to build a better knowledge base prior to reading the excerpt. 1. As a class or in small groups, generate a list on a flip chart of the information and previous knowledge your students have about the *Titanic*. Is their knowledge based primarily on fiction (the popular movie, for example) or on nonfiction? Note the source by each item on the list. 2. After compiling the list, ask students to discuss why this disaster still captures our imaginations more than a century later. 3. If you feel that students need more information on the disaster, have them do additional research or provide photocopies of research materials to provide a basic overview of the *Titanic* catastrophe.	**English Learners All Levels & Approaching Access Prior Knowledge.** Have students fill in the KWL graphic organizer on the Access 1, 2, 3, and 4 handouts. Call on students to discuss their charts. Talk about the common ideas as a class.
	Extend **Tech Infusion** **Learning Network.** *The New York Times* offers a variety of ways to learn the history of the *Titanic*, including eyewitness accounts. Visit http://tinyurl.com/oy4ldpm and choose among the many introductory options there, or bring the site up on a SMART Board and let students decide what to view.

2. READ

Core Path	Access Path
Make Predictions about Vocabulary. There are 5 bold vocabulary words in the text. As students read the text, ask them to make predictions about what they think each bold vocabulary word means based on the context clues in the sentence. If you are in a low tech classroom and students are reading from printed copies or a projected text, ask students to record predictions in their notes, so they can be easily referenced in class. If your students have access to technology, they can use the annotation tool to make their predictions.	**Note:** This exercise, which extends vocabulary instruction, should be completed when the class shifts from whole group instruction to individual work during the "Read and Annotate" exercise.

Make Predictions about Vocabulary. There are 5 bold vocabulary words in the text. As students read the text, ask them to make predictions about what they think each bold vocabulary word means based on the context clues in the sentence. If you are in a low tech classroom and students are reading from printed copies or a projected text, ask students to record predictions in their notes, so they can be easily referenced in class. If your students have access to technology, they can use the annotation tool to make their predictions.

It might be helpful to model this for students before they begin reading. Either using the board or projecting the actual text, focus in on the sentence that uses the word "detached":

- "Thank you," acknowledged the voice with curiously **detached** courtesy. Nothing more was said.

Model for the class how to use the overall structure and meaning of the sentence and the sentences around it, the word's position, and other clues to define the unfamiliar vocabulary word. In this case, point out these context keys:

1. Look at the structure of the sentence. What is the subject (voice) and what is the first verb? (acknowledged) We can determine that with the words "thank you," the voice is acknowledging something it has been told, and we can see that the prepositional phrase "with curiously detached courtesy" tells us that the voice is polite, and that the detachment is curious, or surprising and unexpected.

2. To understand why the voice's being detached is so curious, we must look to the sentences surrounding this one. We can see that the preceding sentence announced an iceberg ahead, and that the sentence following tells us that the voice didn't say anything besides "thank you." It is surprising that the voice doesn't say anything more about the iceberg and doesn't ask any other questions about it.

Note: This exercise, which extends vocabulary instruction, should be completed when the class shifts from whole group instruction to individual work during the "Read and Annotate" exercise.

Beginner, Intermediate, & Approaching Pair Practice.

1. Pair Beginning, Intermediate, and Approaching students with more proficient readers.

2. Give them an additional sentence that contains the new vocabulary word.

3. Ask Beginning, Intermediate, and Approaching students to complete a Think Aloud using the teacher-led Make Predictions about Vocabulary activity as a model, while the proficient reader actively listens.

4. The less proficient readers should use the context clues in the sentence to try to determine the meaning of the new vocabulary word.

5. After the student has completed the Think Aloud and made a prediction about the word's meaning, allow time for the proficient reader to add his/her own thoughts and clarify any points of confusion.

6. Once they've completed this Think Aloud, encourage them to use a dictionary to confirm the definition of the new vocabulary word. Have them refer to the Text Glossary on their Access 1, 2, and 4 handouts for definitions of key vocabulary terms in the text. Encourage them to add any additional vocabulary words or idioms they find in the text and look up definitions for those words and idioms online or in a dictionary.

Beginner & Approaching
Complete a Multiple-Meaning Word Chart. Have pairs complete the Multiple-Meaning Word Chart in their Access 1 handout based on the multiple-meaning words in the text.

Core Path	Access Path
3. So now that we understand why being detached is "curious," we're left to figure out what "detached" means. If we would expect a strong, worried reaction to news of an iceberg, the adverb "curiously" tells us that the voice's reaction was the opposite of what we would expect. That means it's not a strong reaction: the voice doesn't seem to be concerned or worried about the iceberg. Remind students that they can check for precise meanings by consulting print or digital dictionary or other credible resource.	**Intermediate & Advanced** **Complete a Multiple-Meaning Word Chart.** Have pairs complete the Multiple-Meaning Word Chart in their Access 2 and 3 handouts based on the multiple-meaning words in the text. **Approaching** **Complete a Multiple-Meaning Word Chart.** Have pairs complete the Multiple-Meaning Word Chart in their Access 4 handout based on the multiple-meaning words in the text.
	Extend **Track the Narrative.** Have students work in pairs to make a story map that shows what happened first, next, and so on, over the course of the events described. They may use any format they like to make their map but should include the names of the key witnesses. Suggest that they keep their maps to refer to later during the Close Read.
Model Reading Comprehension Strategy. Before students begin reading, model the reading comprehension strategy of visualizing by using this Think Aloud that talks students through the first paragraph of the text. First explain to students that visualizing is: *forming a mental picture of something as you read, and using new details from the text to add to or change the mental images you have created.* Explain to students how visualizing will help them better comprehend the selection and help drive their discussions. • In the first sentence, I read details about "the crow's-nest of the New White Star Liner *Titanic*," and about "Lookout Frederick Fleet" peering "into a dazzling night." That gives me a vivid picture of a big ship cruising on the sea at night, and a sailor high up the mast, looking out.	**Note:** This exercise, which extends vocabulary instruction, should be completed when the class shifts from whole group instruction to individual work during the "Read and Annotate" exercise. **Beginner, Intermediate, & Approaching** **Apply Reading Comprehension Strategy.** 1. Have students complete the Visualization Sentence Frames exercise in the Access 1, 2, and 4 handouts. These sentence frames help students to apply a reading comprehension strategy. 2. Then, have students pair up in order to discuss their visualizations in this exercise. Visit each pair of students and ask which specific vocabulary words help them create a visualization that helps to better understand the more global meaning of the story in order to check reading comprehension. Are there any words or phrases that further confuse or complicate their summary?

Please note that excerpts and passages in the StudySync® library, workbooks, and PDFs are intended as touchstones to generate interest in an author's work. The excerpts and passages do not substitute for the reading of entire texts, and StudySync® strongly recommends that teachers and students seek out and purchase the whole literary or informational work in order to experience it as the author intended. Links to online resellers are available in our digital library. In addition, complete works may be ordered through an authorized reseller by filling out and returning to StudySync® the order form enclosed in this workbook.

Teacher's Edition   **167**

Core Path	Access Path
• The second and third sentences add many specific details: The night is "calm, clear, and bitterly cold"; the sky is "cloudless" and blazing "with stars," but there's no moon. This gives me a clearer picture. • The last sentence in the paragraph compares the sea to "polished plate glass." The figurative language makes me see smooth, clear, polished glass and see the same traits in the water. The people say it was the smoothest they'd ever seen the Atlantic. This makes me wonder why the night is special.	
Read and Annotate. Read and annotate the excerpt. Ask students to use the annotation tool as they read to: 1. use context clues to analyze and determine the meaning of the bolded vocabulary terms 2. ask questions about passages of the text that are unclear 3. identify key information, events, and individuals and the connections between and among them 4. note unfamiliar vocabulary 5. capture their reactions to the events in the text	**Beginner** **Coach the Reading.** While other students read, annotate, and discuss the text independently, work with Beginning students, listening to the audio of the text and pausing periodically or when any student has a question. Coach students in highlighting and annotating the text. Have students refer to the Annotation Guide on the Access 1 handout as they annotate the text. **Intermediate & Advanced** **Listen to the Audio.** Have student pairs listen to the audio of the text as they annotate the text. If pairs need help with annotating the text, have them use the Annotation Guide on the Access 2 and 3 handouts. After working with the Beginning students, you may wish to check this group's progress and provide support as needed. **Approaching** **Use the Annotation Guide.** Have students use the Annotation Guide on the Access 4 handout to support them as they highlight and annotate the text.

Core Path

Discuss. In small groups or pairs, have students discuss the questions and inferences they made while reading. Make sure students follow the rules for collegial discussions. Refer to Collaborative Discussions in the Speaking & Listening Handbook.

1. What exactly happened to the ship in this scene? What textual details helped you visualize the event? (It struck and scraped along an iceberg. Textual details include the break in the rhythm of the engines, the iceberg towering above the water and then disappearing, the grinding, jarring shudder from deep in the ship, and the rattling of the silver, the falling of the pan of rolls, and various passengers' sensory recollections.)

2. How can you tell that most of the passengers are wealthy? (The author refers to the ship as *glamorous* and describes the glamorous dogs and the passengers' important jobs.)

3. Why was Frederick Fleet's job important? (As a lookout, he watched for dangers to the ship.)

4. When Fleet called the bridge, what was the response? (The voice at the other end was calm and detached and thanked him for the information.)

5. Why did the steward say, "Another Belfast trip!" (He thought the shudder meant the ship had undergone a small mishap that would send it to the shipyard for repair.)

Access Path

English Learners All Levels & Approaching
Use the extra time while on- and beyond- grade-level students are discussing their first reads of the text to work individually and in small groups with English Learners and Approaching readers as previously outlined. If those students complete their first reads quickly, integrate them into the on- and beyond- grade-level discussion groups. Otherwise English Learners and Approaching readers will be given an opportunity to participate in text discussions with their peers later in the lesson.

Extend
Tech Infusion
Record. Use a voice recording app (Voice Memo on the iPhone or Smart Voice Recorder for Androids) or VoiceThread (http://tinyurl.com/4m389hy) to capture each group's ideas.

3. SYNCTV

Core Path	Access Path
Watch. As a class, watch the SyncTV video on *A Night to Remember*. Pause the video at these key moments to discuss the information with your students:	**Beginner & Intermediate** **Analyze the Discussion.** Have students use the Analyze the Discussion chart in the Access 1 and 2 handouts to identify key points in the discussion and the evidence the students use to determine those points. Sample answers are located online.

Watch. As a class, watch the SyncTV video on *A Night to Remember*. Pause the video at these key moments to discuss the information with your students:

1. 1:28 - One of the students says, "Right away we see that this is a big story with lots of characters involved." What made the sinking of the *Titanic* such an enormous news story? (The ship was the largest and most glamorous in the world, and this was its maiden voyage, carrying hundreds of wealthy, important people.)

2. 2:52 - One of the students says, "If I were writing this, I'd be worried about keeping it suspenseful." How does suspense add to your interest in a story? (Not quite knowing what will happen makes you want to read on to find out.)

3. 3:53 - One student asks, "As readers, our emotions go up and down." How does the author make the readers' emotions change? (He makes the collision seem minor and major, depending on the point of view.)

Beginner & Intermediate

Analyze the Discussion. Have students use the Analyze the Discussion chart in the Access 1 and 2 handouts to identify key points in the discussion and the evidence the students use to determine those points. Sample answers are located online.

Approaching

Analyze the Discussion. Have students complete the Analyze the Discussion chart on the Access 4 handout by listing textual evidence cited by the students in the video. Sample answers are located online.

Extend

SyncTV-Style Discussion. Put students into small groups and give them a prompt to discuss. Remind them to model their discussions after the SyncTV episodes they have seen. Stress the importance of citing textual evidence in their conversations to support their ideas.

Discussion prompt:

1. What was the attitude of the passengers toward danger?

2. Were the passengers on the *Titanic* too trusting or appropriately cautious?

Core Path	Access Path
	Extend **Tech Infusion** **Record.** Ask one student in each group to videotape their conversation. They can upload their videos to YouTube, share them via Google Drive or email them to you for review. They can also play the video back and critique their own conversations to continually improve.

4. THINK

Core Path	Access Path
Answer and Discuss. Have students complete the Think questions and then use the peer review instructions and rubric to complete the peer reviews. Refer to the sample answers online to discuss responses with your students. Remind students to come to the discussion prepared, to follow guidelines for collegial discussions, to acknowledge and respond to others' questions and ideas.	**Beginner & Intermediate** **Sentence Frames.** Have students use the sentence frames exercise on the Access 1 and 2 handouts to support their responses to the Think questions. If necessary, distribute sentence frames to Advanced students as well. **Approaching** **Find the Evidence.** Have students use Find the Evidence on the Access 4 handout to help them identify the evidence needed to answer the Think questions.
	Extend **Do Research.** In small groups, choose one of the passengers mentioned in the passage (John Jacob Astor, Henry Sleeper Harper, Marguerite Frolicher, etc.). Find more information about the passenger using the Internet or other reference materials. Write a short biography of the passenger including relevant information.
	Extend **Present Findings.** Have one student from each group share their findings with the class by reading the short biography of each passenger. Make sure to use appropriate eye contact, adequate volume, and clear pronunciation.

OVERVIEW

Students have been introduced to the concepts of author's purpose and author's point of view, but here they will learn about shifting points of view in a work of narrative nonfiction. This lesson plan provides follow-up questions and useful enrichments to help teachers guide students toward a usable, repeatable method for analyzing shifting points of view.

OBJECTIVES

1. Learn the definition of author's purpose and author's point of view.
2. Practice using concrete strategies for identifying and analyzing author's purpose and author's point of view.
3. Participate effectively in a range of conversations and collaborations to express ideas and build upon the ideas of others.

ELA Common Core Standards:
Reading: Informational Text - RI.8.1, RI.8.6
Speaking & Listening - SL.8.1.A, SL.8.1.B, SL.8.1.C, SL.8.1.D, SL.8.2
Language - L.8.6

RESOURCES

Access 1 handout (Beginner)
Access 2 handout (Intermediate)
Access 3 handout (Advanced)
Access 4 handout (Approaching)

1. DEFINE

Core Path	Access Path
Watch. Watch the Concept Definition video on author's purpose and author's point of view with your students. Make sure students understand why it's critical to know an author's purpose or author's point of view when trying to unlock the meaning of a text. Pause the video at these key moments to discuss the information with your students:	**Beginner, Intermediate, & Approaching** **Match.** Have students complete the Match activity on the Access 1, 2, and 3 handouts as they watch the video. Then, have students complete the Define chart after they watch the video.

Core Path

Watch. Watch the Concept Definition video on author's purpose and author's point of view with your students. Make sure students understand why it's critical to know an author's purpose or author's point of view when trying to unlock the meaning of a text. Pause the video at these key moments to discuss the information with your students:

1. 1:00 - Can you think of any other purpose (or purposes) an author might have? How does genre affect purpose; i.e., how might the purpose of a fiction text differ from that of an informational text? How might it stay the same?

2. 1:18 - Are there any other elements of a text that might offer clues into an author's purpose or author's point of view? What are some additional resources we can use if we're having trouble deciphering the purpose or point of view?

3. 2:03 - Why don't authors of fiction or poetry state their purpose clearly in the same way a politician or an essayist might?

Read and Discuss. After watching the Concept Definition video, have students read the definition of author's purpose or author's point of view. Either in small groups or as a whole class, use these questions to engage students in a discussion about author's purpose and author's point of view. Make sure students follow the rules for collegial discussions, use academic language correctly, and respond to others' questions and comments with relevant evidence, observations, and ideas.

1. How can authors express their purpose and their point of view? (An author writing to persuade may want to stress an opinion or idea with the help of emotional or figurative language. He or she may also rely on facts and statistics to support an opinion.)

Access Path

Beginner, Intermediate, & Approaching
Match. Have students complete the Match activity on the Access 1, 2, and 3 handouts as they watch the video. Then, have students complete the Define chart after they watch the video.

Advanced
Complete a Chart. Based on the discussion in the video, have students fill in the Complete a Chart exercise on their Access 4 handout.

Beginner & Approaching
Fill in the Blanks. Have these students work together to complete the fill-in-the-blanks activity in the Access 1 and 4 handouts as they read the definition of author's purpose or author's point of view. Have them use the completed sentences to help them participate in the discussion.

Intermediate & Advanced
Generate Examples. To help these students participate in the discussion, encourage them to work in pairs and share simple arguments, similar to the argument about cats and dogs in the concept definition video. Ask students on each side to provide details. Partners can determine if the details are claims, reasons and evidence, or counter arguments. Students can practice these sample arguments before joining the class discussion.

Core Path	Access Path
2. When your point of view differs from that of an author, are you more interested in his or her writing or less interested? Why? (Answers will vary. Some students may say they are less interested because they already hold a strong point of view on a specific topic, and feel that nothing can change it. Others may be interested in seeing the other side of an issue or topic.) 3. Have you ever read something where two points of view are expressed and contrasted? What was it? Did it make you change your mind about an issue? Why or why not? (Answers will vary.)	
	Extend **Tech Infusion** **Contrast Points of View.** Find an op-ed column that has comments attached and display it using a projector or SMART board. Ask students to identify the author's opinions and feelings about the subject and then to determine which of the commenters share his or her point of view and which have differing points of view. What about the commenters' backgrounds or experiences might cause them to view things from different perspectives?

2. MODEL

Core Path	Access Path
Read and Annotate. Have students independently read the Model section. As they read, ask students to use the annotation tool to: • highlight key points • ask questions • identify places where the Model is applying the strategies laid out in the Identification and Application section on point of view	**Note:** During this portion of the lesson, instruction shifts from whole group to individual work. Use this time to work one-on-one or in small groups with Beginning, Intermediate, Advanced, and Approaching students.

Copyright © BookheadEd Learning, LLC

Core Path	Access Path
	Beginner & Intermediate **Coach the Reading.** Work with these students (either individually or in small groups) to fill out the Guided Reading questions on the Access 1 and 2 handouts. Have Beginning students refer to the Model Glossary on the Access 1 handout to help them determine the meaning of difficult words (Note: Provide the Access 1 handout glossary to Intermediate students if necessary). Let students know they'll use these answers to help participate in the discussion about the Model. Sample answers for this exercise are located online. **Advanced** **Identify Evidence.** Provide these students with the same instructions to read and annotate as on- and beyond- grade-level students. In addition, ask Advanced students to complete the Identify Evidence exercise on the Access 3 handout. Let students know that they'll use these answers to help participate in the discussion about the Model. **Approaching** **Guided Reading.** Have students complete the Guided Reading questions on the Access 4 handout as they read. Let them know that they'll use these answers to help participate in the discussion about the Model. Sample answers for this exercise are located online.
Discuss. After students read the Model text, use the following questions to facilitate a whole group discussion that helps students understand how to evaluate point of view in the passage. Make sure students follow the rules for collegial discussions. 1. According to the Model, what is the difference between expository and narrative nonfiction? (Expository nonfiction is concerned only with facts. Narrative nonfiction pays close attention to such elements of fiction as plot structure and character development to make the story as interesting as possible.)	

Core Path	Access Path
2. How is the author's point of view revealed in narrative nonfiction? (Narrative nonfiction is usually told from the viewpoint of the characters in the story, as if readers were walking around in their shoes and seeing the action unfold through their eyes. To express his or her point of view, the author must get inside the heads of one or more people in the narrative.) 3. According to the Model text, author Walter Lord had two purposes for writing *A Night to Remember*. What were they? (Lord wanted to inform people about what happened the night *Titanic* sank in the North Atlantic, but he also wanted to write a suspenseful story about people trapped on a sinking ship.) 4. How does Lord go about creating suspense in *A Night to Remember*? (After *Titanic* collides with the iceberg, Lord records what different crew members and passengers felt about what had happened. Suspense is created because readers know what will eventually happen but, at this point in the retelling, the passengers do not.)	
	Extend **Analyze.** Write this sentence on the board: *The iceberg looked bigger as the ship moved closer.* Have students contrast that sentence with the point of view of Frederick Fleet as illustrated in the Model. How does the author's choice to use Fleet's point of view make the impending collision seem more real and more personal?

3. YOUR TURN

Core Path	Access Path
Assess and Explain. Have students answer the comprehension questions to test for understanding. Share the explanations for Parts A and B (located online) with your students.	

Core Path	Access Path
	Extend **Share and Discuss.** Have students complete the Your Turn section in class. Poll students about their responses and as a class discuss the different strategies they used to determine the correct answers. Most students will notice the thought phrases that represent shifts in the point of view. Tell students to think about how the central idea of a text can help establish the point of view. Ask the following questions: 1. What central idea do the multiple points of view contribute to? (The people on board *Titanic* had different reactions to the ship striking the iceberg, but very few thought it was a serious problem.) 2. What evidence supports your answer to the first question? (Steward James Johnson thought only a propeller blade needed replacing. Mrs. John Jacob Astor thought it was some mishap in the kitchen.)

OVERVIEW

A Night to Remember by Walter Lord takes the reader step-by-step through one of the most devastating disasters of the 20th century, the wreck of the *Titanic*. The author uses interviews with survivors to paint a picture of the final, tragic night of the great, "unsinkable" ship.

OBJECTIVES

1. Complete a close reading of an informational text.
2. Practice and apply concrete strategies for identifying author's purpose and author's point of view in an informational text.
3. Participate effectively in a range of conversations and collaborations to express ideas and build upon the ideas of others.
4. Prewrite, plan, and produce clear and coherent writing in response to a prompt.

ELA Common Core Standards:
Reading: Informational Text - RI.8.1, RI.8.4, RI.8.6
Writing - W.8.4, W.8.5, W.8.6, W.8.10
Speaking & Listening - SL.8.1.A, SL.8.1.C, SL.8.6
Language - L.8.2.C, L.8.4.A, L.8.4.C, L.8.4.D, L.8.6

RESOURCES

A Night to Remember Vocabulary handout
Access 1 handout (Beginner)
Access 2 handout (Intermediate)
Access 3 handout (Advanced)
Access 4 handout (Approaching)

INTRODUCTION

Core Path	Access Path
Define and Compare. Project the vocabulary words and definitions onto the board or provide students with a handout, so they can copy the vocabulary into their notebooks. Suggest that students consult general and specialized reference materials, both print and digital, to compare the precise meaning of a specific word with their initial vocabulary predictions from the First Read. Review words that students defined incorrectly to understand why they were unable to use context clues to develop usable definitions.	**Beginner & Intermediate** **Complete the Sentences.** In order to review the bold key vocabulary terms and the multiple-meaning vocabulary terms from the First Read, have student pairs work together on the Complete the Sentences exercise on the Access 1 and 2 handouts. **Advanced & Beyond** **Write in Journals.** Have students write a news article describing the sinking of the *Titanic* using at least three bold vocabulary words and at least three multiple-meaning words. Remind them to write sentences that communicate the meaning of the words they are using. **Approaching** **Define and Review.** Have students complete the Graphic Organizer exercise on the Access 4 handout by defining and using the vocabulary terms (both the bold key terms and the multiple-meaning terms) from the First Read. Call on students to read aloud their example sentences for the class.
Review. Have students complete the fill-in-the-blank vocabulary handout for this selection. Answers for the handout are listed online.	
	Extend **Converse.** Have students work in pairs. Challenge them to have a conversation about a topic of their choice that includes all five of the bold vocabulary words from the selection.
	Extend **Crazy Connections.** Write the vocabulary words on index cards. Pick two at a time and ask students to write a sentence that connects the two in as likely or unlikely a way as they find interesting. For example, *myriads* is connected to *stewards* because the stewards on a ship may serve myriads of foods.

Copyright © BookheadEd Learning, LLC

READ

Core Path	Access Path
Model Close Reading. Project the text onto the board and model a close reading of the first six paragraphs using the annotation strategies mentioned below. While modeling annotation strategies, make notes that tie the text to the focus skill and demonstrate what students are looking for as they read. Here is some guidance for you as you annotate for your students: • As the Skills lesson that precedes this text makes clear, *A Night to Remember* is an example of narrative nonfiction. The author, Walter Lord, pays close attention to such elements of fiction as plot structure and character development to make the story as interesting as possible. Let's take a close look at the first paragraph. Which sentence in this paragraph reveals to the reader that this is a work of nonfiction? (The phrase "people later said they had never seen it so smooth." This is a statement that indicates the author has verified weather conditions that night with eyewitnesses who survived the disaster.) • Now let's jump ahead to the sixth paragraph. Lord writes that lookout Frederick Fleet sees something directly ahead, "even darker than the darkness." Then, suddenly, Lord is inside Fleet's head, revealing his thoughts the way an author of fiction might do. He writes that at first what Fleet saw "was small, about the size, he thought, of two tables put together." He then interprets how the voice on the phone sounded when Fleet phoned the bridge. The man who answers thanks Fleet "with curiously detached courtesy." The author is using factual information from *Titanic*'s last night to write a nonfiction account that reads like a narrative, or story. • As we continue to read, it becomes apparent that this is how Lord creates suspense. Readers know what will eventually happen but, at this point in the retelling, the passengers and the crew do not.	

Copyright © BookheadEd Learning, LLC

Core Path	Access Path
Read and Annotate. Read the Skills Focus questions as a class, so your students know what they should pay close attention to as they read. Then have students read and annotate the excerpt. Ask students to use the annotation tool as they read to: 1. respond to the Skills Focus section 2. ask questions 3. make connections between the author's use of point of view and the way he creates suspense in the text 4. identify key information, descriptive words, and details that distinguish the selection as an example of narrative nonfiction 5. note unfamiliar vocabulary 6. capture their reaction to the events in the text and they way they are presented. As they read the text, remind students to use the comprehension strategy of Visualizing that they learned in the First Read.	**Note:** While on- grade-level students are reading and annotating, work one-on-one or in small groups with Beginning, Intermediate, Advanced, and Approaching students to support them as they read and annotate the text. **Beginner** **Summary Choice.** In small groups, have students complete the Summary Choice exercise on the Access 1 handout. Encourage students to then use the Summary Choice handouts to help them annotate the text and answer the Skills Focus questions. **Intermediate & Advanced** **Summary Choice.** In pairs, have students complete the Summary Choice exercise in the Access 2 and 3 handouts. When annotating the text and answering the Skills Focus questions, those students who need more support can use the completed Summary Choice exercise. **Approaching & Beginner** **Summary Choice.** In small groups, have students complete the Summary Choice exercise on the Access 4 handout. Encourage students to then use the Summary Choice handouts to help them annotate the text and answer the Skills Focus questions.
Discuss. After students have read the text, use the sample responses to the Skills Focus questions online to discuss the reading and the process of searching for the author's purpose and author's point of view. Make sure that students have acquired and accurately use academic-specific words and phrases related to the skill, and demonstrate a command of formal English appropriate to the discussion.	**Extend** **Pair and Share.** In small, heterogeneous groups or pairs, ask students to share and discuss their annotations with a focus on the point of view presented in the selection. You can provide students with questions to guide their discussion: 1. How does Steward Johnson's perspective on the problem differ from that of Major Peuchen? Why? (Major Peuchen is a passenger and isn't terribly concerned with the jarring event. He thinks it is a heavy wave that hit against the ship. However, Steward Johnson recognized that kind of sound and jarring as the ship dropping a propeller blade.)

Please note that excerpts and passages in the StudySync® library, workbooks, and PDFs are intended as touchstones to generate interest in an author's work. The excerpts and passages do not substitute for the reading of entire texts, and StudySync® strongly recommends that teachers and students seek out and purchase the whole literary or informational work in order to experience it as the author intended. Links to online resellers are available in our digital library. In addition, complete works may be ordered through an authorized reseller by filling out and returning to StudySync® the order form enclosed in this workbook.

Teacher's Edition   181

Core Path	Access Path
	2. How do the passengers' own ages and life experiences affect the way they experience the collision? (Most of the surviving passengers interviewed were rich and didn't think there was a major problem. Some thought it was just a big wave, some thought it was commotion in the kitchen, and some thought it was the ship landing. An older lady thought it felt like the San Francisco earthquake, which was relevant since it had happened a few years prior. Another passenger said it sounded like calico being ripped; calico is an expensive fabric.)
	3. How do the different perspectives combine to give the reader a clear picture of what has happened? Cite specific evidence from the text to support your ideas. (Because the author includes many different perspectives, from those of the ship's crew to the rich passengers, it gives a clear picture of what happened. Most of the passengers didn't even think they hit anything or that they were in immediate danger. The crew knew that the ship hit something and that it was a dangerous situation. For example, Ismay, the ship's Managing Director "...felt sure the ship struck something, but he didn't know what.")
	After the discussion, have the groups create a simple line graph showing each person's response to the collision, on a range from positive to negative. The stewards who are happy because they think they'll get to return to the shipyard at Belfast, for instance, have a very positive reaction. Have one member of each group share their graph, and facilitate a discussion about any differences of opinion between groups.
	Extend **Revise.** Challenge students to find the five vocabulary words in the passage and to write a synonym that could replace each one. Discuss their solutions and talk about the author's choice of words—were his words the best choices possible? How does specific word choice make a point or create a mood?

Core Path	Access Path
	Extend **Analyze.** Ask students to work in small groups to analyze the final paragraph in depth and to explain what about that paragraph makes the collision seem suddenly real. Have one member of each group share their findings with the class.

WRITE

Core Path	Access Path
Prewrite and Plan. Read the prompt as a class and ask students to brainstorm their reactions to *A Night to Remember.*How is this selection different from reading an account of the disaster composed only of facts and details, without the reactions of the crew and passengers on board *Titanic*? Students can brainstorm together either as a class or in small groups to begin planning their responses about the importance of point of view in texts. Remind students to look at the excerpt and their annotations to find textual evidence to support their ideas.	**Beginner & Intermediate** **Answer and Discuss.** Have students complete the prewriting questions on the Access 1 and 2 handouts and then explain their answers to a partner before they write. Explain to students that when they answer a question—such as *What are the central ideas from the text?*—they need to include a detail, example, or quote from the text that supports the statement. For example, students could include the line, "'Thank you,' acknowledged the voice with curiously detached courtesy. Nothing more was said," which shows that even the ship's crew wasn't concerned about the iceberg and the ship potentially sinking. **Approaching** **Answer Prewriting Questions.** Have students complete the prewriting questions on the Access 4 handout to summarize their thoughts before they write.
	Extend **Analyze the Prompt.** Explain that the prompt in this case contains multiple requirements. Suggest that students copy the prompt and number or circle the elements they are expected to include in their writing. (1. How the reactions of the passengers affect my understanding/ feelings; 2. How this kind of writing differs from a straight description; 3. What this tells me about the importance of primary sources in learning history.)

Please note that excerpts and passages in the StudySync® library, workbooks, and PDFs are intended as touchstones to generate interest in an author's work. The excerpts and passages do not substitute for the reading of entire texts, and StudySync® strongly recommends that teachers and students seek out and purchase the whole literary or informational work in order to experience it as the author intended. Links to online resellers are available in our digital library. In addition, complete works may be ordered through an authorized reseller by filling out and returning to StudySync® the order form enclosed in this workbook.

Teacher's Edition   **183**

Core Path	Access Path
Discuss. Project these instructions for the peer review onto the board and review them with your class, so they know what they are looking for when they begin to provide their classmates with feedback: • How has this essay helped you understand how the author's purpose and author's point of view affect readers' understanding of the sinking of *Titanic*? • How did the writer's use of textual details support his or her points? • Did the writer cite specific connections among individuals, ideas, or events to support his or her response? In what ways were the connections helpful? • Does the writer write using standard grammar and punctuation? Are there any weak spots? • What specific suggestions can you make to help the writer improve the response? • What thing(s) does this paper do especially well? Be sure to tell the writer what he or she did well and what he or she needs to work on. Remember that your comments are most useful when they are constructive. After you've looked at the peer review instructions, review the rubric with students before they begin writing. Allow time for students to briefly raise and discuss questions they may have about the peer review instructions and the rubric. Tell students how many peer reviews they will need to complete once they submit their writing.	
Write. Ask students to complete the writing assignment using textual evidence to support their answers. If possible, have students use technology to produce and publish their writing. Once they have completed their writing, they should click "Submit."	

Core Path	Access Path
	Extend **Critique**. Project a writing sample on the board and ask the class to identify the elements of writing that are strong, as well as those that are weak or in need of improvement. Alternatively, you can put students in small groups and give them photo copies of a writing sample to collaboratively evaluate. After students have had an opportunity to evaluate each others' samples, ask each student to identify an example of strong writing they reviewed in a classmates' writing sample. Together, make a list on the board of traits of strong writing.
Review. Once students complete their writing assignment, they should submit substantive feedback to two peers. If possible, have students use technology to interact and collaborate with others.	
	Extend **Tech Infusion** **Track Changes**. If you wish, make student writing available in Word and turn on Track Changes so that reviewers may add their comments in the margins using New Comment. Remind students that they need not make all changes unless they agree with them.

BLAST:
How They Saw It

OVERVIEW

The driving question for this unit is "What attracts us to stories of suspense?" In the excerpt from the account *A Night to Remember*, suspense builds when the *Titanic* passengers feel the ship hit the iceberg and react based on their own understandings and experiences. In this Blast, students will learn more about the passengers, some of their reactions to the collision, and then respond to a driving question about the passage.

OBJECTIVES

1. Explore background information about the passengers on board the *Titanic*.
2. Research using hyperlinks to a range of information about the *Titanic,* including survivor stories and photographs from the events.

ELA Common Core Standards:

Reading: Informational Text - RI.8.1, RI.8.2
Writing - W.8.1.A, W.8.3.A, W.8.4, W.8.5, W.8.6, W.8.10
Speaking & Listening - SL.8.1.A, SL.8.1.C, SL.8.1.D, SL.8.2

RESOURCES

Access 1 handout (Beginner)
Access 2 handout (Intermediate)
Access 4 handout (Approaching)

TITLE/DRIVING QUESTION

Core Path	Access Path
Discuss. As a class read aloud the title and driving question for this Blast. Ask students what they know about the *Titanic* passengers from reading the excerpt. What do students think causes so many different reactions to the same event? Remind students that their initial response to the question will not be their final answer. They'll be returning to this question after they've read the Background and some of the Research Links.	**English Learners All Levels** **Discuss a Visual.** Have students view photographs of the *Titanic*. http://tinyurl.com/o6l2gfq http://tinyurl.com/o3aswrz http://tinyurl.com/ae8b7yw Discuss how the pictures represent the central idea of *A Night to Remember*: • What can you tell about the ship's sleeping quarters in the First Class, Second Class, and Third Class? • What can you tell about the ship's passengers? • What kind of reactions do the passengers have?
Draft. In their notebooks or on scrap paper, have students draft their initial responses to the driving question. This will provide them with a baseline response that they will be developing as they gain more information about the topic in the Background and Research Links sections of the assignment.	**Beginner & Intermediate** **Draft with Sentence Frame.** When drafting their initial response to the driving question, have students refer to this Blast sentence frame on their Access 1 and 2 handouts: • All of the passengers' reactions to the accident share common qualities because_____. Point out these two key features of the sentence frame: 1. The introductory clause "All of the passenger's reactions to the accident share common qualities" borrows language directly from the Blast driving question to provide a response. 2. Ask students to make special note of the conjunction "because," which prompts students to provide evidence to support their claim.
	Extend **Discuss *A Night to Remember* Movie Poster.** Have students view the movie poster. How does the poster differ from the photographs and the real reactions? Discuss as a class. http://tinyurl.com/qj8gz8f

BACKGROUND

Core Path	Access Path
Read. Have students read the Blast Background to provide context for the driving question.	**Beginner & Intermediate** **Read with Support.** Have students read the Blast Background to provide context for the driving question. When they encounter unfamiliar words or phrases, have students refer to the glossary on their Access 1 and 2 handouts. If there are unfamiliar words that are not included in their glossary, encourage students to check a dictionary or online reference tool, like http://tinyurl.com/6ytby. **Approaching** **Read and Summarize.** Have students read the Blast Background to provide context for the driving question. As they read, ask students to complete the fill-in-the-blank summary of the Background provided on their Access 4 handout. When they encounter unfamiliar words or phrases, have students refer to the glossary on their Access 4 handout.
Discuss. Either in small groups or as a whole class use these questions to spur discussion among your students about Background Information. 1. What's the author's topic in this Blast? (to explain how/why the accounts of first-class passengers reveal information about those passengers) 2. There was controversy over so many more lower class passengers dying in the *Titanic* tragedy than passengers of higher social classes. What do you think about this? Is it fair to assign blame to first-class passengers or is this simply the way of the world? (Answers will vary, but all answers should include specific examples to defend the reasons for their opinions. Some students may say that it is fair to assign blame to first-class passengers because they were the first to board the lifeboats; others may say that it is not fair to blame first-class passengers because they paid more to be near the top of the deck and being close to the lifeboats was an advantage they had.)	

Core Path	Access Path
3. Ask students if they've seen the popular film *Titanic*. Explain that while the film was well-researched from a technical standpoint, it is a fictionalized version of true events. By contrast, *A Night to Remember* is an account relying on primary sources. Why do students think the *Titanic* disaster continues to inspire retellings? (Answers will vary, but should include that the main interest lies in how the disaster affected individual people.)	
Imagine. Ask students to share examples of natural disasters that either have affected or could affect their community. Ask them to choose one, as a class, and imagine that, years later, a historian tracks down members of their local community to ask them about their recollections of that day. What types of details might they recall? How would their own personal experiences, ages, and other factors color their descriptions of the event? Have students write an imaginative account of the very first moments of the event from the point of view of a member of the community. Remind students that this is a creative writing assignment, and while they are free to stretch their imaginations, they need to avoid being derogatory. They should write the kinds of anecdotes that a historian would want to include in a book. Some sample answers might include: 1. "I've been at rallies where the applause shook the stage, but nothing ever shook the ground beneath me like the earthquake of 2015," recalled local mayor Renee Patterson. 2. "I was standing in the living room at home, and all of a sudden the whole world felt just like the inside of the truck when we fire up the trash compactor," said local sanitation worker Rick Cobb. 3. "It's funny, but at the time I was so worried about my Honors English exam, my only thought through all the shaking was whether Ms. French would cancel our afternoon exam!" remembered Robert Higgins, an eighth grade student at the time of the quake.	

RESEARCH LINKS

Core Path	Access Path
Explore and Summarize. Ask students to explore the first Research Link, entitled "Encyclopedia Titanica." Have them read up on one of the individuals who appears in *A Night to Remember* to find out exactly how that passenger or crewmember survived the tragedy. After they've read about this individual, ask students to write (either in their notebooks or via a StudySync Writing assignment you create) a short summary that tells how this individual survived the *Titanic* tragedy.	

	Extend
	 Research, Discuss, and Present.
	
	 1. Assign each group one link to explore in depth.
	
	 2. Ask them to discuss the information:
	   a. What are the key points?
	   b. What inferences did you make as you read?
	   c. What did you learn about this "big idea" from reading this research?
	   d. How did this help you to better understand the topic?
	   e. What questions does your group have after exploring this link?
	
	 3. Allow students time to present what they learned informally.

	Extend **Tech Infusion** **Share.** As students explore the links, allow them to crowdsource their findings using a backchannel tool like TodaysMeet (http://tinyurl.com/psef72j). Students can post the research they find individually or in groups to share with the class.

Copyright © BookheadEd Learning, LLC

QUIKPOLL

Core Path	Access Path
Participate. Answer the poll question. Have students discuss their reasons for their answers. Students should refer to evidence from the Background and Research Links to defend their answer.	

NUMBER CRUNCH

Core Path	Access Path
Predict, Discuss, and Click. Before students click on the number, break them into pairs and have them make predictions about what they think the number is related to. After they've clicked the number, ask students if they are surprised by the revealed information.	

CREATE YOUR BLAST

Core Path	Access Path
Blast. Ask students to write their Blast response in 140 characters or less.	**Beginner** **Blast with Support.** Have students refer back to the sentence frame on their Access 1 handout that they used to create their original Blast draft. Ask them to use this frame to write and enter their final Blast. **Intermediate** **Blast with Support.** Have students attempt to draft their Blast without the sentence frame on their Access 2 handout. If students struggle to compose their Blast draft without the sentence frame, remind them to reference it for support.

Core Path	Access Path
	Beyond **Write a Claim.** Ask students to use their answer to the poll question to write a strong claim that could be used as the foundation for a piece of argumentative writing. Once students have written their claims, ask them to read the claims to a small group of their peers. This activity will provide them practice writing claims, as well as expose them to claims written by their peers.
Review. After students have completed their own Blasts, ask them to review the Blasts of their peers and provide feedback. If possible, have students use technology to present information and ideas efficiently as well as to interact and collaborate with others.	**Extend** **Discuss.** As a whole class or in groups, identify a few strong Blasts and discuss what made those responses so powerful. As a group, analyze and discuss what characteristics make a Blast interesting or effective.
	Extend **Revise.** Resend a second version of this Blast assignment to your students and have them submit revised versions of their original Blasts. Do the same responses make the Top 10? How have the answers improved from the first submissions?

OVERVIEW

The novel *Cujo* by Stephen King uses classic elements of the horror genre to grab the reader's interest and not let go. In this excerpt, in which a rabid dog attacks a mother and her young son, the reader reads a vivid description of the grisly attack. Students should make inferences to understand how the author uses descriptive details and elements of suspense to construct a scene that will get your heart racing.

OBJECTIVES

1. Perform an initial reading of a text and demonstrate comprehension by responding to short analysis and inference questions with textual evidence.
2. Practice defining vocabulary words using context.
3. Participate effectively in a range of conversations and collaborations to express ideas and build upon the ideas of others.

ELA Common Core Standards:

Reading: Literature - RL.8.1, RI.8.4, RL.8.10
Writing - W.8.10
Speaking & Listening - SL.8.1.A, SL.8.1.B, SL.8.1.C, SL.8.1.D, SL.8.2, SL.8.6
Language - L.8.4.A, L.8.4.C, L.8.4.D, L.8.6

RESOURCES

Access 1 handout (Beginner)
Access 2 handout (Intermediate)
Access 3 handout (Advanced)
Access 4 handout (Approaching)

Please note that excerpts and passages in the StudySync® library, workbooks, and PDFs are intended as touchstones to generate interest in an author's work. The excerpts and passages do not substitute for the reading of entire texts, and StudySync® strongly recommends that teachers and students seek out and purchase the whole literary or informational work in order to experience it as the author intended. Links to online resellers are available in our digital library. In addition, complete works may be ordered through an authorized reseller by filling out and returning to StudySync® the order form enclosed in this workbook.

Teacher's Edition   **193**

ACCESS COMPLEX TEXT

This excerpt from *Cujo* focuses on a suspenseful scene at a remote car repair shop, where Donna Trenton and her four-year-old son Tad are confronted by a St. Bernard named Cujo that is wild with rabies. In this excerpt, Donna freezes in panic when confronted by Cujo and barely manages to get safely back inside the car. The excerpt ends with mother and child trapped inside their car with a violent "monster" clawing to get in and no help in sight. The challenges of the text are reflected in the limited third-person narrative, which reveals the sequence of events as well as Donna's thoughts. To help students understand Donna's responses to the fear she experiences, use the following ideas to provide scaffolded instruction for an initial reading of the more complex features of this text.

- **Organization** - The text is organized chronologically around a rapidly unfolding event. However, the narration of events is interrupted by the italicized thoughts of Donna, the main character. Remind readers that a limited third-person narrator focuses on one character, who, in this case, is Donna.

- **Purpose** - The text is structured to build suspense and fear. Readers will need to focus on how the author focuses on sensory details, beginning with sound and followed sequentially by touch and sight, to achieve this purpose.

- **Sentence Structure** - Some of Donna's italicized thoughts are written as sentence fragments. Readers should recognize that this structure mimics real thought, which does not always occur in complete sentences.

1. INTRODUCTION

Core Path	Access Path
Read. Individually or as a class, read and listen to the Introduction for *Cujo*. The Introduction provides context for this excerpt from the Stephen King novel.	**English Learners All Levels & Approaching** **Fill in the Blanks.** Have students fill in the blanks in the Access 1, 2, 3, and 4 handouts as they read and listen to the Introduction to *Cujo*. Answers are located online.

Copyright © BookheadEd Learning, LLC

Core Path	Access Path
Access Prior Knowledge. To begin thinking about what makes a great horror story, ask students to share some of the things they fear, such as a monster under the bed, the dark, speaking in public, or falling from a cliff.	**Beginner & Intermediate** **Imagine.** Have students work in groups to complete the pre-reading chart in the Access 1 and 2 handouts.
1. As a class or in small groups, generate a list (on the board or on paper) of the most common events or situations that almost everyone fears using previous knowledge your students.	**Advanced** **Imagine.** Have students complete the pre-reading chart in the Access 3 handout, and then discuss their responses with a partner.
2. After compiling a list, ask students to divide the list into two categories: Fears of Places, those fears we all share; and Fears of Situations. Have them discuss their opinions about what these universal fears have in common. Why do so many of us fear the same things?	**Approaching** **Imagine.** Work with students as a group to complete the pre-reading chart in the Access 4 handout. Guide students through each of the questions.
3. Finally, ask students why people like to write and read books or stories about fear. Have students discuss the uses of fear in storytelling.	
	Extend **Make Predictions.** Based on the Introduction, ask students to make predictions about the central ideas they would expect to encounter in this text.
	Extend **Tech Infusion** **Word Cloud.** Make a word cloud (http://tinyurl.com/6a5f6a) of students' fears and the words associated with them. Ask groups of students to gather the words associated with their worst fears, input them into the Wordle tool, and prepare a Common Fears word cloud. Share the word clouds with your other classes and identify similarities and differences.

2. READ

Core Path	Access Path
Make Predictions about Vocabulary. There are five bold vocabulary words in the text. As students read the text, ask them to make predictions about what they think each bold vocabulary word means based on the context clues in the sentence. If you are in a low-tech classroom and students are reading from printed copies or a projected text, ask students to record predictions in their notes, so they can be easily referenced in class. If your students have access to technology, they can use the annotation tool to make their predictions.	**Note:** This exercise, which extends vocabulary instruction, should be completed when the class shifts from whole group instruction to individual work during the "Read and Annotate" exercise.

English Learners All Levels & Approaching Pair Practice.

Core Path:

It might be helpful to model this for students before they begin reading. Either using the board or projecting the actual text, focus in on the sentence that uses the word "rheumy":

- They were red and **rheumy**.

Model for the class how to use the overall structure and meaning of the sentence and the sentences around it, the word's position, and other clues to define the unfamiliar vocabulary word. In this case, point out these context keys:

1. Look at the structure of the sentence. What is the subject and what is the first verb? (they; were) There aren't many words in this sentence, so we can easily surmise that "rheumy" describes whatever "they" is. We can also tell that "they" are red.

2. If we look at the sentences surrounding this one, we can see that "they" refers to the dog's eyes, because that's the subject of the preceding sentence. "Eyes" is the antecedent of the pronoun "they." We know that the dog's eyes are red and rheumy then, and based on our knowledge of dogs, we know that's not normal.

3. Next, look at the sentence following ours, which tells us "they" (the dog's eyes) were leaking some "viscous substance," and even if we don't know what viscous means, we know that the eyes are leaking something. If we put all these clues together, we know that the dog's eyes are red and leaking something, and since the conjunction "and" between red and rheumy tells

Access Path:

1. Pair Beginning, Intermediate, and Approaching students with Advanced students.

2. Give them a sentence that contains each new boldfaced vocabulary word.

3. Ask students to complete a Think Aloud using the teacher-led Make Predictions about Vocabulary activity as a model, while the Advanced student actively listens.

4. Students should use the context clues in the sentence to try to determine the meaning of the new vocabulary word.

5. After the Beginning, Intermediate, and Approaching students have completed the Think Aloud and made a prediction about the word's meaning, allow time for the Advanced student to add his/her own thoughts and clarify any points of confusion.

6. Once they've completed this Think Aloud, encourage them to use a dictionary to confirm the definition of the new vocabulary words. Have them refer to the Text Glossary in their Access 1, 2, 3, and 4 handouts for definitions of key vocabulary terms in the text. Encourage them to add any additional vocabulary words or idioms they find in the text and look up definitions for those words and idioms online or in a dictionary.

Core Path	Access Path
us they're similar, we can infer that "rheumy" means eyes that are red and wet, like when someone has a cold or allergies.	
Model Reading Comprehension Strategy. Before students begin reading, model the reading comprehension strategy of rereading by using this Think Aloud that talks students through the first paragraph of text. First explain to your students that rereading is:	**Note** This exercise, which extends instruction around reading comprehension strategies, should be completed when the class shifts from whole group instruction to individual work during the "Read and Annotate" exercise.

Core Path (continued):

stopping during a reading selection or after you have completed it to read sections of it again to check for comprehension.

Explain to students how rereading will help them better comprehend the selection and help drive their discussions.

- When I read the first two paragraphs, I can tell that there is a sound that the character is hearing, but I'm not sure what it is or where it is coming from.

- I reread the text to make sure I understand. She hears it when she crosses in front of the car, but then realizes that it is coming from inside the garage.

- I can also reread to remember details better. The noise is described as "directionless." It is coming from nowhere and everywhere. This makes it sound mysterious and even scary.

- I can infer that the author is trying to use the sound to build up to something terrifying happening. I can keep reading to see if I am correct.

Access Path (continued):

Beginner & Intermediate
Apply Reading Comprehension Strategy in Groups. Have these students read the first two paragraphs from the excerpt of *Cujo* independently. Encourage students to think of questions they may have about what they just read. Then, have students work in groups to reread and discuss the excerpt, and answer their questions.

Advanced
Apply Reading Comprehension Strategy in Pairs. Have these students read the first two paragraphs of the excerpt from *Cujo* independently. Encourage students to think of questions they may have about what they just read. Then, have students work with a partner to reread and discuss the excerpt, and answer their questions.

Approaching
Coach the Reading Comprehension Strategy. Have these students read the first three paragraphs from the excerpt of *Cujo*. Then, discuss with students what questions they may have about the reading. Have students reread the first three paragraphs, and coach them as they attempt to answer their questions.

Beyond
Have students write a one-paragraph response comparing their initial read of the excerpt with the reread. Did they learn anything new the second time? Did rereading the excerpt help them better understand the situation Donna and Tad are in, or what is wrong with Cujo?

Core Path	Access Path
Read and Annotate. Read and annotate the excerpt. Ask students to use the annotation tool as they read to:	**Beginner** **Coach the Reading.** Work with students as a group as they read and listen to the text. Help students annotate the text as they go through each line on the Annotation Guide in the Access 1 handout. Pause the audio recording of the text when necessary.

1. make predictions about the meaning of the bold vocabulary words using context clues
2. ask questions about passages of the text that may be unclear or unresolved
3. identify key information, events, characters, and connections between them
4. note unfamiliar vocabulary
5. capture reactions to the events in the text

Intermediate

Annotate in Pairs. Have students work in pairs or small groups to annotate the text using the Annotation Guide in the Access 2 and 3 handouts.

Approaching

Coach the Reading. Work with students as a group as they read and listen to the text. Help students annotate the text as they go through each line on the Annotation Guide in the Access 4 handout. Pause the audio recording of the text when necessary.

Discuss. In small groups or pairs, have students discuss the questions and inferences they made while reading. Remind students to follow guidelines for having collegial discussions.

1. Based on the description of the dog, what can you infer about its health? (Its "red and rheumy" eyes, "gummy tears," and fur "caked and matted with mud" suggest the dog is ill. From what I know about dogs, Cujo may have rabies or may have been poisoned in some way.)

2. Why is Donna paralyzed when she first sees the growling St. Bernard? (She is terrified. She even says she has read about people being "paralyzed by fear," and now she knows it can happen.)

3. What does Tad mean when he asks, "How did the monster in my closet get out?" (Tad must have experienced the fear of a monster in the closet, as so many little children do. This fear may have resulted from being near a raging animal, but we don't know for sure.)

4. What do you predict will happen after Donna rolls up both windows? (She must wait for help inside the car. Maybe a car will drive up, or she can honk for help.)

English Learners All Levels & Approaching

Use the extra time while on- and beyond- grade-level students are discussing their first reads of the text to work individually and in small groups with Approaching readers and English Learners as outlined above. Should those students complete their first reads quickly, integrate them into the on- and beyond- grade-level discussion groups. Otherwise Approaching readers and English Learners will be given an opportunity to participate in text discussions with their peers later in the lesson.

Core Path	Access Path
	Extend **Identify and Define.** After reading the text, compile a list of additional vocabulary words. Ask students to reference their annotations and share any vocabulary words that were unfamiliar. 1. As a class, compile a list of unknown words on the board. 2. In small groups, ask students to make predictions about what they think these words mean based on how they are used in the sentence. Note: They will need access to StudySync to read the words in context and make predictions. 3. Each group should work together using dictionaries or devices to define the words and write the definitions in their notebooks.

3. THINK

Core Path	Access Path
Answer and Discuss. Have students complete the Think questions and then use the peer review instructions and rubric to complete the peer reviews. Refer to the sample answers online to discuss responses with your students. Remind students to follow guidelines for collegial discussions.	**Beginner & Intermediate** **Sentence Frames.** Have students use the sentence frames on the Access 1 and 2 handouts to support their responses to the Think questions. If necessary, distribute sentence frames to Advanced students as well. **Approaching** **Find the Evidence.** Have students use Find the Evidence on the Access 4 handout to help them identify the evidence needed to answer the questions. **Extend** **Debate.** Show students the clip from the 1983 film version of this scene. Invite students to compare how the director changed the details of the novel. Allow students to debate the issue as a class or in smaller groups.

Core Path	Access Path
	Debate prompts: 1. When should a director change the content of the novel he or she is interpreting for film? What liberties can be taken with a script? 2. Does the film version create greater suspense or terror than the novel? Why or why not?
	Extend **Write a Claim.** Ask students to write a strong claim that clearly states their position in relation to the topic they debated. Once students have written their claims, ask them to read their claims to a small group of their peers. This activity will provide them practice writings claims, as well as expose them to claims written by their peers.

OVERVIEW

Students may find it challenging to move beyond what is directly stated in a text in order to make inferences. This lesson provides follow-up questions and useful enrichments to help teachers guide students in making inferences and citing text evidence to support them.

OBJECTIVES

1. Learn the definition of textual evidence.
2. Practice using concrete strategies for identifying textual evidence.
3. Participate effectively in a range of conversations and collaborations to express ideas and build upon the ideas of others.

ELA Common Core Standards:

Reading: Literature - RL.8.1, RL.8.3
Speaking & Listening - SL.8.1.A, SL.8.1.B, SL.8.1.C, SL.8.1.D, SL.8.2
Language - L.8.6

RESOURCES

Access 1 handout (Beginner)
Access 2 handout (Intermediate)
Access 3 handout (Advanced)
Access 4 handout (Approaching)

Please note that excerpts and passages in the StudySync® library, workbooks, and PDFs are intended as touchstones to generate interest in an author's work. The excerpts and passages do not substitute for the reading of entire texts, and StudySync® strongly recommends that teachers and students seek out and purchase the whole literary or informational work in order to experience it as the author intended. Links to online resellers are available in our digital library. In addition, complete works may be ordered through an authorized reseller by filling out and returning to StudySync® the order form enclosed in this workbook.

Teacher's Edition   201

1. DEFINE

Core Path	Access Path
Watch. Watch the Concept Definition video on textual evidence with your students. Make sure students understand the purpose of finding textual evidence in an informational or literary text, as well as the difference between explicit and inferred evidence. Pause the video at these key moments to discuss the information with your students:	**English Learners All Levels & Approaching** **Fill in the Blanks.** Have students complete the fill-in-the-blanks activity on the Access 1, 2, 3, and 4 handouts as they watch the video. Answers are located online.

1. 0:50 - Why aren't authors always as explicit as possible in stating their meaning or purpose? Why do you think they often leave evidence to be inferred?

2. 1:11 - How can readers be sure if an inference is valid? Think of a few ways to test the validity of an inference, in addition to the examples given in the video.

3. 1:49 - Why is inference an important skill when reading both informational and literary works? How can this skill help us deepen our understanding of works in both genres?

Read and Discuss. After watching the Concept Definition video, have students read the definition of textual evidence. Either in small groups or as a whole class, use the following questions to engage students in a discussion about finding and interpreting textual evidence. Make sure students follow the rules for collegial discussions, use academic language correctly, and respond to others' questions and comments with relevant evidence, observations, and ideas.

1. How can textual evidence help readers understand the author's intent? (When you make inferences, you read closely and critically and think about why an author gives particular details and information. Finding textual evidence to support an inference can better help you understand the author's intent, or reason for writing.)

Beginner
Finish the Sentences. Have these students work in groups to complete the sentence frames on the Access 1 handout as they read the definition. Have them use the completed sentence frames to help them participate in the discussion. Sample answers for this exercise are located online.

Intermediate & Advanced
Discuss Prompts. To help these students participate in the discussion, prompt them with questions that can be answered with a few words, such as:

- What is explicit evidence? (Evidence stated directly in the text.)

- How can inferred evidence help readers? (It can deepen their understanding.)

- What can inferences help readers understand? (intent, meaning, and context)

Core Path	Access Path
2. How can your own experiences, or prior knowledge, help you to make inferences? (Possible answer: If an author is describing an activity I am familiar with, or a setting I know about or have experienced, I can use this experience to identify what the author is writing about even if he or she does not identify it directly in the text.) 3. How can related facts in a text help readers make inferences? (Possible answer: Putting related facts together can help readers reach a new understanding about a character or an event in a story, and make inferences about how one affects the other.) 4. Why is citing textual evidence particularly important when you are writing an analysis of a work of literature or a nonfiction text? (Textual evidence is the most important tool for helping you explain your ideas or proving a specific point of view. Any analysis is strengthened by presenting text evidence to support it.)	Students can note their responses on the blank space provided on the Access 2 and 3 handouts. **Approaching** **Complete a Chart.** To prepare students to participate in the discussion, work with them as a group to complete the chart on the Access 4 handout as they read the definition. Correct answers are located online. **Beyond** **Discuss.** Have students select a book, poem, or article they have read, and describe inferred evidence they discovered while reading. Have students discuss how they made inferences while reading, and how these inferences deepened their understanding of the text.
	Extend **Look for the Clues.** Have students look at an illustrated scene from a classic myth, or, alternatively, have them watch a scene from a television show or movie with the volume off. Ask them to make inferences about what they think is happening. Discuss the clues they used to make inferences. Point out that they can apply these same strategies when they read.
	Extend **Blast.** Create a Blast and ask students to "blast out" the definition of making inferences in their own words. Use the poll question to ask students why they think authors don't always state everything directly.

2. MODEL

Core Path	Access Path
Read and Annotate. Have students independently read the Model section. As they read, ask students to use the annotation tool to: • highlight key points • ask questions • identify places where the Model applies the strategies laid out in the Application and Identification section on make inferences	**Note:** During this portion of the lesson, instruction shifts from whole group to individual work. Use this time to work one-on-one or in small groups with Beginning, Intermediate, Advanced, and Approaching students. **Beginner & Intermediate** **Coach the Reading.** Work with these students (either individually or in small groups) to fill out the Guided Reading questions on the Access 1 and 2 handouts. Have Beginning students refer to the Model Glossary on the Access 1 handout to help them determine the meaning of difficult words. (Note: Provide the Access 1 handout Model Glossary to Intermediate students if necessary.) Let students know that they'll use these answers to help participate in the discussion about the Model. Sample answers for this exercise are located online. **Advanced** **Identify Evidence.** Provide these students with the same instructions to read and annotate as on- and beyond- grade-level students. In addition, ask Advanced students to complete the Identify Evidence exercise on the Access 3 handout. Let students know that they'll use these answers to help participate in the discussion about the Model. Sample answers for this exercise are located online. **Approaching** **Guided Reading.** Have students complete the Guided Reading questions on the Access 4 handout as they read. Let them know that they'll use these answers to help participate in the discussion about the Model. Sample answers for this exercise are located online.

Core Path	Access Path
Discuss. After students read the Model text, use these questions to facilitate a whole group discussion that helps students understand how to make inferences while reading the excerpt and find text evidence to support the inferences they make. Make sure students follow the rules for collegial discussions.	

Core Path

1. What inferences does the Model assume readers can make after reading the first sentence of the excerpt? (The Model states that readers can infer that Donna must know Joe Camber, is familiar with his garage, and has been there at least once.)

2. What textual evidence does the Model point to in order to support these inferences? (The Model points to the fact that Donna says "it was the same dog." This is textual evidence that she knows Cujo and has met him, or seen him, at least once before. Otherwise, she wouldn't have been able to know whether Cujo had always been in this state, or if he had changed since she had last seen him. Also, since this is being written in the third person, from Donna's point of view, the fact that she identifies the garage as belonging to Joe Camber is textual evidence that she must know the man.)

3. How are readers able to infer that Donna was not expecting to see Cujo in this condition? What textual evidence does the Model present to support this inference? (The fact that Donna is "paralyzed with fear" is textual evidence that she obviously was not expecting Cujo to be in this condition when she got out of her car near the garage. If she had, readers can infer that she would have been prepared for the sight and taken precautions.)

4. How does having readers make inferences build suspense in the story? (By not stating everything directly, readers become engaged in the action and identify with everyday scenes — such as driving into a garage — that grow into horrible nightmares. By using familiar settings and situations, author Stephen King allows readers to make inferences based on their own experiences.)

Core Path	Access Path
	Extend **Pair and Share.** As a whole group, discuss real-world situations in which students might have to make inferences. Then pair or group students and have them make two or three additional inferences. Ask them to cite text evidence that supports their inferences. Have pairs or groups share their inferences and the text evidence that supports them.

3. YOUR TURN

Core Path	Access Path
Assess and Explain. Have students answer the comprehension questions to test for understanding. Share the explanations for Parts A and B (located online) with your students.	
	Extend **Share and Discuss.** Have students complete the Your Turn section in class. Poll students about their responses, and as a class discuss the different strategies they used to determine the correct answers. Make sure students understand how the movement of the dog presents a threat. Point out that usually a dog is not a threat, but because we know that this dog is sick, and that it has already made an attack on the car, we can infer that it will make another attack.
	Extend **Apply.** Put students into small groups of three or four to design a silent skit. They will need to act out a scene without talking. The class will watch each skit then make inferences about what they thought was happening in the scene based on the details of the performance. After each skit, allow the other groups time to talk about the scene and what they thought was happening. Each group in the audience can share their inferences with the class, then the group that acted out the scene can tell the class which group(s) made the best inferences.

OVERVIEW

The novel *Cujo* by Stephen King uses classic elements of the horror genre to grab the reader's interest and not let go. This lesson plan enables students to explore suspenseful elements in the text in more depth.

OBJECTIVES

1. Complete a close reading of a passage from literature.
2. Practice and apply concrete strategies for identifying textual evidence to support an analysis of an excerpt from a novel.
3. Participate effectively in a range of conversations and collaborations to express ideas and build upon the ideas of others.
4. Prewrite, plan, and produce clear and coherent writing in response to a prompt.

   ELA Common Core Standards:
   Reading: Literature - RL.8.1, RL.8.3, RL.8.4, RL.8.7
   Writing - W.8.4, W.8.5, W.8.6, W.8.10
   Speaking & Listening - SL.8.1.A, SL.8.1.C, SL.8.6
   Language - L.8.2.C, L.8.4.A, L.8.4.C, L.8.4.D, L.8.6

RESOURCES

Cujo Vocabulary handout
Access 1 handout (Beginner)
Access 2 handout (Intermediate)
Access 3 handout (Advanced)
Access 4 handout (Approaching)

Please note that excerpts and passages in the StudySync® library, workbooks, and PDFs are intended as touchstones to generate interest in an author's work. The excerpts and passages do not substitute for the reading of entire texts, and StudySync® strongly recommends that teachers and students seek out and purchase the whole literary or informational work in order to experience it as the author intended. Links to online resellers are available in our digital library. In addition, complete works may be ordered through an authorized reseller by filling out and returning to StudySync® the order form enclosed in this workbook.

Teacher's Edition   207

1. INTRODUCTION

Core Path	Access Path
Define and Compare. Project the vocabulary words and definitions onto the board or provide students with a handout, so they can copy the vocabulary into their notebooks. Ask students to compare their initial vocabulary analysis from the First Read with the actual definitions. Review words that students defined incorrectly to understand why they were unable to use context clues or other tools to develop usable definitions.	**Beginner & Intermediate** **Complete the Sentences.** Have students complete the sentence frames on the Access 1 and 2 handouts using the vocabulary words. Point out that some of the words are in the questions and some will be in the answers. Sample answers are located online. **Advanced & Beyond** **Write in Journals.** Have students use the space provided on the Access 3 handout to write a journal entry using all of their vocabulary words. Remind them to write sentences that communicate the meaning of the words they are using. Have students exchange their completed journal entry with a partner to see more examples of the words in context. **Approaching Graphic Organizer.** To support students in comparing their predictions with the correct meanings, have them complete the graphic organizer on the Access 4 handout to record the vocabulary words, their predictions, and the definitions. Then have them write sentences using the words.
Review. Have students complete the fill-in-the-blank vocabulary handout for this selection. Answers for the handout are listed online.	**Extend** **Skit.** Break students into small groups, assign each group a vocabulary word, and ask them to design a short skit to demonstrate the meaning of the word for their peers.
	Extend **Tech Infusion** **Record.** Record skits and post them to your class YouTube Channel, so they can be reviewed.

2. READ

Core Path	Access Path
Model Close Reading. Project the text onto the board and model a close reading of the excerpt using the annotation strategies mentioned below. While modeling annotation strategies, make notes that tie the text to the focus skill and demonstrate what students should be looking for as they read. Here is some guidance for you as you annotate with your students:	
• As the Skills lesson that precedes this text makes clear, author Stephen King allows readers to make inferences based on their own experiences by using familiar settings and situations. A woman named Donna Trenton, along with her young son Tad, is parked near a garage. As Donna gets out of the car, she hears a "low, thick growling" sound. At this point, we can't be sure if Donna has been to this garage before or not, or what is making the growling sound.	
• Now let's reread paragraphs 6–9. There are some clues here that will allow us to make some inferences about Donna and her situation. As she steps backward and puts her hand on the hood of her car, Donna thinks to herself, "it didn't growl before." This is textual evidence that will allow us as readers to infer that this isn't the first time Donna has been to this garage. She also seems to know what is making the sound.	
• What does Donna think to herself when Cujo comes out of Joe Camber's garage? (She thinks to herself, "It was the same dog. It was Cujo. But — *But oh my.*") How is this further evidence that Donna has met Cujo before, although not in these conditions? (Donna recognizes the dog, but is paralyzed with fear at the condition Cujo is in now, with his coat caked with mud and blood.)	
Read and Annotate. Read the Skills Focus questions as a class, so your students know what they should pay close attention to as they read. Then have students read and annotate the excerpt. Ask students to use the annotation tool as they read to:	**Note:** While on-grade-level students are reading and annotating, work one-on-one or in small groups with Beginning, Intermediate, Advanced, and Approaching students to support them as they read and annotate the text.

Core Path	Access Path
1. respond to the Skills Focus section 2. ask questions 3. make connections 4. identify key information, examples, and themes 5. note unfamiliar vocabulary 6. capture their reaction to the ideas and examples in the text As they reread the text, remind students to use the comprehension strategy of Rereading that they learned in the First Read.	**Beginner & Intermediate** **Summarize and Analyze the Text.** Work with these students to complete the Summarize and Analyze the Text exercise on the Access 1 and 2 handouts (Note: The sentence frames for Intermediate students on the Access 2 handout may contain fewer scaffolds). They will then use the completed sentence frames to help them analyze and annotate the text so that they can then complete the Skills Focus questions. Refer students to the sample Skills Focus answers online to help them complete their summaries. **Advanced** **Work in Pairs.** Pair these students with more proficient English speakers to work together on analyzing and annotating the text to complete the Skills Focus questions. If these students need more support, have them use the sentence frames on the Access 3 handout as they work with their more proficient peers. **Approaching Summarize the Text.** Have these students discuss and complete the text summary on the Access 4 handout. Encourage students to use their summaries to help them analyze and annotate the text so they can then complete the Skills Focus questions. Correct answers for the summary are online. Also refer to the sample Skills Focus answers to aid students with their annotations.
Discuss. After students have read the text, use the sample responses to the Skills Focus questions online to discuss the reading and the process of searching for textual evidence in order to make inferences. Make sure that students have acquired and accurately use academic-specific words and phrases related to the skill, and demonstrate a command of formal language.	**Extend** **Pair and Share.** In small, heterogeneous groups or pairs, ask students to discuss their annotations with a focus on how to make inferences. You can provide students with questions to guide their discussion: 1. How has the dog changed since the last time that Donna saw it? How can you tell? Donna was not used to Cujo growling, because he did not growl when she had seen him before. When Donna hears Cujo growling, she thinks, *It didn't growl before*. Cujo looks different than Donna remembers. She recognizes Cujo, but notices how much he has changed. His eyes are red and rheumy, and his coat is caked and matted with blood.

Core Path	Access Path
	2. **What can you infer about Donna from her initial reaction to the scary dog?** Based on her initial reaction to Cujo, readers can infer that Donna is confused, and then scared. She takes tentative backward steps, and her nerves are "on tripwires." She is "not panicked but in a state of heightened alertness." When she sees Cujo, she becomes really scared. She stops breathing, and cannot move. When she is finally able to move, she is very clumsy. She bangs into the car, and almost slips and falls. She also starts to panic, thinking about how she will not be able to get the car door open in time to escape from Cujo. 3. **What text evidence can you find that establishes Donna's connection to Tad?** The text does not tell you that Donna is Tad's mother. What did you use to make the inference? Readers can tell that Donna is Tad's mother because he calls out "Mommy?" to her from the car. He also calls her "Mommy" and "Momma" later on in the excerpt. And, it is obvious that Donna is very concerned about Tad.
	Extend **Make Predictions.** Have students use their inferences and the text evidence they have gathered to make a prediction about what will happen to Donna and her son after they are safely in the car.

3. WRITE

Core Path	Access Path
Prewrite and Plan. Read the prompt as a class and show the short clip from the film *Cujo* to the full class. http://tinyurl.com/lkelfvk. Ask students to brainstorm their reactions to the film clip, and how it compares to the excerpt from the novel they have just read. Students can brainstorm together either as a class or in small groups to begin planning their responses. Then show the clip again, this time prompting students to take notes as they watch. Remind them to	**Beginner** **Answer Prewriting Questions.** Work with students as a group to complete the prewriting questions on the Access 1 handout. Allow time for students to ask questions and revise their work.

Core Path	Access Path
pay attention to ways in which the clip and Stephen King's text are similar and different. For example, point out that the director, Lewis Teague, creates suspense as Cujo approaches the car by using a "point of view shot." This is a sequence that is shot as if the viewer were looking through the eyes of a specific character.	
	Intermediate & Advanced Have students complete the prewriting questions on the Access 2 and 3 handouts and then explain their answers to a partner before they write. Explain to students that when they answer a question—such as "How does the author build suspense in *Cujo*?"—they need to include a detail, example, or quote from the text that supports the statement. For example, students could include the lines: *Cujo came out of Joe Camber's garage. Donna stared at him, feeling her breath come to a painless and yet complete stop in her throat. It was was the same dog. It was Cujo.* This shows that the dog has changed, in a scary way, but readers do not yet know exactly how the dog has changed, or what it looks like. Allow time for students to revise their work based on the partner discussions. **Approaching** **Answer Prewriting Questions.** Work with students as a group to complete the prewriting questions on the Access 1 and 2 handouts. Allow time for students to ask questions and revise their work.
	Extend **Organize.** Encourage students to complete a two-column chart graphic organizer to organize their ideas before they type their responses.
Discuss. Project these instructions for the peer review onto the board and review them with your class, so they know what they are looking for when they begin to provide their classmates with feedback: • Has he or she made inferences from the text and explained whether they are present in the film? • Has the writer explained the effect of the differences on the film's level of suspense?	

Core Path	Access Path
• Has the writer used evidence from the text and the film to support his or her writing? Does the evidence support the writer's ideas? • Are the writer's ideas clear and well-organized? • What specific suggestions can you make to help the writer improve the response? • What thing(s) does this paper do especially well?	
Be sure to tell the writer what he or she did well and what he or she needs to work on. Remember that your comments are most useful when they are constructive. After you've looked at the peer review instructions, review the rubric with students before they begin writing. Allow time for students to briefly raise and discuss questions they may have about the peer review instructions and the rubric. Tell students how many peer reviews they will need to complete once they submit their writing.	
Write. Ask students to complete the writing assignment using text evidence to support their answers. Remind them that the question asks the writer to focus on whether the changes the director made make a difference in the suspense the scene creates. If possible, have students use technology to produce and publish their writing. Once they have completed their writing, they should click "Submit."	
	Extend **Critique.** Project a writing sample on the board and ask the class to identify the elements of writing that are strong, as well as those that are weak or in need of improvement. Alternatively, you can put students in small groups and give them photo copies of a writing sample to collaboratively evaluate. After students have had an opportunity to evaluate student samples, work as a class to generate strategies students can use as they complete their peer reviews to ensure they are substantive.
Review. Once students complete their writing assignment, they should submit substantive feedback to two peers. If possible, have students use technology to interact and collaborate with others.	

Please note that excerpts and passages in the StudySync® library, workbooks, and PDFs are intended as touchstones to generate interest in an author's work. The excerpts and passages do not substitute for the reading of entire texts, and StudySync® strongly recommends that teachers and students seek out and purchase the whole literary or informational work in order to experience it as the author intended. Links to online resellers are available in our digital library. In addition, complete works may be ordered through an authorized reseller by filling out and returning to StudySync® the order form enclosed in this workbook.

BLAST:
Are You a Smart Consumer?

OVERVIEW

Students will learn about how smart consumers use online tools like consumer buying guides to make sure they are getting the most out of their money, and make an attempt at responding to the Blast's driving question. Students will explore Research Links to some actual consumer buying guides.

OBJECTIVES

1. Explore background information about how consumers use online tools to make sure they are getting the most out of their money.
2. Research using hyperlinks to two different consumer buying guides.
3. Use technology to produce and publish writing.

ELA Common Core Standards:
Reading: Informational Text - RI.8.1, RI.8.5, RI.8.10
Writing - W.8.1.A, W.8.1.B, W.8.4, W.8.6, W.8.10
Speaking & Listening - SL.8.1.A, SL.8.1.C, SL.8.1.D
Language - L.8.4.A, L.8.4.C, L.8.6

RESOURCES

Access 1 handout (Beginner)
Access 2 handout (Intermediate)
Access 4 handout (Approaching)

TITLE/DRIVING QUESTION

Core Path	Access Path
Discuss. As a class read aloud the title and driving question for this Blast. These correspond to the title/driving question for the unit as a whole. Ask students what they think it means to be a smart consumer. Ask what they already know about consumer buying guides. Do they have an idea of how a buying guide can help a consumer shop smart? Remind students that they should not immediately reply to this question. They'll be returning to this question and responding after they've read the Background and some of the Research Links.	**English Learners All Levels & Approaching Discuss a Visual.** Have students view a photograph of Times Square in New York City, such as the photograph seen here: http://tinyurl.com/l4squmb. Discuss the presence of billboards and advertisements in the photograph. Prompt students with the following questions: • What do you notice about the buildings in this photograph? • What information do these billboards provide? • Do you feel the billboards provide quality and unbiased information? • How does this photograph emphasize the need to conduct research as a consumer?
Draft. In their notebooks or on scrap paper, have students draft their initial responses to the driving question. This will provide them with a baseline response that they will be developing as they gain more information about the topic in the Background and Research Links sections of the assignment.	**Beginner & Intermediate Draft with Sentence Frame.** When drafting their initial response to the driving question, have students refer to this Blast sentence frame on their Access 1 and 2 handouts: • A buying guide can help you shop smart because _____ _____. Point out these two key features of the sentence frame: 1. The introductory clause "A buying guide can help you shop smart" borrows language directly from the Blast driving question to provide a response. 2. Ask students to make special note of the conjunction "because" since it requires students to provide reasons and evidence for their claim.

BACKGROUND

Core Path	Access Path
Read. Have students read the Blast Background to provide context for the driving question: How can a buying guide help you shop smart?	**Beginner & Intermediate** **Read with Support.** Have students read the Blast Background to provide context for the driving question. When they encounter unfamiliar words or phrases, have students refer to the Blast Glossary on their Access 1 and 2 handouts. If there are unfamiliar words that are not included in their glossary, encourage students to check a dictionary or online reference tool, like http://tinyurl.com/3qe7. **Approaching** **Read and Summarize.** Have students read the Blast Background to provide context for the driving question. As they read, ask students to complete the fill-in-the-blank summary of the Background provided on their Access 4 handout. When they encounter unfamiliar words or phrases, have students refer to the Blast Glossary on their Access 4 handout.
Discuss. Pair students and have them discuss the following questions: 1. What is ConsumerReports.org? (a nonprofit webzine that tests and rates thousands of different items and helps consumers make decisions, based on several different criteria) 2. What can you do to make sure you're getting the most out of your money if you're buying dog food? What do you do once you locate a good website? (One option is to visit a site like ConsumerReports.org and search for dog food. Once there, you can use text features on the site to locate the specific information you need.) 3. Look at this sentence from near the end of the Blast: "Since a home theater system is a compilation of many components, this guide rates the individual components so consumers can pick and choose the ones they want."	**Beginner** **Discuss.** Pair Beginning with Advanced (or Beyond) students and have them use the dialogue starter on their Access 1 handout to discuss the topic. Advise them to return to the dialogue and switch roles if they get stuck. **Intermediate** **Discuss.** Pair Intermediate with Advanced (or Beyond) students and have them use the dialogue starter on their Access 2 handout to discuss the topic. Advise them to return to the dialogue and switch roles if they get stuck. If their conversation is progressing smoothly, encourage them to continue the discussion beyond the dialogue starter sheet. They can expand their conversations to discuss other situations where buying guides would provide information to help consumers shop smart.

Core Path	Access Path

What does the word *compilation* mean? What context clues helped you? (collection or assortment; the clues include "many components," "individual components," and the idea of being able to "pick and choose")

4. How does the sentence above from that paragraph better help consumers understand the way this buying guide works? (The sentence explains that this buying guide rates the parts of a home entertainment center separately. This tells the consumer reading the site that there is no single "entertainment center" to learn about, and that the consumer will have to research many items.)

5. What are some benefits of a buying guide that is more conversational in tone? (The sentences might be shorter and easier to understand, developing the key ideas in a way that ordinary people can relate to.)

Brainstorm. Remind students about the driving question for this Blast: How can a buying guide help you shop smart?

In their notebooks, ask students to make a list of possible benefits to using a buying guide. What kinds of information would they look for to help them? Here's a short of example of how this might look:

-saving money
-thinking carefully about what you really want
-making sure you get what you actually want and need
-knowing where to go to find what you need
-saving time

Ask students to identify the kinds of details they would expect to find to develop key concepts about consumer items.

-information about what a product does, how much it costs, and how long it lasts
-details about safety features
-any guarantees and warranties

Core Path	Access Path
Ask students to identify how they might use text features to determine which resources might be the most helpful. -title of publication or website -dates of publication -categories located on bars -sidebars -charts of information	

RESEARCH LINKS

Core Path	Access Path
Examine and Explore. Before asking students to explore the Research Links, use these questions to guide their exploration: 1. Look at the chart in the first Research Link, located beneath the picture of the dog. What does the number in the last column to the right tell you? (the potential percentage of money you could save by purchasing the least expensive option) 2. Notice that in some boxes in the chart, it says "NA." What does this mean? (the store in that particular column doesn't carry the product in that row) 3. Read the passage titled "Getting Started" in the second Research Link. Why might a consumer choose to purchase a more expensive item? (because they have a very large room, or because they like to listen to music through their TV, or they want a better quality speaker for some other reason) 4. Which type of buying guide do you prefer, the chart from the first link, or the more conversational type in the second link? (Answers will vary, but should include a discussion of the way the writing develops a key concept, the use of text features for information and ease of use, and other details to support their answers.)	

Core Path	Access Path

	Extend
	Research, Discuss, and Present. Pair or group Beginning and Intermediate students with Advanced students, and assign each pair or group one link to explore.
	
	1. Assign each group one link to explore in depth.
	2. Ask them to discuss the information:
	  a. What are the key points in this resource?
	  b. What inferences did you make as you read?
	  c. What did you learn about this topic from reading this research?
	  d. How did this help you to better understand buying guides?
	  e. What questions does your group have after exploring this link?
	3. Allow students time to informally present what they learned.

	Extend **Tech Infusion** **Share.** As students explore the links, allow them to create a buying guide of their own for a product they are interested in purchasing. Have them do web research to collect data about several models and prices of the item in which they are interested. They can use Glogster to make the buying guide as interesting and informative as possible. (http://tinyurl.com/plm72a). Students can combine text, music, photos, and video before they share their buying guides with the class.

QUIKPOLL

Core Path	Access Path
Participate. Answer the poll question. Have students discuss their reasons for their answers. Students should refer to evidence from the Background and Research Links to defend their answer.	

NUMBER CRUNCH

Core Path	Access Path
Predict, Discuss, and Click. Before students click on the number, break them into pairs and have them make predictions about what they think the number is related to. After they've clicked the number, ask students if they are surprised by the revealed information.	

CREATE YOUR BLAST

Core Path	Access Path
Blast. Ask students to write their Blast response in 140 characters or less.	**Beginner** **Blast with Support.** Have students refer back to the sentence frame on their Access 1 handout that they used to create their original Blast draft. Ask them to use this frame to write and enter their final Blast. **Intermediate** **Blast with Support.** Have students attempt to draft their Blast without the sentence frame on their Access 2 handout. If students struggle to compose their Blast draft without the sentence frame, remind them to reference it for support. **Beyond** **Write a Claim.** Ask students to use their answer to the poll question to write a strong claim that could be used as the foundation for a piece of argumentative writing. Once students have written their claims, ask them to read their claims to a small group of their peers. This activity will provide them practice writing claims, as well as expose them to claims written by their peers.
Review. After students have completed their own Blasts, ask them to review the Blasts of their peers and provide feedback.	**Extend** **Discuss.** As a whole class or in groups, identify a few strong Blasts and discuss what made those responses so powerful. As a group, analyze and discuss what characteristics make a Blast interesting or effective.

Core Path	Access Path
	Extend **Revise.** Resend a second version of this Blast assignment to your students and have them submit revised versions of their original Blasts. Do the same responses make the Top 10? How have the answers improved from the first submissions?

OVERVIEW

The novel *Lord of the Flies* by William Golding exposes human nature when a group of boys are stranded on a deserted island. The First Read gives students the opportunity to experience the text with a limited context.

OBJECTIVES

1. Perform an initial reading of a text and demonstrate comprehension by responding to short analysis and inference questions with textual evidence.
2. Practice defining vocabulary words using context.
3. Participate effectively in a range of conversations and collaborations to express ideas and build upon the ideas of others.

   ELA Common Core Standards:
   Reading: Literature - RL.8.1, RL.8.4, RL.8.10
   Writing - W.8.10
   Speaking & Listening - SL.8.1.A, SL.8.1.B, SL.8.1.C, SL.8.1.D, SL.8.2, SL.8.6
   Language - L.8.4.A, L.8.4.C, L.8.4.D, L.8.6

RESOURCES

Access 1 handout (Beginner)
Access 2 handout (Intermediate)
Access 3 handout (Advanced)
Access 4 handout (Approaching)

ACCESS COMPLEX TEXT

This excerpt from *Lord of the Flies* is set on a remote island where a group of British schoolboys have crash-landed. With no adults present, the boys realize that they will have to look after themselves. Tension builds as some boys are singled out as weak or different, sides are chosen, and a leader is elected. Ambiguous dialogue and complex characterization are reflected in the challenges of the text. To help students familiarize themselves with the characters, use the following ideas to provide scaffolded instruction for an initial reading of the more complex features of this text.

- **Connection of Ideas** - Readers have to figure out that there are two potential rivals, Jack and Ralph, and that this rivalry is cause for conflict, even at this early stage in the story.

- **Sentence Structure** - The excerpt includes untagged dialogue from many different speakers. Readers will have to determine who is speaking in order to follow the action and characterization. It may help readers to read aloud the excerpt with a different speaker assigned to each boy's dialogue.

- **Specific Vocabulary** - Certain terms, such as "Gib," "Addis," and "precentor," will most likely be unfamiliar to most readers. In the thirteenth paragraph, after one of the boys flops onto the sand, Merridew says "He's always throwing a faint. He did in Gib.; and Addis; and at matins over the precentor." "Gib" and "Addis" are shortened terms for Gibraltar and Addis Ababa, in Ethiopia, refueling stops for the plane that was carrying the boys. A precentor is a choir master. Also, words such as "chapter chorister" and "head boy" are meant to show Jack's authority, but these terms, and their connections, may not be clear to readers. They are choir terms meant to disclose Jack's high standing in the choir. Students may also be unfamiliar with the word "conch." A conch is a large tropical marine mollusk with a spiral shell. One of the boys, Ralph, uses the shell to make a trumpet-like sound. Finally, the author uses British slang of the period, as in the fourteenth paragraph that begins, "This last piece of shop brought sniggers from the choir." The word "shop" is slang for "information."

1. INTRODUCTION

Core Path	Access Path
Watch. As a class, watch the video preview of *Lord of the Flies*.	**English Learners All Levels** **Fill in the Blanks.** Ask students to use their Access 1, 2, and 3 handouts to fill in the blanks of the transcript for the preview's voiceover as they watch the preview along with their classmates. Answers are located online.

Core Path	Access Path
Read. Individually or as a class, read the Introduction for *Lord of the Flies*. The Introduction provides context for the excerpts taken from Chapter 1.	**English Learners All Levels & Approaching** **Read and Listen.** Ask students to read and listen to the Introduction for *Lord of the Flies*. Have them refer to the vocabulary listing on their Access 1, 2, 3, and 4 handouts for definitions of key vocabulary terms. If there are unfamiliar words that are not included in their glossary, encourage students to check a dictionary or online reference tool, like http://tinyurl.com/6ytby.
Access Prior Knowledge. Explain that *Lord of the Flies* explores the idea of survival through boys who attend an all-boys school in England. Find out what your students think about how leaders are chosen and how they develop in school settings. 1. In pairs or small groups, or as a class, generate a list or a web of leadership positions among students and staff in a school setting. 2. Next, ask students to put themselves in the boys' situation (stranded on an island) and generate a list (on the board or on paper) of material things they think they would need to survive. 3. Finally, ask students to consider situations they've been in where they have had to work with a team of people to achieve a goal (for example on a sports team or in a club). What problems did they encounter along the way? Did they reach their goal? Why or why not? Remind students to keep these ideas in mind as they read the excerpt.	**Beginner & Intermediate** **Imagine.** Have students work in small groups to complete the pre-reading chart on the Access 1 and 2 handouts. **Advanced** **Imagine.** Have students complete the pre-writing chart on the Access 3 handout, and then discuss their responses with a partner. **Approaching** **Imagine.** Work with students as a group to complete the pre-reading chart on the Access 4 handout. Guide students through each of the questions. Call on students to share their thoughts.
	Extend **Make Predictions.** Based on the Introduction, ask students to make predictions about the themes they would expect to encounter in this text.

2. READ

Core Path	Access Path
Make Predictions about Vocabulary. There are five bold vocabulary words in the text. As students read the text, ask them to make predictions about what they think each bold vocabulary word means based on the context clues in the sentence. If you are in a low-tech classroom and students are reading from printed copies or a projected text, ask students to record predictions in their notes, so they can be easily referenced in class. If your students have access to technology, they can use the annotation tool to make their predictions.	**Note.** This exercise, which extends instruction around reading comprehension strategies, should be completed when the class shifts from whole group instruction to individual work during the "Read and Annotate" exercise.

Core Path (continued)

It might be helpful to model this for students before they begin reading. Either using the board or projecting the actual text, focus in on the sentence that uses the word "furtive":

- There was a slight, **furtive** boy whom no one knew, who kept to himself with an inner intensity of avoidance and secrecy.

Model for the class how to use the overall structure and meaning of the sentence and the sentences around it, the word's position, and other clues to define the unfamiliar vocabulary word. In this case, point out these context clues:

1. Look at the structure of the sentence. What is the subject (there) and what is the first verb? (was) We can look at the next few words in the sentence to see that "there was" describes a boy, who is also described as "slight" and "furtive." Because "furtive" precedes the word "boy," we know that it's an adjective that describes him.

2. To begin to understand what furtive actually means though, we need to look at the next part of the sentence. We also learn that this boy "kept to himself" and that he has an internal "avoidance and secrecy."

3. If we put all these together, we know that this boy avoids other people and has an air of secrecy about him, thus "furtive" must describe someone who is secretive and avoids others.

Have students use a print or digital resource to check the meaning.

Access Path (continued)

Beginner, Intermediate, & Approaching Pair Practice.

1. Pair Beginning, Intermediate, and Approaching students with more proficient readers.

2. Give them an additional sentence that contains a new vocabulary word.

3. Ask the Beginning, Intermediate, and Approaching students to complete a think aloud using the teacher-led Make Predictions about Vocabulary activity as a model, while the proficient students actively listen.

4. The Beginning, Intermediate, and Approaching students should use the context clues in the sentence to try to determine the meaning of the new vocabulary word.

5. After the Beginning, Intermediate, and Approaching students have completed the think aloud and made a prediction about the word's meaning, allow time for the proficient readers to add their own thoughts and clarify any points of confusion.

6. Once they've completed this think aloud, encourage them to use a dictionary to confirm the definition of the new vocabulary word. Have them refer to the Text Glossary on their Access 1, 2, and 4 handouts for definitions of key vocabulary terms in the text. Encourage them to add any additional vocabulary words or idioms they find in the text and look up definitions for those words and idioms online or in a dictionary.

Core Path

Model Reading Comprehension Strategy.
Before students begin reading, model the reading comprehension strategy of asking and answering questions by using this Think Aloud that talks students through the first paragraph of text. First explain to your students that asking and answering questions is:

a way to stop and consider what you don't understand about a text and trying to direct yourself to find the answer to your own questions about it.

Explain to students how asking and answering questions about a text will help them better comprehend the selection and help drive their discussions.

- When I read the first two paragraphs, I can tell that someone is asking a question about a ship, and then a character is being described in detail. I can ask myself who is doing the talking, and who is being described.

- To answer my own questions, I have to keep reading to get more details. As I read, I realize that it is children who are talking and being described.

- I can ask and answer questions about their relationships. Who is in charge? Why aren't there any grownups? When I ask myself questions as I read, I can understand the text better by looking for the answers

Read and Annotate. Have students independently read and annotate the excerpt. Ask students to use the annotation tool as they read to:

1. use context clues to analyze and determine the meaning of the bolded vocabulary terms

2. ask questions about passages of the text that may be unclear or unresolved

3. identify key information, events, characters, and connections between

4. note unfamiliar vocabulary

Access Path

Note: This exercise, which extends vocabulary instruction, should be completed when the class shifts from whole group instruction to individual work during the "Read and Annotate" exercise.

Beginner, Intermediate & Approaching
Apply Reading Comprehension Strategy.

1. Have pairs or small groups of students complete a think-pair-share about questions they have about this text before they read it. Students can write their questions to be shared.

2. Have students listen to the audio version of the excerpt from *Lord of the Flies*. As they listen to the audio recording, ask them to write down at least one more question.

3. Once they have listened to the audio version, have the students write down at least one more question based on the reading.

4. Complete another think-pair-share, allowing students to add to their list if someone had a question that they didn't. Give students time to explain why they asked the questions and how they found the answers to them when they reread or listened to the story again.

Beginner
Coach the Reading. While other students read, annotate, and discuss the text independently, work with Beginning students, listening to the audio of the text and pausing periodically or when any student has a question. Coach students in articulating their questions for the group and in highlighting and annotating the text. Have students use the Annotation Guide on the Access 1 handout to support them as they highlight and annotate the text.

For further support, ask questions about the text such as:

Core Path	Access Path
	• Is there anything about the story that you don't understand?
	• What do you think will happen to the boys?
	• Do you think that Ralph and Jack will get along?
	Intermediate
	Listen to the audio. Have these students listen to the audio of the text and use the definitions on the Access 2 handout to help them with words or idioms that may be unfamiliar. If students need help with annotating the text, have them use the Annotation Guide on the Access 2 handout. After working with the Beginning students, you may wish to check this group's progress and provide support as needed.
	Advanced
	Pair with Proficient Peers. Have Advanced students work with English proficient peers to read, annotate, and discuss the text. Have students use the Annotation Guide in the Access 3 handout to support them as they highlight and annotate the text. Encourage them to listen to the audio of the text if needed.
	Approaching
	Use the annotation guide. Have students use the Annotation Guide on the Access 4 handout to support them as they highlight and annotate the text.
Discuss In small groups or pairs, have students discuss the questions and inferences they made while reading. 1. At the beginning of the excerpt, who is Jack leading? (He is leading the choir boys.) 2. Why are the boys holding a meeting? (They are stranded on a deserted island, and they are trying to figure out what to do.) 3. Which two boys want to be the leaders? How do you know? (Ralph and Jack seem to want to be the leaders. Ralph suggests choosing a chief to decide things, and Jack automatically assumes that he should be chief because he is the chapter chorister.)	

Core Path	Access Path
4. Why does Ralph say that the choir can be Jack's? (He is trying to make Jack feel better after Jack loses the vote.) 5. At the end of the excerpt, how do the three boys feel about their situation? (For the moment, they see their situation as glamorous and are made happy by it.)	**English Learners All Levels & Approaching** Use the extra time while on- and beyond- grade-level students are discussing their first reads of the text to work individually and in small groups with Approaching readers and English Learners as previously outlined. Should those students complete their first reads quickly, integrate them into the on- and beyond- grade-level discussion groups. Otherwise Approaching readers and English Learners will be given an opportunity to participate in text discussions with their peers later in the lesson.
	Extend **Brainstorm.** Pair students and ask them to brainstorm how the boys might survive on the island. Students who have access to a backchannel tool such as TodaysMeet (http://tinyurl.com/nogqjow/) may enjoy brainstorming in that medium.
	Extend **Identify and Define.** After reading the text, compile a list of additional vocabulary words. Ask students to reference their annotations and share any vocabulary words that were unfamiliar. 1. As a class, compile a list of unknown words on the board. 2. In small groups, ask students to make predictions about what they think these words mean based on how they are used in the sentence. (Note: They will need access to StudySync to read the words in context and make predictions.) 3. Each group should work together using dictionaries or devices to define the words and write the definitions in their notebooks.

3. SYNCTV

Core Path	Access Path
Watch As a class, watch the SyncTV video on *Lord of the Flies*. Pause the video at these key moments to discuss the information with your students: 1. 1:18 – One of the students says, "How do you determine whether something is a nightmare scenario or a great opportunity?" Brainstorm possible pros and cons of the situation that the boys find themselves in. 2. 2:02 – One of the students says, "So it sounds to me like an ideal society." Why might this society seem ideal to the boys? 3. 5:40 – One student says, "There's definitely going to be a power struggle at some point." What evidence does the text provide that suggests she might be right?	**Beginner & Intermediate** **Analyze the Discussion.** Have students use the "Analyze the Discussion" guide in the Access 1 and 2 handouts to identify key points in the discussion and the evidence the students use to determine those points. Sample answers are online.
	Extend **SyncTV-Style Discussion.** Put students into small groups and give them a prompt to discuss. Remind them to model their discussions after the SyncTV episodes they have seen. Stress the importance of citing textual evidence in their conversations to support their ideas. Discussion prompt: 1. What does the election represent? 2. What are some symbols in this story? What do they represent?

4. THINK

Core Path	Access Path
Answer and Discuss Have students complete the Think questions and then use the peer review instructions and rubric to complete the peer reviews. Refer to the sample answers online to discuss responses with your students. Remind students to follow guidelines for collegial discussions.	**Beginner** **Find the Evidence.** Guide students through the Find the Evidence activity on the Access 1 handout to help them identify the evidence needed to answer the questions.

Core Path	Access Path
	Intermediate **Complete Sentence Frames.** Have students work in groups to complete the sentence frames activity on the Access 2 handout. **Advanced** **Complete Sentence Frames and Review.** Have students complete the sentence frames activity on the Access 3 handout. Then, students should exchange their handout with a partner to review each other's work. **Approaching** **Find the Evidence.** Have students use Find the Evidence on the Access 4 handout to help them identify the evidence needed to answer the questions.
	Extend **Write an Alternative Proposal.** Ask students to consider a different way that the boys might have gone about organizing themselves. Break the class up into smaller groups and have each group discuss the following questions: 1. Is choosing a leader the best way to begin organizing? What problems might arise out of the decision to make one boy a leader? 2. Why do you think the boys automatically felt they should choose someone to lead the group? Would you have the same instinct if you were in this situation? 3. What other ways might the boys choose to organize themselves? Is there a better alternative? Have each group write a proposal for another way the boys could have chosen to organize themselves. Have each group share their proposal with the class. Have the class vote on the group with the best solution.

OVERVIEW

Determining the theme of a text can be a challenging skill for students to master. This lesson plan provides follow-up questions and useful enrichments to help teachers guide students toward a usable, repeatable method for uncovering theme in a work of fiction.

OBJECTIVES

1. Learn the definition of theme.
2. Practice using concrete strategies for identifying theme.
3. Participate effectively in a range of conversations and collaborations to express ideas and build upon the ideas of others.

   ELA Common Core Standards:
   Reading: Literature - RL.8.1, RL.8.2
   Speaking & Listening - SL8.1.A, SL8.1.B, SL8.1.C, SL8.1.D, SL.8.2
   Language - L.8.6

RESOURCES

Access 1 handout (Beginner)
Access 2 handout (Intermediate)
Access 3 handout (Advanced)
Access 4 handout (Approaching)

Please note that excerpts and passages in the StudySync® library, workbooks, and PDFs are intended as touchstones to generate interest in an author's work. The excerpts and passages do not substitute for the reading of entire texts, and StudySync® strongly recommends that teachers and students seek out and purchase the whole literary or informational work in order to experience it as the author intended. Links to online resellers are available in our digital library. In addition, complete works may be ordered through an authorized reseller by filling out and returning to StudySync® the order form enclosed in this workbook.

Teacher's Edition   231

1. DEFINE

Core Path	Access Path
Watch. Watch the Concept Definition video on theme with your students. Ask students to write the definitions and the key evidence they can examine to determine theme in their notes. Pause the video at these key moments to discuss the information with your students: 1. 1:00 – Why would authors choose to have readers infer stories' themes? Why don't all authors just come out and state the theme like they do in fables? 2. 1:25 – What are some other real-life examples of when inference skills are important? 3. 2:37 – Can you think of any evidence that might help a reader identify theme that the students in the video don't mention? Are some pieces of evidence more important for determining theme?	**English Learners All Levels & Approaching** **Match.** Have students complete the matching exercise on the Access 1, 2, 3, and 4 handouts as they watch the video. Answers are located online.
Read and Discuss. After watching the Concept Definition video, have students read the definition of theme. Either in small groups or as a whole class, use the following questions to spur discussion among your students about theme. Make sure students follow the rules for collegial discussions, use academic-specific words and phrases correctly, and respond to others' questions and comments with relevant evidence, observations, and ideas. 1. What are some common themes in works of literature? (Answers will vary, but students may mention universal themes such as the individual pitted against society, the pain and pleasure of growing into adulthood, or man vs. nature.) 2. What strategies have you used to determine theme? Which ones were most helpful? (Answers will vary, but students should mention examining the thoughts and actions of the characters as well as the dialogue in the story.)	**Beginner** **Finish the Sentences.** Have students work in groups to complete the sentence frames on the Access 1 handout as they read the definition of theme. Have them use the completed sentence frames to help them participate in the discussion. Sample answers for this exercise are located online. **Intermediate & Advanced** **Discuss Prompts.** To help students participate in the discussion, prompt them with questions that can be answered with a few words, such as: • What is theme? (the central idea or message in a work of literature) • What are some examples of themes? (love, luck, family, and justice) • What can the author use to explicitly state a theme? (a title, characters' words, descriptive phrases)

Copyright © BookheadEd Learning, LLC

Core Path	Access Path
3. Is it possible to determine the overall theme of a story from the very first chapter of a novel? (Possible answer: While a theme may begin to develop in the first chapter, the resolution of the conflict in the plot of the story often has a significant impact on the development of the theme, and this does not take place in the first chapter.)	• What can themes unite? (plots and subplots in literature, and language and ideas in poetry) Students can note their responses in the space provided on the Access 2 and 3 handouts.
	Approaching **Complete a Chart.** To prepare students to participate in the discussion, have them work in groups to complete the chart on the Access 4 handout as they read the definition of theme. Correct answers are located online. **Beyond** **Discuss.** Have students select a book they've read and describe its theme. Compile a list of examples. Have students discuss how they determined the theme. How did determining the theme impact their understanding or enjoyment of the story?
	Extend **Tech Infusion** **Brainstorm.** Compile a list of common themes in works of literature as a class using a whiteboard or a Padlet Wall http://tinyurl.com/n7l7cyy. Ask students why they think that many stories share a common theme.
	Extend **Tech Infusion** **Blast.** Create a Blast and ask students to "blast out" the definition of theme in their own words and/or provide examples of theme that they've seen in other books or movies. Use the poll question to ask students which common theme they most enjoy reading about.

2. MODEL

Core Path	Access Path
Read and Annotate. Have students independently read the Model section. As they read, ask students to use the annotation tool to: • highlight key points • ask questions • identify places where the Model applies the strategies laid out in the Define section on theme	**Note:** During this portion of the lesson, instruction shifts from whole group to individual work. Use this time to work one-on-one or in small groups with Beginning, Intermediate, Advanced, and Approaching students. **Beginner & Intermediate** **Coach the Reading.** Work with these students (either individually or in small groups) to fill out the guided reading questions on the Access 1 and 2 handouts. Have students refer to the Model Glossary on the Access 1 and 2 handouts to help them determine the meaning of difficult words. Let students know they'll use these answers to help participate in the discussion about the Model. Sample answers for this exercise are located online. **Advanced** **Identify Evidence.** Provide these students with the same instructions to read and annotate as on- and beyond- grade-level students. In addition, ask Advanced students to complete the identifying evidence exercise on the Access 3 handout. Let students know that they'll use these answers to help participate in the discussion about the Model. If needed, have students refer to the Model Glossary on the Access 3 handout to help them determine the meaning of difficult words. Sample answers for this exercise are located online. **Approaching** **Guided Reading.** Have students complete the guided reading questions on the Access 4 handout as they read. Let them know that they'll use these answers to help participate in the discussion about the Model. Refer students to the Model Glossary on the Access 4 handout to help them determine the meaning of difficult words. Sample answers for this exercise are located online.

Core Path	Access Path
Discuss. After students read the Model text, use the questions below to facilitate a whole group discussion that helps students understand how to determine and analyze theme in the excerpt. Remind students to follow rules for collegial discussions and to use academic vocabulary correctly:	

Core Path (continued):

1. According to the Model text, readers can start to determine possible themes from the very first pages of a novel. How is this possible? (Although themes are developed over the course of an entire story, sometimes the foundations for those themes are built right at the beginning of the text.)

2. Why does the Model start by examining a main character's words and thoughts instead of just stating a possible theme? (Authors rarely state a theme directly in a work of fiction, so examining a character's words and thoughts are one way readers can begin to infer it.)

3. Besides dialogue in a story, what else can help readers begin to infer possible themes in a work of fiction? (Characters' actions also help reveal potential themes. Readers can make inferences about themes based on what characters do and what they learn from their behavior.)

4. From the bulleted list included on the Identification and Application section of the definition, which strategy for determining theme do you think is most helpful for determining the theme in this excerpt? Why? (Paying attention to the characters' words, thoughts, and actions. They show the problems and tensions between the boys that might be further developed into a theme.)

Access Path:

Extend

Tech Infusion

Pair and Share. Pair or group students and ask each group to identify a possible theme that is not mentioned in the Model, for example good vs. evil or weak vs. strong. Have each group tell which strategies they used to identify a possible additional theme. Here are the strategies:

- point-of-view of the narration
- character thoughts and actions
- character dialogue

Please note that excerpts and passages in the StudySync® library, workbooks, and PDFs are intended as touchstones to generate interest in an author's work. The excerpts and passages do not substitute for the reading of entire texts, and StudySync® strongly recommends that teachers and students seek out and purchase the whole literary or informational work in order to experience it as the author intended. Links to online resellers are available in our digital library. In addition, complete works may be ordered through an authorized reseller by filling out and returning to StudySync® the order form enclosed in this workbook.

Teacher's Edition   235

Core Path	Access Path
	• events in the story's plot • details about the setting or characters • titles and chapter headings Ask the groups to share their findings with the class. If possible, have students capture pair shares on video using their mobile devices so they can watch their conversations and critique the content.

3. YOUR TURN

Core Path	Access Path
Assess and Explain. Have students answer the comprehension questions to test for understanding. Share the explanations for Parts A and B (located online) with your students.	
	Extend **Share and Discuss.** Have students complete the Your Turn section in class. Poll students about their responses and as a class discuss the different strategies they used to determine the correct answers. Make sure students make the connection between the words "the delicate thing" in the answer to question 2 and the conch shell. Have students think about the possible themes that could be explored in *Lord of the Flies* and ask the following questions: 1. Through which aspects of a work of literature is the author most likely to reveal his themes in this story? (dialogue; character thoughts and actions) 2. How do you think Jack and Ralph will differ in the way they will attempt to solve problems that arise? (Based on the way they seek to choose a leader, Jack will want to have control and make unilateral decisions while Ralph will want to let the group decide as a whole.)
	Extend **Apply.** Review some of the test-taking tips students have compiled on whiteboards, tablets, or chart paper. Discuss which ones are particularly helpful in answering point-of-view test questions.

SKILL:
Character

OVERVIEW

Most students will have little difficulty identifying characters in a story, but getting to know and really understand them is a little more challenging. This lesson provides follow-up questions and useful enrichments to help teachers guide students toward a usable, repeatable method of identifying main characters and analyzing their traits, which can help them unlock the theme of a story.

OBJECTIVES

1. Learn the definition of character.
2. Practice using concrete strategies for analyzing character in a literature selection.
3. Participate effectively in a range of conversations and collaborations to express ideas and build upon the ideas of others.

ELA Common Core Standards:
Reading: Literature - RL.8.1, RL.8.3
Speaking & Listening - SL8.1.A, SL8.1.B, SL8.1.C, SL8.1.D, SL.8.2
Language - L.8.6

RESOURCES

Access 1 handout (Beginner)
Access 2 handout (Intermediate)
Access 3 handout (Advanced)
Access 4 handout (Approaching)

Please note that excerpts and passages in the StudySync® library, workbooks, and PDFs are intended as touchstones to generate interest in an author's work. The excerpts and passages do not substitute for the reading of entire texts, and StudySync® strongly recommends that teachers and students seek out and purchase the whole literary or informational work in order to experience it as the author intended. Links to online resellers are available in our digital library. In addition, complete works may be ordered through an authorized reseller by filling out and returning to StudySync® the order form enclosed in this workbook.

Teacher's Edition   237

1. DEFINE

Core Path	Access Path
Watch. Watch the Concept Definition video on character with your students. Make sure students write down and understand the definition of character traits, focusing in particular on how these traits may change or evolve over the course of a story's plot. Pause the video at these key moments to discuss the information with your students:	**English Learners All Levels & Approaching** **Match.** Have students complete the matching exercise on the Access 1, 2, 3, and 4 handouts as they watch the video. Answers are located online.

1. 0:18 – Who are some of your favorite characters from literary works you've read? Share a few of your favorite characters and discuss what it is about these characters that make them interesting or likable.

2. 0:30 – Can you think of any other ways to understand character traits, aside from dialogue and action? How does a story's point of view determine how character traits are revealed?

3. 0:51 – Which characters in a story change or evolve over the course of a story's plot, and which ones don't? Why is this the case?

Read and Discuss. After watching the Concept Definition video, have students read the definition of character. Either in small groups or as a whole class, use the following questions to spur discussion among your students about character. Make sure students follow the rules for collegial discussions, use academic words and phrases correctly, and respond to questions and comments from others in the classroom with relevant evidence, observations, and ideas.

1. Who are some of the main characters in books you've read? (Answers will vary.)

2. Do characters usually change in a story? If so, what often causes this change? (Answers may vary, but students should note that characters often change as a result of trying to solve a problem or conflict in the plot. They may learn something new or go through an experience that changes their point of view.)

Beginner
Finish the Sentences. Have students work in groups to complete the sentence frames on the Access 1 handout as they read the definition. Have them use the completed sentence frames to help them participate in the discussion. Sample answers for this exercise are located online.

Intermediate & Advanced
Discuss Prompts. To help students participate in the discussion, prompt them with questions that can be answered with a few words, such as:

- What do characters do?

  (move the action forward/create drama)

- How do authors construct characters?

  (through description, dialogue, or situations that reveal their personalities)

- What does a protagonist do?

  (move a story's action forward)

Core Path	Access Path
3. How do the words authors choose affect the way we think about characters? (As the Model states, unlike in movies, television, or real-life, readers can't see or hear the characters in works of literature. In order to tell what a character is like, readers must pay close attention to the words the author uses to describe the characters as well the things the characters think, say, or do.) 4. How can what "drives" a character – what he or she wants in a story – help reveal a character's traits? (Possible answer: What drives or motivates a character to solve a problem or achieve something can reveal a great deal about the character's traits. They may turn out to be sneaky and devious, or honorable and fair, depending on the actions they take to achieve a goal.)	• Who is an antagonist? (someone who works against a protagonist) Students can note their responses in the space provided on the Access 2 and 3 handouts. **Approaching** **Complete a Chart.** To prepare students to participate in the discussion, have them work in groups to complete the chart on the Access 4 handout as they read the definition. Correct answers are located online. **Beyond** **Discuss.** Have students select a book they've read. Ask students to describe the protagonist, antagonist, and at least one minor character. How did these characters move the action in the story forward or create drama?
	Extend **View.** After watching the Concept Definition video with students, analyze a character from a popular television show or movie. Point out that since these types of media don't directly tell us what characters are like, viewers have to base their analysis on things the character says or does or how others respond to the character.
	Extend **Tech Infusion** **Blast.** Create a Blast and ask students to "blast out" the name of a favorite character followed by a hashtag with a word that describes what that character is like.

2. MODEL

Core Path	Access Path
Read and Annotate. Have students independently read the Model section. As they read, ask students to use the annotation tool to: • highlight key points • ask questions • identify places where the Model applies the strategies laid out in the Identification and Application section on character	**Note:** During this portion of the lesson, instruction shifts from whole group to individual work. Use this time to work one-on-one or in small groups with Beginning, Intermediate, Advanced, and Approaching students.
	Beginner & Intermediate **Coach the Reading.** Work with these students (either individually or in small groups) to fill out the guided reading questions on the Access 1 and 2 handouts. Have students refer to the Model Glossary on the Access 1 and 2 handouts to help them determine the meaning of difficult words. Let students know they'll use these answers to help participate in the discussion about the Model. Sample answers for this exercise are located online. **Advanced** **Identify Evidence.** Provide these students with the same instructions to read and annotate as on- and beyond- grade-level students. In addition, ask Advanced students to complete the identifying evidence exercise on the Access 3 handout. Let students know that they'll use these answers to help participate in the discussion about the Model. If needed, have students refer to the Model Glossary on the Access 3 handout to help them determine the meaning of difficult words. Sample answers for this exercise are located online. **Approaching** **Guided Reading.** Have students complete the guided reading questions on the Access 4 handout as they read. Have students refer to the Model Glossary on the Access 4 handout to help them determine the meaning of difficult words. Let them know that they'll use these answers to help participate in the discussion about the Model. Sample answers for this exercise are located online.

Core Path	Access Path
Discuss. After students read the Model text, use the questions below to facilitate a whole group discussion that helps students understand how to identify the theme of the passage. Remind students to follow rules for collegial discussions and to use academic vocabulary correctly:	

1. According to the Model, what is the first step readers must take in order to begin analyzing a character? Why? (Readers can't see or hear the characters in a work of literature. In order to tell what a character is like, readers must pay close attention to the words the author uses to describe the characters as well the things the characters think, say, or do.)

2. Why does the Model point out that the author uses many words with negative connotations to describe Jack? (to help readers understand that Golding is not portraying Jack in a positive way. He may turn out to be "a bad guy.")

3. The Model uses Jack Merridew as an example of one way an author can use a character's actions to reveal what he or she is like. Look back at the excerpt. What do Jack's actions reveal about his character? (Jack likes to exert control and behaves badly toward the other boys. He shows no sympathy when one of the boys faints onto the sand.)

4. What are some other examples of Jack's actions, not cited in the Model, that show what his character is like? (Possible response: Jack tells Piggy to shut up and calls him "Fatty." He also tells him that he "talks too much," though he isn't talking any more than Jack.)

5. From the list under the Identification and Application section of the skill, which strategy for making inferences about characters is most helpful for determining what the characters are like in this excerpt? Why? (Paying attention to the characters' words, thoughts and actions. We still don't know much about their relationships with others or how they go about trying to solve problems.)

Core Path	Access Path
	Extend **Dramatize.** Have students choose a character from *Lord of the Flies* or another familiar book to dramatize. Explain that their dramatization should reveal a fundamental trait of the character they choose, such as power or shyness. They may wish to record their dramatizations using audio-visual equipment, iPads, or mobile devices.

3. YOUR TURN

Core Path	Access Path
Assess and Explain. Have students answer the comprehension questions to test for understanding. Share the explanations for Parts A and B (located online) with your students.	
	Extend **Share and Discuss.** Have students complete the Your Turn section in class. Poll students about their responses and, as a class, discuss the different strategies they used to determine the correct answers. Make sure students make the connection between the correct answer to Part A (A.) and Piggy's actions. Conduct your poll by asking your students to complete a handout with questions or using Poll Everywhere (http://tinyurl.com/5grl69) or Socrative (http://tinyurl.com/nfz427v).
	Extend **Apply.** Challenge students to write their own character test questions and answers about this passage or another story with which the class is familiar. You may want to use quiz software such as Flubaroo (http://tinyurl.com/4ueah2v) to compile students' questions into a quiz.

OVERVIEW

Lord of the Flies by William Golding exposes human nature when a group of young boys are stranded on a deserted island. The Close Read gives students the opportunity to focus on how the author develops central ideas.

OBJECTIVES

1. Complete a close reading of a passage from literature.
2. Practice and apply concrete strategies for analyzing theme and character in an excerpt from a novel.
3. Participate effectively in a range of conversations and collaborations to express ideas and build upon the ideas of others.
4. Prewrite, plan, and produce clear and coherent writing in response to a prompt.

ELA Common Core Standards:
Reading: Literature - RL.8.1, RL.8.2, RL.8.3, RL.8.4
Writing - W.8.4, W.8.5, W.8.6, W.8.10
Speaking & Listening - SL.8.1.A, SL.8.1.C, SL.8.6
Language - L.8.2.C, L.8.4.A, L.8.4.C, L.8.4.D, L.8.6

RESOURCES

Lord of the Flies Vocabulary handout
Access 1 handout (Beginner)
Access 2 handout (Intermediate)
Access 3 handout (Advanced)
Access 4 handout (Approaching)

Please note that excerpts and passages in the StudySync® library, workbooks, and PDFs are intended as touchstones to generate interest in an author's work. The excerpts and passages do not substitute for the reading of entire texts, and StudySync® strongly recommends that teachers and students seek out and purchase the whole literary or informational work in order to experience it as the author intended. Links to online resellers are available in our digital library. In addition, complete works may be ordered through an authorized reseller by filling out and returning to StudySync® the order form enclosed in this workbook.

Teacher's Edition   243

1. INTRODUCTION

Core Path	Access Path
Define and Compare. Project the vocabulary words and definitions onto the board or provide students with a handout, so they can copy the vocabulary into their notebooks. Ask students to compare their initial vocabulary analysis from the First Read with the actual definitions. Review words that students defined incorrectly to understand why they were unable to use context clues or other tools to develop usable definitions. **Review.** Have students complete the fill-in-the-blank vocabulary handout for this selection. Answers for the handout are listed online.	**Beginner & Intermediate** **Complete the Sentences.** Have students complete the sentence frames on the Access 1 and 2 handouts using the vocabulary words. Point out that some of the words are in the questions and some will be in the answers. Sample answers are located online. **Advanced & Beyond** **Write in Journals.** Have students write a journal entry using all of their vocabulary words. Remind them to write sentences that communicate the meaning of the words they are using. **Approaching** **Complete a Graphic Organizer.** To support students in comparing their vocabulary predictions with the correct meanings, have them complete the graphic organizer on the Access 4 handout to record the vocabulary words, their predictions, and the definitions. Then have them write sentences using the words.
	Extend **Tech Infusion** **Create.** Create a vocabulary review quiz using Google Forms. Design multiple choice and/or fill-in-the-blank questions that require students to apply their understanding of the vocabulary. After the students have completed the quiz, install Flubaroo (http://tinyurl.com/4ueah2v). It will automatically grade the quizzes, and you can email students their scores. You will be given the option to include an answer key and short message for each student.

2. READ

Core Path	Access Path
Model Close Reading. Project the text onto the board and model a close reading of certain sections of the excerpt using the annotation strategies mentioned below. While modeling annotation strategies, make notes that tie the text to the focus skills and demonstrate what students should be looking for as they read. Here is some guidance for you as you annotate with your students:	

- As the Skills lessons that precede this text makes clear, We can make inferences about the theme by paying close attention to the words, thoughts, and actions of the main characters. What kind of questions does Jack ask Ralph in the opening paragraphs? (Jack asks if there are any grownups on the island, or if there is a ship.) When Jack realizes that the answer to all of his questions is "no," what does this reveal about a possible theme in the selection? (Possible answer: one theme developed in this story will relate to survival.)

- Let's look back at the second paragraph, and read how the author. William Golding, describes Jack. He writes that "out of this face stared two light blue eyes, frustrated now, and turning, or ready to turn, to anger." He is also "tall, thin, and bony" underneath his "floating cloak," a description that makes him seem almost ghoulish. So from the very beginning, Golding sets Jack up as a character of whom others need to be wary, or careful.

- Now let's skip ahead to the fortieth paragraph. Ralph lifts the conch and says "seems to me we ought to have a chief to decide things." The other boys get excited about this idea and as they all cry out for a vote, Golding writes, "this toy of voting was almost as pleasing as the conch." What do you think the author means by this phrase? (Possible answer: The author sees the boys voting for a leader as a kind of play acting, as if this is a game and they are not really taking the issue as seriously as they should.) What seems to be the deciding

Copyright © BookheadEd Learning, LLC

Core Path	Access Path
factor for some of the boys who vote for Ralph? (The fact that Ralph has the conch in his possession. "Let him be the chief with the trumpet-thing," says one of the boys.) **So one of the themes here seems to be a universal desire, even among children, for leadership, rules, and order. Yet how seriously the children view these concerns may cause trouble as the story continues**	

Core Path	Access Path
Read and Annotate. Read the Skills Focus questions as a class, so your students know what they should pay close attention to as they read. Then have students read and annotate the excerpt. Ask students to use the annotation tool as they read to: 1. respond to the Skills Focus section 2. ask questions 3. make connections 4. identify key information, examples, and themes 5. note unfamiliar vocabulary 6. capture their reaction to the ideas and examples in the text As they reread the text, remind students to use the comprehension strategy of Asking and Answering Questions that they learned in the First Read.	**Note:** While on-grade-level students are reading and annotating, work one-on-one or in small groups with Beginning, Intermediate, Advanced, and Approaching students to support them as they read and annotate the text. **Beginner & Intermediate** **Summarize and Analyze the Text.** Work with these students to complete the sentence frames on the Access 1 and 2 handouts. They will then use the completed sentence frames to help them analyze and annotate the text by completing the Skills Focus questions. Refer to the sample Skills Focus answers online to help them complete the sentence frames and annotate the text. **Advanced** **Work in Pairs.** Pair these students with more proficient English speakers to work together on analyzing and annotating the text to complete the Skills Focus questions. If these students need more support, have them use the sentence frames on the Access 3 handout as they work with their more proficient peers. **Approaching** **Summarize the Text.** Have these students discuss and complete the text summary on the Access 4 handout. Encourage students to use their summary to help them analyze and annotate the text by completing the Skills Focus questions. Correct answers for the summary are online. Also refer to the sample Skills Focus answers to aid students with their annotations.

Core Path	Access Path
	Beyond **Compare and Contrast.** Ask students to compare and contrast Ralph and Jack using a Venn diagram. Encourage students to discuss themes that might arise from the similarities and differences between these characters, for example, leadership or good vs. evil.
Discuss After students have read the text, use the sample responses to the Skills Focus questions of this lesson plan online to discuss the reading and the process of searching for the theme and how dialogue and incidents in the plot reveal aspects of a character. Make sure that students have acquired and accurately use academic-specific words and phrases related to the skill, and demonstrate a command of formal English appropriate to the discussion.	**Extend** **Pair and Share.** In small, heterogeneous groups or pairs, ask students to share and discuss their annotations with a focus on the analyzing characters and theme presented in the selection. You can provide students with these questions to guide their discussion: 1. What is Jack like? What kind of characteristics does the author use to represent him? He is pushy and mean. He feels entitled to lead the group. 2. How is the conch shell important? How does it relate to theme? It symbolizes power and authority. Because Jack holds the conch shell, he becomes the leader of the group.
	Extend **Vote.** 1. Break the class into smaller groups. Have each member cast a vote by secret ballot for who they think should be the leader of the boys. 2. After they tally the votes, have each group discuss and respond to the following questions: Why do you think your results were the same or different from the boys in the excerpt? What does this tell you about how we choose our leaders? Did the group choose a leader based on widely held beliefs about what qualities make a good leader? How valid are these beliefs? 3. Have each group present its findings to the class.

3. WRITE

Core Path	Access Path
Prewrite and Plan. Read the prompt as a class and ask students to brainstorm their reactions to *Lord of the Flies,* and the relationship between the characters Ralph and Piggy. How does Jack Merridew affect this relationship, and what does it suggest about the rules and challenges of friendship? Students can brainstorm together either as a class or in small groups to begin planning their responses. Remind students to look at the excerpt and their annotations to find textual evidence to support their ideas.	**Beginner, Intermediate & Advanced** **Answer and Discuss.** Have students complete the prewriting questions on the Access 1, 2, and 3 handouts and then explain their answers to a partner before they write. Explain to students that when they answer a question—such as "What is a theme in *Lord of the Flies?*" — they need to include a detail, example, or quote from the text that supports the statement. For example, students could include the line, "'Then we'll have to look after ourselves,'" which shows that the boys do not have adults around to help them figure out how to survive on the island.

Approaching **Answer Prewriting Questions.** Work with students as a group to complete the prewriting questions on the Access 4 handout to summarize their thoughts before they write. |
| | **Extend** **Tech Infusion** **Map.** Students can create concept maps online using http://tinyurl.com/5u2koto. Google drawing can also be used to design a concept map. |
| **Discuss.** Project these instructions for the peer review onto the board and review them with your class, so they know what they are looking for when they begin to provide their classmates with feedback:

• How thoroughly and accurately does the writer explain how Jack Merridew affects this relationship?

• How effectively does the writer use his or her understanding of character and theme to explore the relationship between Ralph and Piggy and what it might suggest about the rules and challenges of friendship? | |

Core Path	Access Path
• What evidence from the text does the writer include to support his or her writing? Be sure to include positive feedback on sections you liked or thought were well done. After you've looked at the peer review instructions, review the rubric with students before they begin writing. Allow time for students to briefly raise and discuss questions they may have about the peer review instructions and the rubric. Tell students how many peer reviews they will need to complete once they submit their writing.	
Write. Ask students to complete the writing assignment using textual evidence to support their answers. If possible, have students use technology to produce and publish their writing. Once they have completed their writing, they should click "Submit."	
	Extend **Critique.** Invite students to share general ideas about what makes a piece of writing strong or weak. Elicit responses about use of textual evidence, development, organization, and conventions. Then work as a class to generate strategies students can use as they complete their peer reviews to ensure they are substantive. You may want to record their responses in a checklist format on a whiteboard or Padlet Wall. Have students highlight their favorite section of the response they reviewed. Have them explain to the class why they thought it was particularly good.
Review. Once students complete their writing assignment, they should submit substantive feedback to two peers. If possible, have students use technology to interact and collaborate with others.	

BLAST:
Follow the Leader

OVERVIEW

The concept of power, including who leads and who follows, plays an important role in suspense narratives. Students will learn about leadership and think critically about characteristics that good leaders have in common. Research Links explore aspects of leadership, including what it means to be a good leader, characteristics that leaders have in common, and how leaders influence people.

OBJECTIVES

1. Provide background information about the traits that great leaders have in common and ask students to analyze and respond to the driving question: "What would you expect from a leader during a crisis?"
2. Encourage research with hyperlinks to a range of information about leaders and leadership, including biographies, essays, interviews, and databases.

ELA Common Core Standards:
Reading: Informational Text - RI.8.1, RI.8.6
Writing - W.8.1.A, W.8.1.B, W.8.5, W.8.6
Speaking & Listening - SL.8.1.A, SL.8.1.C, SL.8.1.D, SL.8.2
Language - L.8.6

RESOURCES

Access 1 handout (Beginner)
Access 2 handout (Intermediate)
Access 4 handout (Approaching)

TITLE/DRIVING QUESTION

Core Path	Access Path
Discuss. As a class read aloud the title and driving question for this Blast. Ask students to share their ideas about leadership. Do they have an opinion about what makes someone a good leader or what they expect from their leaders? Remind students that they should not immediately reply to the driving question. They'll be returning to this question and responding after they've read the Background and some of the Research Links.	**English Learners All Levels** **Discuss a Visual.** Have students view this photograph from the Library of Congress: Coretta Scott King holding a candle and leading a march at night to the White House as part of the Moratorium to End the War in Vietnam which took place on October 15, 1969 http://tinyurl.com/qefdlky. Discuss how the picture represents leadership, prompting students with questions such as: • What is happening in the photo? • What makes this person seem like a leader? • Why might this person make a good leader?
Draft. In their notebooks or on scrap paper, have students draft their initial responses to the driving question. This will provide them with a baseline response that they will be developing as they gain more information about the topic in the Background and Research Links sections of the assignment.	**Beginner & Intermediate** **Draft with Sentence Frame.** When drafting their initial response to the driving question, have students refer to this Blast sentence frame on their Access 1 and 2 handouts: • A good leader is someone who has certain qualities, like _____ _____. Point out these two key features of the sentence frame: 1. The introductory clause "A good leader is someone who has certain qualities" borrows language directly from the Blast driving question to provide a response. 2. Ask students to make special note of the determiner "like," which is a word that serves to express the reference of the noun phrase "A good leader" in the context.

BACKGROUND

Core Path	Access Path
Read. Have students read the Blast Background to provide context for the driving question.	**Beginner & Intermediate** **Read with Support.** Have students read the Blast Background to provide context for the driving question. When they encounter unfamiliar words or phrases, have students refer to the glossary on their Access 1 and 2 handouts. If there are unfamiliar words that are not included in their glossary, encourage students to check a dictionary or online reference tool, like http://dictionary.reference.com. **Approaching** **Read and Summarize.** Have students read the Blast Background to provide context for the driving question. As they read, ask students to complete the fill-in-the-blank summary of the Background provided on their Access 4 handout. When they encounter unfamiliar words or phrases, have students refer to the glossary on their Access 4 handout.
Discuss. Pair students and have them discuss the following questions: 1. If you were writing about a great leader, what words would you use to describe her or him? (Possible responses: fair, wise, brave, courageous, decisive, wise, kind, bold, innovative) 2. Who are some good leaders you have read about? What qualities identified in the Background do they possess? (Answers will vary, but should include some specific names. Adjectives might include charismatic, proactive, great communicator.) 3. What, in your experience, are qualities of poor or ineffective leaders? What characteristics of an ineffective leader would you add to the Background to show contrast with a great leader? (Answers will vary, but might include secretive, vengeful, spiteful, afraid, distrustful, bullying, not knowledgeable.)	**Beginner & Intermediate** **Discuss.** Pair Beginning and Intermediate students and have them use the dialogue starter on their Access 1 and 2 handouts to discuss the topic. Advise them to return to the dialogue and switch roles if they get stuck. **Beyond** **Discuss.** Have students work in pairs to discuss a leader of their choice. Students should engage in a dialogue about the leader based around the information in the Blast Background.

Core Path	Access Path
Brainstorm and Research. Remind students about the driving question for this Blast: "What makes a good leader?" In their notebooks ask students to make two columns. In the first column, have them list traits they associate with leaders. In the second column, have them provide examples of leaders they know and how they've embodied this trait. Here's an example:	

Trait	Example
Makes difficult decisions and sticks to them even when they are unpopular	Coach Cline. He made a rule that everyone has to be on time to basketball practice. The punishment for being late for practice was to sit out a quarter of the next game. When our best player was late, Coach Cline made her sit out the first quarter of the next game even though it was against our biggest rival.

RESEARCH LINKS

Core Path	Access Path
Examine and Explore. Before asking students to explore the Research Links, use these activities and questions to guide their exploration:	
1. Have students examine either the "Leadership Database" or the "Great Women Rulers" link. Most of the people here will be unrecognizable to them. Ask students to read about at least 5 leaders they have never heard of.	

Please note that excerpts and passages in the StudySync® library, workbooks, and PDFs are intended as touchstones to generate interest in an author's work. The excerpts and passages do not substitute for the reading of entire texts, and StudySync® strongly recommends that teachers and students seek out and purchase the whole literary or informational work in order to experience it as the author intended. Links to online resellers are available in our digital library. In addition, complete works may be ordered through an authorized reseller by filling out and returning to StudySync® the order form enclosed in this workbook.

Teacher's Edition   253

Core Path	Access Path
2. After they've read about at least 5 leaders, ask students to think about any commonalities or overlaps that they read in the biographies of those 5 leaders. What do these leaders have in common? If time permits, make a list of responses as a class. 3. Were they surprised to find so many leaders listed on these sites? When we think of leaders, we often think of great leaders like Lincoln or King or Gandhi or Mandela, but do we make note of the other leaders at work in our world every day?	
	Extend **Research, Discuss and Present.** Assign each group one link to explore in depth. Ask them to discuss the information: • What are the key points? • What inferences did you make as you read? • What did you learn about this "big idea" from reading this research? • How did this help you to better understand the topic? • What questions does your group have after exploring this link? Allow students time to informally present what they learned.
	Extend **Tech Infusion** **Word Clouds.** As students explore the links, allow them to paste them into an online site such as Wordle to create word clouds. Have students discuss the important ideas and concepts about leadership in the links based on the most prominent words in the clouds.

QUIKPOLL

Core Path	Access Path
Participate. Answer the poll question. Have students use information from the Background and Research Links to explain their answers.	

NUMBER CRUNCH

Core Path	Access Path
Predict, Discuss, and Click. Before students click on the number, break them into pairs and have them make predictions about what they think the number is related to. After they've clicked the number, ask students if they are surprised by the revealed information.	

CREATE YOUR BLAST

Core Path	Access Path
Blast. Ask students to write their Blast response in 140 characters or less.	**Beginner** **Blast with Support.** Have students refer back to the sentence frame on their Access 1 handout that they used to create their original Blast draft. Ask them to use this frame to write and enter their final Blast. **Intermediate** **Blast with Support.** Have students attempt to draft their Blast without the sentence frame on their Access 2 handout. If students struggle to compose their Blast draft without the sentence frame, remind them to reference it for support.

Core Path	Access Path
	Beyond **Write a Claim.** Ask students to use their answer to the poll question to write a strong claim that could be used as the foundation for a piece of argumentative writing. Once students have written their claims, ask them to read the claims to a small group of their peers. This activity will provide them practice writing claims, as well as expose them to claims written by their peers.
Review. After students have completed their own Blasts, ask them to review the Blasts of their peers and provide feedback. If possible, have students use technology to present information and ideas efficiently as well as to interact and collaborate with others.	**Extend** **Discuss.** As a whole class or in groups, identify a few strong Blasts and discuss what made those responses so powerful. As a group, analyze and discuss what characteristics make a Blast interesting or effective.
	Extend **Revise.** Resend a second version of this Blast assignment to your students and have them submit revised versions of their original Blasts. Do the same responses make the Top 10? How have the answers improved from the first submissions?

FIRST READ:
Ten Days in a Mad-House

OVERVIEW

In 1887, reporter Nellie Bly went on an undercover assignment for a New York newspaper, the *World*, for which she feigned insanity to get committed to the Blackwell Island's Insane Asylum. This excerpt describes how she attempted to get herself sent to the asylum. The First Read gives students the opportunity to experience the text with a limited context.

OBJECTIVES

1. Perform an initial reading of a text and demonstrate comprehension by responding to short analysis and inference questions with textual evidence.
2. Practice defining vocabulary words using context.
3. Participate effectively in a range of conversations and collaborations to express ideas and build upon the ideas of others.

ELA Common Core Standards:

Reading: Informational Text - RI.8.1, RI.8.4, RI.8.10
Writing - W.8.7, W.8.10
Speaking & Listening - SL.8.1.A, SL.8.1.B, SL.8.1.C, SL.8.1.D, SL.8.2, SL.8.6
Language - L.8.4.A, L.8.4.B, L.8.4.C, L.8.6

RESOURCES

Access 1 handout (Beginner)
Access 2 handout (Intermediate)
Access 3 handout (Advanced)
Access 4 handout (Approaching)

ACCESS COMPLEX TEXT

In this excerpt from *Ten Days in a Mad-House,* reporter Nellie Bly pretends to be affected by a mental illness in front of a judge for the purpose of gaining admittance to the Women's Lunatic Asylum on Blackwell Island. At the turn of the 19th century, people did not understand the severity and characteristics of mental illnesses. For this reason, Nellie Bly endeavors to uncover the conditions and treatments within the "mad-house" while gaining valuable insight to push for change. To help students understand Bly's undercover investigation, use the following ideas to provide scaffolded instruction for an initial reading of the more complex features of this text.

- **Organization** - The first-person narrative switches back and forth between the plot of Bly's feigned insanity and her thoughts regarding the success of this plot. For example, "'I did not come to New York,' I replied (while I added, mentally, 'because I have been here for some time.')" Readers may benefit by highlighting Bly's thoughts to separate them from the insanity plot.

- **Specific Vocabulary** - Some idiomatic expressions, such as a description of a judge "dealing out the milk of human kindness by wholesale," may present challenges for some readers. In this case, it refers to a judge who is exceedingly kind.

- **Prior Knowledge** - Students may be unfamiliar with the practice of court-ordered assignment to an insane asylum without the commission of a crime.

1. INTRODUCTION

Core Path	Access Path
Watch. As a class, watch the video preview of *Ten Days in a Mad-House.* Have students share their ideas about the story to come based on the preview.	**English Learners All Levels** **Fill in the Blanks.** Ask students to use their Access 1, 2, and 3 handouts to fill in the blanks of the transcript for the preview's voiceover as they watch the preview along with their classmates. Answers are located online.
Read and Listen. Individually or as a class, read and discuss the Introduction for *Ten Days in a Mad-House.* The Introduction provides context for the excerpts taken from Chapter IV.	**English Learners All Levels & Approaching** **Fill in the Blanks.** Ask students to complete the fill-in-the-blank exercise on the Access 1, 2, 3, and 4 handouts as they read and listen to the *Ten Days in a Mad-House* excerpt.

Core Path	Access Path

Build Background. Have your students investigate the treatment of people with mental illness throughout history.
 	
1. To pairs or small groups, assign one of the subjects below. Have them focus on the following issues in terms of the 19th Century in the United States:
 	
   a. medical definitions and symptoms of mental illness
 	
   b. medical and social views of the mentally ill, including how large a problem it was and where it was most often found and treated
 	
   c. prescribed treatments or other attempts to deal with the mentally ill
 	
2. Have them write a brief summary of their research. Then have them share their findings.
 	
3. As a class, list the findings that were most unsettling or surprising.
	English Learners All Levels & Approaching Targeted Background Research Questionnaire. Ask students to complete the specified Targeted Background Research Questionnaire as they research different aspects of the mental illness in small groups. These questionnaires are on the Access 1, 2, 3 and 4 handouts. Sample answers are provided online.

	Extend **Discuss the Introduction.** After reading the Introduction, use the information provided to facilitate a pre-reading discussion to get students thinking about the events and point of view in *Ten Days in a Mad-House*. • How does the author view the officials she comes into contact with? • How does she view the people on the streets? • Does it surprise you that someone would want to get committed to a mental institution? • Why do you think the author wanted to do this?
	Extend **Multimedia.** Ask students to read and discuss *Life Magazine*'s article titled "Strangers to Reason: LIFE Inside a Psychiatric Hospital, 1938." What do they learn about life in psychiatric hospitals in the 1930s from the article and pictures? Give them time to discuss their reactions to this article. (http://tinyurl.com/pfjkco6)

Copyright © BookheadEd Learning, LLC

2. READ

Core Path	Access Path
Make Predictions about Vocabulary. There are five bold vocabulary words in the text. As students read the text, ask them to make predictions about what they think each bold vocabulary word means based on the context clues in the sentence. If you are in a low tech classroom, ask students to record their predictions in their notes, so they can be easily referenced in class. If your students have access to technology, they can use the built in annotation tool to make their predictions.	**Note**: This exercise, which extends vocabulary instruction, should be completed when the class shifts from whole group instruction to individual work during the "Read and Annotate" exercise.

Make Predictions about Vocabulary. There are five bold vocabulary words in the text. As students read the text, ask them to make predictions about what they think each bold vocabulary word means based on the context clues in the sentence. If you are in a low tech classroom, ask students to record their predictions in their notes, so they can be easily referenced in class. If your students have access to technology, they can use the built in annotation tool to make their predictions.

Point out that two of the vocabulary terms—*the milk of human kindness* and *ferret out*—are actually idioms, or expressions used over time. The sources of idiomatic expressions are often lost over time. Explain that these idioms are not often used in the present day, but that they were common at the time Nellie Bly was writing.

It might be helpful to model this for students before they begin reading. Either using the board or projecting the actual text, focus on the sentence that uses the word "incredulous":

- "No," I said, looking as **incredulous** as I thought a crazy person could, "I did not come to New York."

Model for the class how to use the overall structure and meaning of the sentence and the sentences around it, the word's position, and other clues to define the unfamiliar vocabulary word. In this case, point out these context clues:

1. Look at the structure of the sentence. What is the subject (I) and what is the first verb (said)? We know that Nelly Bly is speaking about herself as she talks to someone else here, and we know from the participial phrase that begins with "looking as" that she's trying to look incredulous; it's an act.

2. We also know from the last part of the participial phrase "as I thought a crazy person could" that Bly is trying to look and act like a crazy person, and that she thinks crazy people often act and look incredulous.

Note: This exercise, which extends vocabulary instruction, should be completed when the class shifts from whole group instruction to individual work during the "Read and Annotate" exercise.

Beginner, Intermediate, & Approaching Pair Practice.

1. Pair students with more proficient readers.

2. Give them an additional sentence that contains a new vocabulary word.

3. Ask the students to complete a Think Aloud using the teacher-led Make Predictions about Vocabulary activity as a model, while the more proficient readers actively listen.

4. The students should use the context clues in the sentence to try to determine the meaning of the new vocabulary word.

5. After the students have completed the Think Aloud and made a prediction about the word's meaning, allow time for the more proficient readers to add their own thoughts and clarify any points of confusion.

6. Once they've completed this Think Aloud, encourage them to use a dictionary to confirm the definition of the new vocabulary word. Have them refer to the Text Glossary on their Access 1, 2, and 4 handouts for definitions of key vocabulary terms in the text. Encourage them to add any additional vocabulary words or idioms they find in the text and look up definitions for those words and idioms online or in a dictionary.

Core Path	Access Path

3. If we look at the sentences surrounding this one, we can see that Bly is pretending like she doesn't know that she's in New York, and when other people tell her that she is in New York, she pretends not to believe them. Thus, if she's acting crazy by not accepting that she's in New York, we can infer that "incredulous" means "unwilling to accept something as true."

Model Reading Comprehension Strategy.

Before students begin reading, model the reading comprehension strategy of summarizing by using this Think Aloud that talks students through the first paragraph of text. First explain to your students that summarizing is:

using your own words to briefly state the important points in a text by recalling and synthesizing key ideas in an objective manner.

Explain to students how summarizing will help them better comprehend the selection and help drive their discussions.

- When I read the first few paragraphs of the text, I try to understand the key ideas. The story is a first person account of a person whose name we believe to be Nellie Bly, although she is not certain. Based on the details in the text, she is confused about who she is or what is happening to her.

- As I think about objectively summarizing this part of the story, I take note of the key characters (Nellie, the policemen) and the setting (a public street). I ask myself which details are important to understanding the main idea of the selection. If I need them in order to understand, they should be included in my summary.

- I can now develop a summary in my own words, placing the key ideas in a logical order, such as chronological or order of importance. My summary will include only objective details about the events and characters from the selection, and not my own opinion.

Note: This exercise, which extends vocabulary instruction, should be completed when the class shifts from whole group instruction to individual work during the "Read and Annotate" exercise.

Beginner, Intermediate, & Approaching Apply Reading Comprehension Strategy.

1. Have students complete the summary sentence frames that guide the summarization *Ten Days in a Mad-House*. Refer students to the summary sentence frames on their Access 1, 2, and 4 handouts.

2. Then, have students pair up in order to discuss their summaries in a Think Aloud session. Visit each pair of students and ask which specific vocabulary words help them understanding a more global meaning in order to check reading comprehension. Are there any words or phrases that further confuse or complicate their summarization?

Please note that excerpts and passages in the StudySync® library, workbooks, and PDFs are intended as touchstones to generate interest in an author's work. The excerpts and passages do not substitute for the reading of entire texts, and StudySync® strongly recommends that teachers and students seek out and purchase the whole literary or informational work in order to experience it as the author intended. Links to online resellers are available in our digital library. In addition, complete works may be ordered through an authorized reseller by filling out and returning to StudySync® the order form enclosed in this workbook.

Teacher's Edition   261

Core Path	Access Path
Read and Annotate. Read and annotate the excerpt. Ask students to use the annotation tool as they read to: • use context clues to analyze and determine the meaning of the bolded vocabulary terms • ask questions about passages of the text that may be unclear or unresolved • identify key information, events, and individuals and connections between them • note unfamiliar vocabulary • capture their reaction to the events in the text	**Beginner** **Coach the Reading.** While other students read, annotate, and discuss the text independently, work with Beginning students, listening to the audio of the text and pausing periodically or when any student has a question. Coach students in highlighting and annotating the text. Have students refer to the Annotation Guide on the Access 1 handout as they annotate the text.
	Intermediate & Advanced **Listen to the Audio.** Have student pairs listen to the audio of the text as they annotate the text. If pairs need help with annotating the text, have them use the Annotation Guide on the Access 2 and 3 handouts. After working with the Beginning students, you may wish to check this group's progress and provide support as needed. **Approaching** **Use the Annotation Guide.** Have students use the Annotation Guide on the Access 4 handout to support them as they highlight and annotate the text.
Discuss. In small groups or pairs, have students discuss the questions and inferences they made while reading. 1. Why does Nellie keep talking about her trunks? (She is trying to sound like she is mentally ill.) 2. What did Nellie think about the statements of the people they passed in the street? (She was interested and amused by them.) 3. What does Nellie think about the officers in the courtroom? (She thinks they are passive and indifferent.) 4. What is Nellie's reaction to the judge? Why does she react that way? (paragraph 19) (She thinks he is kind-looking, and this upsets her because she is afraid he won't send her to the asylum.)	**Extend** **Tech Infusion** **Define.** Use a downloadable idioms dictionary such as the Beiks English Idioms Dictionary (http://tinyurl.com/k8kkp5c) to check the meaning of the vocabulary idioms and any other idioms in the text.

Core Path	Access Path
5. Why does it frighten Nellie when the judge mentions bringing reporters in? (paragraphs 41–42) (She knows reporters are good at getting to the truth, and she doesn't want to be exposed.)	

3. THINK

Core Path	Access Path
Answer and Discuss. Have students complete the Think questions and then use the peer review instructions and rubric to complete the peer reviews. Refer to the sample answers online to discuss responses with your students. Remind students to follow guidelines for collegial discussions.	**Beginner & Intermediate** **Sentence Frames.** Have students use the sentence frames on the Access 1 and 2 handouts to support their responses to the Think questions. **Approaching** **Find the Evidence.** Have students use Find the Evidence on the Access 4 handout to help them identify the evidence needed to answer the questions.
	Extend **State an Opinion.** Point out to students that Nellie Bly chose to lie about her mental state to ensure that she would be able to spend time in the mental hospital. Ask each student to state his or her opinion about whether this lie was acceptable, given Bly's motives, and explain why he or she holds that opinion. As students prepare to answer, revisit with them the core Think questions about Bly to help students sharpen their understanding of her motives and the purpose of her deception.

Please note that excerpts and passages in the StudySync® library, workbooks, and PDFs are intended as touchstones to generate interest in an author's work. The excerpts and passages do not substitute for the reading of entire texts, and StudySync® strongly recommends that teachers and students seek out and purchase the whole literary or informational work in order to experience it as the author intended. Links to online resellers are available in our digital library. In addition, complete works may be ordered through an authorized reseller by filling out and returning to StudySync® the order form enclosed in this workbook.

Teacher's Edition   **263**

OVERVIEW

Determining the author's purpose and author's point of view helps readers better understand what they are reading and why. It also helps them become critical readers and clarify their own point of view. This lesson provides follow-up questions and useful enrichments to help teachers guide students toward identifying and analyzing an author's point of view.

OBJECTIVES

1. Learn the definition of author's purpose and author's point of view.
2. Practice using concrete strategies for identifying author's purpose and author's point of view.
3. Participate effectively in a range of conversations and collaborations to express ideas and build upon the ideas of others.

ELA Common Core Standards:

Reading: Informational Text - RI.8.1, RI.8.6
Speaking & Listening - SL.8.1.A, SL.8.1.B, SL.8.1.C, SL.8.1.D, SL.8.2
Language - L.8.6

RESOURCES

Access 1 handout (Beginner)
Access 2 handout (Intermediate)
Access 3 handout (Advanced)
Access 4 handout (Approaching)

1. DEFINE

Core Path	Access Path
Watch. Watch the Concept Definition video on author's purpose and author's point of view. Make sure students understand why it's critical to know an author's purpose or author's point of view when trying to unlock the meaning of a text. Pause the video at these key moments to discuss the information with your students: 1. 1:00 - Can you think of any other purpose (or purposes) an author might have? How does genre affect purpose; i.e., how might the purpose of a fiction text differ from that of an informational text? How might it stay the same? 2. 1:18 - Are there any other elements of a text that might offer clues into an author's purpose or author's point of view? What are some additional resources we can use if we're having trouble deciphering the purpose or point of view? 3. 2:03 - Why don't authors of fiction or poetry state their purpose clearly in the same way a politician or an essayist might?	**English Learners All Levels & Approaching** **Match.** Have students complete the matching exercise on the Access 1, 2, 3, and 4 handouts as they watch the Concept Definition video. Correct answers are located online.
Read and Discuss. After watching the Concept Definition video, have students read the definition of author's purpose and author's point of view. Either in small groups or as a whole class, use the following questions to spur discussion among your students about author's purpose and author's point of view. Make sure students follow the rules for collegial discussions and respond to the questions and comments of others in the classroom with relevant evidence, observations, and ideas. 1. According to the Introduction, what are the different purposes a writer might have for writing? (Authors generally write to inform, persuade, or entertain. Some writers have more than one purpose, and may write to inform and persuade, or any combination of the three.)	**Beginner & Approaching** **Complete a Chart.** To prepare students to participate in the discussion, have them complete the chart on the Access 1 and 4 handouts as they read the definition of author's purpose and author's point of view. Correct answers are located online. **Intermediate & Advanced** **Discuss Prompts.** To help these students participate in the discussion, prompt them with questions that can be answered with a few words, such as: • What is an author's purpose? (the author's intention) • What are some examples of an author's purpose? (to persuade, to entertain, to inform) • What kinds of texts are clear in presenting the author's purpose? (speeches, personal essays)

Core Path	Access Path
2. How can authors express their purpose and their point of view? (Authors writing to inform might offer readers facts and statistics that they can easily analyze. An author writing to persuade may want to stress an opinion or idea with the help of emotional or figurative language.) 3. What are some other kinds of writing in which authors express their point of view? (Possible response: Authors of fiction often express their point of view about a topic or event through the actions of characters in the work.) 4. Describe a time you have used one of the strategies described to identify and evaluate an author's point of view. (Answers will vary.)	**Beyond** **Discuss.** After watching the video with students, discuss the author's purpose in a print or online advertisement or article. Have students point out the main idea, specific words, and imagery that express the author's purpose.

2. MODEL

Core Path	Access Path
Read and Annotate. As students read the Model text, ask them to use the annotation tool to: • Highlight key points • Ask questions • Identify places where the Model is applying the strategies laid out in the Identification and Application section on author's purpose and author's point of view	**Note:** During this portion of the lesson, instruction shifts from whole group to individual work. Use this time to work one-on-one or in small groups with Beginning, Intermediate, Advanced, and Approaching students. **Beginner & Intermediate** **Coach the Reading.** Work with these students in pairs to fill out the Guided Reading questions on the Access 1 and 2 handouts. Let students know they'll use these answers to help participate in the discussion about the Model. Sample answers for this exercise are located online. **Advanced** **Identify Evidence.** Provide these students with the same instructions to read and annotate as on- and beyond- grade-level students. In addition, ask Advanced students to complete the identifying evidence exercise on the Access 3 handout. Let students know that they'll use these answers to help participate in the discussion about the Model. Correct answers for this exercise are online.

Core Path	Access Path
	Approaching **Guided Reading.** In small groups, have students complete the Guided Reading questions on the Access 4 handout as they read. Let them know that they'll use these answers to help participate in the discussion about the Model. Sample answers for this exercise are located online.

Discuss. After students read the Model text, use the following questions to facilitate a whole group discussion that helps students understand how to determine and analyze the author's point of view in the excerpt. Remind students to follow the rules for collegial discussions and to use academic vocabulary correctly:

1. What's the first step this Model uses to begin looking for the author's point of view? (The Model presents and discusses information presented in the Overview. It notes that *Ten Days in a Mad-House* was originally published as a series of newspaper articles and that Nellie Bly was a reporter. This information suggests that Bly's purpose for writing was to inform readers about the true conditions within the Women's Lunatic Asylum from an insider's perspective.)

2. According to the Model, why is it important that Nellie Bly chose to write her account from the first person point of view? (Bly uses first person to describe her own vivid reactions to being admitted to the asylum. She writes that she "commenced to shake with more than the cold." As the Model states, "such a detail makes Bly a relatable narrator, as it demonstrates that she does not take her assignment lightly.")

3. The Model gives an example of how the author uses signal words and phrases. How can signal words and phrases help readers identify the point of view? (Possible response: Signal words make it clear that the author is expressing an opinion, or point of view.) What signal words and phrases does Bly use to express how she feels

Core Path	Access Path
about the people in the courtroom? (She writes of faces printed with "stories" of "hard lives, abuse and poverty" and people whose expressions often betray "utter helplessness." By contrast, Bly describes the officers in charge as "well-dressed" and "well-fed.") 4. Look back at the passage. Are there other examples of places where the author specifically states her point of view? (Possible response: Judge Duffy sat behind the high desk, wearing a look which seemed to indicate that he was dealing out the milk of human kindness by wholesale. I rather feared I would not get the fate I sought, because of the kindness I saw on every line of his face.)	
	Extend **Mock Interview.** Pair or group students and have them work together to write a mock interview with Nellie Bly about her experiences trying to enter the madhouse. Students should ask questions about why she wanted to go there and answer them as if they were Nelly Bly. They may wish to act out and record their interviews using audio visual equipment, tablets, or mobile devices.

3. YOUR TURN

Core Path	Access Path
Assess and Explain. Have students answer the comprehension questions to test for understanding. Share the explanations for Parts A and B (located online) with your students.	
	Extend **Apply.** Review some of the test-taking tips students have compiled on whiteboards, tablets, or chart paper. Discuss which ones are particularly helpful in answering point of view test questions.

OVERVIEW

In 1887, reporter Nellie Bly went on an undercover assignment for a New York newspaper, the *World*, for which she feigned insanity in order to get committed to the Blackwell Island's Insane Asylum. This excerpt describes how she attempted to get herself sent to the asylum. The Close Read gives students the opportunity to more deeply analyze the author's purpose and author's point of view toward those faced with going to Blackwell Island.

OBJECTIVES

1. Complete a close reading of a passage from an informational text.
2. Practice and apply concrete strategies for identifying author's purpose and author's point of view in an excerpt in an informational text.
3. Participate effectively in a range of conversations and collaborations to express ideas and build upon the ideas of others.
4. Prewrite, plan, and produce clear and coherent writing in response to a prompt.

ELA Common Core Standards:
Reading: Informational Text - RI.8.1, RI.8.4, RI.8.6, RI.8.10
Writing - W.8.4, W.8.5, W.8.6, W.8.10
Speaking & Listening - SL.8.1.A, SL.8.1.C, SL.8.6
Language - L.8.2.C, L.8.4.A, L.8.4.C, L.8.4.D, L.8.6

RESOURCES

Graphic Organizer: Point of View Chart
Ten Days in a Mad-House Vocabulary handout
Access 1 handout (Beginner)
Access 2 handout (Intermediate)
Access 3 handout (Advanced)
Access 4 handout (Approaching)

Please note that excerpts and passages in the StudySync® library, workbooks, and PDFs are intended as touchstones to generate interest in an author's work. The excerpts and passages do not substitute for the reading of entire texts, and StudySync® strongly recommends that teachers and students seek out and purchase the whole literary or informational work in order to experience it as the author intended. Links to online resellers are available in our digital library. In addition, complete works may be ordered through an authorized reseller by filling out and returning to StudySync® the order form enclosed in this workbook.

Teacher's Edition　269

1. INTRODUCTION

Core Path	Access Path
Define and Compare. Project the vocabulary words and definitions onto the board or provide students with a handout, so they can copy the vocabulary into their notebooks. Suggest that students consult general and specialized reference materials, both print and digital, to compare the precise meaning of a specific word with their initial vocabulary predictions from the First Read. Review words that students defined incorrectly to understand why they were unable to use context clues to develop usable definitions.	**Beginner & Intermediate** **Complete the Sentences.** Have students complete the sentence frames on the Access 1 and 2 handouts using the vocabulary words. Point out that some of the words are in the questions and some will be in the answers. Correct answers are located online. **Advanced & Beyond** **Write in Journals.** Have students write a journal entry using all of their vocabulary words. Remind them to write sentences that communicate the meaning of the words they are using. **Approaching** **Complete a Graphic Organizer.** To support students in comparing their vocabulary predictions with the correct meanings, have them complete the graphic organizer on the Access 4 handout to record their original vocabulary predictions. Students will then write sentences using the words.
Review. Have students complete the fill-in-the-blank vocabulary handout for this selection. Answers for the handout are listed online.	
	Extend **Comic Strip.** Have students create a comic strip in which one of the characters uses a vocabulary word in context.
	Extend **Tech Infusion** **Create.** Have students create their comic strip online, using a site such as Make Belief's Comix (http://tinyurl.com/aagmbj).

2. READ

Core Path	Access Path
Model Close Reading. Project the text onto the board and model a close reading of the excerpt using the annotation strategies mentioned below. While modeling annotation strategies, make notes that tie the text to the focus skill and demonstrate what students are looking for as they read. Here is some guidance for you as you annotate for your students:	

- As the Skills lesson that precedes this text makes clear, an author's purpose for writing might be to inform, persuade, or entertain. Many times an author writes for a combination of reasons. We also know that it is often necessary to identify the author's point of view, or perspective, on the subject he or she writes about, and how it is conveyed in the text, in order to fully understand an author's purpose or intention.

- We know that Nellie Bly was a reporter, and that she pretended to be insane in order to get herself admitted to a mental institution. Her intention was to write a series of newspaper articles about conditions inside one of these places. So we know that at least one of her purposes for writing was to inform readers.

- Let's skip down to the nineteenth paragraph. How does Nellie Bly describe the "strange crowd" that surrounds her? (She mentions "poorly dressed men and women with stories printed on their faces of hard lives, abuse and poverty.") What does she write about the police officers watching this scene? (They watch the scene "passively and almost indifferently." These people are just "one more unfortunate added to a long list which had long since ceased to be of any interest or concern to them.") This suggests that Nellie Bly is sympathetic to the people held in these mental institutions. It is a clue that one of the purposes for Bly's articles is to persuade people to share the sympathy she feels.

Core Path	Access Path
Read and Annotate. Read the Skills Focus questions as a class, so your students know what they should pay close attention to as they read. Then have students read and annotate the excerpt. Ask students to use the annotation tool as they read to:	**Note:** While on grade-level students are reading and annotating, work one-on-one or in small groups with Beginning, Intermediate, Advanced, and Approaching students to support them as they read and annotate the text.

Core Path

Read and Annotate. Read the Skills Focus questions as a class, so your students know what they should pay close attention to as they read. Then have students read and annotate the excerpt. Ask students to use the annotation tool as they read to:

1. respond to the Skills Focus section

2. ask questions

3. make connections between Nellie Bly's purpose for writing and her point of view.

4. identify key information, events, and points of view

5. note unfamiliar vocabulary

6. capture their reactions to the events in the text

As they reread the text, remind students to use the comprehension strategy of Summarizing that they learned in the First Read.

Discuss. After students have read the text, use the sample responses to the Skills Focus questions online to discuss the reading and the process of searching for the author's purpose and author's point of view. Make sure that students have acquired and accurately use academic-specific words and phrases related to the skill, and demonstrate a command of formal English appropriate to the discussion.

Access Path

Note: While on grade-level students are reading and annotating, work one-on-one or in small groups with Beginning, Intermediate, Advanced, and Approaching students to support them as they read and annotate the text.

Beginner
Summary Choice. In small groups, have students complete the Summary Choice exercise on the Access 1 handout. Encourage students to then use the Summary Choice handouts to help them annotate the text and answer the Skills Focus questions.

Intermediate & Advanced
Summary Choice. In pairs, have students complete the Summary Choice exercise in the Access 2 and 3 handouts. When annotating the text and answering the Skills Focus questions, those students who need more support can use the completed Summary Choice exercise.

Approaching
Summary Choice. In small groups, have students complete the Summary Choice exercise on the Access 4 handout. Encourage students to then use the Summary Choice handouts to help them annotate the text and answer the Skills Focus questions.

Extend
Pair and Share. In small groups or pairs, ask students to share and discuss their annotations with a focus on the author's point of view.

You can provide students with questions to guide their discussion:

1. What was the author's opinion of the judge and the other officials she met? Cite specific textual evidence to support your statements.

2. Given your understanding of point of view and a second reading of the text, what do you think the author's opinion of the mental health system is? Cite specific textual evidence to support your statements.

Core Path	Access Path
	Extend **Other Points of View.** Have students look for evidence showing the opinions of the other characters in the text about the author. Encourage them to work with partners to identify the opinions of one of these: • The people in the street • The judge • Mrs. Stanard • The court officials In discussion, have students provide evidence from the text that supports their interpretation of the characters' opinions.

3. WRITE

Core Path	Access Path
Prewrite and Plan. Read the prompt as a class and ask students to brainstorm their reactions to Nellie Bly's point of view and purpose for writing in *Ten Days in a Mad-House*. Students can brainstorm together either as a class or in small groups to begin planning their responses, and discuss how Bly uses humor, dramatic irony, and descriptive adjectives to reveal her opinions. Remind students to look at the excerpt and their annotations to find textual evidence to support their ideas.	**Beginner, Intermediate & Advanced** **Answer and Discuss.** Have students complete the prewriting questions on the Access 1, 2, and 3 handouts and then explain their answers to a partner before they write. **Approaching** **Answer Prewriting Questions.** Work with students as a group to complete the prewriting questions on the Access 4 handout to summarize their thoughts before they write.
Discuss. Project these instructions for the peer review onto the board and review them with your class, so they know what they are looking for when they begin to provide their classmates with feedback: • Has the writer identified the author's point of view about the plight of the poor and mentally ill and the attitude of the officials toward these people? • Has the writer explained how the author's use of humor, dramatic irony, and descriptive adjectives reveals her point of view? • What sort of evidence did the writer use from the text to support his or her writing?	

Core Path	Access Path
• How well does the writer explain how that evidence supports his or her arguments? • Does the writer use standard grammar and punctuation? What weak spots might need to be addressed? • What specific suggestions can you make to help the writer improve the response? • What thing(s) does this paper do especially well? Be sure to tell the writer what he or she did well and what he or she needs to work on. Remember that your comments are most useful when they are constructive. After you've looked at the peer review instructions, review the rubric with students before they begin writing. Allow time for students to briefly raise and discuss questions they may have about the peer review instructions and the rubric. Tell students how many peer reviews they will need to complete once they submit their writing.	
Write. Ask students to complete the writing assignment using textual evidence to support their answers. If possible, have students use technology to produce and publish their writing. Once they have completed their writing, they should click "Submit."	
Review. Once students complete their writing assignment, they should submit substantive feedback to two peers. If possible, have students use technology to interact and collaborate with others.	

OVERVIEW

The excerpt from *Ten Days in a Mad-House* reveals the problem of mental illness and its treatments in the United States in the late nineteenth century. The subject of mental illness is a major feature of many stories and movies of suspense. Around the world and for many centuries, the victims of mental illness have been treated as people to be feared, punished, or hidden away. To develop a better understanding of mental illness, students will learn about the history of mental health care and the advances that have been made over the years.

OBJECTIVES

1. Explore background information about the history of the treatment of mental illness.
2. Research using hyperlinks to a range of information about mental illness, treatment options, and the effectiveness of those options.

ELA Common Core Standards:
Reading: Informational Text - RI.8.1, RI.8.6
Writing - W.8.1.A, W.8.5, W.8.6
Speaking & Listening - SL.8.1.A, SL.8.1.C, SL.8.1.D

RESOURCES

Access 1 handout (Beginner)
Access 2 handout (Intermediate)
Access 4 handout (Approaching)

Please note that excerpts and passages in the StudySync® library, workbooks, and PDFs are intended as touchstones to generate interest in an author's work. The excerpts and passages do not substitute for the reading of entire texts, and StudySync® strongly recommends that teachers and students seek out and purchase the whole literary or informational work in order to experience it as the author intended. Links to online resellers are available in our digital library. In addition, complete works may be ordered through an authorized reseller by filling out and returning to StudySync® the order form enclosed in this workbook.

Teacher's Edition   275

TITLE/DRIVING QUESTION

Core Path	Access Path
Discuss. As a class read aloud the title and driving question for this Blast. These correspond to the title/driving question for the unit as a whole. Ask students what they know about the way mental students what they know about the way mental health problems were treated in the past. Do they have a sense of how treatments for mental illness have changed over time? Remind students that they should not immediately reply to this question. They'll be returning to this question and responding after they've read the Background and some of the Research Links.	**English Learners All Levels & Approaching Discuss Visuals.** As a class, view the following visuals to learn about how those with mental health problems were treated in the past: Timeline: Treatments for Mental Illness: http://tinyurl.com/mvprslk Images from the U.S. National Library of Medicine: http://tinyurl.com/n38gkzm http://tinyurl.com/ng86jkd Discuss the visuals by prompting students with the following questions: • How can you see the progression of mental health problems from the past to the present? What do you notice? • What does the image of Mrs. Packard suggest? How does it relate to *Ten Days in a Mad-House*? • What does the image of the man suggest about people's knowledge of cures?
Draft. In their notebooks or on scrap paper, have students draft their initial responses to the driving question. This will provide them with a baseline response that they will be altering as they gain more information about the topic in the Background and Research Links sections of the assignment.	**Beginner & Intermediate Draft with Sentence Frame.** When drafting their initial response to the driving questions, have students refer to this Blast sentence frame on their Access 1 and 2 handouts: • Mental health care can continue to improve by __ _____ _____. Point out that the introductory clause "Mental health care can continue to improve" borrows language directly from the Blast driving question to provide a response.

BACKGROUND

Core Path	Access Path
Read. Have students read the Blast Background to provide context for the driving question.	**Beginner & Intermediate** **Read with Support.** Have students read the Blast Background to provide context for the driving question. When they encounter unfamiliar words or phrases, have students refer to the glossary on their Access 1 and 2 handouts. If there are unfamiliar words that are not included in their glossary, encourage students to check a dictionary or online reference tool, like http://tinyurl.com/3qe7.
	Approaching **Read and Summarize.** Have students read the Blast Background to provide context for the driving question. As they read, ask students to complete the fill-in-the-blank summary of the Background provided on their Access 4 handout. When they encounter unfamiliar words or phrases, have students refer to the glossary on their Access 4 handout.
Discuss. Pair students and have them answer the following questions. 1. Why do you think people in the Middle Ages and after isolated or mistreated those who were mentally ill? (Because they didn't understand what was wrong with them; they were afraid.) 2. In what way were psychiatric hospitals both a good and a bad idea? (They provided a place where the mentally ill could be treated, but they also increased isolation and became overcrowded, leading to abuse and neglect.) 3. What was the result of de-institutionalization? (It led to homelessness for many of the mentally ill.) 4. How have treatments for mental illness changed over the last hundred years? Has it been enough? (Medications and talk therapies have been developed, but there is still more to do.)	**Beginner** **Discuss.** Pair Beginning with more proficient readers and have them use the dialogue starter on their Access 1 handout to discuss the topic. Advise them to return to the dialogue and switch roles if they get stuck. **Intermediate** **Discuss.** Pair Intermediate with more proficient readers and have them use the dialogue starter on their Access 2 handout to discuss the topic. Advise them to return to the dialogue and switch roles if they get stuck. If their conversation is progressing smoothly, encourage them to continue the discussion beyond the dialogue starter sheet. They can expand their conversations to discuss ways mental health care can continue to improve.

Core Path	Access Path

Brainstorm. Remind students about the driving question for this Blast: "How can mental health care continue to improve?"

In their notebooks, have students make three columns. They will make some inferences based on the information presented in the Background. In the first column, have students list their ideas of what they think "mental illness" means and examples of symptoms as they understand them. In the second column, students can list possible sources of mental illness based on what they may have read about or learned. In the third column, list ideas to explain why it would be important to find treatments for mental illness. Here's an example of how the chart might look:

What is mental illness?	What might cause mental illness?	Why is it important to treat mental illness?
Mental illness has to do with the way the brain works. I know that sometimes people get depressed or sad, but if you are so sad it makes it impossible to live normally, that is mental illness.	I've read about war veterans who have PTSD, which means that war caused them to lose their sense of themselves and make them feel very depressed.	Without getting help, a mentally ill person would miss out on feeling good about his or her life, enjoying things. An ill person might even commit suicide.

RESEARCH LINKS

Core Path	Access Path
Examine and Explore. Use these questions to guide students' exploration of the Research Links: 1. Ask students to look at "Dorothea Dix Pleads for a State Mental Hospital." Why were mentally ill people put in prisons and jails? (for security) How were the mentally ill treated in jails and poor-houses? (often in chains or confined in groups, some worse than others) Why does Dorothea Dix argue that mental hospitals are crucial? (a "blessing and a benefit"; to give them better treatment) 2. Have students read the article, "Why Not to Shut Down a Mental Hospital." As a class discuss the main reasons for closing mental institutions as well as the three negative consequences of doing so on both the patients and society as a whole. What is motivating the decision to shut down mental hospitals? (saving money, $12.5 million) What happens to patients when a mental hospital closes? (disrupts treatment; families cannot be near loved ones; patients may end up in prison) 3. Have students explore "How Do We Cure Mental Illness?" and "The Future of Treatment." Given your understanding of these two pieces, do you think there is a "cure" for mental illness? Debate this in small groups or as a class.	

	Extend
	Research, Discuss and Present.
	
	1. Assign each group one link to explore in depth.
	
	2. Ask them to discuss the information:
	    a. What are the key points?
	    b. What inferences did you make as you read?
	    c. What did you learn about this topic from reading this research?
	    d. How did this help you to better understand the topic?
	    e. What questions does your group have after exploring this link?
	
	Allow students time to informally present what they learned.

QUIKPOLL

Core Path	Access Path
Participate. Answer the poll question. Have students discuss the reasons for their answers. Students should refer to evidence from the Background and Research Links to defend their answer.	

NUMBER CRUNCH

Core Path	Access Path
Predict, Discuss and Click. Before students click on the number, break them into pairs and have them make predictions about what they think the number is related to. After they've clicked the number, ask students if they are surprised by the revealed information.	

CREATE YOUR BLAST

Core Path	Access Path
Blast. Ask students to answer the Blast question in 140 characters.	**Beginner** **Blast with Support.** Have students refer back to the sentence frame on their Access 1 handout that they used to create their original Blast draft. Ask them to use this frame to write and enter their final Blast. **Intermediate** **Blast with Support.** Have students attempt to draft their Blast without the sentence frame on their Access 2 handout. If students struggle to compose their Blast draft without the sentence frame, remind them to reference it for support.

Core Path	Access Path
	Beyond **Write a Claim.** Ask students to use their answer to the poll question to write a strong claim that could be used as the foundation for a piece of argumentative writing. Once students have written their claims, ask them to read the claims to a small group of their peers. This activity will provide them practice writing claims, as well as expose them to claims written by their peers.
Review. After students have completed their own Blasts, ask them to review the Blasts of their peers and provide feedback. If possible, have students use technology to present information and ideas efficiently as well as to interact and collaborate with others.	**Extend** **Discuss.** As a whole class or in groups, identify a few strong Blasts and discuss what made those responses so powerful. As a group, analyze and discuss what characteristics make a Blast interesting or effective.
	Extend **Revise.** Resend a second version of this Blast assignment to your students and have them submit revised versions of their original Blasts. Do the same responses make the Top 10? How have the answers improved from the first submissions?

OVERVIEW

This short story, "The Tell-Tale Heart" by Edgar Allan Poe, is a Gothic tale of psychological horror in which a demented first-person narrator recounts his murder of an old man to satisfy his need to rid himself of scrutiny from the old man's "evil eye." The First Read gives students the opportunity to experience making inferences when dealing with an unreliable first-person narrator.

OBJECTIVES

1. Perform an initial reading of a text and demonstrate comprehension by responding to short analysis and inference questions with textual evidence.
2. Practice defining vocabulary words using context.
3. Participate effectively in a range of conversations and collaborations to express ideas and build upon the ideas of others.

ELA Common Core Standards:

Reading: Literature - RL.8.1, RL.8.10
Writing - W.8.10
Speaking & Listening - SL.8.1.A, SL.8.1.B, SL.8.1.C, SL.8.1.D, SL.8.2, SL.8.6
Language - L.8.1.C, L.8.4.A, L.8.4.B, L.8.4.D, L.8.6

RESOURCES

Grammar handout: Verb Moods
Access 1 handout (Beginner)
Access 2 handout (Intermediate)
Access 3 handout (Advanced)
Access 4 handout (Approaching)

ACCESS COMPLEX TEXT

Edgar Allan Poe's Gothic short story "The Tell-Tale Heart" is set in the home of the story's narrator as he comes to entertain three police officers who have been called by a neighbor in response to a shriek heard during the night. In the end, Poe's narrator confesses to killing an old man in his care because he becomes convinced that officers can hear the dead man's heart beating through the floorboards. The first-person point of view and the narrator's gradual confession and descent into madness are reflected in the challenges of the text. To help students understand the narrator's unfolding mental state, use the following ideas to provide scaffolded instruction for an initial reading of the more complex features of this text.

- **Organization** - The text is organized so as to gradually reveal the narrator's murder of the old man. The text's first-person point of view may challenge some students as the narrator alternates between external description and internal thought. Readers will need to distinguish between fact and perception.

- **Sentence Structure** - Long sentences are broken by dashes and capital letters to indicate the narrator's anxious, fragmented thinking. In addition, point out to students that Poe is using nonstandard font, punctuation, and other devices as visual cues to the narrator's emotional state. While this kind of style is evident today in text messages and other communications, Poe's use of these devices was quite innovative at the time..

- **Specific Vocabulary** - Difficult vocabulary, such as unperceived and over-acuteness, may present a challenge to readers. Remind readers to use context clues, as well as knowledge of Greek and Latin roots and affixes, to help them define unknown words. When needed, students should use a print or digital resource to help them.

1. INTRODUCTION

Core Path	Access Path
Watch. As a class, watch the video preview of "The Tell-Tale Heart." Discuss with students how the graphics and audio features, including music, provide context for the selection they are about to read and contribute to the mood and tone.	**English Learners All Levels** **Fill in the Blanks.** Ask students to use their Access 1, 2, and 3 handouts to fill in the blanks of the transcript for the preview's voiceover as they watch the preview along with their classmates. Answers are located online.

Please note that excerpts and passages in the StudySync® library, workbooks, and PDFs are intended as touchstones to generate interest in an author's work. The excerpts and passages do not substitute for the reading of entire texts, and StudySync® strongly recommends that teachers and students seek out and purchase the whole literary or informational work in order to experience it as the author intended. Links to online resellers are available in our digital library. In addition, complete works may be ordered through an authorized reseller by filling out and returning to StudySync® the order form enclosed in this workbook.

Teacher's Edition **283**

Core Path	Access Path
Read and Listen. Individually or as a class, read and listen to the Introduction for "The Tell-Tale Heart." The Introduction provides context for this classic tale of horror and suspense.	**English Learners All Levels & Approaching** **Read and Listen.** Ask students to read and listen to the Introduction for "The Tell-Tale Heart." Have them refer to the vocabulary listing on their Access 1, 2, 3, and 4 handouts for definitions of key vocabulary terms. If there are unfamiliar words that are not included in their glossary, encourage students to check a dictionary or online reference tool, like http://tinyurl.com/6ytby.

Build Background. To prepare to enter the world of master storyteller Edgar Allan Poe, have students research the author as well as the genre.

1. Divide the class into groups. Have one group of your students investigate the genre of Gothic fiction—when it emerged, who its major authors were, and what its major characteristics were. Have the second group research Poe's life and work.

2. Have each group make a list of three to five interesting facts about their subjects to share with the class. Use this as a basis for a class discussion. What have they learned that is interesting or surprising?

3. Finally, ask your students if they can think of any contemporary examples of Gothic fiction (TV, movies, books). Or, have them choose a contemporary story (movie, TV show) and consider how they could "Gothify" it by inserting characteristics of Gothic fiction into it.

4. Have them share their ideas with the class.

English Learners All Levels & Approaching **Select.** Have students complete the Select activity on the Access 1, 2, 3, and 4 handouts, making predictions about Gothic fiction based on the Introduction. Answers are located online.

Extend
Make Predictions. Based on the Introduction, ask students to make predictions about the themes they would expect to encounter in this text. In what way would a first-person narrator contribute to the need for the reader to make inferences?

Core Path	Access Path
	Extend **Discuss the Introduction.** After reading the Introduction, use the information provided to facilitate a pre-reading discussion to get students thinking about the plot and themes in "The Tell-Tale Heart." 1. Have you ever heard a character in a play or in a poem deliver a monologue? 2. Does it surprise you that an author might use the short story as a dramatic monologue? Explain. 3. What some elements of "horror" and "suspense" associated with Gothic stories?

2. READ

Core Path	Access Path
Make Predictions about Vocabulary. There are six bold vocabulary words in the text. As students read the text, ask them to make predictions about what they think each bold vocabulary word means based on the context clues in the sentence. If you are in a low tech classroom, ask students to record their predictions in their notes, so they can be easily referenced in class. If your students have access to technology, they can use the built in annotation tool to make their predictions. It might be helpful to model this for students before they begin the reading. Either using the board or projecting the actual test, focus in on the sentence that uses the word "dissimulation": • You should have seen how wisely I proceeded—with what caution—with what foresight, with what **dissimulation**, I went to work! Model for the class how to use the overall structure and meaning of the sentence and the sentences around it, the word's position, and other clues to define the unfamiliar vocabulary word. In this case, point out these context keys: 1. Look at the structure of the sentence. Who is the narrator talking about? (himself) We also know that he's describing how he "went to work" on something.	**Note:** This exercise, which extends vocabulary instruction, should be completed when the class shifts from whole group instruction to individual work during the "Read and Annotate" exercise. **Beginner, Intermediate, & Approaching Pair Practice.** 1. Pair Beginning, Intermediate, and Approaching students with more proficient readers. 2. Give the less-proficient students an additional sentence that contains a new vocabulary word. 3. Ask those students to complete a Think Aloud using the teacher-led Make Predictions about Vocabulary activity as a model, while the proficient student actively listens. 4. The students should use the context clues in the sentence to try to determine the meaning of the new vocabulary word. 5. After the less-proficient student has completed the Think Aloud and made a prediction about the word's meaning, allow time for the proficient reader to add his/her own thoughts and clarify any points of confusion.

Please note that excerpts and passages in the StudySync® library, workbooks, and PDFs are intended as touchstones to generate interest in an author's work. The excerpts and passages do not substitute for the reading of entire texts, and StudySync® strongly recommends that teachers and students seek out and purchase the whole literary or informational work in order to experience it as the author intended. Links to online resellers are available in our digital library. In addition, complete works may be ordered through an authorized reseller by filling out and returning to StudySync® the order form enclosed in this workbook.

Teacher's Edition   **285**

Core Path	Access Path
2. Look at the other parts of the sentence as well: count the number of times he uses the word "with." (three) The repetition of prepositional phrases using "with" could be used to show three similar ideas or three separate but equally important ideas. We know that "caution" and "foresight" are different, since one means carefulness and the other means planning. This tells us that "dissimulation" probably means something different as well. 3. If we look to the sentence that follows, we see that the narrator claims that he was "never kinder to the old man than during the whole week before [he] killed him" and so we see that the narrator is pretending to be nice to the old man. Since we know that neither "caution" or "foresight" relate to lying or pretending, we can conclude that "dissimulation" has to do with pretending or bluffing. Remind students that they can check for precise meanings as well as pronunciations in a dictionary.	6. Once they've completed this Think Aloud, encourage them to use a dictionary to confirm the definition of the new vocabulary word. Have them refer to the vocabulary listing on their Access handouts 1, 2, and 3 for definitions of key vocabulary terms in the text. Encourage them to add any additional vocabulary words or idioms they find in the text and look up definitions for those words and idioms online or in a dictionary.
Model Reading Comprehension Strategy. Before students begin reading, explain that asking and answering questions is just what Sherlock Holmes does when he has a case—it's the perfect strategy when you read a mystery or suspense story, because it helps you keep track of the clues and make accurate predictions. Model the reading comprehension strategy of asking and answering questions by using this Think Aloud that talks students through the first paragraph of the story: • The narrator begins by asking "why WILL you say that I am mad?" In Poe's time, *mad* meant *insane*. Is the narrator in a mental hospital? Is he under restraint? To whom is he speaking? • In the second sentence, the narrator says "the disease had sharpened my senses." So he is sick in some way. This makes me say yes to my earlier question; he probably is in a mental hospital.	**Note:** This exercise, which extends vocabulary instruction, should be completed when the class shifts from whole group instruction to individual work during the "Read and Annotate" exercise. **Beginner, Intermediate & Approaching Asking & Answering Questions.** 1. To practice asking and answering questions, have students listen to the audio version of "The Tell-Tale Heart." Pause the audio after the first paragraph. Have them write down a question they have about the text in their Access 1, 2, and 4 handouts. If students struggle to come up with one, prompt them by asking: *Why is the narrator nervous? Is the narrator truly mad?*

Core Path	Access Path
• When the narrator says he hears things in heaven and hell, this is still more evidence that he is mentally and emotionally unbalanced. I think the person he's speaking to is probably a doctor or maybe a policeman.	2. Resume the audio, pausing periodically to allow students to ask new questions as well as take notes on their Access handouts, as clues to their previous questions arise. Offer guidance to help them notice answers, such as: *In paragraph 3 the narrator says that his dissimulation means he is not mad.* 3. Once all their questions have been answered, pair students with more proficient readers and ask them to discuss the strategies they used. What led you to ask certain questions? What details answered your questions? Encourage groups to share their findings with the class.

Read and Annotate. Direct students to independently read and annotate the excerpt. Before they begin, have them read the text aloud or play the voiceover (using either the Audio or the Audio Text Highlight tool). Ask students to use the annotation tool as they read to:

1. use context clues to analyze and determine the meaning of the bolded vocabulary terms

2. ask questions about passages of the text that may be unclear or unresolved

3. identify key details, events, characters, and connections between them

4. note unfamiliar vocabulary

5. capture reactions to the events

Beginner
Coach the Reading. While other students read, annotate, and discuss the text independently, work with Beginning students, listening to the audio of the text and pausing periodically or when any student has a question. Coach students in articulating their questions for the group and in highlighting and annotating the text. Have students use the Annotation Guide in the Access 1 handout to support them as they highlight and annotate the text.

For further support, ask questions about the text such as:

• Is there anything about the story that you don't understand?

• What do you think will happen to narrator?

• Why do you think "The Tell-Tale Heart" is the title of the story?

Intermediate
Listen to the Audio. Have these students listen to the audio of the text and use the definitions on the Access 2 handout to help them with words or idioms that may be unfamiliar. If students need help with annotating the text, have them use the Annotation Guide on the Access 2 handout. After working with the Beginning students, you may wish to check this group's progress and provide support as needed.

Core Path	Access Path
	Advanced **Pair with Proficient Peers.** Have Advanced students work with English proficient peers to read, annotate, and discuss the text. Have students use the Annotation Guide in the Access 3 handout to support them as they highlight and annotate the text. Encourage them to listen to the audio of the text if needed. **Approaching** **Use the Annotation Guide.** Have students use the Annotation Guide in the Access 4 handout to support them as they highlight and annotate the text.
Discuss. In small groups or pairs, have students discuss the questions and inferences they made while reading. Remind students to follow guidelines for collegial conversations. 1. What does the narrator want the reader to understand about his state of mind? (The narrator wants the reader to understand that he is sane and not mad.) 2. What evidence does the narrator provide to convince the reader of his sanity? (The narrator notes that his sense of hearing was heightened and that he performed each action cautiously.) 3. Why didn't the narrator commit the murder before the eighth night? What happened on the eighth night that provoked the narrator to finally act? (The narrator could not commit the murder on the first seven nights because he could not see the "vulture eye" of the old man. He finally sees the eye on the eighth night, and this spurs the narrator into action.) 4. How does the narrator kill the old man? (The narrator suffocates the old man with the mattress from his bed.) 5. What does narrator do with the old man's dead body? (The narrator hides the body beneath some floor boards in the old man's bedroom.)	**English Learners All Levels & Approaching** Use the extra time while on- and beyond- grade-level students are discussing their first reads of the text to work individually and in small groups with English Learners and Approaching readers as previously outlined. Should those students complete their first reads quickly, integrate them into the on- and beyond- grade-level discussion groups. Otherwise English Learners and Approaching readers will be given an opportunity to participate in text discussions with their peers later in the lesson.

Core Path	Access Path
6. Why does the narrator think the police are mocking him? (The narrator thinks if he can hear the old man's heartbeat getting louder and louder, then so can the police. However, the officers seem to be pretending that they don't hear the sound. The narrator becomes increasingly paranoid and thinks the police are mocking him.)	
7. Why does the narrator confess to the crime at the end of the story? (As the sound of the heartbeat grows louder and louder in the narrator's mind, he becomes more and more outraged that the police are mocking him by not acknowledging that they can hear it too.)	

(G) **Grammar, Usage, and Mechanics.** Distribute the Grammar handout: Verb Moods. Review with students the use of verb moods as explained in the handout. Then have students complete the practice exercise. (Answers for the practice exercise appear online.) Finally, encourage students to apply what they have learned by analyzing the use of the verb moods in "The Tell-Tale Heart." Ask students:

1. What verb mood does Poe use throughout the first paragraph? (imperative mood)

2. Rewrite a passage from the first paragraph using subjunctive mood. How does it alter the meaning? (Sample answer: "If the disease had sharpened, not destroyed or dulled, my senses, then above all, my hearing would be acute." Using the subjunctive mood weakens the narrator's point significantly, as he is arguing, without a doubt, that he is sane.)

3. How does the subjunctive mood function in writing? (to express an idea that is contrary to fact, is doubtful or uncertain, or is an assumption or a wish)

Beginner & Intermediate
Work with the Teacher. Remind these students that the mood of a verb refers to the manner in which a thought is expressed.

Write the following statement on the board:
Why did you do that?
Ask: *What is the verb mood?* (indicative)

Ask students what word in the sentence below is an indicative verb.
She ran to the store. (ran)

Allow time for students to share their answers. Then have these students participate in the short lesson above with Approaching students. Then work with them to complete the Grammar handout.

Advanced & Beyond
Extend the Search. Challenge these students to work in pairs or small groups to find the different types of verb moods in the text.

Core Path	Access Path
4. How would use of the subjunctive mood throughout the first paragraph of "The Tell-Tale Heart" undermine one of the central ideas of the first paragraph? (Poe's narrator is trying to convince his readers that he is not mad, that he absolutely did witness all that he is about to describe. The use of the subjunctive mood, which would introduce doubt into his retelling of the events, would undermine his point that he is not mad.)	**Approaching** **Analyze an example.** If students need more support identifying verb moods, call their attention to these words in paragraph 2: *It is impossible to say how first the idea entered my brain, but, once conceived, it haunted me day and night.* Ask: *What is the verb mood?* subjunctive verb (is) Have students locate a subjunctive verb in paragraph 2. Then have students complete the Grammar handout.
	Extend **Identify and Define.** After reading the text, compile a list of additional vocabulary words. Ask students to reference their annotations and share any vocabulary words that were unfamiliar. 1. As a class, compile a list of unknown words on the board. 2. In small groups, ask students to make predictions about they think these words mean based on how they are used in the sentence. Note: Students will need access to StudySync to read the words in context and make predictions. 3. Member of each group should work together using dictionaries or devices to define the words and write the definitions in their notebooks.
	Extend **Tech Infusion** **Record.** Use a voice recording app (Voice Memo on the iPhone or Smart Voice Recorder for Androids) or VoiceThread (https://voicethread.com) to capture the answers given by the members in each group or pair.

3. SYNCTV

Core Path	Access Path
Watch. As a class, watch the SyncTV video on "The Tell-Tale Heart." Pause the video at these key moments to discuss the information with your students:	**Beginner & Intermediate** **Analyze the Discussion.** Have students use the Analyze the Discussion guide in the Access 1 and 2 handouts to identify key points in the discussion and the evidence the students use to determine those points. Sample answers are located online.
1. 0:52 – Katie asks, "So, what exactly is an unreliable narrator?" From what point of view does the narrator tell the story? How does this point of view affect the reliability of the narrator's story?	**Advanced** **Narrators.** Have students discuss and complete the Narrators chart on the Access 3 handout, referring back to the SyncTV video as needed to clarify their answers. Sample answers appear online.
2. 2:34 – Olivia says, "Yeah, or maybe he's trying to convince himself that he's awesome, which might mean he is actually insecure." Do you agree or disagree with Olivia's interpretation? Why or why not?	**Approaching** **Analyze the Discussion.** Have students complete the chart on the Access 4 handout by listing textual evidence cited by the students in the video. Sample answers are located online.
3. 4:48 – Katie comments, "It's really interesting how the narrative focuses on these two body parts—the eye and the heart." What reasons do the students give to explain the narrator's focus on these two symbols? What other symbolic objects appear in the story?	
	Extend **SyncTV-Style Discussion.** Place students into small groups and have each group discuss one of the prompts provided below. Remind students to model their discussions after the SyncTV episodes they have seen. Stress the importance of citing textual evidence in their conversations to support their ideas. Discussion prompt: 1. The narrator is frightened by the old man's eye. Think of an image that has frightened you, whether from a picture, movie, or something you saw in person. Describe the image, how you first saw it, and why you found it scary. 2. If you were a lawyer, how would you go about defending or prosecuting the narrator in the story? What argument would you use? What evidence would you cite?

Please note that excerpts and passages in the StudySync® library, workbooks, and PDFs are intended as touchstones to generate interest in an author's work. The excerpts and passages do not substitute for the reading of entire texts, and StudySync® strongly recommends that teachers and students seek out and purchase the whole literary or informational work in order to experience it as the author intended. Links to online resellers are available in our digital library. In addition, complete works may be ordered through an authorized reseller by filling out and returning to StudySync® the order form enclosed in this workbook.

Teacher's Edition   **291**

4. THINK

Core Path	Access Path
Answer and Discuss. Have students complete the Think questions and then use the peer review instructions and rubric to complete the peer reviews. Refer to the sample answers online to discuss responses with your students. Remind students to follow guidelines for collegial discussions.	**Beginner & Intermediate** **Sentence Frames.** Have students use the sentence frames on the Access 1 and 2 handouts to support their responses to the Think questions. If necessary, distribute sentence frames to Advanced students as well. **Approaching** **Find the Evidence.** Have students use Find the Evidence on the Access 4 handout to help them identify the evidence needed to answer the questions.
	Extend **Closing Arguments.** Organize students into pairs and have each member chose to be the defending attorney or prosecutor in the trial of the narrator of "The Tell-Tale Heart." Students must prepare a closing statement based on one of the two situations listed below. Closing argument prompts: 1. Prosecutor's Closing Statement: The narrator is guilty of premeditated murder. 2. Defendant Attorney's Closing Statement: The narrator is not guilty of premeditated murder by reason of insanity. Encourage students to include supporting details from the story as well as reasonable inferences to support the claim made in their closing argument. Have students deliver their closing statement to a small group of their peers acting as "jurors." This activity will provide student with practice in writing arguments to support claims. If time permits, have "jurors" decide to convict or acquit the narrator based on the closing statements.
	Extend **Tech Infusion** **Record.** Use a voice recording app (Voice Memo on the iPhone or Smart Voice Recorder for Androids) or VoiceThread (http://tinyurl.com/4m389hy) to capture each student's closing argument.

OVERVIEW

Students may find it challenging to move beyond what is directly stated in a text to make inferences. This lesson provides follow-up questions and useful enrichments to help teachers guide students toward making inferences and citing textual evidence to support them.

OBJECTIVES

1. Learn the definition of textual evidence.
2. Practice using concrete strategies for identifying textual evidence.
3. Participate effectively in a range of conversations and collaborations to express ideas and build upon the ideas of others.

ELA Common Core Standards:
Reading: Literature - RL.8.1
Speaking & Listening - SL.8.1.A, SL.8.1.B, SL.8.1.C, SL.8.1.D, SL.8.2
Language - L.8.6

RESOURCES

Access 1 handout (Beginner)
Access 2 handout (Intermediate)
Access 3 handout (Advanced)
Access 4 handout (Approaching)

Please note that excerpts and passages in the StudySync® library, workbooks, and PDFs are intended as touchstones to generate interest in an author's work. The excerpts and passages do not substitute for the reading of entire texts, and StudySync® strongly recommends that teachers and students seek out and purchase the whole literary or informational work in order to experience it as the author intended. Links to online resellers are available in our digital library. In addition, complete works may be ordered through an authorized reseller by filling out and returning to StudySync® the order form enclosed in this workbook.

Teacher's Edition   293

1. DEFINE

Core Path	Access Path
Watch. Watch the Concept Definition video on textual evidence with your students. Make sure students understand the purpose of finding textual evidence in an informational or literary text, as well as the difference between explicit and inferred evidence. Pause the video at these key moments to discuss the information with your students: 1. 0:50 - Why aren't authors always as explicit as possible in stating their meaning or purpose? Why do you think they often leave evidence to be inferred? 2. 1:11 - How can readers be sure if an inference is valid? Think of a few ways to test the validity of an inference, in addition to the examples given in the video. 3. 1:49 - Why is inference an important skill when reading both informational and literary works? How can this skill help us deepen our understanding of works in both genres?	**English Learners All Levels & Approaching** **Match.** Have students complete the matching exercise on the Access 1, 2, 3, and 4 handouts as they watch the video. Answers are located online.
Read and Discuss. After watching the Concept Definition video, have students read the definition of textual evidence. Either in small groups or as a whole class, use these questions to spur discussion among your students about finding textual evidence to make inferences, making sure they follow the rules for collegial discussions, use academic language correctly, and respond to the questions and comments of others in the class with relevant evidence, observations, and ideas: 1. Why do readers sometimes need to make inferences? (Authors do not always state directly in a text everything they want readers to know.)	**Beginner & Approaching** **Complete a Chart.** To prepare students to participate in the discussion, have them complete the chart on the Access 1 and 4 handouts as they read the definition. The correct answers are located online. **Intermediate & Advanced** **Discuss Prompts.** To help these students participate in the discussion, prompt them with questions that can be answered with a few words, such as: • Another word for inference is _____. (guess) • What can readers use to understand a text? (textual evidence) • What can readers use as textual evidence? (words, pictures, characters)

Core Path	Access Path
2. How can using what you know help you make an inference or a reasonable guess? (Using what you already know, or your own prior knowledge, can help you make an inference about a situation or event. For example, if you know that characters are in a big city, and the author refers to a "towering stone giant 110 stories tall," you might infer that the author is referring to a tall building even if the author doesn't use the word "building." This is because you know tall buildings are often made of stone and are located in big cities.) 3. Why is locating textual evidence important when making an inference? (Textual evidence is used to support any inferences a reader makes. When analyzing and interpreting a text, being able to support inferences by citing text evidence is an important part of a literary analysis.) 4. Describe a time you made an inference, either when reading or watching a movie or TV show. Explain how you made it. (Answers will vary.)	**Beyond** **Discuss.** Have students select a book they've read and describe textual evidence they could use to understand the text. Compile a list of examples. Have students discuss how the textual evidence of each work affects how the reader understands the text. Write examples on the board.
	Extend **Play Detective.** Have students watch a scene from a suspenseful TV show or detective series, or from a movie based on these genres. Ask them to make inferences about what they see happening and what they think is actually happening. Discuss how the writer and director reveal clues to spark viewers' involvement. Have students discuss the clues they used to make inferences. Point out that they can apply these same strategies when they read.
	Extend **Blast.** Create a Blast and ask students to "blast out" the definition of making inferences in their own words. Use the poll question to ask students why they think that authors don't always state everything directly.

2. MODEL

Core Path	Access Path
Read and Annotate. Have students independently read the Model section. As they read, ask students to use the annotation tool to: • highlight key points • ask questions • identify places where the Model is applying the strategies laid out in the Identification and Application section on textual evidence.	**Note:** During this portion of the lesson, instruction shifts from whole group to individual work. Use this time to work one-on-one or in small groups with Beginning, Intermediate, Advanced, and Approaching students. **Beginner & Intermediate** **Coach the Reading.** Work with these students (either individually or in small groups) to fill out the guided reading questions on the Access 1 and 2 handouts. Have Beginning students refer to the glossary on the Access 1 handout to help them determine the meaning of difficult words (Note: Provide the Access 1 handout glossary to Intermediate students if necessary). Let students know they'll use these answers to help participate in the discussion about the Model. Sample answers for this exercise are located online. **Advanced** **Identify Evidence.** Provide these students with the same instructions to read and annotate as on- and beyond- grade-level students. In addition, ask Advanced students to complete the identifying evidence exercise on the Access 3 handout. Let students know that they'll use these answers to help participate in the discussion about the Model. Sample answers for this exercise are located online. **Approaching** **Guided Reading.** Have students complete the guided reading questions on the Access 4 handout as they read. Let them know that they'll use these answers to help participate in the discussion about the Model. Sample answers for this exercise are located online.
Discuss. After students read the Model text, use these questions to facilitate a whole group discussion that helps students understand how to make inferences and find textual evidence to support them in the excerpt. Remind students to follow rules for collegial discussions and to use academic vocabulary correctly. In addition, make sure students have read the selection and draw on	

Core Path	Access Path
that preparation by referring to evidence from the text during the discussion. 1. Instead of trying to deny his guilt, the murderer in "The Tell-Tale Heart" tries to prove to readers that he is sane. How does Edgar Allan Poe use this plot device to create suspense? (Instead of accepting as truth what the narrator says, readers must use clues from his account to make inferences about his mental state and the events that have taken place.) 2. Poe uses a dramatic monologue to tell the story in "The Tell-Tale Heart." How does Poe force readers to make inferences in order to discover the narrator's real motivation? (Readers do not know if the narrator is talking to a psychologist, a reporter, an investigator or other law official, or a lawyer hired to defend him. They must make inferences to interpret the narrator's true nature and motivation. What the narrator says, how he says it, and what is left out, all provide clues.) 3. According to the Model text, what statements does the narrator make in the story that could lead readers to infer he is not in his right mind? (If the narrator is hearing things, and especially if he believes he is hearing "all things in the heaven and in the earth" and "many things in hell," then this could be used as text evidence that he is not in his right mind.) 4. What other evidence does the text provide that proves the "sanity" of the narrator's actions exists only in his own mind? (The narrator takes a whole hour to put his head in a door opening. He also puts a dark lantern into his victim's room, "all closed, so that no light shone out." If he is not using the lantern to provide light, why put it into the room at all? All of this evidence points to the fact that the narrator is not in his right mind.)	

Please note that excerpts and passages in the StudySync® library, workbooks, and PDFs are intended as touchstones to generate interest in an author's work. The excerpts and passages do not substitute for the reading of entire texts, and StudySync® strongly recommends that teachers and students seek out and purchase the whole literary or informational work in order to experience it as the author intended. Links to online resellers are available in our digital library. In addition, complete works may be ordered through an authorized reseller by filling out and returning to StudySync® the order form enclosed in this workbook.

Teacher's Edition   **297**

Core Path	Access Path
	Extend **Pair and Share.** Pair or group students and have them make two or three additional inferences from other sections of the story. Have each group apply inference making strategies that deal with • point of view • character development • events in the story's plot • the story's title Ask students to cite text evidence that supports their inferences. Have pairs or groups share their inferences and the text evidence that supports them. As a whole group, discuss real-world situations in which students might also have to make inferences.

3. YOUR TURN

Core Path	Access Path
Assess and Explain. Have students answer the comprehension questions to test for understanding. Share the explanations for Parts A and B (located online) with your students.	
	Extend **Tech Infusion** **Share and Discuss.** Have students complete the Your Turn section in class. Poll students about their responses and, as a class, discuss the different strategies they used to determine the correct answers. Make sure students understand that they are to cite evidence about whether or not the narrator/murderer is insane or sane. Conduct your poll by asking your students to complete a handout with questions or using Poll Everywhere (http://tinyurl.com/3zyw33) or Socrative (http://tinyurl.com/3bxbjpt)

Core Path	Access Path
	Extend **Apply.** Put students into small groups of three or four and have them apply the inference-making skills they learned to an excerpt from another selection by Edgar Allan Poe such as "The Cask of Amontillado" or "The Pit and the Pendulum." Point out that both these stories, like "The Tell-Tale Heart," are told from the point of view of an unreliable first-person narrator. Select passages for students to work with or have each group select its own passage to analyze after a first read of the selection. Then have students work in groups to analyze the excerpt, noting examples of inferences they made. As a class, have students discuss how the inference making strategies learned when reading "The Tell-Tale Heart" can be readily applied

Greek and Latin Affixes and Roots

OVERVIEW

Using common Greek and Latin affixes and roots as clues to the meanings of unfamiliar words is crucial for a reader's ability to read complex texts. This lesson plan provides follow-up questions and enrichments to help teachers guide students toward a usable, repeatable method for determining the meanings of unfamiliar words based on a knowledge of common Greek and Latin affixes and roots.

OBJECTIVES

1. Learn the definition of Greek and Latin affixes and roots.
2. Practice and apply concrete strategies for using Greek and Latin affixes and roots, as well as etymological information provided by a dictionary, as clues to the meanings of words.
3. Participate effectively in a range of conversations and collaborations to express ideas and build upon the ideas of others.

ELA Common Core Standards:
Reading: Literature - RL.8.1
Speaking & Listening - SL.8.1.A. SL.8.1.B, SL.8.1.C, SL.8.1.D, SL.8.2
Language - L.8.4.B, L.8.4.C, L.8.4.D

RESOURCES

Access 1 handout (Beginner)
Access 2 handout (Intermediate)
Access 3 handout (Advanced)
Access 4 handout (Approaching)

1. DEFINE

Core Path	Access Path

Core Path

Read and Discuss. Have students read the definition of Greek and Latin affixes and roots. Either in small groups or as a whole class, use the following questions to engage students in a discussion about Greek and Latin affixes and roots. Remind students to follow the rules for collegial discussions.

1. How is the meaning of a word related to its root?

2. What are the purposes of prefixes and suffixes?

3. Even though Latin is a "dead" language, or a language not currently in use, why might studying it be just as useful as learning a foreign language?

4. How might you improve your knowledge of Greek and Latin roots and affixes?

5. For what reasons might English be a collection of borrowed words?

6. How might examining a word's etymology, or origin, be useful?

7. How can you use these parts to build a word: *de-*("not or opposite"), *-struct-* ("build"), and *-tion* ("act or process")? Based on the meanings of the parts, what does the resulting word mean?

8. How can you confirm the meaning of a word whose preliminary meaning you determined by using Greek and Latin roots and affixes?

Access Path

Beginner
Finish the Sentences. Have these students complete the sentence frames on the Access 1 handout as they read the definition of Greek and Latin affixes and roots. Have them use the completed sentence frames to help them participate in the discussion. Sample answers for this exercise are located online.

Intermediate & Advanced
Discuss Prompts. To help these students participate in the discussion, prompt them with questions that can be answered with a few words, such as:

- If the root *spir* means "breath," then what can you infer about the meaning of the word "respiration"? (The word "respiration" is related to the subject of breathing.)

- Why are prefixes and suffixes important? (They change the meanings of words.)

- Based on the affixes in the word "vulcanology," what might the word mean? (The suffix *-ology* means "the study of" something and the root word looks like it relates to volcanoes. So, the word probably means the study of volcanoes.)

Approaching
Complete a Chart. To prepare students to participate in the discussion, have them complete the chart on the Access 4 handout as they read the definition. Correct answers are located online.

Beyond
Discuss. Have partners read the excerpt from "The Tell-Tale Heart" to find one example of a word that contains a common Greek or Latin affix (should look for words other than "acute" because is covered in the Model section). When they select a word, have them identify the root or affix. Students should look up the meaning of the root or affix, and then use that meaning to infer the word's definition. Students should write down their predictions before using a print or digital dictionary to check the word's definition. Then have them present their example to the class.

Core Path	Access Path
	Extend **Know Affixes.** Tell students that researchers have determined that there are 20 prefixes and 20 suffixes that account for over 90% of the prefix and suffix usage in English. If students memorize these 40 affixes, they will be well-prepared to tackle unfamiliar vocabulary. Do an Internet search to find these affixes. Have students form small groups; provide each group with a copy of the affixes. Tell students to discuss memory techniques they might employ that will help them remember these affixes. Ask each group to share some of its ideas aloud with the class.

2. MODEL

Core Path	Access Path
Read and Annotate. Have students independently read the Model section. As they read, ask students to use the annotation tool to: • highlight key points • ask questions • identify places where the Model applies the strategies laid out in the Identification and Application section • comment on the relationships between affixes and roots and meaning in the text	**Note:** During this portion of the lesson, instruction shifts from whole group to individual work. Use this time to work one-on-one or in small groups with Beginning, Intermediate, Advanced, and Approaching students. **Beginner & Intermediate** **Coach the Reading.** Work with these students (either individually or in small groups) to fill out the Guided Reading questions on the Access 1 and 2 handouts. Have Beginning students refer to the Model Glossary on the Access 1 and 2 handouts to help them determine the meaning of difficult words. Let students know they'll use these answers to help participate in the discussion about the Model. Sample answers for this exercise are located online. **Advanced** **Identify Evidence.** Provide these students with the same instructions to read and annotate as on- and beyond- grade-level students. In addition, ask Advanced students to complete the Identify Evidence exercise on the Access 3 handout. Let students know that they'll use these answers to help participate in the discussion about the Model. Sample answers for this exercise are located online.

Core Path	Access Path
	Approaching **Guided Reading.** Have students complete the Guided Reading questions on the Access 4 handout as they read. Let them know that they'll use these answers to help participate in the discussion about the Model. Sample answers for this exercise are located online.

Discuss. After students read the Model text, use the following questions to facilitate a whole group discussion that helps students understand how to use Greek and Latin affixes and roots as clues to the meanings of unfamiliar words. Remind students to follow the rules for collegial discussions.

1. Why doesn't the Model begin by breaking the unfamiliar word *acute* into its parts? (The word is based on one root without prefixes or suffixes.)

2. How does the meaning of *-acuere-* add to the definition of *acute*? (The Latin verb "to sharpen" is used to build an English adjective to describe something as "sharp or highly developed.")

3. How is the definition of the word *acute* supported by the context? (The narrator argues that his sense of hearing is sharp—he hears everything, which may explain why only the narrator is able to hear the beating heart later in the story.)

4. How does the narrator show dissimulation toward the old man? (He treats the old man with kindness while plotting his murder.)

5. How might you research the similarities and differences in origin and meaning between the words *dissimulation* and *simulation*? (Consult a dictionary.) What do you think the word *simulation* means? (Answers will vary, but should touch on the idea of imitation.) Verify this preliminary meaning using a dictionary.

6. What are some other adjectives that you might convert to nouns using the suffix *-ity*? (civil, loyal, honest)

Core Path	Access Path
	Extend **Find the Origin.** Point out that Poe's story contains many challenging words. Ask each student to identify another unfamiliar word. Model for students how to determine the origin of a word using a dictionary entry. Then, ask students to research the origins of their selected words. Have students display their findings in the form of print or digital one-panel annotated cartoon sketches. Ask students to post and present their words to the class. **Extend** **Tech Infusion** **Research.** Point out that *echo* is also the name of a Greek mythological character. Form small student groups to research and read the myth of Echo. Students may use print or digital resources. Then have students discuss the connections among the myth, the Greek root, and the modern meanings of the word. Ask each group to present a summary of its ideas to the class.

3. YOUR TURN

Core Path	Access Path
Assess and Explain. Have students answer the comprehension questions to test for understanding of Greek and Latin roots and affixes and their uses. Share the explanations for Parts A and B (located online) with your students.	
	Extend **Roleplay.** Ask students to form groups of four: one student should play the narrator and the other three should play police officers. Tell each group to develop a short skit of the scene from paragraph 17, making sure to include "violent (but classroom safe) gesticulations" as a featured part of the skit. Have each group perform its skit for the class. Lead the class to discuss the importance of the gesticulations and its root meaning in helping readers assess whether or not the narrator is mad.

Copyright © BookheadEd Learning, LLC

OVERVIEW

"The Tell-Tale Heart" by Edgar Allan Poe, is a Gothic tale of psychological horror in which a demented first-person narrator recounts his murder of an old man to satisfy his need to rid himself of scrutiny from the old man's "evil eye." The Close Read gives students the opportunity to experience making inferences when dealing with an unreliable first-person narrator. It also provides practice in analyzing dialogue and story incidents that reveal aspects of the narrator's character and actions.

OBJECTIVES

1. Complete a close reading of a passage from literature.
2. Practice and apply concrete strategies for analyzing a short story using textual evidence.
3. Participate effectively in a range of conversations and collaborations to express ideas and build upon the ideas of others.
4. Prewrite, plan, and produce clear and coherent writing in response to a prompt.

ELA Common Core Standards:

Reading: Literature - RL.8.1, RL.8.2, RL.8.3, RL.8.4
Writing - W.8.4, W.8.5, W.8.6, W.8.9.A, W.8.10
Speaking & Listening - SL.8.1.A, SL.8.1.B, SL.8.1.C, SL.8.1.D, SL.8.2, SL.8.6
Language - L.8.2.C, L.8.4.A, L.8.4.B, L.8.4.C, L.8.4.D, L.8.6

RESOURCES

"The Tell-Tale Heart" Vocabulary handout
Access 1 handout (Beginner)
Access 2 handout (Intermediate)
Access 3 handout (Advanced)
Access 4 handout (Approaching)

1. INTRODUCTION

Core Path	Access Path
Define and Compare. Project the vocabulary words and definitions onto the board or provide students with a handout, so they can copy the vocabulary into their notebooks. Ask students to compare their initial vocabulary predictions from the First Read with the actual definitions. Review words that students defined incorrectly to understand why they were unable to use context clues or other tools to develop usable definitions.	**Beginner & Intermediate** **Complete the Sentences.** Have students complete the sentence frames on the Access 1 and 2 handouts using the vocabulary words. Point out that some of the words are in the questions and some will be in the answers. Sample answers are located online. **Advanced & Beyond** **Write in Journals.** Have students write a journal entry using all of their vocabulary words. Remind them to write sentences that communicate the meaning of the words they are using. **Approaching** **Graphic Organizer.** To support students in comparing their predictions with the correct meanings, have them complete the graphic organizer on the Access 4 handout to record the vocabulary words, their initial analysis, and the definitions. Then have them write sentences using the words.
Review. Have students complete the fill-in-the-blank vocabulary handout to practice using the domain-specific vocabulary acquired (see answers online).	**Beyond** **Converse.** After students complete the handout, have them work in pairs. Challenge them to have a conversation about a topic of their choice that includes all five of the vocabulary words from the selection.
	Extend **Tech Infusion** **Skit.** Break students into small groups, assign each group a vocabulary word, and ask them to design a short skit to demonstrate the meaning of the word for their peers. Have one student record the skits and post them to your class YouTube Channel so they can be reviewed.

Core Path	Access Path
	Extend **Tech Infusion** **Verbi-Visual Flashcards.** Challenge students to search photo databases to locate photographs that illustrate the vocabulary words. Have them create online flashcards for vocabulary words using StudyBlue (http://tinyurl.com/6aqluw7).

2. READ

Core Path	Access Path
Model Close Reading. Project the text onto the board and model a close reading of the opening paragraphs using the following annotation strategies. While modeling annotation strategies, make notes that tie the text to the focus skill and demonstrate what students should be looking for as they read. Here is some guidance for you as you annotate with your students: • As the Skills lesson that precedes this text makes clear, readers can summarize to demonstrate a general understanding of the plot and characters in a story, in this case the role of the narrator in "The Tell-Tale Heart." However, readers need to identify textual evidence that supports their understanding. • This story opens with several paragraphs of dialogue from the narrator, but Poe uses some carefully chosen words to lead us to question the narrator's reliability. • In the first sentence, the narrator asks why his audience (we're not sure who it is) thinks that he's "mad." He wants to convince the listener, whoever it is, to believe just the opposite. Textual evidence, such as "Hearken! and observe how healthily, how calmly, I can tell you the whole story," supports this.	

Core Path	Access Path
<ul><li>Poe is employing a form called dramatic monologue, in which a narrator tells his own story to a silent listener. This technique allows the narrator to share his thoughts and feelings in his own words, so the reader needs to analyze the textual details to determine what exactly sounds true, and what does not.</li><li>As the story progresses, the difference between a sane narrator and an insane one begin to intensify. For example, the time the narrator says he spent merely to open the door of the old man's room needs analysis. The narrator believes himself to be "wise," but a careful reader will realize that patience on that order makes him unhinged.</li><li>Knowledge of Greek and Latin affixes and roots might help readers define unfamiliar terms. For example, the narrator says that the sound of the old man's heart that "beat on" did not "vex" him. *Vex* comes from the Latin *vexare,* meaning "to agitate or trouble." This detail is important, because no one should hear the sound of a heart beating as the narrator does, and this sound will in fact go on to "vex" him terribly.</li><li>Reading the words carefully, a reader gains deeper insights into Poe's narrator, and textual supports those insights.</li></ul>	
Read and Annotate. Read the Skills Focus questions as a class, so your students know what they should pay close attention to as they read. Then have students read and annotate the excerpt. Ask students to use the annotation tool as they read to: 1. respond to the Skills Focus section 2. ask questions 3. make connections 4. identify textual evidence, including key details and word choices, that supports an understanding of character	**Note:** While on- grade-level students are reading and annotating, work one-on-one or in small groups with Beginning, Intermediate, Advanced, and Approaching students to support them as they read and annotate the text.

Core Path	Access Path
5. use Greek and Latin affixes and roots to help define words in context 6. use correctly any academic vocabulary and note unfamiliar vocabulary 7. capture their reactions to the ideas and examples in the text Remind students to use the strategy they learned (such as visualizing) as as they reread the text.	**Beginner & Intermediate** **Summarize and Analyze the Text.** Work with these students to complete the sentence frames on the Access 1 and 2 handouts (Note: The sentence frames for Intermediate students on the Access 2 handout contain fewer scaffolds). They will then use the completed sentence frames to help them analyze and annotate the text by completing the Skills Focus questions. Refer to the sample Skills Focus answers online to help them complete the sentence frames and annotate the text. **Advanced** **Work in Pairs.** Pair these students with more proficient English speakers to work together on analyzing and annotating the text to complete the Skills Focus questions. If these students need more support, have them use the sentence frames on the Access 3 handout as they work with their more proficient peers. **Approaching** **Summarize the Text.** Have these students discuss and complete the text summary on the Access 4 handout and use their summary to help them analyze and annotate the text by completing the Skills Focus questions. Correct answers for the summary are online. Also refer to the sample Skills Focus answers to aid students with their annotations.
Discuss Either after students have read the text or while they are reading, use the sample responses to the Skills Focus questions online to discuss the reading and the process of citing textual evidence and making inferences. Remind students to follow guidelines for collegial discussions.	**Extend** **Pair and Share.** In small, heterogeneous groups or pairs, ask students to share and discuss their annotations with a focus on the point of view presented in the selection. You can provide students with questions to guide their discussion:

Core Path	Access Path
	1. What inference can you make about the state of the narrative's mind based on the words he uses in the first paragraph of the story? (He is troubled and mad.)
	2. What can you infer about the reliability of the narrator's statement based on his obsession of the old man's eye as described in paragraph 2 of the story? (He cannot be fully trusted to convey reality.)
	3. What can you infer by the fact that Poe takes more than half the story (paragraphs 4-11) to set up the key event that takes place on the eighth night? How does this affect the development of suspense in the story? (He is more interested in character and suspense than plot.)
	Extend **Tech Infusion** **Draw Conclusions.** Have students work in groups to brainstorm key pieces of evidence to support their conclusion about the beating heart heard by the narrator at the end of the story. Use a voice recording app (Voice Memo on the iPhone or Smart Voice Recorder for Androids) to capture students' ideas. Have students play back their discussion and decide which three pieces of evidence provide the best support for their conclusion.

3. WRITE

Core Path	Access Path
Prewrite and Plan. Read the prompt as a class and ask students to brainstorm ideas about Poe's "scary and creepy effects" in "The Tell-Tale Heart." Remind your students to look at the excerpt and their annotations to find textual evidence to support their ideas.	**Beginner & Intermediate** **Answer and Discuss.** Have students complete the prewriting questions on the Access 1 and 2 handouts and then explain their answers to a partner before they write. Explain to students that when they answer a question they need to include a detail, example or quote from the text that supports the statement. **Approaching** **Answer Prewriting Questions.** Have students complete the prewriting questions on the Access 4 handout to summarize their thoughts before they write. **Extend** **Tech Infusion** **Graphic Organizers.** Encourage students to complete a graphic organizer to help identify reasonable evidence they can use to make inferences. You may want to use the organizers available at http://tinyurl.com/ptyb95u or at http://tinyurl.com/kzg4tbc.

Discuss. Project these instructions for the peer review onto the board and review them with your class, so they know what they are looking for when they begin to provide their classmates with feedback:

- What textual evidence of the narrator's psychological state before, during, and after the murder does the writer provide?

- How effectively does this evidence illustrate the narrator's insanity?

- What details in the narrator's account of the events does the writer identify as reflecting most poorly upon his character?

- How convincing are the writer's "closing arguments" in offering a defense for the narrator by reason of insanity?

Teacher's Edition

Core Path	Access Path
• What specific suggestions can you make to help the writer improve the essay? • What thing(s) does this paper do especially well? After you've looked at the peer review instructions, review the rubric with students before they begin writing. Tell students how many peer reviews they will need to complete once they submit their writing. If feedback is given orally, remind students to follow guidelines for collegial discussions.	
Write. Ask students to complete the writing assignment using textual evidence to support their responses. Once they have completed their writing, they should click "Submit."	
	Extend **Critique.** Project a writing sample on the board and ask the class to identify the elements of writing that are strong, as well as those that are weak or in need of improvement. Alternatively, you can put students in small groups and give them photo copies of a writing sample to collaboratively evaluate. After students have had an opportunity to evaluate student samples, work as a class to generate strategies students can use as they complete their peer reviews to ensure they are substantive.
Review. After students have completed their writing assignment, they should submit substantive feedback to five peers.	

FIRST READ:
"Annabel Lee"

OVERVIEW

The poem "Annabel Lee" is about love and love lost. The First Read gives students the opportunity to experience the text with limited context.

OBJECTIVES

1. Perform an initial reading of a text and demonstrate comprehension by responding to short analysis and inference questions with textual evidence.
2. Practice defining vocabulary words using context.
3. Participate effectively in a range of conversations and collaborations to express ideas and build upon the ideas of others.

ELA Common Core Standards:

Reading: Literature - RL.8.1, RL.8.4, RL.8.10
Writing - W.8.10
Speaking & Listening - SL.8.1.A, SL.8.1.B, SL.8.1.C, SL.8.1.D, SL.8.2, SL.8.6
Language - L.8.4.A, L.8.4.C, L.8.4.D, L.8.6

RESOURCES

Access 1 handout (Beginner)
Access 2 handout (Intermediate)
Access 3 handout (Advanced)
Access 4 handout (Approaching)

ACCESS COMPLEX TEXT

In "Annabel Lee," Edgar Allan Poe explores themes of loss and love as the speaker tells about losing his young beloved to death. Students are asked to analyze poetic elements. To help students master this skill, use the following ideas to provide scaffolded instruction for an initial reading of the more complex features of this text.

- **Organization** - The poem establishes and then breaks structural patterns. For example, a long line followed by a short line or rhyming short lines. Readers should question the effects of both the patterns and the changes to these patterns.

- **Genre** - The poem contains many symbols, or items that represent ideas beyond their literal meanings. There are natural symbols: the sea, the moon, and the stars. There are religious symbols: angels and seraphs. There are fairy tale symbols: the kingdom and the kinsmen.

  Readers should consider how these images represent the speaker's emotional state following the death of his beloved.

- **Specific Vocabulary** - Difficult vocabulary, such as *coveted* and *sepulchre*, may present a challenge for some readers.

1. INTRODUCTION

Core Path	Access Path
Watch. As a class, watch the video preview of "Annabel Lee." Have students share their ideas about the story to come based on the preview.	**English Learners All Levels** **Fill in the Blanks.** Ask students to use their Access 1, 2, and 3 handouts to fill in the blanks of the transcript for the preview's voiceover as they watch the preview along with their classmates. Answers are located online.
Read and Listen. Individually or as a class, read and listen to the Introduction for "Annabel Lee." The Introduction provides context for the poem.	**English Learners All Levels & Approaching** **Read and Listen.** Ask students to read and listen to the Introduction for "Annabel Lee." Have them refer to the vocabulary listing on their Access 1, 2, 3, and 4 handouts for definitions of key vocabulary terms. If there are unfamiliar words that are not included in their glossary, encourage students to check a dictionary or online reference tool, like http://tinyurl.com/6ytby.

Core Path	Access Path
Access Prior Knowledge. Poe wrote "Annabel Lee" for a woman, and many people believe that he wrote it to honor his late wife. Ask your students to think of other songs (or stories or poems) that they know were written to or for another person. Suggest contemporary songs that are suitable for class.	**Beginner** **Inspiration.** Pair Beginning and more proficient (Beyond) readers. Have these groups complete the "Inspiration" sentence frames on their Access 1 handout that asks students to describe how they would write about another person. Have the pairs generate ideas and complete the sentences together.

Core Path:

- In pairs or small groups, have students generate a list of popular songs, the lyrics of which speak about a person.

- As a class, break the songs into categories of love songs, tribute songs, and story songs, for example.

- Have students identify key words in the lyrics that describe the subject of the song as well has how the speaker (the song writer or singer) feels about that person. How might an author's feelings for someone else impact the poem or song lyric he or she chooses to write?

- Ask: What makes a poem different from a song? How are they similar? Have students discuss the way music and a singer's voice affect a song's lyrics.

Access Path:

Intermediate & Advanced
Inspiration. Pair Intermediate and Advanced students. Have these groups complete the "Inspiration" sentence frames on their Access 2 and 3 handouts that asks students to describe how they would write about another person. Have the pairs generate ideas and complete the sentences together.

Extend
Make Predictions. Based on the Introduction, ask students to make predictions about the poem.

Discuss. After students have read the text, use the sample responses to the Skills Focus questions online to discuss the reading and the process of searching for the theme and how dialogue and incidents in the plot reveal aspects of a character. Make sure that students have acquired and accurately use academic-specific words and phrases related to the skill, and demonstrate a command of formal English appropriate to the discussion.

Extend
Discuss the Introduction. After reading the Introduction, use the information provided to facilitate a pre-reading discussion to get students thinking about the theme in "Annabel Lee."

1. How does one deal with grief?

2. What other stories or songs have you heard that helped writers give meaning to the loss of those they loved?

2. READ

Core Path	Access Path

Make Predictions about Vocabulary. There are four bold vocabulary words in the text. As students read the text, ask them to make predictions about what they think each bold vocabulary word means based on the context clues in the sentence. If you are in a low-tech classroom, ask students to record their predictions in their notes, so they can be easily referenced in class. If your students have access to technology, they can use the built in annotation tool to make their predictions.

It might be helpful to model this for students before they begin the reading. Either using the board or projecting the actual text, focus in on the lines of the poem that uses the word "sepulchre":

- So that her high-born kinsmen came
  And bore her away from me,
  To shut her up in a **sepulchre**
  In this kingdom by the sea.

Model for the class how to use the overall structure and meaning of the sentence and the sentence around it, the word's position, and other clues to define the unfamiliar vocabulary word. In this case, point out these context keys:

1. Look at the structure of the line that contains the word "sepulchre." What is its part of speech (object of a preposition), and what preposition precedes it? (in) From this, then, we know that a sepulchre is something that a person can fit in.

2. If we look at the two lines before, we learn that "high-born" people took Annabel Lee away from the narrator and shut her in that sepulchre. This means that the sepulchre is something away from other people, and something that one might not willingly enter, because the people "bore her away" from the narrator, implying that she didn't leave on her own.

3. To figure out exactly what a sepulchre is though, we need to look at the next stanza. The narrator's reference to "angels" and "heaven" clue us into Annabel Lee's location, and the last line tells us very clearly that Annabel Lee is no

Note: This exercise, which extends vocabulary instruction, should be completed when the class shifts from whole group instruction to individual work during the "Read and Annotate" exercise.

Beginner, Intermediate, & Approaching Pair Practice.

1. Pair Beginning, Intermediate, and Approaching students with more proficient readers.

2. Give them an additional sentence that contains a new vocabulary word.

3. Ask the students to complete a Think Aloud using the teacher-led Make Predictions about Vocabulary activity as a model, while the proficient student actively listens.

4. The students should use the context clues in the sentence to try to determine the meaning of the new vocabulary word.

5. After the student has completed the Think Aloud and made a prediction about the word's meaning, allow time for the proficient reader to add his/her own thoughts and clarify any points of confusion.

6. Once they've completed this Think Aloud, encourage them to use a dictionary to confirm the definition of the new vocabulary word. Have them refer to the vocabulary listing on their Access 1, 2, and 4 handouts for definitions of key vocabulary terms in the text. Encourage them to add any additional vocabulary words or idioms they find in the text and look up definitions for those words and idioms online or in a dictionary.

Core Path	Access Path

longer alive. Thus, we're able to infer that a sepulchre is some sort of tomb or place for people to go when they're deceased.

Remind students that they can check precise meanings as well as parts of speech and pronunciations in a dictionary.

Model Reading Comprehension Strategy. Before students begin reading, model the reading comprehension strategy of visualizing by using this Think Aloud that talks students through the first three stanzas of the poem. First explain to your students that visualizing is:

forming a mental picture of something as you read, and using new details from the text to add to or change the mental images you have created.

Explain to students how visualizing will help them better comprehend the selection and help drive their discussions.

- When I read the first stanza, I see a castle on a cliff overlooking the ocean. There's a young woman—maybe a princess?—standing in front of the castle. She's looking out at the waves crashing against the cliffs while her hair blows in the breeze.

- In the next stanza, I see the same young woman, but as a child. She's playing with a young boy on the beach, drawing pictures in the sand and attempting to skip rocks in the ocean. I also see an angel off to the side, watching them with affection.

- Then I see another scene, where this same young woman—about the age she was in the first stanza—being kidnapped by some men on horseback and locked up in a burial vault. This is actually a little confusing, because I don't know exactly what's going on. Are they burying her alive? I'll keep reading to find out what happens to her.

Note: This exercise, which extends vocabulary instruction, should be completed when the class shifts from whole group instruction to individual work during the "Read and Annotate" exercise.

Beginner, Intermediate, & Approaching Apply Reading Comprehension Strategy.

1. Have Beginning, Intermediate, and Approaching students listen to the audio version of the poem "Annabel Lee." As they listen to the audio recording, ask them to draw or sketch a picture of what they see in their minds as they visualize the story. Encourage them to include as much detail as possible in the time allowed.

2. Once they have listened to the audio version and created a picture or series of pictures based on what they heard, pair Beginning, Intermediate, and Approaching students with more proficient readers and ask them to describe what they drew and why. Why did they include particular images and/or colors?

3. Allow pairs time to discuss the pictures. Were there any details from the text that were not included in the picture? If so, encourage them to add details to the drawing based on their conversations.

Core Path	Access Path
Read and Annotate. Read and annotate the excerpt. Ask students to use the annotation tool as they read to: 1. use context clues to analyze and determine the meaning of the bolded vocabulary terms 2. ask questions about passages of the text that may be unclear or unresolved 3. identify key details, events, characters, and connections between them 4. note unfamiliar vocabulary 5. capture their reaction to the language and subject of the poem	**Beginner** **Coach the Reading.** While other students read, annotate, and discuss the text independently, work with Beginning students, listening to the audio of the text and pausing periodically or when any student has a question. Coach students in articulating their questions for the group and in highlighting and annotating the text. Have students use the Annotation Guide in their Access 1 handout to support them as they highlight and annotate the text. For further support, ask questions about the text such as: • Is there anything about the poem that you don't understand? • Why do you think the narrator is convinced the angels in heaven envied him and Annabel Lee? • What do you think this narrator's life is like at the time he's telling this story? **Intermediate** **Listen to the Audio.** Have these students listen to the audio of the text and use the definitions in the Access 2 handout to help them with words or idioms that may be unfamiliar. If students need help with annotating the text, have them use the Annotation Guide in their Access 2 handout. After working with the Beginning students, you may wish to check this group's progress and provide support as needed.
	Advanced **Pair with Proficient Peers.** Have Advanced students work with English proficient peers to read, annotate, and discuss the text. Have students use the Annotation Guide in their Access 3 handout to support them as they highlight and annotate the text. Encourage them to listen to the audio of the text if needed. **Approaching** **Use the Annotation Guide.** Have students use the Annotation Guide in their Access 4 handout to support them as they highlight and annotate the text.

Core Path	Access Path
Discuss. In small groups or pairs, have students discuss the questions and inferences they made while reading. Have them also note new vocabulary. Make sure students follow rules for collegial discussions.	**English Learners All Levels & Approaching** Use the extra time while on- and beyond- grade-level students are discussing their first reads of the text to work individually and in small groups with English Learners and Approaching readers as outlined above. Should those students complete their first reads quickly, integrate them into the on- and beyond- grade-level discussion groups. Otherwise English Learners and Approaching readers will be given an opportunity to participate in text discussions with their peers later in the lesson.

1. Why do you think the speaker tell the story he does? (The speaker seems to want to share his grief over the death of a woman he loved. Maybe by telling the story as a poem gives a reason and a meaning for her death.)

2. Do you think writing can be a useful way to understand, find reasons, or make meaning out of personal or public tragedies? Refer to the poem as an example. (Answers will vary, but should refer to examples in the world, personal examples, or lines from the poem to show ways this may or may not be true.)

3. What are some ways that people comfort themselves in times of loss? Where in the poem does the speaker do this? (Answers will vary, but should include the images that Poe's speaker creates of angels, the comfort of the sea, and the kingdom to show that his loss is important.)

Extend
Pair and Share. Have pairs of students choose a stanza and choose a word or phrase that sums up the feeling of the stanza.

Extend
Tech Infusion
Audio. Have students use the StudySync audio text highlight feature to choose the word or phrase that builds the suspense in the poem.

Extend
Identify and Define.
Ask students to reference their annotations and share any vocabulary words that were unfamiliar.

1. As a class, compile a list of unknown words on the board.

Core Path	Access Path
	2. In small groups, ask students to make predictions about they think these words mean based on how they are used in the sentence. (Note: They will need access to StudySync to read the words in context and make predictions.)
	3. Each group should work together using dictionaries or devices to define the words and write the definitions in their notebooks.
	Extend
	Tech Infusion
	Record. Use a voice recording app (Voice Memo on the iPhone or Smart Voice Recorder for Androids) or VoiceThread (http://tinyurl.com/4m389hy) to capture each group's ideas.

3. SYNCTV

Core Path	Access Path
Watch. As a class, watch the SyncTV video on "Annabel Lee." Pause the video at these key moments to discuss the information with your students:	**Beginner & Intermediate** **Analyze the Discussion.** Have students use the "Analyze the Discussion" guide in the Access 1 and 2 handouts to identify key points in the discussion and the evidence the students use to determine those points. Sample answers are online.
1. 2:25 – What do you think? Is repetition a form of figurative language? Provide textual evidence to support your answer.	
2. 3:32 – What is the significance of this example of personification in the poem? Does it show the depth of the narrator's feelings for Annabel Lee? Do you agree with Morgan's explanation?	**Advanced** **Figurative Language.** Have students discuss and complete the *Figurative Language Chart* on the Access 3 handout, referring back to the SyncTV video as needed to clarify their answers. Sample answers appear online.
3. 4:50 – Morgan concludes that the narrator is more obsessed with the *death* of Annabel Lee than with her. Do you agree? Use supporting evidence from the text.	**Approaching** **Analyze the Discussion.** Have students complete the chart on the Access 4 handout by listing textual evidence cited by the students in the video. Sample answers are online.

Core Path	Access Path
	Extend **Tech Infusion** **Record.** Ask one student in each group to video record their conversation. They can upload their videos to YouTube, share them via Google Drive, or e-mail them to you for review. They can also play the video back and critique their own conversations to continually improve.

4. THINK

Core Path	Access Path
Answer and Discuss. Have students complete the Think questions and then use the peer review instructions and rubric to complete the peer reviews. Refer to the sample answers online to discuss responses with your students. Remind students to follow guidelines for collegial discussions.	**Beginner & Intermediate** **Sentence Frames.** Have students use the sentence frames on the Access 1 and 2 handouts to support their responses to the Think questions. If necessary, distribute sentence frames to Advanced students as well. **Approaching** **Find the Evidence.** Have students use Find the Evidence on the Access 4 handout to help them identify the evidence needed to answer the questions.
SyncTV-Style Discussion. Put students into heterogeneous small groups and give them a prompt to discuss. Remind them to model their discussions after the SyncTV episodes they have seen. Stress the importance of citing textual evidence in their conversations to support their ideas. Discussion prompt options: 1. The narrator seems to have a stronger obsession with Annabel Lee's death than the woman herself. Is this effective in expressing the narrator's feelings accurately or is it too extreme? Consider textual evidence when stating your opinion.	**Beginner & Intermediate** **Use Sentence Frames.** Have these students use the sentence frames on the Access 1 and 2 handouts to help them participate in the discussion. **Approaching** **Use Think Questions.** Remind these students to refer back to their answers to the Think questions to help them participate in the group discussion.

Core Path	Access Path
2. Consider the purpose of a hyperbole in writing. When is it most effective and when would it be unnecessary? Think of examples to support your answer.	
	Extend **Debate.** Present students with an issue from the text that can be debated. Allow students to debate the issue as a class or in smaller groups. Debate prompts: 1. Can a great loss change someone's life for the better? 2. By looking for meaning and cause for a tragedy, does that keep someone from appreciating and moving on?
	Extend **Write a Claim.** Ask students to write a strong claim that clearly states their position in relation to the topic they debated. Once students have written their claims, ask them to read their claims to a small group of their peers. This activity will provide them practice writings claims, as well as expose them to claims written by their peers.

OVERVIEW

Understanding the form of a poem is the first step in comprehension. Repetition, meter, and the use of rhyme are all important devices that contribute to the meaning of a poem. This lesson plan provides follow-up questions and useful enrichments to help teachers guide students toward a usable, repeatable method for understanding poetic elements.

OBJECTIVES

1. Learn the definition of poetic elements.
2. Practice using concrete strategies for identifying poetic elements.
3. Participate effectively in a range of conversations and collaborations to express ideas and build upon the ideas of others.

ELA Common Core Standards:

Reading: Literature - RL.8.1, RL.8.4

Speaking & Listening - SL.8.1.A, SL.8.1.B, SL.8.1.C, SL.8.1.D, SL.8.2

Language - L.8.6

RESOURCES

Access 1 handout (Beginner)

Access 2 handout (Intermediate)

Access 3 handout (Advanced)

Access 4 handout (Approaching)

Please note that excerpts and passages in the StudySync® library, workbooks, and PDFs are intended as touchstones to generate interest in an author's work. The excerpts and passages do not substitute for the reading of entire texts, and StudySync® strongly recommends that teachers and students seek out and purchase the whole literary or informational work in order to experience it as the author intended. Links to online resellers are available in our digital library. In addition, complete works may be ordered through an authorized reseller by filling out and returning to StudySync® the order form enclosed in this workbook.

Teacher's Edition   323

1. DEFINE

Core Path	Access Path
Watch. Watch the Concept Definition video on poetic elements with your students. Make sure students write down and are familiarized with the basic elements of poetry, including meter, rhyme, stanza, and figurative language. Pause the video at these key moments to discuss the information with your students:	**English Learners All Levels & Approaching** **Match.** Have students complete the matching exercise on the Access 1, 2, 3, and 4 handouts as they watch the video. Answers are located online.

1. 0:21 - Discuss what separates rap lyrics, for instance, from a random grouping of words. What do you think it takes for a random "arrangement of words" to become a poem?

2. 1:07 - Why do you think newer poems are less likely to rhyme? Do song or rap lyrics always rhyme? In the absence of a rhyming pattern, what other kinds of word patterns can be found in poetry?

3. 1:47 - What are some different kinds of poems? Break down the rhyme scheme, meter, and number of lines in the stanza for each different type of poem.

Read and Discuss. After watching the Concept Definition video, have students read the definition of poetic elements. Either in small groups or as a whole class, use these questions to spur discussion among your students about identifying and analyzing poetic elements, making sure they follow the rules for collegial discussions, use academic language correctly, and respond to the questions and comments of others in the class with relevant evidence, observations, and ideas:	**Beginner & Approaching** **Complete a Chart.** To prepare students to participate in the discussion, have them complete the chart on the Access 1 and 4 handouts as they read the definition. The correct answers are located online. **Intermediate & Advanced** **Discuss Prompts.** To help these students participate in the discussion, prompt them with questions that can be answered with a few words, such as:

1. Which poetic elements do you feel are most obvious when you are reading? (Answers will vary, but students will probably say rhyme is the most obvious.) Which are the most challenging to identify? (Answers will vary, but may include identifying specific types of figurative language.)

- What is another name for the rhythm of the words in a poem? (meter)

- What poetic element tends to come at the ends of lines, and is often used in older poems? (rhyme)

Core Path	Access Path
2. Beyond poetry, where is repetition frequently used? (Students should note that writers of nonfiction often use repetition to stress or underscore a specific point they want to make.) 3. In general, what effect does repeating words and phrases have on a reader or listener? (It contributes to the mood and feeling the poet wishes to create, and can make certain lines and phrases stay in the reader's mind.) 4. Why might a poet prefer to use a nontraditional form when writing? (Answers will vary.) What might the impact of this decision be on the reader? (Answers will vary.)	• Can you think of a poem you have read that has used one of the poetic elements mentioned on the previous page? (Answers will vary.) **Beyond** **Discuss.** Have students select a poem they've read and describe the poetic elements used. Compile a list of examples. Have students discuss how the poetic elements of each work affect what the reader learns about the characters and poem's structure. How might different poetic elements affect the theme or style of the poem?
	Extend **Tech Infusion** **Pair and Share.** Pair or group students and ask each group to do a Google search for a modern ballad. Then ask them to compare the song they found with "Annabel Lee." How are they alike and different? Ask each group to share their findings with the class.

2. MODEL

Core Path	Access Path
Read and Annotate. Have students independently read the Model section. As they read, ask students to use the annotation tool to: • highlight key points • ask questions • identify places where the Model is applying the strategies laid out in the Application and Identification section on poetic elements.	**Note:** During this portion of the lesson, instruction shifts from whole group to individual work. Use this time to work one-on-one or in small groups with Beginning, Intermediate, Advanced, and Approaching students. **Beginner & Intermediate** **Coach the Reading.** Work with these students (either individually or in small groups) to fill out the guided reading questions on the Access 1 and 2 handouts. Have Beginning students refer to the glossary on the Access 1 handout to help them determine the meaning of difficult words. (Note: Provide the Access 1 handout glossary to Intermediate students if necessary.)

Please note that excerpts and passages in the StudySync® library, workbooks, and PDFs are intended as touchstones to generate interest in an author's work. The excerpts and passages do not substitute for the reading of entire texts, and StudySync® strongly recommends that teachers and students seek out and purchase the whole literary or informational work in order to experience it as the author intended. Links to online resellers are available in our digital library. In addition, complete works may be ordered through an authorized reseller by filling out and returning to StudySync® the order form enclosed in this workbook.

Teacher's Edition   325

Core Path	Access Path
	Let students know they'll use these answers to help participate in the discussion about the Model. Sample answers for this exercise are located online. **Advanced** **Identify Evidence.** Provide these students with the same instructions to read and annotate as on- and beyond- grade-level students. In addition, ask Advanced students to complete the Identify Evidence exercise on the Access 3 handout. Let students know that they'll use these answers to help participate in the discussion about the Model. Sample answers for this exercise are located online
	Approaching **Guided Reading.** Have students complete the guided reading questions on the Access 4 handout as they read. Let them know that they'll use these answers to help participate in the discussion about the Model. Sample answers for this exercise are located online.
Discuss. After students read the Model text, use the following questions to facilitate a whole group discussion that helps students understand how to identify and analyze poetic elements. Remind students to follow rules for collegial discussions and to use academic vocabulary correctly. In addition, make sure students have read the selection and draw on that preparation by referring to evidence from the text during the discussion. 1. Why does the Model maintain that the rhythm of "Annabel Lee" might mislead some readers? (The poem has a sing-song rhythm and the repetition of certain words and phrases make the poem sound more like a nursery rhyme than an expression of grief.) 2. According to the Model text, how does Poe suggest that his love for Annabel Lee was, in some ways, like a fairy tale? (Poe uses words and phrases, such as "It was many and many a year ago" and "maiden" that recall typical fairy	

Copyright © BookheadEd Learning, LLC

Core Path	Access Path
tale beginnings such as "once upon a time." He also hints at a supernatural threat in the form of "winged seraphs of heaven" who are jealous of his love. This recalls characters such as the witch in "Sleeping Beauty.")	

3. According to the Model, how does Poe use meter and rhythm in the poem? (The poem's regular meter, established by a pattern of stressed and unstressed syllables, creates an effect that mirrors the sound of waves on the beach. For this reason it is closely connected to the poem's setting.)

4. What kinds of things are repeated in the poem? (Annabel Lee's name, the kingdom by the sea; people, places, i.e. names to invoke memory)

5. How does this repetition affect the way readers understand the poem? (By repeating things over and over, the speaker seems to be obsessive and perhaps unable to let go of his grief.)

Extend

Tech Infusion

Pair and Share. Pair or group students. Have each group explore http://tinyurl.com/n54ypy and choose a poem they like. Then, have each group answer the following questions about its poem:

- What type of form or rhythm does your poem have?

- How does the form of the poem add to or impact its meaning?

- What examples of repetition do you see?

- What impact does this repetition have on the meaning of the poem?

Ask the groups to share their findings with the class. If possible, have students capture pair shares on video using their mobile devices so they can watch their conversations and critique the content.

Core Path	Access Path
Assess and Explain. Have students answer the comprehension questions to test for understanding. Share the explanations for Parts A and B (located online) with your students.	
	Extend **Share and Discuss.** Have students complete the Your Turn section in class. Poll students about their responses and as a class discuss the different strategies they used to determine the correct answers.
	Extend **Tech Infusion** **Music and Rhythm.** Play a song for your class that has a strong rhythm and repetition, and provide your students with the lyrics. Have pairs or groups mark stressed and unstressed syllables throughout the song. Have them use the information provided in the Model to determine what sort of foot the songwriter used. Challenge them to research different types of meter and rhythm to find the one that best matches the song. Allow students time to share their ideas with the class. You could also use a screen capture or recording tool like Educreations (http://tinyurl.com/k6wl3aw) to allow students the chance to record themselves explaining the lyrics, and how they determined the song's rhythm.

OVERVIEW

The poem "Annabel Lee" is about love and love lost. The Close Read gives students the opportunity to more deeply analyze the poet's choices of poetic elements and repetition and their effect on the reader's interpretation of the poem.

OBJECTIVES

1. Complete a close reading of a work of literature.
2. Practice and apply concrete strategies for analyzing poetic elements in a poem.
3. Participate effectively in a range of conversations and collaborations to express ideas and build upon the ideas of others.
4. Prewrite, plan, and produce clear and coherent writing in response to a prompt.

ELA Common Core Standards:
Reading: Literature - RL.8.1, RL.8.3, RL.8.4
Writing - W.8.4, W.8.5, W.8.6, W.8.10
Speaking & Listening - SL.8.1.A, SL.8.1.C, SL.8.6
Language - L.8.2.C, L.8.4.A, L.8.4.C, L.8.4.D, L.8.6

RESOURCES

"Annabel Lee" Vocabulary handout
Access 1 handout (Beginner)
Access 2 handout (Intermediate)
Access 3 handout (Advanced)
Access 4 handout (Approaching)

Please note that excerpts and passages in the StudySync® library, workbooks, and PDFs are intended as touchstones to generate interest in an author's work. The excerpts and passages do not substitute for the reading of entire texts, and StudySync® strongly recommends that teachers and students seek out and purchase the whole literary or informational work in order to experience it as the author intended. Links to online resellers are available in our digital library. In addition, complete works may be ordered through an authorized reseller by filling out and returning to StudySync® the order form enclosed in this workbook.

Teacher's Edition **329**

1. INTRODUCTION

Core Path	Access Path
Define and Compare. Project the vocabulary words and definitions onto the board or provide students with a handout, so they can copy the vocabulary into their notebooks. Suggest that students consult general and specialized reference materials, both print and digital, to compare the precise meaning of a specific word with their initial vocabulary predictions from the First Read. Review words that students defined incorrectly to understand why they were unable to use context clues to develop usable definitions.	**Beginner & Intermediate** **Fill in the Blanks.** Have students fill in the blanks on the Access 1 and 2 handouts using the vocabulary words. Sample answers are located online. **Advanced & Beyond** **Write in Journals.** Have students write a journal entry using all of their vocabulary words. Remind them to write sentences that communicate the meaning of the words they are using. **Approaching** **Graphic Organizer.** To support students in comparing their predictions with the correct meanings, have them complete the graphic organizer on the Access 4 handout to record the vocabulary words, their initial analysis, and the definitions. Then have them write sentences using the words.
Review. Have students complete the fill-in-the-blank vocabulary handout for this selection. Answers for the handout are listed online.	
	Extend **Word Web.** Break students into small groups, assign each group a vocabulary word, and ask them to fill out a word web with the vocabulary word in the center and the associating words in bubbles around the center word. Have them use dictionaries and thesauruses to find words related to the vocabulary word.
	Extend **Tech Infusion** **Draw.** Create artwork to visually represent the words using an iPad or Android art app. Alternatively, students can draw on paper.

Core Path	Access Path
	Extend **Charades.** Have groups of students work together to create a pantomime that shows as many of the vocabulary words as they can incorporate into the skit. Have groups present their pantomime as the class tries to guess the vocabulary words that are being acted out.
	Extend **Tech Infusion** **Create.** Create online flashcards for the vocabulary using Quizlet (http://tinyurl.com/2vdfxf) or StudyBlue (http://tinyurl.com/ov6xbl). Alternatively, have students use index cards to review and memorize the words.

2. READ

Core Path	Access Path
Model Close Reading. Project the text onto the board and model a close reading of the first five stanzas using the following annotation strategies. While modeling annotation strategies, make notes that tie the text to the focus skill and demonstrate what students are looking for as they read. Here is some guidance for you as you annotate for your students: • As the Skills lesson that precedes this text makes clear, the elements, or features, of poetry include figurative language, rhythm, rhyme, repetition, and stanza length and organization. Let's look for these elements in the first two stanzas of "Annabel Lee." What kind of mood does the poem's regular meter, established by a pattern of stressed and unstressed syllables, create? (Possible response: A hypnotic, sing-song effect that almost recalls waves going in and out on a beach.)	

Core Path	Access Path
• Poe uses elements of fairy tales in the poem, too. He writes that he fell in love with Annabel Lee "many and many a year ago," recalling the many fairy tales that begin with the words "Once upon a time." There are also hints of supernatural characters, as he hints of "winged seraphs" in heaven who are jealous of the love he shares with Annabel Lee. • Now let's reread the fourth stanza. Poe is writing about the cause of Annabel Lee's death here, and this too has supernatural overtones. In what way does Poe suggest that Annabel Lee did not die of natural causes? (He writes that "the wind came out of the cloud, chilling, and killing my Annabel Lee.") Poe blames the angels, who envied the love he shared with Annabel Lee, and the lines "Yes!--that was the reason (as all men know/In this kingdom by the sea)" indicate that he sees her death as an event known far and wide. It's as if Poe must describe the death of his love as some great, mythic event because of the grief he still feels over it.	
Read and Annotate. Read the Skills Focus questions as a class, so your students know what they should pay close attention to as they read. Then have students read and annotate the excerpt. Ask students to use the annotation tool as they read to: 1. respond to the Skills Focus section 2. ask questions 3. make connections 4. identify key information, examples of figurative language and other poetic elements, and themes 5. note unfamiliar vocabulary 6. capture their reaction to the ideas and poetic elements in the text As they reread the text, remind students to use the comprehension strategy of Visualising that they learned in the First Read.	**Note:** While on-grade-level students are reading and annotating, work one-on-one or in small groups with Beginning, Intermediate, Advanced, and Approaching students to support them as they read and annotate the text. **Beginner & Intermediate** **Summarize and Analyze the Text.** Work with these students to complete the Summarize and Analyze the Text exercise in the Access 1 and 2 handouts (Note: The sentence frames for Intermediate students on the Access 2 handout contain fewer scaffolds). They will then use the completed sentence frames to help them analyze and annotate the text by completing the Skills Focus questions. Refer to the sample Skills Focus answers online to help them complete the sentence frames and annotate the text.

Core Path	Access Path
	Advanced **Work in Pairs.** Pair these students with more proficient English speakers to work together on analyzing and annotating the text to complete the Skills Focus questions. If these students need more support, have them use the Summarize and Analyze the Text exercise in the Access 3 handout as they work with their more proficient peers. **Approaching** **Summarize and Text.** Have these students discuss and complete the Summarize the Text exercise in the Access 4 handout and use their summary to help them analyze and annotate the text so as to complete the Skills Focus questions. Correct answers for the summary are online. Also refer to the sample Skills Focus answers to aid students with their annotations.
Discuss After students have read the text, use the sample responses to the Skills Focus questions online to discuss the reading and the process of searching for and analyzing poetic elements. Make sure that students have acquired and accurately use academic-specific words and phrases related to the skill, and demonstrate a command of formal English appropriate to the discussion.	**Extend** **Pair and Share.** In small, heterogeneous groups or pairs, ask students to share and discuss their annotations with a focus on the point of view presented in the selection. You can provide students with these questions to guide their discussion: 1. How does the narrator describe Annabel Lee? How does he describe himself? 2. Why do you think the author used rhymes and repeated words in the poem? 3. Do you trust this narrator? Why or why not?
	Extend **Connect.** Start a discussion with the class about what it might take to have a relationship that becomes a story that people tell hundreds of years after the people who lived it are dead. Is it possible in this era for there to be eternal stories? Or are things as fleeting as websites and friend requests?

Core Path	Access Path
	Extend **Discuss.** In small groups or pairs, ask students to discuss their annotations with a focus on form and repetition. You can provide students with questions to guide their discussion: 1. What form is the poem in? (ballad) 2. Does the repetition of words and phrases make the poem sadder or more unsettling? (Answers will vary.) 3. Is the "plot" of the poem understandable? Does the form make it easier or harder to understand? (Answers will vary.) 4. What is the theme of the poem? (love is stronger than death) 5. Do you agree or disagree with the author's theme? Why or why not?

3. WRITE

Core Path	Access Path
Prewrite and Plan. Read the prompt as a class and ask students to brainstorm their reactions to Edgar Allan Poe's poem "Annabel Lee." Have students work in pairs to identify lines in the poem that most clearly allow readers to follow its narrative, or "story." Students can then brainstorm what the poem loses when it becomes a prose story rather than a poem, and how the poem's rhythm and rhyme, as well as other poetic elements, support its theme or message. Remind students to look at the poem and their annotations to find textual evidence to support their ideas.	**Beginner & Intermediate** **Answer and Discuss.** Have students complete the prewriting questions in the Access 1 and 2 handouts and then explain their answers to a partner before they write. Explain to students that when they answer a question—such as *How does the narrator describe Annabel Lee? What does this tell you about her? About him?*—they need to include a detail, example, or quote from the text that supports the statement. For example, students could include the lines, "She was a child," "she lived with no other thought/Than to love and be loved by me", and "The beautiful Annabel Lee," which show the narrator's devotion and admiration, but also that he is very single-minded and convinced that their love was perfect, equal, and like no other.

Core Path	Access Path
	Approaching **Answer Prewriting Questions.** Have students complete the prewriting questions in the Access 4 handout to summarize their thoughts before they write.
	Extend **Organize.** Encourage students to complete a graphic organizer or concept map to organize their ideas before they type their responses. Students can create concept maps online using http://tinyurl.com/yceu2jg or Google drawing.

Discuss. Project these instructions for the peer review onto the board and review them with your class, so they know what they are looking for when they begin to provide their classmates with feedback:

- How accurate was the writer's retelling of the story in prose?
- How has this essay helped you understand how the poem's form supports its theme or message?
- What evidence did the writer use from the text to support his or her writing?
- How well does the writer explain how that evidence supports his or her analysis?
- Does the writer use standard grammar and punctuation? What weak spots should be addressed?
- What specific suggestions can you make to help the writer improve the response?
- What thing(s) does this paper do especially well?

Be sure to tell the writer what he or she did well and what he or she needs to work on. Remember that your comments are most useful when they are constructive.

After you've looked at the peer review instructions, review the rubric with students before they begin writing. Allow time for students to briefly raise and discuss questions they may have about the peer review instructions and the rubric. Tell students how many peer reviews they will need to complete once they submit their writing.

Core Path	Access Path
Write. Ask students to complete the writing assignment using textual evidence to support their answers. If possible, have students use technology to produce and publish their writing. Once they have completed their writing, they should click "Submit."	
	Extend **Critique.** Project a writing sample on the board and ask the class to identify the elements of writing that are strong, as well as those that are weak or in need of improvement. Alternatively, you can put students in small groups and give them photocopies of a writing sample to collaboratively evaluate. After students have had an opportunity to evaluate student samples, work as a class to generate strategies students can use as they complete their peer reviews to ensure they are substantive.
Review. Once students complete their writing assignment, they should submit substantive feedback to two peers. If possible, have students use technology to interact and collaborate with others.	

FIRST READ:
"The Bells"

OVERVIEW

The poem "The Bells" is as much about sound and feeling as it is about a story. The First Read gives students the opportunity to experience the text with limited context.

OBJECTIVES

1. Perform an initial reading of a text and demonstrate comprehension by responding to short analysis and inference questions with textual evidence.
2. Practice defining vocabulary words using context.
3. Participate effectively in a range of conversations and collaborations to express ideas and build upon the ideas of others.

ELA Common Core Standards:

Reading: Literature - RL.8.1, RL.8.4, RL.8.10
Writing - W.8.10
Speaking & Listening - SL.8.1.A, SL.8.1.B, SL.8.1.C, SL.8.1.D, SL.8.2, SL.8.6
Language - L.8.4.A, L.8.4.C, L.8.4.D, L.8.6

RESOURCES

Access 1 handout (Beginner)
Access 2 handout (Intermediate)
Access 3 handout (Advanced)
Access 4 handout (Approaching)

ACCESS COMPLEX TEXT

In "The Bells," Edgar Allan Poe's speaker describes the sounds of four different types of bells embedded within particular settings. The mood shifts from happiness to misery as readers hear sleigh bells, then wedding bells, then alarm bells, and finally ghoulish iron bells. Students are asked to analyze poetic elements. To help students master this skill, use the following suggestions to provide scaffolded instruction for an initial reading of the more complex features of this text.

- **Purpose** - Rather than tell a story, the poem moves readers through an emotional range via sound. This purpose may challenge some readers. Remind them that poetry may create an emotion or an experience rather than address a traditional topic or storyline.

- **Genre** - The poem relies heavily on onomatopoeia. Readers must consider the effect of this sound device on the poem.

- **Specific Vocabulary** - The mood shifts from stanza to stanza. Readers should analyze how Poe achieves these shifts.

1. INTRODUCTION

Core Path	Access Path
Read and Listen. Individually or as a class, read and listen to the Introduction for "The Bells." The Introduction provides context for the inspiration for the poem.	**English Learners All Levels & Approaching** **Read and Listen.** Ask students to read and listen to the Introduction for "The Bells." Have them refer to the vocabulary listing on their Access 1, 2, 3, and 4 handouts for definitions of key vocabulary terms. If there are unfamiliar words that are not included in their glossary, encourage students to check a dictionary or online reference tool, like http://tinyurl.com/6ytby.
Access Prior Knowledge. Put your students into small groups or pairs. Remind them of the meaning of the word "onomatopoeia," giving "buzz" as an example. Then have each group list as many examples of onomatopoeia as they can in two minutes. You could even offer some sort of prize for the winning group.	**Beginner** **Complete and Discuss the Chart.** Pair Beginning and more proficient (Beyond) readers. Have these groups complete the "Onomatopoeia Match" exercise on the Access 1 handout that asks students to provide an example of onomatopoeia for each sound source. Have the pairs generate ideas, discuss the chart, and complete it together.

Core Path	Access Path
1. Next, challenge each group to write and perform a brief conversation using only their examples of onomatopoeia. Encourage them to make the sounds in ways that suggest particular emotions as well as the source objects or creatures.	Encourage students to act out how these words would sound coming from the animal. Ask students: *How would the use of onomatopoeia in a poem or story affect you as a reader?*
2. After each group performs the conversations, have the listeners identify the source of the onomatopoeias. Extend the conversation by discussing the emotions the sounds suggested, or caused, for the listeners.	**Intermediate & Advanced** **Complete and Discuss the Chart.** Pair Intermediate and Advanced students. Have these groups complete the "Onomatopoeia Chart" exercise on the Access 2 and 3 handouts that asks students to provide an example of onomatopoeia for each animal. Have the pairs generate ideas, discuss the chart, and complete it together. Encourage students to act out how these words would sound coming from the animal. Ask students: *How would the use of onomatopoeia in a poem or story affect you as a reader?*
3. Ask students about writers they are familiar with and which ones have used onomatopoeia in poems or stories. How does onomatopoeia affect a text?	
	Approaching **Draw Responses.**
	1. First, explain that onomatopoeia is a word that mimics the sound it is describing. For example the word "moo" sounds like the noise a cow makes. The word "moo" is an example of onomatopoeia.
	2. Have students create a comic strip of three or four frames showing a scene on a farm. Students should include as many animals as they can and use only onomatopoeia in the speech bubbles that match the sound of each animal.
	3. After they've completed their comic strips, have students complete the "Onomatopoeia Match" exercise on the Access 4 handout.
	Extend **Discuss the Introduction.** After reading the Introduction, use the information provided to facilitate a pre-reading discussion to get students thinking about the theme in "The Bells."
	1. What are some of the different types of bells you hear ringing everyday?
	2. What types of associations do you have when you hear the ringing of bells?

Teacher's Edition

2. READ

Core Path	Access Path
Make Predictions about Vocabulary. There are seven bold vocabulary words in the text. As students read the text, ask them to make predictions about what they think each bold vocabulary word means based on the context clues in the sentence. If you are in a low-tech classroom, ask students to record their predictions in their notes, so they can be easily referenced in class. If your students have access to technology, they can use the built in annotation tool to make their predictions.	**Note:** This exercise, which extends vocabulary instruction, should be completed when the class shifts from whole group instruction to individual work during the "Read and Annotate" exercise.

Core Path (continued)

It might be helpful to model this for students before they begin the reading. Either using the board or projecting the actual text, focus in on the lines around one that uses the word "runic":

- And he dances, and he yells;
  Keeping time, time, time,
  In a sort of **Runic** rhyme,

Model for the class how to use the overall structure and meaning of the sentence and the sentences around it, the word's position, and other clues to define the unfamiliar vocabulary word. In this case, point out these context keys:

1. Look at the structure of the lines. The word "runic" follows what preposition (In) and precedes which noun? (rhyme) From this, we know that runic is part of a prepositional phrase, and since it's placed before the noun, it's an adjective that describes the rhyme of the bells.

2. We have to look several lines above to find the antecedent for "he," but we can determine that "he" refers to the king of "ghouls."

3. A king of ghouls would be spooky and mysterious, and so maybe the "runic rhyme" he yells is something the ghouls can understand. Therefore, we can infer that "runic" describes something that's mysterious or whose meaning is secret to most people.

Remind students to use a print or digital resource, such as a dictionary, to verify precise word meanings, parts of speech, and pronunciations.

Access Path (continued)

Beginner, Intermediate, & Approaching Pair Practice.

1. Pair Beginning, Intermediate and Approaching students with more proficient readers.

2. Give them an additional sentence that contains a new vocabulary word.

3. Ask the Beginning, Intermediate and Approaching students to complete a Think Aloud using the teacher-led Make Predictions about Vocabulary activity as a model, while the proficient student actively listens.

4. The students should use the context clues in the sentence to try to determine the meaning of the new vocabulary word.

5. After the less-proficient student has completed the Think Aloud and made a prediction about the word's meaning, allow time for the proficient reader to add his/her own thoughts and clarify any points of confusion.

6. Once they've completed this Think Aloud, encourage them to use a dictionary to confirm the definition of the new vocabulary word. Have them refer to the vocabulary listing on their Access handouts 1, 2, and 4 for definitions of key vocabulary terms in the text. Encourage them to add any additional vocabulary words or idioms they find in the text and look up definitions for those words and idioms online or in a dictionary.

Core Path	Access Path

Model Reading Comprehension Strategy. Before students begin reading, model the reading comprehension strategy of rereading by using this Think Aloud that talks students through the first paragraph of text. First explain to your students that rereading is:

reading an entire passage more than once, or reading certain excerpts multiple times in order to uncover meaning and improve comprehension.

Explain to students how rereading will help them understand the selection and better prepare them to remember and find textual evidence to support their ideas in discussions.

- When I reread the first section, I see the author describing the sound of bells. The words he chooses are cheerful.

- By rereading the second section, I can sense the author's excitement building. I can study his word choices—such as "gush of euphony"—to determine this.

- Rereading the third section shows me how the author achieves a dramatic shift in tone. Poe uses words such as "loud," "brazen," "terror," and "scream" to create a horrific scene.

Note: This exercise, which extends instruction around reading comprehension strategies, should be completed when the class shifts from whole group instruction to individual work during the "Read and Annotate" exercise.

Beginner, Intermediate & Approaching Rereading Chart. Have students work in mixed-level pairs to complete the Rereading Chart on their Access 1, 2, and 4 handouts. They will read the first section of the poem twice, noticing new details and refining their understanding with each read. Prompt students to notice other themes or images that are important to your reading of the poem, and to discuss with their partner how their last reading of the text differs from their first.

Read and Annotate. Read and annotate the excerpt. Ask students to use the annotation tool as they read to:

1. use context clues to analyze and determine the meaning of the bolded vocabulary terms

2. ask questions about passages of the text that may be unclear or unresolved

3. identify key details, events, characters, and connections between them

4. note unfamiliar vocabulary

5. capture their reaction to the language and subject of the poem

Beginner
Coach the Reading. While other students read, annotate, and discuss the text independently, work with Beginning students, listening to the audio of the text and pausing periodically or when any student has a question. Coach students in articulating their questions for the group and in highlighting and annotating the text. Have students use the Annotation Guide in the Access 1 handout to support them as they highlight and annotate the text.
For further support, ask questions about the text such as:

Please note that excerpts and passages in the StudySync® library, workbooks, and PDFs are intended as touchstones to generate interest in an author's work. The excerpts and passages do not substitute for the reading of entire texts, and StudySync® strongly recommends that teachers and students seek out and purchase the whole literary or informational work in order to experience it as the author intended. Links to online resellers are available in our digital library. In addition, complete works may be ordered through an authorized reseller by filling out and returning to StudySync® the order form enclosed in this workbook.

Teacher's Edition   341

Core Path	Access Path
	• Is there anything about the story that you don't understand?
	• Why do you think the author describes different kinds of bells?
	• Why do you think the word "bells" is repeated so many times at the end of each stanza?
	Intermediate
	Listen to the Audio. Have these students listen to the audio of the text and use the definitions on the Access 2 handout to help them with words or idioms that may be unfamiliar. If students need help with annotating the text, have them use the Annotation Guide on the Access 2 handout. After working with the Beginning students, you may wish to check this group's progress and provide support as needed.
	Advanced
	Pair with Proficient Peers. Have Advanced students work with English proficient peers to read, annotate, and discuss the text. Have students use the Annotation Guide in the Access 3 handout to support them as they highlight and annotate the text. Encourage them to listen to the audio of the text if needed.
	Approaching
	Use the Annotation Guide. Have students use the Annotation Guide in the Access 4 handout to support them as they highlight and annotate the text.
Discuss. In small groups or pairs, have students discuss the questions and inferences they made while reading. Have them also note new vocabulary. Make sure students follow guidelines for collegial discussions.	
1. Skim the poem to look at the line lengths, punctuation, and number of lines in each section. What changes or patterns do you notice? (The sections I-IV get progressively longer. Also, the lines are in irregular lengths, mostly fairly short. The beginning line of each section ends with a dash, and the next lines announce the kinds of bells and end in exclamation points.)	

Core Path	Access Path
2. What is the overall emotion of the poem? For example, does it feel cheerful or angry? Does it change? (Each section or stanza seems to show a different state of mind. The poem seems to begin cheerfully, but by the long final section it feels repetitive and unhappy.) 3. What are some examples of onomatopoeia? (Answers include *tinkle, tintinnabulation, jingling, shriek, twanging, clanging, jangling, moaning,* and *groaning*)	**English Learners All Levels & Approaching** Use the extra time while on- and beyond- grade-level students are discussing their first reads of the text to work individually and in small groups with English Learners and Approaching readers as previously outlined. Should those students complete their first reads quickly, integrate them into the on- and beyond- grade-level discussion groups. Otherwise English Learners and Approaching readers will be given an opportunity to participate in text discussions with their peers later in the lesson.
	Extend **Tech Infusion.** Have students use the StudySync audio text highlighter to listen for and mark the use of onomatopoeia and make annotations about its effect on the poem.
	Extend **Identify and Define.** Ask students to reference their annotations and share any vocabulary words that were unfamiliar. 1. As a class, compile a list of unknown words on the board. 2. In small groups, ask students to make predictions about they think these words mean based on how they are used in the sentence. Note: They will need access to StudySync to read the words in context and make predictions. 3. Each group should work together using dictionaries or devices to define the words and write the definitions in their notebooks.
	Extend **Tech Infusion** **Record.** Use a voice recording app (Voice Memo on the iPhone or Smart Voice Recorder for Androids) or VoiceThread (http://tinyurl.com/4m389hy) to capture each group's ideas.

Teacher's Edition

3. THINK

Core Path	Access Path
Answer and Discuss. Have students complete the Think questions and then use the peer review instructions and rubric to complete the peer reviews. Refer to the sample answers online to discuss responses with your students. Remind students to follow guidelines for collegial discussions.	**Beginner & Intermediate** **Fill in the Blanks.** Have students use the fill-in-the-blank activity on the Access 1 and 2 handouts to support their responses to the Think questions. If necessary, distribute the activity to Advanced students as well. **Approaching** **Find the Evidence.** Have students use Find the Evidence on the Access 4 handout to help them identify the evidence needed to answer the questions.
	Extend **Debate.** Present students with an issue from the text that can be debated. Allow students to debate the issue as a class or in smaller groups. Debate prompts: 1. When two people look at the same thing, do they ever see it in the same way? 2. How do pieces of art convey meaning if meaning is dependent on the person?
	Extend **Write a Claim.** Ask students to write a strong claim that clearly states their position in relation to the topic they debated. Once students have written their claims, ask them to read their claims to a small group of their peers. This activity will provide them practice writings claims, as well as expose them to claims written by their peers.

SKILL:
Poetic Elements

OVERVIEW

Understanding how poetic elements such as line and stanza work together to provide a framework for meaning is vital to the comprehension of a poem. Onomatopoeia is a sound device that can be used to modulate and add meaning and enjoyment to a poem. This lesson plan provides follow-up questions and useful enrichments to help teachers guide students toward a usable, repeatable method for apprehending both.

OBJECTIVES

1. Learn the definition of poetic elements.
2. Practice using concrete strategies for identifying poetic elements.
3. Participate effectively in a range of conversations and collaborations to express ideas and build upon the ideas of others.

ELA Common Core Standards:
Reading: Literature - RL.8.1, RL.8.4
Speaking & Listening - SL.8.1.A, SL.8.1.B, SL.8.1.C, SL.8.1.D, SL.8.2
Language - L.8.6

RESOURCES

Access 1 handout (Beginner)
Access 2 handout (Intermediate)
Access 3 handout (Advanced)
Access 4 handout (Approaching)

Please note that excerpts and passages in the StudySync® library, workbooks, and PDFs are intended as touchstones to generate interest in an author's work. The excerpts and passages do not substitute for the reading of entire texts, and StudySync® strongly recommends that teachers and students seek out and purchase the whole literary or informational work in order to experience it as the author intended. Links to online resellers are available in our digital library. In addition, complete works may be ordered through an authorized reseller by filling out and returning to StudySync® the order form enclosed in this workbook.

Teacher's Edition   345

1. DEFINE

Core Path	Access Path
Watch. Watch the Concept Definition video on poetic elements with your students. Make sure students write down and are familiarized with the basic elements of poetry, including meter, rhyme, stanza, and figurative language. Pause the video at these key moments to discuss the information with your students:	**English Learners All Levels & Approaching Match.** Have students complete the matching exercise on the Access 1, 2, 3, and 4 handouts as they watch the video. Answers are located online.
1. 0:21 - Discuss what separates rap lyrics, for instance, from a random grouping of words. What do you think it takes for a random "arrangement of words" to become a poem?	
2. 1:07 - Why do you think newer poems are less likely to rhyme? Do song or rap lyrics always rhyme? In the absence of a rhyming pattern, what other kinds of word patterns can be found in poetry?	
3. 1:47 - What are some different kinds of poems? Break down the rhyme scheme, meter, and number of lines in the stanza for each different type of poem.	
Read and Discuss. After watching the Concept Definition video, have students read the definition of Poetic Elements. Either in small groups or as a whole class, use these questions to spur discussion among your students about identifying and analyzing poetic elements, making sure they follow the rules for collegial discussions, use academic language correctly, and respond to the questions and comments of others in the class with relevant evidence, observations, and ideas:	**Beginner** **Finish the Sentences.** Have these students work in pairs to complete the sentence frames on the Access 1 handout as they read the definition. Have them use the completed sentence frames to help them participate in the discussion.
1. What is the difference between a line and a stanza? (A line is a group of words arranged in a single row and ends either at the margin, a pause or at punctuation. Lines have a particular number of syllables, stresses and metrical feet. In contrast, a stanza is a group of lines—not just one—forming the basic recurring metrical unit in a poem. A stanza may combine lines of varied length.)	**Intermediate & Advanced** **Discussion Prompts.** To help these students participate in the discussion, prompt them with questions that can be answered with a few words, such as: • What is another word for meter? (rhythm) • For poems that rhyme, where are the rhyming words usually found? (end of the lines) • What kind of language is metaphor? (figurative language) • What does figurative language help develop? (theme)

Core Path	Access Path
2. In the context of the poem, how do the line lengths add to the meaning? (Some forms of poetry, like iambic pentameter, dictate the specific length of a line. However, the line length in free verse can vary dramatically and impact how the poem is read, as well as the impact on the reader.) 3. What do sound devices like onomatopoeia do that other types of figurative language cannot do? (Writers use sensory details to bring writing to life for the reader, but describing sounds with words can be difficult. Onomatopoeia allows the writer to create the actual sound and immerse the reader in that sensory experience. Also, examples of onomatopoeia are often single syllable words that can have a large impact on the rhythm and meter of a poem allowing poets to emphasize a point or evoking an emotion.)	• What is a group of lines organized in a certain way? (stanza) **Approaching** **Complete a Chart.** To prepare students to participate in the discussion, have them complete the chart on the Access 4 handout as they read the definition. **Beyond** **Discuss.** Have students select a poem they've read and describe poetic elements used in the text. Compile a list of examples. Have students discuss what poetic elements are used in each work and what effect each has on the reader. If the author had not included one of the poetic elements, how might this affect the reader's enjoyment of the story?
	Extend **Tech Infusion** **Pair and Share.** Pair or group students and ask each group to do a Google search to find a song that has an inconsistent rhythm. • How does the rhythm change how you hear the song? • Does it add or detract from your enjoyment of the song? Ask the groups to share their findings with the class. If possible, have students capture pair shares on video using their mobile devices so they can watch their conversations and critique the content.

2. MODEL

Core Path	Access Path
Read and Annotate. Have students independently read the Model section. As they read, ask students to use the annotation tool to: • highlight key points • ask questions • identify places where the Model applies the strategies laid out in the Identification and Application section on Poetic Elements	**Note:** During this portion of the lesson, instruction shifts from whole group to individual work. Use this time to work one-on-one or in small groups with Beginning, Intermediate, Advanced, and Approaching students. **Beginner & Intermediate** **Coach the Reading.** Work with these students (either individually or in small groups) to fill out the guided reading questions on the Access 1 and 2 handouts. Have Beginning students refer to the glossary on the Access 1 handout to help them determine the meaning of difficult words. (Note: Provide the Access 1 handout glossary to Intermediate students if necessary.) Let students know they'll use these answers to help participate in the discussion about the Model. Sample answers for this exercise are located online. **Advanced** **Identify Evidence.** Provide these students with the same instructions to read and annotate as on- and beyond- grade-level students. In addition, ask Advanced students to complete the identifying evidence exercise on the Access 3 handout. Let students know that they'll use these answers to help participate in the discussion about the Model. Sample answers for this exercise are located online. **Approaching** **Guided Reading.** Have students complete the guided reading questions on the Access 4 handout as they read. Let them know that they'll use these answers to help participate in the discussion about the Model. Sample answers for this exercise are located online.

Core Path	Access Path
Discuss. After students read the Model text, use the questions below to facilitate a whole group discussion that helps students understand how to identify and analyze poetic elements. Remind students to follow rules for collegial discussions and to use academic vocabulary correctly. In addition, make sure students have read the selection and draw on that preparation by referring to evidence from the text during the discussion.	

1. According to the Model, how does Poe's poem "The Bells" differ in format from other published poems of the period? (In the 19th century, most poetry was written according to established forms and was organized into stanzas that looked uniform and orderly on the page. "The Bells," however, exhibits great variety in its line and stanza length, in addition to its rich use of figurative language and sound devices.)

2. How does inconsistency and variation in the format of the poem add to its meaning? (The inconsistency in line and stanza length is linked to the idea that while the bells may always be ringing, their sound may appear to be different depending on what event they are intended to signal. They can also be seen to reflect the unpredictability of life.)

3. What other poetic elements does the author use to keep the poem unpredictable? (He uses a variety of rhyme schemes, as well as repetition and an inconsistent rhythm.)

4. How does Poe use onomatopoeia to create a disturbing, frightening mood in the third stanza? (When Poe uses words like *jangling, wrangling, clang, clash, roar,* and *shriek,* readers can hear the harsh noise of the bells. It is no longer a sweet sound, but something that jars the senses, like a car or fire alarm.)

Core Path	Access Path
	Extend **Tech Infusion** **Pair and Share.** Pair or group students. Have each group explore http://tinyurl.com/n54ypy and choose a poem they like. Then, have each group answer the following questions about its poem:
	• Does your poem have consistent rhythm? • How does the form of the poem add to or impact its meaning? • What examples of repetition do you see? • How do those repetitions add to or impact the poem's meaning? Ask the groups to share their findings with the class. If possible, have students capture pair shares on video using their mobile devices so they can watch their conversations and critique the content.

3. YOUR TURN

Core Path	Access Path
Assess and Explain. Have students answer the comprehension questions to test for understanding. Share the explanations for Parts A and B (located online) with your students.	
	Extend **Share and Discuss.** Have students complete the Your Turn section in class. Poll students (using or http://tinyurl.com/nfz427v) about their responses and as a class discuss the different strategies they used to determine the correct answers.

Core Path	Access Path
	Extend **Model.** Have students choose a sound they hear regularly in their lives (text message notifications, the bell at the beginning or end of class, honking horns, dogs barking, etc). Challenge them to write a poem about the sound in their lives, using Poe's poem as a model. Alternatively, you can give your students a modified version of "The Bells" that has all of Poe's original sounds removed and ask them to fill in the blank portions of the poem with sounds from their own lives. Have students produce a display copy of their poem to hang in the classroom, and have them do a "gallery walk" where they circulate around the classroom, reading what their classmates have written. Allow volunteers to perform their poems. Encourage students to draw comparisons between their poems and Poe's poem.

OVERVIEW

The poem "The Bells" is as much about sound and feeling as it is about a story. This Close Read lesson provides an opportunity for students to identify poetic elements and how they help clarify the poem's meaning.

OBJECTIVES

1. Complete a close reading of a passage of literature.
2. Practice and apply concrete strategies for analyzing elements in a poem.
3. Participate effectively in a range of conversations and collaborations to express ideas and build upon the ideas of others.
4. Prewrite, plan, and produce clear and coherent writing in response to a prompt.

   ELA Common Core Standards:
   Reading: Literature - RL.8.1, RL.8.2, RL.8.4
   Writing - W.8.4, W.8.5, W.8.6, W.8.10
   Speaking & Listening - SL.8.1.A, SL.8.1.C, SL.8.6
   Language - L.8.2.C, L.8.4.A, L.8.4.C, L.8.4.D, L.8.5.A, L.8.6

RESOURCES

"The Bells" Vocabulary handout
Access 1 handout (Beginner)
Access 2 handout (Intermediate)
Access 3 handout (Advanced)
Access 4 handout (Approaching)

1. INTRODUCTION

Core Path	Access Path
Define and Compare. Project the vocabulary words and definitions onto the board or provide students with a handout, so they can copy the vocabulary into their notebooks. Suggest that students consult general and specialized reference materials, both print and digital, to compare the precise meaning of a specific word with their initial vocabulary predictions from the First Read. Review words that students defined incorrectly to understand why they were unable to use context clues to develop usable definitions.	**Beginner & Intermediate** **Complete the Sentences.** Have students complete the sentence frames on the Access 1 and 2 handouts using the vocabulary words. Point out that some of the words are in the questions and some will be in the answers. Sample answers are located online. **Advanced & Beyond** **Write in Journals.** Have students write a journal entry using all of their vocabulary words. Remind them to write sentences that communicate the meaning of the words they are using. **Approaching** **Complete a Graphic Organizer.** To support students in comparing their predictions with the correct meanings, have them complete the graphic organizer on the Access 4 handout to record the vocabulary words, their predictions, and the definitions. Then have them write sentences using the words.
Review Have students complete the fill-in-the-blank vocabulary handout for this selection. Answers for the handout are listed online.	
	Extend **Word Web.** Break students into small groups, assign each group a vocabulary word, and ask them to fill out a word web with the vocabulary word in the center and the associating words in the bubbles around the center word. Have them use dictionaries and thesauruses to find words related to the vocabulary word.

Core Path	Access Path
	Extend **Tech Infusion** **Draw.** Have students create artwork to visually represent the words using an iPad or Android art app. Alternatively, you can ask students to draw images on paper.
	Extend **Tech Infusion** **Tunes.** Assign groups of students one of the vocabulary words. Have students use a music library on a mobile device or on a computer to find a piece of music that they feel defines the word. Have the groups share their selection and explain how it relates to the definition of the word.

2. READ

Core Path	Access Path
Model Close Reading. Project the text onto the board and model a close reading of the first stanza using the following annotation strategies. While modeling annotation strategies, make notes that tie the text to the focus skill and demonstrate what students should be looking for as they read. Here is some guidance for you as you annotate with your students: • As the Skills lesson that precedes this text makes clear, writers make use of a number of different poetic elements when they write poetry, including assonance, alliteration, personification, and onomatopoeia. When Edgar Allan Poe published "The Bells," he probably intended its presentation on the page to surprise readers. In the 19th century, most poetry was written according to established forms and was organized into stanzas that looked uniform and orderly on the page. "The Bells," however, exhibits great variety in its line and stanza length. Let's look at the first two stanzas.	

Core Path	Access Path
• What is similar in the first two stanzas? (The first and the last three lines are similar in each stanza.) **How are they different?** (The first stanza is 14 lines, while the second is 21 lines. The line lengths are not consistent between or within both stanzas. While both stanzas contain a great deal of end rhyme, there is no predictable rhyme scheme.) **These differences may have something to do with the theme of the poem. Poe may be saying that while the bells are always ringing, their sound may appear to be different depending on what event they are intended to signal—and what state of mind the listener is in as a result.** • What is the mood in the first two stanzas of the poem? (Possible answer: Positive and cheerful. The silver bells symbolize a "world of merriment" and the golden bells ring out on the occasion of a wedding.) **How does this mood change in the third stanza?** (The bells warn of danger.) **What poetic element does Poe use in this stanza to create a harsh, upsetting kind of mood? Give some examples.** (He uses onomatopoeia. With words such as *jangling, wrangling, clang, clash, roar,* and *shriek,* readers can hear the harsh noise of the bells. It is no longer a sweet sound.) • How long is the fourth and final stanza, and how does it differ from the previous three? (It is 43 lines, much longer than the first and second stanzas and ten lines longer than the third stanza.) **Perhaps through the different line lengths, as well as the length of each stanza, Poe is saying that life is unpredictable. Everyone will experience joy, sorrow, and death, but no one knows how or when.**	
Read and Annotate. Read the Skills Focus questions as a class, so your students know what they should pay close attention to as they read. Then have students read and annotate the excerpt. Ask students to use the annotation tool as they read to: 1. respond to the Skills Focus section 2. ask questions about Poe's use of poetic elements, specifically onomatopoeia.	**Note:** While on- grade-level students are reading and annotating, work one-on-one or in small groups with Beginning, Intermediate, Advanced, and Approaching students to support them as they read and annotate the text.

Core Path	Access Path
3. make connections between the mood in each of the four stanzas, and how they are similar and different. 4. identify key examples of poetic elements that Poe makes use of, including rhyme and repetition. 5. note unfamiliar vocabulary 6. capture their reaction to the ideas and poetic elements in the text As they reread the text, remind students to use the comprehension strategy of Rereading that they learned in the First Read.	**Beginner & Intermediate** **Summarize and Analyze the Text.** Work with these students to complete the sentences on the Access 1 and 2 handouts (Note: The activity for Intermediate students on the Access 2 handout contains fewer scaffolds). They will then use the completed sentences to help them analyze and annotate the text by completing the Skills Focus questions. Refer to the sample Skills Focus answers onine to help them complete the sentences and annotate the text. **Advanced** **Work in Pairs.** Pair these students with more proficient English speakers to work together on analyzing and annotating the text to complete the Skills Focus questions. If these students need more support, have them complete the sentences on the Access 3 handout as they work with their more proficient peers. **Approaching** **Summarize the Text.** Have these students discuss and complete the text summary on the Access 4 handout and use their summary to help them analyze and annotate the text by completing the Skills Focus questions. Correct answers for the summary are online. Also refer to the sample Skills Focus answers to aid students with their annotations.
Discuss After students have read the text, use the sample responses to the Skills Focus questions online to discuss the reading and the process of identifying and analyzing poetic elements. Make sure that students have acquired and accurately use academic-specific words and phrases related to the skill, and demonstrate a command of formal English appropriate to the discussion.	**Extend** **Pair and Share.** In small, heterogeneous groups or pairs, ask students to share and discuss their annotations with a focus on the poetic elements used in the selection. You can provide students with these questions to guide their discussion: 1. How does the author's use of onomatopoeia affect the mood throughout the poem? Cite specific textual evidence to support your statements. (In the first stanza, the word "tinkle"

Copyright © BookheadEd Learning, LLC

Core Path	Access Path
	reflects "merriment" because it is a light sound. By the third stanza, the mood has changed: "What a tale of terror, now, their turbulency tells!" The words "twanging" and "clanging" make the sounds of these bells seem loud and unpleasant, which helps create a mood that reflects the unpleasant purpose of the alarm bells.)

2. The type of bell used in each stanza can help the reader to understand the author's theme or central idea for each section. What is the theme or central idea in each stanza? Cite specific textual evidence to support your answer. (The theme of the first stanza is happiness or fun because the bells "tinkle" and the stars "twinkle with a crystalline delight." The theme of the second stanza is the promise of a happy future because people are getting married. In the third stanza, the theme changes to a realistic view of what actually happens in life. "How the danger ebbs and flows" describes how life is filled with periods of danger or tough challenges. The theme of the final stanza is death. The word "monody" is used to describe the sound of the "iron bells." The bells are creating a mood of sadness.)

3. How does the author create suspense in the poem? (The poem starts out in a light, happy tone, but suddenly changes in the third stanza with alarm bells ringing. The reader wonders what is causing alarm and what will happen next. This, along with the idea that the bells in the fourth stanza represent death, creates a spooky, suspenseful mood.)

Extend
Connect. Start a discussion with the class about how the same thing can look or feel or sound different depending on your circumstances. Is there a song or a book or a piece of art that has changed its meaning from one time of your life to another? Why might that be? |

Core Path	Access Path
	Extend **Discuss.** In small groups or pairs, ask students to discuss their annotations with a focus on line and stanza and onomatopoeia. You can provide students with questions to guide their discussion: 1. How is each stanza different? (The mood of each one is different.) 2. What work does the onomatopoeia do in the poem? (It tells the reader how the speaker is experiencing the bells depending on his outlook.) 3. Is the "plot" of the poem understandable? Does the form make it easier or harder to understand? (Answers will vary.) 4. What is the theme of the poem? (Our attitude changes the way we see the world.) 5. Do you agree or disagree with the author's theme? Why or why not?
	Extend **Search.** Use http://tinyurl.com/em5yc to find another poem that shifts its mood or tone as it progresses. Which poem do you prefer? Why? Present your thoughts with the class.

3. WRITE

Core Path	Access Path
Prewrite and Plan. Read the prompt as a class and ask students to brainstorm their reactions to Edgar Allan Poe's "The Bells." Students can brainstorm together either as a class or in small groups to begin planning their responses as to whether the poem's theme is about the changing of the seasons, as opposed to the story of a tragic loss and subsequent grief. Remind students to look at the excerpt and their annotations to find textual evidence to support their ideas.	**Beginner & Intermediate** **Answer and Discuss.** Have students complete the prewriting questions on the Access 1 and 1 handouts and then explain their answers to a partner before they write. Explain to students that when they answer a question—such as *What is an example of onomatopoeia in "The Bells?"*—they need to include a detail, example or quote from the text that supports the statement. For example, students could include the fourth line, "how they tinkle, tinkle, tinkle," which describes the sound made by the silver bells on the sleighs.

Core Path	Access Path
	Approaching **Answer Prewriting Questions.** Have students complete the prewriting questions on the Access 4 handout to summarize their thoughts before they write.
	Extend **Organize.** Ask students to complete the Idea Map Graphic Organizer (see Resources online) to organize their ideas before they type their responses.
	Extend **Tech Infusion** **Map.** Students can create concept maps online using http://tinyurl.com/yceu2jg. Google drawing can also be used to design a concept map.

Discuss. Project these instructions for the peer review onto the board and review them with your class, so they know what they are looking for when they begin to provide their classmates with feedback:

- How has this essay helped you understand an interpretation of one of the poem's themes?
- What theme did the writer identify?
- Did the writer support the interpretation of the theme with specific text evidence?
- How well does the writer explain how that evidence supports his or her arguments?
- Does the writer write using standard grammar and punctuation? What weak spots could be addressed?
- What specific suggestions can you make to help the writer improve the response?
- What thing(s) does this paper do especially well?

Be sure to tell the writer what he or she did well and what he or she needs to work on. Remember that your comments are most useful when they are constructive.

Core Path	Access Path
After you've looked at the peer review instructions, review the rubric with students before they begin writing. Allow time for students to briefly raise and discuss questions they may have about the peer review instructions and the rubric. Tell students how many peer reviews they will need to complete once they submit their writing.	
Write. Ask students to complete the writing assignment using textual evidence to support their answers. If possible, have students use technology to produce and publish their writing. Once they have completed their writing, they should click "Submit."	
	Extend **Critique.** Project a writing sample on the board and ask the class to identify the elements of writing that are strong, as well as those that are weak or in need of improvement. Alternatively, you can put students in small groups and give them photocopies of a writing sample to collaboratively evaluate. After students have had an opportunity to evaluate student samples, work as a class to generate strategies students can use as they complete their peer reviews to ensure they are substantive.
Review. Once students complete their writing assignment, they should submit substantive feedback to two peers. If possible, have students use technology to interact and collaborate with others.	

When Fear Becomes Phobia

OVERVIEW

As a fun activity to synthesize the material for this unit, students will learn about the psychology of phobias and conduct a short research project to name a phobia one of the characters in the unit might have after his/her suspenseful encounters. Research Links—exploring the science of phobic responses, their relationship to the popularity of horror and suspense fiction, and the Greek-based naming conventions of phobias—are also available.

OBJECTIVES

1. Provide background information about how phobias emerge and ask students to analyze and respond to the question: "What's the worst phobia one of the characters in the Suspense! Unit might develop?"
2. Encourage research with hyperlinks to a range of information about the science of fear and its relationship to works of suspenseful fiction and nonfiction.
3. Recognize uses in tracing the etymology of words.
4. Use technology to produce and publish writing.

   ELA Common Core Standards:
   Reading: Informational Text - RI.8.1
   Writing - W.8.1.A, W.8.1.B, W.8.6
   Speaking & Listening - SL.8.1.A, SL.8.1.C, SL.8.1.D, SL.8.2
   Language - L.8.4.C, L.8.6

RESOURCES

Access 1 handout (Beginner)
Access 2 handout (Intermediate)
Access 4 handout (Approaching)

TITLE/DRIVING QUESTION

Core Path	Access Path
Discuss. As a class, read aloud the title and driving question for this Blast. Ask students what fears they have or what fears they know to be common. Do they have a sense of how and why these fears emerged? (For example, an allergic reaction to a bee sting provoking a later fear of bees.) Remind students that they should not immediately reply to this question. They'll be returning to this question and responding after they've read the Background and some of the Research Links.	**English Learners All Levels** **Define and Discuss an Example.** Discuss with students the difference in meaning between *fear* and *phobia*. Help them see that a phobia is an exaggerated, intense fear that becomes unhealty. Offer an example of a healthy, ordinary fear, and then discuss what could make such a fear a phobia. Discuss these differences using an example from the unit's selections.
Draft. In their notebooks or on scrap paper, have students draft their initial responses to the driving question. This will provide them with a baseline response that they will be developing as they gain more information about the topic in the Background and Research Links sections of the assignment.	**Beginner & Intermediate** **Draft with Sentence Frame.** When drafting their initial response to the driving question, have students refer to this Blast sentence frame on their Access 1 and 2 handouts: • A phobia is much like a fear, but it is_____ _____ _____. Point out these two key features of the sentence frame: 1. The introductory clause "A phobia is much like a fear" borrows language directly from the Blast driving question to provide a response. 2. Ask students to make special note of the comma that separates the two main clauses.

BACKGROUND

Core Path	Access Path
Read. Have students read the Blast Background to provide context for the driving question.	**Beginner & Intermediate** **Read with Support.** Have students read the Blast Background to provide context for the driving question. When they encounter unfamiliar words or phrases, have students refer to the glossary on their Access 1 and 2 handouts. If there are unfamiliar

Core Path	Access Path
	words that are not included in their Blast Glossary, encourage students to check a dictionary or online reference tool, like http://tinyurl.com/6ytby.

Copyright © BookheadEd Learning, LLC

Access Path (continued)

Approaching
Read and Summarize. Have students read the Blast Background to provide context for the driving question. As they read, ask students to complete the fill-in-the-blank summary of the Background provided on their Access 4 handout. When they encounter unfamiliar words or phrases, have students refer to the Blast Glossary on their Access 4 handout.

Beginner & Intermediate
Discuss. Pair students and have them complete the Discuss exercise on the Access 1 and 2 handouts. Encourage students to continue the discussion with their own thoughts and ideas. If students get stuck, have them switch roles.

Core Path

Discuss. Pair students and have them discuss the following questions:

1. When does a fear become a phobia? (when a person experiences anxiety or panic over something, far beyond the actual danger it poses)

2. What did researchers at Emory do with mice? Why is this important to the study of phobias? (Researchers trained mice to fear the smell of cherry blossoms and when the mice's offspring also began to fear cherry blossoms, the researchers could surmise that fear can be passed down genetically.)

3. Why do you think the etymologies of the names of phobias are so complicated or unusual? Where can you learn more about etymologies? (Since the word *phobia* comes from a Greek root, the other phobia name part must also come from roots in Greek or possibly other languages. It makes the words sound scientific, but more important, by using root words to name phobias, the names will be specific. I can learn more about a word's etymology by consulting a dictionary, glossary, or other reference material.)

4. Do you believe we can overcome our phobias, or are we doomed to live with them our entire lives? (I think people can overcome their fears with self-control and determination. Also, it seems that if researchers can train mice to have a phobia, they can teach people to get over a phobia, too.)

Core Path	Access Path
Brainstorm. Remind students about the driving question for this Blast: "What's the worst phobia one of the characters in the Suspense! Unit might develop?" Also remind them of the driving question for this unit: "What attracts us to stories of suspense?" In their notebooks, ask students to make three columns, one for the Blast Background, one for the unit "Suspense!", and one labeled Connect It. Ask students to brainstorm answers to the driving question and the driving question for the unit. In the third column, have students brainstorm to explain the ways that fear plays into our attraction to stories of suspense. Show students how to look up the names of phobias as they identify them, and to use the Research Links. Here's a short example of how it might look:	

Background	Suspense!	Connect It
Narrator of "The Tell-Tale Heart": fear of loud noises, or phono- phobia	The fears characters experience can show us how many different kinds of fears are in the world.	Looking at how characters face fear makes me think that maybe I could learn to be braver myself, and my own fears don't look so big after all.

RESEARCH LINKS

Core Path	Access Path
Examine and Explore. Before asking students to explore the Research Links, use these activities and questions to guide their exploration:	

Core Path

1. To prepare for their actual Blast, have students check out the "Phobias!" and "Totally Normal Phobias" links.

2. What are some of the most surprising phobias listed on these links? Are there any phobias on these links that jump out as possibly relating to characters or individuals from the "Suspense!" unit? (Some of the surprising phobias may include: ablutophobia, which is the fear of bathing and washing; anthophobia, which is the fear of flowers; bathmophobia, which is the fear of stairs, etc. Some phobias that may jump out as possibly relating to characters from this unit may include: cynophobia, which is the fear/dislike of dogs for the story *Cujo*.)

3. Why do we name so many phobias? Are there really so many people with a fear of gravity that we need "barophobia"? What are some of the positives and negatives to giving these fears their own specific names? (People are scared of all kinds of things. There might be some people who are afraid of gravity, but I don't think there's a lot. If we name a fear, we are in some ways empowering that fear, giving it control over somebody. If we don't name a fear, then it seems less real and easier to control for some.)

Access Path

Extend

Research, Discuss, and Present.

1. Assign each group one link to explore in depth.

2. Ask them to discuss the information:
   a. What are the key points made in this resource?
   b. What new information have you learned?
   c. What did you learn about this "big idea" from reading this research?
   d. How did this help you to better understand the topic?
   e. What questions does your group have after exploring this link?

3. Allow students time to informally present what they learned.

Core Path	Access Path
	Extend **Tech Infusion** **Generate Suspense.** As students explore the links, encourage them to make their own suspense stories as Choose Your Own Adventures with CYOCYOA (http://tinyurl.com/q8veexc). Have students read and play with one another's stories.

QUIKPOLL

Core Path	Access Path
Participate. Answer the poll question. Have students use information from the Background and Research Links to explain their answers.	

NUMBER CRUNCH

Core Path	Access Path
Predict, Discuss, and Click. Before students click on the number, break them into pairs and have them make predictions about what they think the number is related to. After they've clicked the number, ask students if they are surprised by the revealed information.	

CREATE YOUR BLAST

Core Path	Access Path
Blast. Ask students to write their Blast response in 140 characters or less.	**Beginner** **Blast with Support.** Have students refer back to the sentence frame on their Access 1 handout that they used to create their original Blast draft. Ask them to use this frame to write and enter their final Blast. **Intermediate** **Blast with Support.** Have students attempt to draft their Blast without the sentence frame on their Access 2 handout. If students struggle to compose their Blast draft without the sentence frame, remind them to reference it for support. **Beyond** **Write a Claim.** Ask students to use their answer to the poll question to write a statement that could be used as the foundation for a piece of explanatory writing. Once students have written their statements, ask them to read the statements to a small group of their peers. This activity will provide them practice writing, as well as expose them to the writing of others.
Review. After students have completed their own Blasts, ask them to review the Blasts of their peers and provide feedback.	

Extended Writing Project

Suspense!

EXTENDED WRITING PROJECT:
Narrative Writing

OVERVIEW

This unit includes a variety of texts and materials that deepen students' knowledge about the art of suspense. For this unit's Extended Writing Project, students will be writing a suspenseful narrative. This lesson provides students with a definition of narrative writing and its major features, as well as a portion of a sample student response.

OBJECTIVES

1. Discuss and demonstrate an understanding of the features of narrative writing.
2. Practice and apply concrete strategies for identifying features of narrative writing.
3. Participate effectively in a range of conversations and collaborations to express ideas and build upon the ideas of others.

ELA Common Core Standards:
Reading: Literature - RL.8.1, RL.8.2, RL.8.3
Reading: Informational Text - RI.8.1, RI.8.2
Writing - W.8.3.A, W.8.4, W.8.5, W.8.10
Speaking & Listening - SL.8.1.A, SL.8.1.B, SL.8.1.C, SL.8.1.D, SL.8.2

RESOURCES

Access 1 handout (Beginner)
Access 2 handout (Intermediate)
Access 3 handout (Advanced)
Access 4 handout (Approaching)

1. INTRODUCTION

Core Path	Access Path
Read and Discuss. Have students read the prompt to the Extended Writing Project on narrative writing. Ask them to look at the various parts of the prompt and respond to the following questions: • What is the prompt asking you to do? • What specific requirements does the prompt lay out for your narrative? • What does the prompt ask you to specifically consider? • Which elements of narrative writing will you need to learn more about in order to respond to the prompt?	**Beginner & Intermediate** **Paraphrase.** Have students follow along with the text as they listen to the audio recording of the prompt. After they've heard the audio recording, have them fill in the blanks on their Access 2 and 3 handouts to create their own paraphrased version of the prompt. After they've completed their prompt paraphrase, have students participate in the whole class discussion of the prompt using the questions provided in the Core Path. A sample paraphrase is located online. **Approaching** **Listen and Discuss.** Have students follow along with the text as they listen to the audio recording of the prompt. Then have them participate in the whole class discussion of the prompt using the questions provided in the Core Path.
Read and Annotate. Individually or as a class, read the Introduction to Narrative Writing. The Introduction defines narrative writing as well as the five features of narrative writing. If you have students read the Introduction as a class, be sure they take notes. They should note the definition of narrative writing, the purpose, and the five features in their own words. If they are reading online, request that they use the StudySync annotation tool to make notes about informative writing. Then divide the class into small groups. Ask each group to collaborate on writing a summary of the purpose and features of the narrative writing form. Remind the class not to include personal opinions in their summary. Have groups trade their summaries and discuss points that are the same and different. What can each group add to or change in its summary that will help students better understand, plan, and produce a strong narrative piece of writing? Remind students to follow the rules of collegial discussions as they exchange ideas.	**Beginner & Intermediate** **Fill in the Blanks.** As they read and listen to the Introduction, have Beginning and Intermediate students work together to fill in the blanks on the Access 1 and 2 handouts. They can also refer to the Introduction glossary provided on those handouts. Provide assistance and clarification as needed. Sample answers are located online. **Approaching & Advanced** **Identify Features of Narrative Writing.** After reading the Introduction, have students list the five features of narrative writing on their Access 3 and 4 handouts in their own words.

Core Path	Access Path
Recall and Connect. Pair or group students and ask each group to recall the elements of narrative writing, without looking at the lesson. Then ask students to list these elements for each of the narratives they have encountered so far in this unit. Have groups share their lists with the class, and discuss any differences in group responses.	
	Extend **Freewrite.** Ask students to take out a sheet of paper and, at the top of the paper, write the following: 1. Someone they would like to visit the Roman Coliseum with 2. The last place they spent money 3. The worst thing about where they live Then, display the following sentence: *[person from #1] walks into [place from #2] and starts complaining loudly about [quality from #3].* For example: LeBron James walks into a movie theater and starts complaining loudly about the traffic. Give students 10 minutes to freewrite, using their sentence as a starting point. Remind them that their writing doesn't have to be perfect; they should **just keep writing** until the 10 minutes are up. After students have finished, give them the chance to share their ideas with a neighbor or the class.

2. READ

Core Path	Access Path
Read and Label. Have students read the student model narrative "The Silver Box." Then have students identify the five features of narrative writing in "The Silver Box" and label them using the annotation tool: • setting • characters	**Beginner** **Coach the Reading.** While other students read, annotate, and discuss the text independently, work with Beginning students, listening to the audio of the text, using the model glossary on their Access 1

Please note that excerpts and passages in the StudySync® library, workbooks, and PDFs are intended as touchstones to generate interest in an author's work. The excerpts and passages do not substitute for the reading of entire texts, and StudySync® strongly recommends that teachers and students seek out and purchase the whole literary or informational work in order to experience it as the author intended. Links to online resellers are available in our digital library. In addition, complete works may be ordered through an authorized reseller by filling out and returning to StudySync® the order form enclosed in this workbook.

Teacher's Edition   373

Core Path	Access Path
<ul><li>plot</li><li>theme</li><li>point of view</li></ul>	handout, and pausing when any student has a question. Coach students in articulating their questions for the group and in highlighting and annotating the text using the Annotation Guide on the Access 1 handout. **Intermediate** **Listen to the Audio.** Have these students listen to the audio of the text and use the model glossary on their Access 2 handout to help them with words or idioms that may be unfamiliar. If students need help with annotating the text, have them use the Annotation Guide on the Access 2 handout. After working with the Beginning students, you may wish to check this group's progress and provide support as needed. **Advanced** **Pair with Proficient Peers.** Have Advanced students work with English proficient peers to read, annotate, and discuss the text. You can also refer them to the model glossary on the Access 3 handout if necessary. Have these student pairs use the Annotation Guide in the Access 3 handout to support them as they highlight and annotate the text. Encourage them to listen to the audio of the text if needed. **Approaching** **Use the Annotation Guide.** Have students use the Annotation Guide on the Access 4 handout to support them as they highlight and annotate the text.
Discuss. In small groups or pairs, have students discuss the observations and annotations they made while reading. Make sure students follow the rules for collegial discussions. Have them examine the "Constructed Response – Narrative" grading rubric this Student Model was written to satisfy. Inform students that this is the same rubric that will be used to evaluate their completed Narrative Extended Writing Project. They should consider how understanding the Student Model can help them as they begin to craft their own suspenseful narrative in response to the prompt.	**English Learners All Levels & Approaching** Use the extra time while on- and beyond- grade-level students are discussing their first reads of the text to work individually and in small groups with Approaching readers and English Learners as outlined above. Should those students complete their first reads quickly, integrate them into the on- and beyond- grade-level discussion groups. Otherwise Approaching readers and English Learners will be given an opportunity to participate in text discussions with their peers in future Extended Writing Project lessons.

Core Path	Access Path
	Extend **Tech Infusion** **Feature ReFocus.** Ask students to each choose one of the five features of narrative writing. Ask each student to identify how the author of the sample student narrative used that feature. What is the setting? Who are the characters? What is the point of view? How is the plot introduced? What possible themes does the author present? Then, using a collaborative whiteboard like Padlet (http://tinyurl.com/nv79c7y), ask students to hypothesize how the story might be different if their feature was changed. For example, the characters are a mother, father, and son, but if the characters were a mother, a son, and a grandmother, the story might open with the son and grandmother playing a card game, as opposed to a video game. Allow students the opportunity to discuss the changes they proposed.

3. THINK

Core Path	Access Path
Answer and Discuss. Have students complete the Think questions. Collect papers or discuss answers as a class. Refer to the sample answers online.	**Beginner** **Answer Questions with Support.** Review all of the Think questions with students to clarify vocabulary and comprehension. Read aloud question 1: then ask students to refer back to their annotations to find key details related to the setting of the story. Once students have identified these key details (paragraphs 3 and 4—"The sun will be coming up soon" and "ignoring his mother's warning of imminent danger"), ask them to determine what is most likely the setting by piecing their annotations of key details together. Once you've completed this instruction with students, have them complete the remaining Think questions using the sentence frames on their Access 1 handout. **Intermediate** **Support.** Have partners review the Think questions and help one another with any terms or concepts that need to be clarified. Tell them that they may ask you about any vocabulary or concepts they cannot

Core Path	Access Path
	clarify for themselves, and then have them use the sentence frames on their Access 2 handout to assist them in writing the answers to the questions. **Advanced** **Discuss.** Have students read and answer the Think questions independently. Then have them discuss their answers to questions with an English-proficient partner. Have them share the ideas they want to develop into their own narrative, the reasons why these ideas are interesting to them, and what sources are available. They can take notes on their discussion and save them for their pre-write. **Approaching** **Rewrite the Think Questions.** Preview the Think questions and ask students to rewrite each question in their own words on the Access 1 handout. Have students use their paraphrased versions of the Think questions to help them respond.
	Extend **Identify.** As a class, watch a suspenseful scene from a movie or television show (the opening scene of *Monsters, Inc.* works well for this, and you can find it on YouTube here: http://tinyurl.com/pdf8mcf, and ask students to compile a list of elements that make the scene suspenseful, for example: • It's dark. • The boy hears strange noises. • He's going to bed – a "scary" time of day. • The boy is alone in his room. • There's a physical threat. • We hear ominous music. • The audience doesn't know what's casting the shadow. Then, ask students (individually, in pairs, or in groups) to think of other suspenseful TV or movie scenes. What other suspenseful elements can they identify? Create a Google Doc so students can create an ongoing list of suspenseful elements that they can refer to as they write their own suspenseful narrative.

Organize Narrative Writing

OVERVIEW

As students begin the planning stage of their Extended Writing Project, they will need to consider an organizational structure for their suspenseful narratives. This lesson identifies the common elements of a narrative and explains how a writer uses these elements to develop a story.

OBJECTIVES

1. Discuss and demonstrate an understanding of organizational structure in narrative writing.
2. Practice and apply concrete strategies for organizing narrative writing.
3. Participate effectively in a range of conversations and collaborations to express ideas and build upon the ideas of others.

ELA Common Core Standards:

Reading: Literature - RL.8.1, RL.8.3

Writing - W.8.3.A, W.8.5

Speaking & Listening - SL.8.1.A, SL.8.1.B, SL.8.1.C, SL.8.1.D

RESOURCES

Access 1 handout (Beginner)

Access 2 handout (Intermediate)

Access 3 handout (Advanced)

Access 4 handout (Approaching)

Please note that excerpts and passages in the StudySync® library, workbooks, and PDFs are intended as touchstones to generate interest in an author's work. The excerpts and passages do not substitute for the reading of entire texts, and StudySync® strongly recommends that teachers and students seek out and purchase the whole literary or informational work in order to experience it as the author intended. Links to online resellers are available in our digital library. In addition, complete works may be ordered through an authorized reseller by filling out and returning to StudySync® the order form enclosed in this workbook.

Teacher's Edition   377

1. DEFINE

Core Path	Access Path
Read and Discuss. Either individually or as a class, read the Define section of the lesson. Then, in small groups or as a class, use the following questions to spur discussion among your students about organizational structure in narratives. Remind students to follow the rules for collegial discussions.	**Beginner** **Use Support.** Read the definition of narrative writing and organizational structure with students, having them refer to the glossary on the Access 1 handout. Pause after each definition to clarify vocabulary and to ask students to restate in their own words what information they think the statement is communicating about the different kinds of organizational structures. Provide clarification as necessary.

Core Path (continued):

1. The definition discusses the role of conflict in a story. How does the conflict of a narrative affect the characters of the story? (It presents the characters with a problem they must face; it forces the characters to take action.)

2. What roles can a narrator serve in a story? How does the narrator's point of view help readers determine the narrator's role? (The narrator is the voice of the story, but the narrator also serves as the reader's eyes, allowing the reader to view the actions of the story. The narrator's point of view allows readers to determine if the narrator is a participant in the story or an outside observer.)

3. The definition states that characters are the driving force of a story. How do characters drive a story forward? (Character actions, thoughts, and dialogue move the plot forward as they deal with the main problem or conflict. Characters also develop and undergo significant change by a story's end.)

Access Path (continued):

Intermediate
Use Support and Discuss. Use the Access 2 handout to introduce and clarify the terms in the lesson. Then allow students to participate in the class discussion.

Advanced
Discuss. Have Advanced students read and then discuss what they have learned with an English-proficient partner or in mixed-proficiency groups about organizational structure and how it might be used in narrative writing. Students can refer to the Access 3 handout for help if necessary.

Approaching
Explain. After participating in the reading and the class discussion, have students state in their own words what organizational structure is and why it is important in narrative writing. Have them explain to a partner what they know about each of the text structures: sequential or chronological, cause and effect, problem and solution, and compare and contrast. They can use the definitions on the Access 4 handout to clarify their understanding.

Beyond
Analyze Narrative Writing. Have small groups read and analyze an online or print narrative story, either fiction or nonfiction. Ask them to identify the theme or big idea, as well as the structure of the text. Then have them evaluate the effectiveness of the writer's structure and discuss what they might do differently

Core Path	Access Path
	Extend **Feature Focus.** Pair or group students and tell them they have ten minutes to brainstorm a list of as many story conflicts as possible. Encourage them to think of conflicts they've encountered before, in stories and in life, as well as conflicts that they've invented. Invite students to share their conflict lists and discuss the conflicts as a class. Discuss which conflicts work best for a suspenseful story and why.

2. MODEL

Core Path	Access Path
Read and Discuss. As students read the Model text, use these questions to help students understand the organizational elements of a narrative. 1. How does the narrator introduce the problem in this story? How does the author heighten the problem at the beginning? (The narrator describes the woman's actions and tells readers that she hears a low, thick growling. This lets readers know that the woman and her son are in danger. The author heightens the problem by revealing that the woman's son is inside the car, while she is outside the car.) 2. How can readers determine the narrator's point of view in this story? What effect does this point of view have on the storytelling? (Readers can tell that the story is written from the third-person point of view because the narrator describes the character's thoughts and actions as an outside observer rather than a participant. This point of view allows the narrator to let readers know what the woman is thinking and feeling, as if readers are inside her head, and experience her shock and fear.)	**Beginner & Intermediate** **Use Support.** Work with students to use and complete the activity on the Access 1 and 2 handouts to support their reading and comprehension of the Model text and instruction. When they have completed the activity, have them join the class discussion. **Advanced** **Discuss.** Have students read and discuss the Model text with a partner or group that includes native English speakers. **Approaching** **Read with Support.** Have students read the Model text aloud with an on-level partner. Work with them to complete the Access 4 handout. Then have them join in the class discussion.

Core Path	Access Path
3. What detail do readers learn at the end of the excerpt that heightens the problem further? How does the author reveal this information? (Through Donna's thoughts, readers learn that the dog is matted with blood. This helps readers infer that Cujo has killed his owner, and that he intends to kill Donna and her son as well.)	
Practice. 1. Ask students to list their favorite suspense stories and to identify the type of narrator and conflict in each. 2. Have students describe trends or patterns in the kinds of stories they like to read and thus might like to write. Do they prefer first-person or third-person narrators? Do they prefer real-life conflicts or more extreme ones? 3. Once students have completed their lists and descriptions either on a piece of paper in class or online, they will need to provide their peers with constructive feedback either on paper or online. (Note: You will need to create a writing assignment if they are going to submit these online.) 4. Students should use their peers' feedback to focus their future prewriting activities.	**Extend** **Write.** Group students and ask each group to rewrite the excerpt from *Cujo* with a first-person point of view, with Donna relating the incidents in the excerpt as they took place. Invite groups to read their scenes aloud to the class. Discuss how the point of view shift changed the story and the reader's understanding of the conflict and characters. Ask students to think about which narrative point of view they would like to use when crafting their own suspenseful narratives.

3. YOUR TURN

Core Path	Access Path
Assess and Explain. Have students answer the comprehension questions to test for understanding of organizing narrative writing. Share the explanations for Parts A and B (located online) with your students.	

Core Path	Access Path
	Extend **Quiz.** Group students and invite each group to write a Your Turn question about conflict in another selection from the unit. Publish student questions on Socrative (http://tinyurl.com/nfz427v) and allow students time to answer the questions generated by each group. Discuss which questions were most effective and why.

OVERVIEW

In this lesson, students will prepare to write their suspenseful narratives by brainstorming and listing ideas for problem, narrator, setting, and characters. Students will present prewriting lists for peer review and receive feedback on their prewriting ideas.

OBJECTIVES

1. Discuss and demonstrate understanding of narrative writing features.
2. Analyze the prompt and generate information for a suspenseful narrative.
3. Participate effectively in a range of conversations and collaborations to express ideas and build upon the ideas of others.

   ELA Common Core Standards:
   Reading: Literature - RL.8.1, RL.8.3, RL.8.6
   Writing - W.8.3.A, W.8.4, W.8.5, W.8.6, W.8.10
   Speaking & Listening - SL.8.1.A

RESOURCES

Graphic Organizer: Story Elements
Access 1 handout (Beginner)
Access 2 handout (Intermediate)

1. WRITE

Core Path	Access Path

Core Path

Brainstorm. Before students begin brainstorming, ask them to discuss the following questions to fuel their prewriting:

- What types of characters and settings do you like to read about? Why?

- Do certain character types seem to encounter more conflict than others?

- What kinds of conflicts are interesting to readers?

- How can a story's setting impact the conflict in the story?

- How can conflict force characters to take action?

- How do writers keep readers in suspense?

- What elements of suspense are enjoyable to readers?

- How does a narrator's point of view affect the reader's experience?

- How is a story different when the narrator is a character in the story rather than an observer?

Encourage students to keep readers in mind when brainstorming for their suspenseful narratives. Remind students that their aim is to engage and entertain readers with their suspenseful narratives.

Then ask students to complete the "Prewrite: Narrative Writing" graphic organizer, which presents students with the following questions regarding their suspenseful narratives:

- What types of characters would I like to write about?

- What types of problems might these characters face?

- How might the setting affect the characters and the problem?

- From which point of view should this story be told? Why?

Access Path

Beginner & Intermediate
Organize and Support the Prewrite.
Before Beginning and Intermediate students complete the graphic organizer, they may benefit from a more structured version of the class discussion.

1. Group students in pairs with proficient English speakers or mixed-proficiency small groups.

2. Having them finish the sentence frames on the Access 1 and 2 handouts.

3. Encourage students to consider movies and television stories as well as those they have read and heard as they complete the sentences.

4. If there is time, have some pairs share their responses to the sentence frames to help other students consider ideas or details they hadn't thought of during the assignment.

Advanced
Share and Evaluate. Ask partners to share and evaluate their finished graphic organizers with an English-proficient partner. Have them discuss the following questions:

- Who are some characters you have enjoyed reading about?

- Why did you like them?

- What are some story settings that you like reading about?

- Why did you like them?

- What kinds of conflicts do you like to read about?

- What stories did you find suspenseful?

- What was it about them that made you anxious or uneasy?

- Does it make any difference who is telling the story? Why?

Core Path	Access Path
Review. Once students complete their writing assignment, they should submit substantive feedback to three peers. Students will use the feedback to develop their writing in different stages of the writing process. Project these instructions for the peer review onto the board and review them with your class, so they know what they are looking for when they begin to provide their classmates with feedback: • How well did they answer the following questions presented in the prewriting chart? • Did they list multiple ideas for each element of narrative writing? • Have they chosen the strongest ideas for each element? • Are there any elements that should be more carefully considered or better planned? • Do their notes reflect the reasons behind their choices? • Do the ideas seem well suited for an engaging suspenseful narrative? • Are there any ideas that could be improved on? How so?	
	Extend **Spotlight on Suspense.** Group students and ask each group to generate a list of words related to suspense. Provide students with the following list to get them started: • fright • worry • tension • mystery Invite groups to share their lists with the class, and compile a comprehensive list of group responses. Use the student word choices to generate a classroom discussion about how authors achieve these effects in writing. Encourage students to review the list and keep these elements in mind as they prewrite for their own suspenseful narratives.

OVERVIEW

Students will learn about the elements of a strong narrative introduction, including exposition to establish setting, characters, and a story problem or conflict. They will then examine the opening paragraph of "The Monkey's Paw" to learn how authors use exposition to establish setting and introduce characters. Students will practice identifying introductory exposition details in familiar narratives and discuss their necessity and effect in narrative writing. They will then practice crafting the introductions to their own suspenseful narratives.

OBJECTIVES

1. Discuss and demonstrate understanding of narrative introductions.
2. Practice using concrete strategies for identifying elements of narrative introductions and apply this knowledge to the development of their own narrative introductions.
3. Participate effectively in a range of conversations and collaborations to express ideas and build upon the ideas of others.

ELA Common Core Standards:
Reading: Literature - RL.8.1, RL.8.3
Writing - W.8.3.A, W.8.3.B, W.8.3.D, W.8.4, W.8.5, W.8.10
Speaking & Listening - SL.8.1.A, SL.8.1.B, SL.8.1.C, SL.8.1.D

RESOURCES

Access 1 handout (Beginner)

Access 2 handout (Intermediate)

Access 3 handout (Advanced)

Access 4 handout (Approaching)

Please note that excerpts and passages in the StudySync® library, workbooks, and PDFs are intended as touchstones to generate interest in an author's work. The excerpts and passages do not substitute for the reading of entire texts, and StudySync® strongly recommends that teachers and students seek out and purchase the whole literary or informational work in order to experience it as the author intended. Links to online resellers are available in our digital library. In addition, complete works may be ordered through an authorized reseller by filling out and returning to StudySync® the order form enclosed in this workbook.

Teacher's Edition   385

1. DEFINE

Core Path	Access Path
Read and Discuss. Either individually or as a class, read the Define section of the lesson. Then, in small groups or as a class, use the following questions to spur discussion among your students about the elements of a good narrative introduction. Remind students to follow the rules for collegial discussions.	**Beginner** **In Your Own Words.** Have students read the definition and then use their Access 1 handouts to pause after each bullet point to rewrite the components of an introduction in their own words. Once students have completed this activity, ask them to complete the fill-in-the-blank activity on the Access 1 handout.
1. The definition states that a narrative introduction "sets the stage for the events that follow." In what ways is a narrative introduction similar to a stage set in a theater performance? (Sample answer: When the curtain rises on a theater production, an audience can often determine where and when the action in a play occurs based on the set design. Similarly, clues in the introduction to a narrative can reveal where and when a story takes place.)	**Intermediate** **In Your Own Words.** Have students read the definition of an introduction and then use their Access 2 handout to pause after each bullet point to rewrite the components of an introduction in their own words. After they've rewritten each of the bullet points in their words, work with students to develop their own definitions of the term.
2. The definition explains that writers often include elements of exposition in a narrative introduction. Why might a writer want readers to have this information at the opening of the story? (Sample answer: The exposition contains information that is essential to the story, such as who the characters are, where the story is set, and what kind of problem or conflict the characters face. Without this information at the beginning of the story, writers would not be able to orient readers and capture their attention.)	**Advanced** **In Your Own Words.** Have Advanced students read and then discuss what they have learned about introductions with an English-proficient partner or in mixed-proficiency groups. After their conversation, have Advanced students write the definition of an introduction on the Access 3 handout.
3. The definition explains that writers use precise language and sensory details in narrative introductions. Why is this important? How does it affect the reader's experience with the story? (Sample answer: Precise language and sensory details can transport a reader into the world of the story. This is especially true in fantasy and science fiction, where the writer is describing an environment completely unlike the real world.)	**Approaching** **Restate the Definition.** Have students read the define section and then use their Access 4 handouts to restate the most important points in their own words. Clarify questions to aid students' comprehension as needed. Then have students participate in mixed-level groups with the class to discuss the purpose of an introduction in an essay.
4. Think about a story that "hooked" you in the first few paragraphs. What was appealing about the introduction? Why did you want to keep reading? (Answers will vary.)	**Beyond** **Jigsaw.** If there is extra time, have students watch the introduction or opening scene to a movie or television show. Challenge students to identify elements of exposition in the opening scene. • Are characters introduced to the viewer?

Core Path	Access Path
	• Does the viewer learn about the setting of the story?
	• Is a problem or conflict revealed to the viewer in the opening scene?
	• If elements of exposition are not presented in the opening scene, why might this be? As a class, briefly discuss why elements of exposition may not be included in the introduction of a story. Then, challenge them to write scenes that would add the missing elements of exposition for the scene presented to the class.
	Extend **Tech Infusion** **Annotate.** Organize the class into groups. Have each group search for and choose a short story in the public domain. (One collection can be found at http://tinyurl.com/pq7v6ud). Ask each group to read the first three paragraphs of the story and identify expository details that introduce setting, character, and conflict. Have students use Diigo (http://tinyurl.com/yo6zoj) or another online annotation tool to highlight and annotate the expository elements of the introduction. Then have groups share their annotations with the class and discuss the effectiveness of the narrative introductions.

2. MODEL

Core Path	Access Path
Read and Discuss. As students read the Model text use these questions to help students understand the features and function of narrative introductions: 1. According to the Model, how does an author engage and orient a reader in a narrative introduction? (by including specific details that reveal important information such as setting and character, as well as a hint of the conflict in the story)	**Beginner, Intermediate & Approaching** **Underline Writing Elements.** Have students look closely at the elements of exposition alongside the Model introduction from the text, "The Monkey's Paw" on the Access 1, 2, and 4 handouts. Then ask them to find and underline the elements of the introduction you learned about in the Define section that are similar to those mentioned in the writing prompt. Make sure students understand these

Please note that excerpts and passages in the StudySync® library, workbooks, and PDFs are intended as touchstones to generate interest in an author's work. The excerpts and passages do not substitute for the reading of entire texts, and StudySync® strongly recommends that teachers and students seek out and purchase the whole literary or informational work in order to experience it as the author intended. Links to online resellers are available in our digital library. In addition, complete works may be ordered through an authorized reseller by filling out and returning to StudySync® the order form enclosed in this workbook.

Teacher's Edition   387

Core Path	Access Path
2. In the opening paragraph of "The Monkey's Paw," how does the author use descriptive language to reveal the atmosphere of the setting? (by contrasting the interior of the home with the "cold and wet" night outside; by including details such as the "drawn" blinds and bright fire; by describing the father and son playing a game and the old woman knitting by the fire)	elements. Explain that they can use elements of exposition similar to those found in the excerpt from "The Monkey's Paw" in their own introductions when they write their narratives. If students come across words they have difficulty with while reading the Model, refer them to the Glossary on the Access 1, 2, and 4 handouts.
3. How does the author reveal information about the characters in the introductory paragraph? (by describing the father's thoughts and actions during the game of chess; by showing the old woman's reaction to the husband's outbursts)	**Advanced** **Identify the Parts.** Have students read the Model and answer the questions on the Access 3 handout. Once they've completed the questions, pair Advanced students with more proficient students to allow them to share their answers.
4. According to the Model, what is the author's aim in crafting a narrative introduction? (The author hopes readers will want to continue reading to find out who the characters are, what kind of problem they face, and how they might solve it.)	
	Extend **Practice.** 1. If students have extra time, have small groups brainstorm a list that contains at least two characters, some important information about the characters, a setting, and a problem. 2. Once each group has finished its list, ask each group to switch lists with another group in the classroom. 3. Allow the groups time to collectively construct an introduction for a narrative based on the details provided on the list they received from another group in the classroom. 4. Then have them share and discuss their introductions with the group that wrote the original list of information. 5. As a class, discuss a few of the introductions generated. Encourage students to analyze and critique the introductions generated during this activity.

Teacher's Edition

Core Path	Access Path

Practice.

1. Ask students to complete a short writing assignment and apply the skills they have learned for writing an introduction paragraph.

2. Students have had a chance to brainstorm and prewrite about characters, setting, conflict, and narrator. Now have them write an introduction for their suspenseful narrative. What details will they include to engage and involve their readers?

3. Remind students that they will be able to use either this introduction or a revised version when they write their narrative.

4. Students can complete this draft of their narrative introduction on paper, or you can create a Write Assignment on StudySync, and they can submit their drafts online for anonymous peer review.

Beginner
Write Your Introduction.

1. Prior to writing their introductions, ask students to complete the sentence frames on the Access 1 handout.

2. After students have finished the sentence frames, ask them to discuss with a partner what they plan to write about, clarifying any language as needed before writing their introductions.

3. Then students should write their own introductions being sure to use precise language when describing their settings or characters. Encourage them to refer back to the Prewrite Worksheet they completed.

Intermediate
Finish Sentences. Have students fill in the sentence frames on the Access 2 handout. Review their answers with them, and after making any clarifications needed, allow them to use their answers to craft their introductions. Then allow them to join Advanced students to discuss and edit their introductions.

Advanced
Clarify and Edit. Have students refer to their Prewrite Worksheet and the writing prompt as they write their introductions. Have them read their introductions aloud to another Intermediate or Advanced student to check for language that needs to be clarified and to answer the following questions:

- Have you introduced characters, setting, and a conflict?

- What information do you provide the reader about the characters? Are the characters simply described by their physical appearances, or did you include details about their personalities?

- What kinds of details did you include about the setting? Does the setting directly or indirectly contribute to the conflict?

Please note that excerpts and passages in the StudySync® library, workbooks, and PDFs are intended as touchstones to generate interest in an author's work. The excerpts and passages do not substitute for the reading of entire texts, and StudySync® strongly recommends that teachers and students seek out and purchase the whole literary or informational work in order to experience it as the author intended. Links to online resellers are available in our digital library. In addition, complete works may be ordered through an authorized reseller by filling out and returning to StudySync® the order form enclosed in this workbook.

Teacher's Edition   **389**

Core Path	Access Path
	• What about your introduction do you think will keep the reader moving forward? Is there a clear hook in your introduction meant to capture the reader's attention? If not, do you think a clear hook is necessary? Allow students time to make edits to their introductions as necessary. **Approaching** **Finish the Sentences.** 1. Prior to writing their introductions, ask students to complete the sentence frames on the Access 4 handout. 2. Once they have completed the statements with the information they plan to write about, have them begin writing their introductions. Remind students that they can begin their introductions by introducing one of their characters, introducing the setting, or introducing the conflict (though typically have students attempt to introduce characters or setting first).
	Extend **Tech Infusion** **Character Chat.** Create a class chat room on Today's Meet (http://tinyurl.com/psef72j) and tell students that they will be chatting as one of the characters in their suspenseful narrative. Encourage students to introduce their characters and ask questions that help them get to know the other characters in the chat room. Ask students to think about what they would want to know about the characters if they were reading a story about them. This activity is designed to foster character development, as well as to encourage students to hone in on which character details they should reveal in their narrative introductions.

3. YOUR TURN

Core Path	Access Path
Assess and Explain. Have students answer the comprehension questions to test for understanding of the functions and features of narrative introductions. Share the explanations for Parts A and B (located online) with your students.	
	Extend **Write.** Have students work in pairs or groups to write two Your Turn questions about the features of the introduction of another story from the unit. The questions should focus on details of character and setting, as well as the author's word choice and descriptive language. Have groups share their questions with other groups. Give the groups time to answer the questions. Then lead a class discussion about what students learned from completing the questions.

Narrative Techniques and Sequencing

OVERVIEW

As students move toward the planning stage of their Extended Writing Project, they'll need to consider the manner in which they choose to tell their story. This lesson identifies the variety of tools that writers use to develop the plot and characters, explore the setting, and engage the reader.

OBJECTIVES

1. Discuss and demonstrate an understanding of narrative techniques and sequencing.
2. Practice identifying narrative techniques and sequencing and apply this understanding to an original piece of writing.
3. Participate effectively in a range of conversations and collaborations to express ideas and build upon the ideas of others.

ELA Common Core Standards:

Reading: Literature - RL.8.1, RL.8.3

Writing - W.8.3.A, W.8.3.B, W.8.5

Speaking & Listening - SL.8.1.A, SL.8.1.B, SL.8.1.C, SL.8.1.D

RESOURCES

Access 1 handout (Beginner)

Access 2 handout (Intermediate)

Access 3 handout (Advanced)

Access 4 handout (Approaching)

1. DEFINE

Core Path	Access Path
Read and Discuss. Either individually or as a class, have students read the Define section of the lesson. Then use the following questions to spur discussion among your students about narrative techniques and sequencing. Remind students to follow the rules for collegial discussions.	**Beginner & Intermediate** **In Your Own Words.** Have students read the definition and then use their Access 1 and 2 handouts to pause after each bullet point to rewrite the definition for narrative techniques and sequencing in their own words. Once students have completed this activity, ask them to complete the fill-in-the-blank activity on the Access 1 and 2 handouts.

Core Path

Read and Discuss. Either individually or as a class, have students read the Define section of the lesson. Then use the following questions to spur discussion among your students about narrative techniques and sequencing. Remind students to follow the rules for collegial discussions.

1. The definition explains that writers manipulate the pacing of a narrative to slow down or speed up the action at certain parts of a story. What do you think this means? How do you think writers can manipulate a story's pacing? (Sample answer: An author can create suspense by pacing and drawing out a moment of uncertainty. For example, in *Cujo,* author Stephen King slows down the pacing when Donna first sees the dog in the garage. He separates her reactions into separate paragraphs, focusing separately on each one of the thoughts that run through her mind as she watches the dog. This forces the reader to slow down, drawing out the suspense. In contrast, action sequences often contain little dialogue and few thoughts from the characters, to quicken the pace.)

2. What essential information do writers give to the audience in the exposition? (Sample answer: Authors introduce the characters, the time and place in which the action occurs, and the problem or conflict the characters must face and attempt to solve.) **Can you think of stories, movies, etc. that don't give some of that information in the exposition?** (Answers will vary.)

3. Can a story have more than one problem for a character to solve? How might a story with multiple problems differ from a story with only one problem or conflict? (Sample answer: Yes. Many novels present characters with more than one problem or conflict. Sometimes the solution to one problem creates another conflict. The difference between a story with one problem for a character to solve or confront and one with multiple problems is mainly one of length. A short story might have only one problem or conflict, where a long novel will have more than one.)

Access Path

Beginner & Intermediate
In Your Own Words. Have students read the definition and then use their Access 1 and 2 handouts to pause after each bullet point to rewrite the definition for narrative techniques and sequencing in their own words. Once students have completed this activity, ask them to complete the fill-in-the-blank activity on the Access 1 and 2 handouts.

Advanced
In Your Own Words. Have Advanced students read and then discuss what they have learned about narrative techniques and sequencing with an English-proficient partner or in mixed-proficiency groups. After their conversation, have Advanced students write the definition of narrative techniques on the Access 3 handout.

Approaching
Complete a Chart. Have students read the Define section of the lesson. As they read, have them complete the chart on their Access 4 handout. If they struggle to fill in a cell, help them by providing an example of each technique to help students see and understand how each technique can be used in a narrative. Once they are finished, have students join the class discussion.

Core Path	Access Path
4. The definition states that narrative techniques follow a certain order: exposition, rising action, climax, falling action, resolution. What would happen to a story if the writer didn't follow that order? (Sample answer: Authors sometimes break these rules to create interesting or unexpected twists in their stories. For example, a writer might open with a flashback, without explaining who the characters are or what exactly is happening until the following chapter or section. This can create interest on the part of the reader, who keeps reading to find out what exactly is going on.) **Can you think of any stories that don't follow that order?** (Answers will vary.)	**Beyond** **Jigsaw.** If students have extra time, put them in small groups and assign each group two different texts from the unit (or a previous unit). Then challenge them to work together to identify the narrative techniques used in those texts and how they are sequenced. • Do the authors use all of the techniques you learned about in the Define section? If not, which techniques are not used? • How are the texts sequenced? Challenge students to discuss how narrative techniques are used in the exposition, middle of the story, and conclusion of each text. Allow each group time to share their findings with the class.
	Extend **Tech Infusion** **Blast.** Create a Blast and ask students to "blast out" the definition of narrative techniques in their own words and/or provide examples of a really strong exposition, climax, etc. that they've seen in other books or movies. Use the poll question to ask students which part of a story they think is the easiest/hardest to write.

2. MODEL

Core Path	Access Path
Read and Discuss. As students read the Model text, use these questions to help students understand how to use narrative techniques:	**Beginner & Intermediate** **Underline Key Words.** Have Beginning and Intermediate students work in pairs. As they read the Model, have them refer to the excerpt as it appears on their Access 1 and 2 handouts. Have students underline words or phrases that represent a narrative technique used by the author. If they encounter any words they find difficult to understand, have them refer to the glossary on the Access 1 and 2 handouts.

Core Path	Access Path
1. The Model presents excerpts from "The Monkey's Paw" that contains dialogue. According to the Model, how do authors use dialogue as a narrative technique? (Authors use dialogue to develop characters and build reader understanding of the characters in a story. Dialogue can also be used to move the action forward and foreshadow events to come.)	**Advanced** **Identify the Parts.** Have students read the Model and answer the questions on the Access 3 handout. Once they've completed the questions, pair Advanced students with more proficient students to allow them to share their answers. If they have trouble with any of the words found in the Model, direct students to the glossary on their Access 3 handout.
2. What types of details has the author of "The Monkey's Paw" used to develop the characters and plot? (The author has used descriptive details to show readers what the characters think and feel. Mr. White looks at the monkey's paw "dubiously," and emits a "shuddering cry" when the paw twists in his hand. The author has also used sensory details to allow readers to experience the events of the story as the characters experience them, such as the high wind outside and the mysterious sound of a banging door.)	**Approaching** **Read with Support.** Have students read the Model. As they read, have them complete the reading activity on the Access 4 handout. If students struggle with some of the vocabulary in the Model, refer them to the glossary on the Access 4 handout.
3. How does the author use pacing in this part of "The Monkey's Paw"? What effect do you think pacing has on the tone of this story? (The author speeds up the action of the scene when Mr. White makes his first wish. Then the action slows down as the family sits in silence before they go to bed. This slowed action helps the author create an oppressive and anxious tone as the family waits to see what will happen now that a wish has been made.)	
4. Why do you think pacing is an important narrative technique? (Pacing is important because it allows writers to control how quickly events are revealed. Without it, writers might rush to the climax, because it's the most exciting part, without developing their characters and conflicts thoroughly. This could make the climax less interesting, and could make the resolution illogical.)	

Core Path	Access Path
Practice. Have students create an outline in order to organize the sequence of events in the rising action section of their suspenseful narratives and consider narrative techniques such as dialogue and pacing. When they are finished, have them exchange their outlines with a partner to offer and receive feedback.	**Beginner** **Use Narrative Techniques.** 1. Prior to creating their outlines, ask students to complete the sentence frames on the Access 1 handout. 2. After students have answered the questions, ask them to discuss with a partner what they need to organize, clarifying any language as needed before beginning to sequence the events contained in the rising action section of the student's suspenseful narratives. 3. Then students should create their outline to sequence the events in the rising action for their suspenseful narratives. Remind students to consider how they can use dialogue and pacing to enhance their writing and add suspense to their narratives. Encourage them to refer back to the writing prompt and to the Prewrite Worksheet they completed. 4. Have them use the sentence frames on the Access 1 handout to help them create their outlines. **Intermediate** **Finish Sentences.** Have students fill in the sentence frames on the Access 2 handout. Review their answers with them, and after making any clarifications needed, allow them to use their answers to create their outline, organizing the sequence of events in the rising action of their narratives. Then allow them to join Advanced students to discuss and edit their outlines. **Advanced** **Clarify and Edit.** Have students refer to their Prewrite Worksheet and the writing prompt as they create their outlines. Have them read the contents of their outlines aloud to another Intermediate or Advanced student to check for elements that need to be developed further and to answer the following questions: • Does the sequence of events seem logical? If not, is there an intended reason for events not to be logically sequenced?

Core Path	Access Path
	• Does the outline include all of the information typically found in the rising action?
	• Does the outline contain information about how dialogue will be used in this section of the narrative? How pacing will be used?
	• Do the events ultimately develop the characters and story enough to reach the climax?
	Allow students time to make edits to their outlines as necessary.

Approaching
Finish the Sentences.

1. Prior to creating their outlines, ask students to complete the sentence frames on the Access 4 handout.

2. Once they have completed the statements with the information they plan to include in their outlines, provide support to students as needed to develop their outlines. Remind students to use the information they plan to include in their own narratives.

Extend
Scramble. Split the class into four or five equal groups and give each group an envelope with slips of paper in it. In the envelope, they'll find slips with the terms *exposition, rising action, climax, falling action,* and *resolution* on them. Mixed in, they'll find slips of paper with details or events from a story in the unit (or a story that everyone in the class is familiar with). For example, you might write "Mrs. Stevenson is unable to contact her husband by telephone" as a piece of exposition from *Sorry, Wrong Number.* You may choose to include several details for each part of the sequence of events, depending on the reading level of your students. Each group will need to put the sequence in order, and group the correct details from the story with the correct part of the sequence. You could turn it into a contest or race, giving the first group to get them all right a reward (or just bragging rights).

Please note that excerpts and passages in the StudySync® library, workbooks, and PDFs are intended as touchstones to generate interest in an author's work. The excerpts and passages do not substitute for the reading of entire texts, and StudySync® strongly recommends that teachers and students seek out and purchase the whole literary or informational work in order to experience it as the author intended. Links to online resellers are available in our digital library. In addition, complete works may be ordered through an authorized reseller by filling out and returning to StudySync® the order form enclosed in this workbook.

Teacher's Edition 397

3. YOUR TURN

Core Path	Access Path
Assess and Explain. Have students answer the comprehension questions to test for understanding of narrative techniques and sequencing. Share the explanations for Parts A and B (located online) with your students.	
	Extend **Write.** Pair or group students and have them write two Your Turn questions about a different text from the unit, using the Your Turn questions from this lesson as a model. They should include multiple-choice answers in their questions. Once all groups are finished, have them trade questions with other groups.
	Extend **Tech Infusion** **Space Race.** Collect the questions and answers from the activity above using a Google Form and create a Space Race activity using Socrative (http://tinyurl. com/nfz427v) so students can compete to answer questions from all the groups.

EXTENDED WRITING PROJECT:
Plan

OVERVIEW

Students will gather previous prewriting lists and plan their suspenseful narratives by completing a plot diagram with information they have brainstormed. Students will present plot diagrams for peer review and receive feedback on their narrative techniques and sequencing.

OBJECTIVES

1. Discuss and demonstrate understanding of narrative techniques and sequencing.
2. Plan a suspenseful narrative by sequencing events of rising action, climax, and falling action.
3. Participate effectively in a range of conversations and collaborations to express ideas and build upon the ideas of others.

ELA Common Core Standards:
Writing - W.8.3.A, W.8.3.B, W.8.5, W.8.6, W.8.10
Speaking & Listening - SL.8.1.A, SL.8.1.B, SL.8.1.C, SL.8.1.D

RESOURCES

Graphic Organizer: Narrative Writing Plot Diagram

Access 1 handout (Beginner)

Access 2 handout (Intermediate)

Access 4 handout (Approaching)

1. WRITE

Core Path	Access Path
Discuss. As a class, review the information about narrative techniques and sequencing. Read through the questions posed by the prompt in the Extended Writing Project Plan lesson:	**Beginner & Intermediate** **Use Sentence Frames.** In small groups, have students discuss their own writing ideas using the following questions and sentence frames below. Clarify unknown vocabulary, answer questions, and provide examples for anything students do not understand.

Core Path (continued):

- What details and events are most important in the exposition of a story?
- What story developments should take place during the rising action of a story?
- What is the purpose of a story's climax?
- How do writers lead readers toward a resolution of a story?
- What narrative techniques are the most effective for creating a feeling of suspense?

Solicit two or three sample texts from the class and, as a group, use these to discuss the questions posed by the prompt. Remind students to follow the rules for collegial discussions. Students should ask themselves these questions as they begin to plan their own suspenseful narratives.

Access Path (continued):

- What details and events are most important in the exposition of a story?
- What story developments should take place during the rising action of a story?
- What is the purpose of a story's climax?
- How do writers lead readers toward a resolution of a story?
- What narrative techniques are the most effective for creating a feeling of suspense?

Then, have students review the characteristics of narrative techniques by completing the sentence frames on the Access 1 and 2 handouts. They may need to reread the Define section of the Narrative Techniques Skill lesson to help them complete the sentences.

Organize. Remind students that as part of the planning process, they should use their prewriting graphic organizer, introductory paragraph drafts, and rising action outlines to complete the "Narrative Writing Plot Diagram." Students may seek out additional plot diagrams or story maps online to help them prepare for the writing assignment.

Note: As the on- and beyond- grade-level students begin the organization and writing stage of this lesson, support Beginning, Intermediate, and Approaching students to ensure they understand what type of information they need to include in their "Narrative Writing Plot Diagram."

Beginner & Intermediate
Preview Road Map. To help Beginning and Intermediate students organize their narratives and prepare to fill in the plot diagram, have them use their prewriting graphic organizers to answer the questions on the Planning Chart on the Access 1 and 2 handouts. Point out that as they organize their ideas for their narratives, they may find it necessary to structure events in a different manner than they had originally planned. Then, refer students to the Narrative Road Map on their Access 1 and 2

Copyright © BookheadEd Learning, LLC

Core Path	Access Path
	handouts and explain what kind of information they will write in each section. Have them review their previously completed assignments to identify and underline information and details they can use in each section of their Narrative Road Map. **Approaching** **Use Organizational Supports.** Make sure students have access to all of their previous assignments to draw upon. Then give them the Narrative Road Map on their Access 4 handout to structure their organization. Go over each of the categories. Explain that as they write they can add additional paragraphs as needed.
Write. Tell students to refer to the ideas they compiled in the previous stage of the writing process and to transfer ideas and details from their prewriting graphic organizers and introductory paragraph drafts into the plot diagram they will be completing. Point out that as they organize their ideas for their narratives, students may find it necessary to structure events in a different manner than they had originally planned. Then ask students to complete the writing assignment using the "Narrative Writing Plot Diagram."	**Beginner** **Complete a Road Map with Support.** Help students use the underlined sections of their previously completed materials to fill in the Narrative Road Map on the Access 1 handout. Before writing, have them state orally what they want to write in each section to evaluate where they may need help with vocabulary, grammar, and sentence structure. You can work with Beginning students individually as needed or in a small group offering support to multiple students at one time. Then have them write, providing assistance as needed. **Intermediate** **Write and Discuss.** Remind students that they can use what they underlined in their previous assignments and Narrative Road Map on the Access 2 handout to plan their writing. Have partners or small groups discuss questions about the content of their completed Narrative Road Maps such as: • When or where will your setting take place? My setting will take place _____. • Who will be your characters? My characters will be _____. • What will be some of the events in your narrative? Some of the events in my narrative will be _____. Have them make any changes necessary before submitting their writing for further peer review.

Copyright © BookheadEd Learning, LLC

Core Path	Access Path
	Advanced **Clarify Organization.** Ask Advanced students to pair up with Beginning, Intermediate, and Approaching students to review their Narrative Road Map. Have them work together to discuss the following questions about their writing. Encourage Beginning, Intermediate, and Approaching students to make changes to their Narrative Road Map if necessary: • Does the exposition introduce the characters, the setting, and the problem? Is this organized in a way that makes sense? • Do the events support the rising action and the falling action? • Are there any other details that should be included? **Approaching** **Complete an Essay Road Map.** Provide students with the following questions to help them complete and review their Narrative Road Map on the Access 4 handout: • Are my characters and setting introduced at the beginning? Do I introduce a problem also? • Do I support the rising action with two or more events? Do I support the falling action with two or more events? • Do I have a clear resolution to the problem? • Are there additional details I should add?
Review. Once students complete their writing assignment, they should submit substantive feedback to three peers. Students will use the feedback to develop their writing in different stages of the writing process. Project these instructions for the peer review onto the board and review them with your class, so they know what they are looking for when they begin to provide their classmates with feedback: • How well do the details on the plot diagram address the writing prompt?	**Beginner & Intermediate** **Review.** Group Beginning and Intermediate students with more proficient writers as they review their plot diagrams. Have them use the following questions to help in the reviews. • Does the exposition introduce the characters and setting? • What is the problem? • Does the rising action lead to the climax? • What is the climax or turning point?

Core Path	Access Path
• How can the sequencing of events be improved? What suggestions can you offer the writer to make the events of the story fall in a more logical order?	• Do the climax and falling action make you wonder how the conflict will be resolved?
• What suggestions can you make to help the writer improve the expository elements listed on the diagram? Do you understand who the characters are and what is happening?	• How is the problem or conflict resolved?
• Is there enough of a plot to keep the reader interested? How can the writer adjust the rising action events to reflect development of character and conflict?	
• What steps might the writer take to improve the climax of the story so that it is more suspenseful and engaging to readers?	
• How could the writer modify the falling action events to create a strong and memorable resolution?	
	Extend
	Building Plot. Ask students to become story architects to build the plots of their stories. Have students write each plot event on an index card or sticky note. Then ask students to arrange plot events in the order in which they will occur in the story. Encourage students to keep the five main parts of a plot diagram in mind as they sequence the events in their stories. Then have students meet with a partner to review one another's story plans and provide feedback.

BLAST:
Descriptive Details

OVERVIEW

Students will learn how writers include descriptive details in a narrative to enhance a story and create a vivid experience for readers. Students will examine how descriptions help a reader understand details about story elements such as character, setting, and conflict. Students will explore a variety of Research Links that allow them to research the craft of narrative writing, practice identifying descriptive details in familiar narratives, and discuss the necessity of and effect of descriptive details in narrative writing.

OBJECTIVES

1. Explore background information about the use of descriptive details and sensory language when writing narratives.
2. Practice the narrative elements of descriptive details and sensory language as well as research using hyperlinks to a range of information about details and sensory language, including articles, videos, audio, as well as informational and educational perspectives.
3. Participate effectively in a range of conversations and collaborations to express ideas and build upon the ideas of others.

   ELA Common Core Standards:
   Reading: Literature - RL.8.1
   Writing - W.8.3.A, W.8.3.B, W.8.3.D, W.8.4, W.8.6, W.8.10
   Speaking & Listening - SL.8.1.A, SL.8.1.B, SL.8.1.C, SL.8.1.D, SL.8.2

RESOURCES

Access 1 handout (Beginner)
Access 2 handout (Intermediate)
Access 4 handout (Approaching)

TITLE/DRIVING QUESTION

Core Path	Access Path
Read and Discuss. As a class read aloud the title and driving question for this Blast: "How can details bring a story to life?" Ask students what they already know about descriptive details and sensory language. What are descriptive details? What is sensory language? Why would an author use details and sensory language when writing a narrative? How are these narrative elements used? Taking into account ideas generated by their classmates and following the rules for collegial discussions, how do they think details can bring a story to life? Remind students that they should not immediately reply to this question. They'll be returning to this question and responding after they've read the Background and some of the Research Links.	**English Learners All Levels & Approaching** **Discuss a Visual.** Have students view a photograph of that shows a scene from nature. The image should be rich and full of details so students can use their senses to describe it, like the example below: http://tinyurl.com/ke8ldvy. Have students imagine they are in the forest where the picture was taken. Discuss how the picture is full of details from nature, and prompt students to use their senses to describe it. Use these questions to prompt discussion: • What do you smell? • What does the water sound like? • How would you describe the green plants? • What does the water feel like? • What would the water taste like? Have students share their list of details and sensory language.
Draft. In their notebooks or on scrap paper, have students draft their initial responses to the driving question: "How can details bring a story to life?" This will provide them with a baseline response that they will be altering as they gain more information about the topic in the Background and Research Links sections of the assignment.	**Beginner & Intermediate** **Draft with Sentence Frame.** When drafting their initial response to the driving question, have students refer to this Blast sentence frame on their Access 1 and 2 handouts: • When writing a story, details can bring it to life because _____. Point out these two key features of the sentence frame: 1. The introductory clause "When writing a story" borrows language directly from the Blast driving question to provide a response. 2. Ask students to make special note of the comma that separates the introductory clause from the subject and predicate ("details can bring").

Please note that excerpts and passages in the StudySync® library, workbooks, and PDFs are intended as touchstones to generate interest in an author's work. The excerpts and passages do not substitute for the reading of entire texts, and StudySync® strongly recommends that teachers and students seek out and purchase the whole literary or informational work in order to experience it as the author intended. Links to online resellers are available in our digital library. In addition, complete works may be ordered through an authorized reseller by filling out and returning to StudySync® the order form enclosed in this workbook.

Teacher's Edition   **405**

BACKGROUND

Core Path	Access Path
Read. Have students read the Blast Background to provide context for the driving question: How can details bring a story to life?	**Beginner & Intermediate** **Read with Support.** Have students read the Blast Background to provide context for the driving question. When they encounter unfamiliar words or phrases, have students refer to the glossary on their Access 1 and 2 handouts. If there are unfamiliar words that are not included in their glossary, encourage students to check a dictionary or online reference tool, like http://tinyurl.com/6ytby. **Approaching** **Read and Summarize.** Have students read the Blast Background to explain the driving question. As they read, ask students to complete the fill-in-the-blank summary of the Background provided on their Access 4 handout. When they encounter unfamiliar words or phrases, have students refer to the glossary.
Discuss. Pair students and have them discuss the following questions about descriptive details: 1. What are descriptive details? (Descriptive details are details that describe story elements such as characters, setting, and conflict.) 2. What is sensory and figurative language? (Sensory language is descriptive language that enhances what the characters are seeing, experiencing, or feeling. Figurative language is a type of sensory language that uses simile and metaphor to aid in description.) 3. Why would an author use details and sensory language when writing a narrative? (Authors use details and sensory language to enhance their descriptions and help readers understand information about the story as well as to help draw a reader into a story and create an engaging experience for the reader.)	**Beginner** **Discuss.** Pair Beginning with Advanced (or Beyond) students and have them use the dialogue starter on their Access 1 handout to discuss the topic. Advise them to return to the dialogue and switch roles if they get stuck. **Intermediate** **Discuss.** Pair Intermediate with Advanced (or Beyond) students and have them use the dialogue starter on their Access 2 handout to discuss the topic. Advise them to return to the dialogue and switch roles if they get stuck. If their conversation is progressing smoothly, encourage them to continue the discussion beyond the dialogue starter sheet. They can expand their conversations to discuss other examples of how descriptive details are used to bring a story to life.

Core Path	Access Path

Core Path

4. How are these narrative elements used? (They are used to describe how a character looks, feels, dresses, and thinks. They describe the time, location, appearance of the place, atmosphere of the setting. They also describe the conflict, the severity of the problem, and whether the problem is getting better or worse). What are some examples of these elements? (adjectives, adverbs, specific nouns, sensory details, strong verbs, and figurative language.)

5. Why are these elements essential to a strong narrative? (These elements are essential because they make the characters, setting, and actions of the story particular to that story and make the story more involving.)

Brainstorm. Remind students about the driving question for this Blast: "How can details bring a story to life?"

Ask students to think of words that are sensory or images that provide details. Have students use this sentence to build a bank of details and sensory words. In their notebooks, ask students to make five columns, one for each sense, and then list the words under the appropriate sense.
Sentence: *The dog ate it.*

Here is an example:

sight	hearing	smell	taste	touch
tears ran down cheeks	the slurping was like a suction cup	it smelled like rotten eggs	thick, hot, and gooey	mushroomy, spongy, and soft

RESEARCH LINKS

Core Path	Access Path
Examine and Explore. Before asking students to explore all of the Research Links, use these activities to guide their exploration of descriptive details: Have students explore "'Hi, ho, Silver!'" Pair them and have each set of partners listen to a different short radio clip. Have one person write down the descriptive details and sensory language, and the other person write down the background sounds. Then, have them collaborate to draw a picture of the main character or action sequence. Then, have them all watch "Adding Details to a Statement." Provide a different simple sentence to the class (ex. "She was going.") and invite each student to craft a new statement comprised of descriptive details and sensory language. Invite students to share their work with the class. Discuss how the details added by different groups make the statement particular in terms of the character, setting, and action.	

	Extend
	Research, Discuss, and Present.
	1. Assign each group one link to explore in depth.
	2. Ask them to discuss the information:
	   a. What are the key points?
	   b. What inferences did you make as you read?
	   c. What did you learn about descriptive detail and sensory language from reading this research?
	   d. How did this help you to better understand the topic?
	   e. What questions does your group have after exploring this link?
	3. Allow students time to informally present what they learned.

QUIKPOLL

Core Path	Access Path
Participate. Answer the poll question. Have students use information from the Background and Research Links to explain their answers. Remind students to follow the rules for collegial discussions.	
	Extend **Discuss.** Once students have posted their response to the poll, ask them to discuss the results in small groups or as a class. Are they surprised by the outcome?

NUMBER CRUNCH

Core Path	Access Path
Predict, Discuss, and Click. Before students click on the number, break them into pairs and have them make predictions about what they think the number is related to. After they have clicked the number, ask students if they are surprised by the revealed information.	

CREATE YOUR BLAST

Core Path	Access Path
Blast. Ask students to write their Blast response in 140 characters or less, answering the driving question: How can details bring a story to life?	**Beginner** **Blast with Support.** Have students refer back to the sentence frame on their Access 1 handout that they used to create their original Blast draft. Ask them to use this frame to write and enter their final Blast.

Core Path	Access Path
	Intermediate **Blast with Support.** Have students attempt to draft their Blast without the sentence frame on their Access 2 handout. If students struggle to compose their Blast draft without the sentence frame, remind them to reference it for support. **Beyond** **Write a Vision.** Ask students to use their answer to the poll question to write a strong descriptive sentence that they could use for either a character, setting, or conflict in their own narrative assignment. Once students have written their sentence, ask them to read share with a group of their peers. This activity will provide them practice writing descriptive sentences, as well as expose them to language written by their peers.
Review. After students have completed their own Blasts, ask them to review the Blasts of their peers and provide feedback.	**Extend** **Discuss.** As a class or in groups, identify a few strong Blasts and discuss what made those responses so powerful. As a group, analyze and discuss what characteristics make a Blast interesting or effective.
	Extend **Revise.** Resend a second version of this Blast assignment to your students and have them submit revised versions of their original Blasts. Do the same responses make the Top 10? How have the answers improved from the first submissions?

Writing Dialogue

OVERVIEW

Students will learn about the elements of effective and engaging dialogue in narrative writing. Students will examine an excerpt from "The Monkey's Paw" to learn how authors use dialogue to reveal information about characters, as well as their thoughts and actions. Students will then draft a scene of their own suspenseful narratives in which two or more characters engage in dialogue.

OBJECTIVES

1. Discuss and demonstrate an understanding of the purpose and mechanics of dialogue in narrative writing.
2. Practice identifying and writing dialogue in a piece of narrative writing.
3. Participate effectively in a range of conversations and collaborations to express ideas and build upon the ideas of others.

ELA Common Core Standards:
Reading: Literature - RL.8.1, RL.8.3, RL.8.4
Writing - W.8.3.B, W.8.4, W.8.5, W.8.10
Speaking & Listening - SL.8.1.A, SL.8.1.B, SL.8.1.C, SL.8.1.D

RESOURCES

Access 1 handout (Beginner)

Access 2 handout (Intermediate)

Access 3 handout (Advanced)

Access 4 handout (Approaching)

Please note that excerpts and passages in the StudySync® library, workbooks, and PDFs are intended as touchstones to generate interest in an author's work. The excerpts and passages do not substitute for the reading of entire texts, and StudySync® strongly recommends that teachers and students seek out and purchase the whole literary or informational work in order to experience it as the author intended. Links to online resellers are available in our digital library. In addition, complete works may be ordered through an authorized reseller by filling out and returning to StudySync® the order form enclosed in this workbook.

Teacher's Edition   411

1. DEFINE

Core Path	Access Path
Read and Discuss. Either individually or as a class, read the Define section of the lesson. Either in small groups or as a class, use the following questions to spur discussion among your students about writing dialogue. Remind students to follow the rules for collegial discussions.	**Beginner** **In Your Own Words.** Have students read the definition and then use their Access 1 handouts to pause after each bullet point to rewrite the components of dialogue in their own words. Once students have completed this activity, ask them to complete the fill-in-the-blank activity on the Access 1 handout.

Core Path (continued):

1. The definition refers to dialogue as a written verbal exchange between two or more characters. How else is dialogue used in a narrative? (Sample answer: Through the use of dialogue, an author can show aspects of a character's personality and advance the plot, revealing details that can give readers information about the conflict or problem in the story. Dialogue can also give readers hints about where the story is set.)

2. Why is direct dialogue important for a character within a narrative? Why is indirect dialogue important for the narrator? (Sample answer: Direct dialogue allows characters to speak for themselves without relying on a narrator to express their feelings and ideas for them. Indirect dialogue is important for the narrator when the reader needs to know that a conversation took place, but the exact words that were spoken are unimportant.)

3. Why is following correct punctuation rules and guidelines important when writing dialogue? (Answers will vary. Students should suggest that remembering to start a new paragraph when the speaker changes will avoid confusion over who is talking in the story, and that using both open and closed quotation marks is important for noting when dialogue begins and ends in a story.)

Access Path (continued):

Intermediate
In Your Own Words. Have students read the definition of dialogue and then use their Access 2 handout to pause after each bullet point to rewrite the components of dialogue in their own words. After they've rewritten each of the bullet point in their words, work with students to develop their own definitions of the term.

Advanced
In Your Own Words. Have Advanced students read and then discuss what they have learned about dialogue with an English-proficient partner or in mixed-proficiency groups. After their conversation, have Advanced students write the definition of dialogue on the Access 3 handout.

Approaching
Restate the Definition. Have students read the define section and then use their Access 4 handouts to restate the most important points in their own words. Clarify questions to aid students' comprehension as needed. Then have students participate in mixed-level groups with the class to discuss the purpose of dialogue in a narrative.

Beyond
Jigsaw. If students have extra time, put them in small groups and assign each group a different text from the unit (or a previous unit). Then challenge them to work together to identify the impact of dialogue in that text.

Core Path	Access Path
	• Is the author using direct or indirect dialogue in the text? Does the author use both?
	• What is the impact of using direct or indirect dialogue in the text? If the author is using both, how does this impact the text?
	• What suggestions can you make about improving how dialogue is used in the story?
	Allow each group time to share their findings with the class.

Extend

Make Conversation. Prior to the lesson, create or print a number of different dialogues. Then, cut them up into the following strips:

• an open quotation mark with a quote following (be sure NOT to include the punctuation and closed quotation mark on this strip)

• a punctuation mark (comma, question mark, exclamation point, period) and closed quotation mark

• any descriptive details regarding who is speaking that would immediately follow the closed quotation mark (examples: "she said," "he said harshly," "they wondered," etc.)

• any indirect dialogue or narrative that runs in between direct dialogue

Organize students into groups of four or five. Provide each group with an envelope filled with the strips of paper comprising a dialogue, as well as a piece of colored construction paper and some tape or glue. Invite each group to work together to reconstruct the dialogue and scene by putting the strips of paper back in order on the construction paper.

Allow students the opportunity to share their dialogues and rationales with the class. You can display the finished products in the classroom.

2. MODEL

Core Path	Access Path
Read and Discuss. As students read the Model text, use these questions to help students understand how to use dialogue in narrative writing:	**Beginner, Intermediate, & Approaching** **Underline Dialogue Elements.** Have students look closely at the elements of dialogue alongside the excerpt from, "The Monkey's Paw" on the Access 1, 2, and 4 handouts. Then ask them to find and underline the elements of dialogue you learned about in the Define section. Make sure students understand these elements. Explain that they can use elements of dialogue similar to those found in the excerpt from "The Monkey's Paw" in their own narratives. If students come across words they have difficulty with while reading the Model, refer them to the Glossary on the Access 1, 2, and 4 handouts.

Core Path (continued)

1. The Model provides examples of both direct and indirect dialogue. What is the difference between them? (Direct dialogue is something a character actually says and is set off by quotation marks. Indirect dialogue is a description within the narrative of something a character says, or it is a paraphrase of something a character said within the direct dialogue of another character.)

2. The definition outline explains that dialogue can help readers better understand a character's appearance, emotions, or intentions. How does the dialogue within the Model do that? (The example in the Model points out that Mr. White's outburst over the weather and the out-of-the-way location of his house is really a reaction to losing a game of chess with his son. He is revealed as being very competitive.)

3. How does the Model indicate that indirect dialogue can be just as important as direct dialogue? Provide an example. (Indirect dialogue can also reveal character traits and drive the plot. Readers learn that Sergeant-Major Morris talks about wild scenes and doughty deeds; of wars and plagues and the strange people he met on his travels, but it is not important to know the precise details. This indirect dialogue helps to explain how Morris came to possess the monkey's paw, and that is all readers really need to know.)

4. How does the use of adjectives, adverbs, and verbs when writing dialogue help to reveal what the characters are feeling? (Adjectives, adverbs, and verbs can help explain how a character said something in a story. In the Model, Sergeant-Major Morris, when asked about the monkey's paw, replies that it is "nothing," but he does so "hastily," which indicates he is not eager to go into further detail and may even be sorry he brought the subject up.)

Access Path (continued)

Advanced
Identify the Parts. Have students read the Model and answer the questions on the Access 3 handout. If students have difficulty during their reading of the Model, refer them to the glossary on the Access 3 handout to clarify the meaning of difficult or unfamiliar words. Once they've completed the questions, pair Advanced students with more proficient students to allow them to share their answers.

Core Path	Access Path
	Extend **Fix It.** Using a whiteboard or an overhead projector, display a direct dialogue containing several examples of incorrect formatting (missing quotes or punctuation, no indication of speaker, etc.). Lead a classroom discussion about how to revise the examples so that they read correctly.
Practice. 1. Ask students to complete a short writing assignment and apply the skills they have learned for writing narrative dialogue. 2. Students have had a chance to brainstorm and prewrite about characters, setting, conflict, and narrator, as well as draft their narrative introductions. Now have them write scenes for their suspenseful narratives in which two or more characters engage in direct and indirect dialogue. What details will they include to develop their characters and story plot? 3. Remind students that they will be able to use this scene or a revised version when they write their narrative. 4. Students can complete this draft of their narrative introduction on paper, or you can create a Write Assignment on StudySync, and they can submit their drafts online for anonymous peer review.	**Beginner** **Write Your Scene.** 1. Prior to writing their scenes, ask students to complete the sentence frames on the Access 1 handout. 2. After students have finished the sentence frames, ask them to discuss with a partner what they plan to write about, clarifying any language as needed before writing their scenes. 3. Then students should write their own scenes being sure to use proper punctuation to indicate direct dialogue when used. Encourage them to refer back to the Prewrite Worksheet they completed. **Intermediate** **Finish Sentences.** Have students fill in the sentence frames on the Access 2 handout. Review their answers with them, and after making any clarifications needed, allow them to use their answers to craft their scenes. Then allow them to join Advanced students to discuss and edit their scenes.
	Advanced **Clarify and Edit.** Have students refer to their Prewrite Worksheet and the writing prompt as they write their scenes. Have them read their scenes aloud to another Intermediate or Advanced student to check for language that needs to be clarified and to answer the following questions:

Core Path	Access Path
	• Are the characters using direct or indirect dialogue in this scene?
	• If using direct dialogue, what information is being given to the reader through the dialogue?
	• If using indirect dialogue, is there enough information provided about the conversation for the reader? If not, is this intentional in your opinion? Why might a writer intentionally provide little information through indirect dialogue?
	Allow students time to make edits to their scenes as necessary.
	Approaching
	Finish the Sentences.
	1. Prior to writing their scenes, ask students to complete the sentence frames on the Access 4 handout.
	2. Once they have completed the statements with the information they plan to write about, have them begin writing their scenes. Remind students that they can use direct or indirect dialogue to convey information to the reader about the characters, setting, or conflict.
	Extend
	What Are These Characters Talking About? Find three different images (can be photos, drawings, paintings, etc.) that show two different people or characters interacting (Note: Each image should be different as far as dress, setting, and facial expressions or body language are concerned). Pair students and have each set of partners work on one of the three images to create a simple dialogue between the characters in the image.
	Invite students to share their dialogues with the class and discuss any differences between dialogues based on the same images. Then, working as a class, comprise a list of character traits for the characters in each image.

Core Path	Access Path
	Extend **Tech Infusion** **Record.** Allow students to record themselves holding their images and reading their dialogues using Educreations (http://tinyurl.com/k6wl3aw). Students can then upload their videos to a class website or YouTube channel.

3. YOUR TURN

Core Path	Access Path
Assess and Explain. Have students answer the comprehension questions to test for understanding. Share the explanations for Parts A and B (located online) with your students.	
	Extend **Write.** Now that students have had practice identifying and formatting the components of direct and indirect dialogue, invite them to draft a scene of their own suspenseful narratives in which two or more characters engage in dialogue. Encourage students to share their dialogues with one another for informal peer reviews.

OVERVIEW

Students will learn how writers consider audience and purpose when crafting suspenseful narratives, as well as how to introduce elements that will appeal to an audience and enhance reader experience. Students will explore a variety of Research Links that allow them to learn about the craft of suspenseful writing and audience appeal. Students will learn how differences in the points of view of the characters and the audience or reader often create a suspenseful effect.

OBJECTIVES

1. Explore background information about the elements and techniques of suspense stories and how writers use those elements when considering their audience, purpose, and style.
2. Research using hyperlinks to a range of information about writing suspense, including articles, audio, video, and informational perspectives in order to determine the connection between audience and purpose in their narratives.
3. Participate effectively in a range of conversations and collaborations to express ideas and build upon the ideas of others.

ELA Common Core Standards:
Writing - W.8.3.A, W.8.3.B, W.8.4, W.8.5, W.8.6, W.8.10
Speaking & Listening - SL.8.1.A, SL.8.1.C, SL.8.1.D, SL.8.2

RESOURCES

Access 1 handout (Beginner)
Access 2 handout (Intermediate)
Access 4 handout (Approaching)

TITLE/DRIVING QUESTION

Core Path	Access Path
Read and Discuss. As a class read aloud the title and driving question for this Blast: "How are audience and purpose connected when writing a suspense story?" Ask students to discuss what they think the purpose of a suspenseful narrative is. How do suspenseful narratives engage an audience? Remind students that they should not immediately reply to this question. They'll be returning to this question and responding after they've read the Background and some of the Research Links. Remind students to follow the rules for collegial discussions.	**English Learners All Levels & Approaching** **Share and Fill In KWL Charts.** To help students prepare for and participate in the discussion, have pairs fill in the KWL charts on their Access handouts. Students can add to the chart during the discussion and throughout the rest of the lesson.
Draft. In their notebooks or on scrap paper, have students draft their initial responses to the driving question. This will provide them with a baseline response that they will be altering as they gain more information about the topic in the Background and Research Links sections of the assignment.	**Beginner & Intermediate** **Draft with Sentence Frame.** When drafting their initial response to the driving question, have students refer to this Blast sentence frame on their Access 1 and 2 handouts: • When writing a suspense story, audience and purpose are connected because _____ _____. Point out these two key features of the sentence frame: 1. The introductory clause "When writing a suspense story" borrows language directly from the Blast driving question to provide a response. 2. Ask students to make special note of the comma that separates the introductory clause from the subject and predicate ("audience and purpose are connected").

BACKGROUND

Core Path	Access Path
Read. Have students read the Blast Background to provide context for the driving question: "How are audience and purpose connected when writing a suspense story?"	**Beginner & Intermediate** **Read with Support.** Have students read the Blast Background to provide context for the driving question. When they encounter unfamiliar words or

Please note that excerpts and passages in the StudySync® library, workbooks, and PDFs are intended as touchstones to generate interest in an author's work. The excerpts and passages do not substitute for the reading of entire texts, and StudySync® strongly recommends that teachers and students seek out and purchase the whole literary or informational work in order to experience it as the author intended. Links to online resellers are available in our digital library. In addition, complete works may be ordered through an authorized reseller by filling out and returning to StudySync® the order form enclosed in this workbook.

Teacher's Edition   419

Core Path	Access Path
	phrases, have students refer to the glossary on their Access 1 and 2 handouts. If there are unfamiliar words that are not included in their glossary, encourage students to check a dictionary or online reference tool, like http://tinyurl.com/6ytby. **Approaching** **Read and Summarize.** Have students read the Blast Background to explain the driving question. As they read, ask students to complete the summary of the Background provided on their Access 4 handout. When they encounter unfamiliar words or phrases, have students refer to the glossary on their Access 1 handout.
Discuss. Pair students and have them discuss the following questions: 1. What is the purpose for a suspenseful narrative? (The purpose for a suspenseful narrative is to engage the audience and keep them entertained.) 2. How does suspense function to serve its purpose? (Suspense engages the reader by keeping them curious and entertained over the course of an entire story by creating tension and interest not only in *what* happened, but *how* it happened.) 3. Who is the audience? (The audience of a suspenseful narrative can be anyone, of any age or background who is interested in the story, but usually readers are drawn to particular genre, such as science fiction.) 4. What role does the audience play in the purpose of suspense? (For suspense to be effective, the audience has to feel as though they are experiencing the events right along with the characters. The audience has to be eager for every turn of the plot, waiting for the payoff of the final outcome.) 5. What is the difference between surprise and suspense? (Surprise occurs in one single moment, while suspense is ongoing.)	**Beginner & Intermediate** **Dialogue.** Pair Beginning and Intermediate students with Advanced (or Beyond) students and have them use the dialogue starter on their Access 1 handout to discuss the topic. Advise them to return to the dialogue and switch roles. If students get stuck, they can refer to the KWL charts from Access 1 and 2 handouts.

RESEARCH LINKS

Core Path	Access Path
Examine and Explore. Before asking students to explore the Research Links, use these activities and questions to guide their exploration:	

1. Which Research Link might provide the best advice for writing suspense? ("Every Step on the Staircase to Suspense" because the breakdown of a suspenseful narrative is so specific that a writer will know exactly how to use each story element of character, setting, plot, and conflict to keep an audience entertained.)

2. Play snippets of a few of the songs from "Suspenseful Soundtrack". Ask students what about this music lends itself to the building of suspense. (Sample answers: The songs start out quiet or slow, more instruments are added as the tempo and volume increases; the instruments create a spooky, eerie feeling; the songs create a tension as their rhythm changes.) How might listening to this type of music help an author writing suspense? (Because of the tense, building nature of the music, the author, as audience to the music, might feel the same anticipatory sensation while writing an anticipatory text.)

3. Have students explore "Tricks for Keeping an Audience in Suspense." Ask them whether suspense can function in storylines other than horror. Following the rules for collegial discussions, have them discuss what the ultimate purpose of suspense is and how suspense should be presented to make it effective. (Students should include specific examples to support their positions.)

Core Path	Access Path

	Extend
	Research, Discuss, and Present.
	
	1. Assign each group one link to explore in depth.
	2. Ask them to discuss the information:
	   a. What are the key points?
	   b. What inferences did you make as you read?
	   c. What did you learn about this "Big Idea" from reading this research?
	   d. How did this help you to better understand the topic?
	   e. What questions does your group have after exploring this link?
	3. Allow students time to informally present what they learned.

	Extend **Tech Infusion** **Create a Cliffhanger.** Separate students into groups of three or four and encourage them to discuss a suspenseful cliffhanger. Then, using Twiddla (http://tinyurl.com/2n8oun), have students draw an image of their cliffhanger and attach a link to some kind of suspenseful audio. Have them share their creations with the class and discuss whether the class, as an audience, was captivated.

QUIKPOLL

Core Path	Access Path
Participate. Answer the poll question. Have students use information from the Background and Research Links to explain their answers. Remind students to follow the rules for collegial discussions.	

Core Path	Access Path
	Extend **Discuss.** Once students have posted their response to the poll, ask them to discuss the results in small groups or as a class. Are they surprised by the outcome?
	Extend **Poll.** Have students ask the QuikPoll questions to another group of students, or to friends and family members. Have them compare the results of the two polls and explain any similarities or differences.

NUMBER CRUNCH

Core Path	Access Path
Predict, Discuss, and Click. Before students click on the number, break them into pairs and have them make predictions about what they think the number is related to. After they've clicked the number, ask students if they are surprised by the revealed information.	

CREATE YOUR BLAST

Core Path	Access Path
Blast. Ask students to write their Blast response in 140 characters or less, answering the driving question: "How are audience and purpose connected when writing a suspense story?"	**Beginner** **Blast with Support.** Have students refer back to the sentence frame on their Access 1 handout that they used to create their original Blast draft. Ask them to use this frame to write and enter their final Blast. **Intermediate** **Blast with Support.** Have students attempt to draft their Blast without the sentence frame on their Access 2 handout. If students struggle to compose their Blast draft without the sentence frame, remind them to reference it for support.

Core Path	Access Path
	Beyond **Write an Outline.** Ask students to use their answer to the poll question to write an outline for a suspense story of that genre. What would happen in the story? Once students have written their outlines, ask them to share with a small group of their peers. How does the group react?
Review. After students have completed their own Blasts, ask them to review the Blasts of their peers and provide feedback.	**Extend** **Discuss.** As a whole class or in groups, identify a few strong Blasts and discuss what made those responses so powerful. As a group, analyze and discuss what characteristics make a Blast interesting or effective.
	Extend **Revise.** Resend a second version of this Blast assignment to your students and have them submit revised versions of their original Blasts. Do the same responses make the Top 10? How have the answers improved from the first submissions?

OVERVIEW

Students will learn about the elements of a strong narrative conclusion, including providing a resolution that follows from and reflects on the experiences, observations, and events of the narrative. They will then examine Edgar Allan Poe's "The Tell-Tale Heart" to learn how authors provide a conclusion that reflects the events of the overall plot and provides a resolution of the problem or conflict in the story. Students will practice identifying conclusive details in familiar narratives and discuss their necessity and effect in narrative writing. They will then practice crafting a suspenseful conclusion to the Student Model narrative.

OBJECTIVES

1. Discuss and demonstrate an understanding of narrative conclusions.
2. Practice concrete strategies for identifying elements of narrative conclusions and apply this understanding to an original narrative piece.
3. Participate effectively in a range of conversations and collaborations to express ideas and build upon the ideas of others.

ELA Common Core Standards:

Reading: Literature - RL.8.1, RL.8.2, RL.8.3
Writing - W.8.3.E, W.8.4, W.8.5, W.8.10
Speaking & Listening - SL.8.1.A, SL.8.1.B, SL.8.1.C, SL.8.1.D

RESOURCES

Access 1 handout (Beginner)

Access 2 handout (Intermediate)

Access 3 handout (Advanced)

Access 4 handout (Approaching)

Please note that excerpts and passages in the StudySync® library, workbooks, and PDFs are intended as touchstones to generate interest in an author's work. The excerpts and passages do not substitute for the reading of entire texts, and StudySync® strongly recommends that teachers and students seek out and purchase the whole literary or informational work in order to experience it as the author intended. Links to online resellers are available in our digital library. In addition, complete works may be ordered through an authorized reseller by filling out and returning to StudySync® the order form enclosed in this workbook.

Teacher's Edition   425

1. DEFINE

Core Path	Access Path
Read and Discuss. Either individually or as a class, read the Define section of the lesson. Either in small groups or as a class use the following questions to spur discussion among your students about the elements of a strong narrative conclusion. Remind students to follow the rules for collegial discussions.	**Beginner** **In Your Own Words.** Have students read the definition and then use their Access 1 handouts to pause after each bullet point to rewrite the components of a conclusion in their own words. Once students have completed this activity, ask them to complete the fill-in-the-blank activity on the Access 1 handout.
1. The definition explains that a narrative conclusion must provide a resolution of the conflict in a story, which does not always result in a positive outcome for the characters. What does this mean? (Sample answer: A story doesn't need to have a happy ending to be considered finished—what is most important is that it is clear that all of the action has stopped and that the driving conflict or problem in the story has been somehow resolved.)	**Intermediate** **In Your Own Words.** Have students read the definition of a conclusion and then use their Access 2 handout to pause after each bullet point to rewrite the components of a conclusion in their own words. After they've rewritten each of the bullet points in their own words, work with students to develop their own definitions of the term.
2. The definition states that the way a problem is resolved can be a surprise to the reader, particularly in a suspense story, but it should still be logical and feel like a natural part of the plot. Do you agree? Why or why not? (Answers will vary. Students should suggest that any successful conclusion should arise logically out of the events in the story and the motivations and actions of the characters throughout the narrative. Having a character solve a money problem by suddenly inheriting money without any warning would not be considered a satisfying conclusion.)	**Advanced** **In Your Own Words.** Have Advanced students read and then discuss what they have learned about conclusions with an English-proficient partner or in mixed-proficiency groups. After their conversation, have Advanced students write the definition of conclusion on the Access 3 handout.
3. The definition states that an author must consider how to leave readers with a lasting impression. What are some ways an author might leave a reader with a lasting impression? (Answers will vary. Students may suggest by creating an emotional experience for the reader; by teaching the reader an important lesson; by entertaining the reader in a memorable way.)	**Approaching** **Restate the Definition.** Have students read the define section and then use their Access 4 handouts to restate the most important points in their own words. Clarify questions to aid students' comprehension as needed. Then have students participate in mixed-level groups with the class to discuss the purpose of a conclusion in a narrative.

Teacher's Edition

Core Path	Access Path
	Beyond **Analyze Narrative Conclusions.** Have students form small groups and provide them with a short story either online or in print. Ask them to identify the climax, and from there to read and identify the key details provided in the falling action. Have them also make notes about the resolution. Once the groups are finished reading the short story, have them evaluate the conclusion based on the characteristics they have learned about good, effective conclusions. If there's time, have a few of the groups share their evaluations with the class and discuss if there could be improvements to the conclusions they read.
	Extend **Feature Focus.** Pair students or form smaller groups and then provide the entire class with a brief introduction to a story and a conflict. Then, have each pair or group brainstorm details or actions that would likely result in the falling action. Once they are done brainstorming, have pairs or groups organize their thoughts into a summary of the conclusion, by listing the key details in the falling action, and then constructing a resolution for the story. Discuss which conclusions work best with the provided introduction and conflict, and why.

2. MODEL

Core Path	Access Path
Read and Discuss. As students read the Model text, use these questions to help students understand the features and function of narrative conclusions: 1. According to the Model, which portion of "The Tell-Tale Heart" comprises the falling action of the story? (the events that take place after the narrator has murdered the old man, when he thinks he has solved his problem)	**Beginner, Intermediate, & Approaching** **Underline Conclusion Elements.** Have students look closely at the elements of a narrative conclusion alongside the Model conclusion from the text, "The Tell-Tale Heart" on the Access 1, 2, and 4 handouts. Then ask them to find and underline the elements of the conclusion they learned about in the Define section. Make sure students understand these elements. Explain that they can use elements of a conclusion similar to those found in the excerpt

Core Path	Access Path
2. How does Poe engage the reader with the falling action of the story? (by using descriptive details to help the reader understand how the narrator is feeling; by using strong verbs and adjectives to describe the narrator's increasingly wild actions, such as "I swung the chair upon which I had been sitting, and grated it upon the boards"; by using emotionally loaded words to describe the narrator's mental state, as in the statement "they were making a mockery of my horror! — this I thought, and this I think. But anything was better than this agony! Anything was more tolerable than this derision!") 3. How does Edgar Allan Poe finally conclude his narrative? (with the narrator's emotional and confessional outburst to the police officers) 4. According to the Model, how might the author have hoped to leave his readers feeling at the end of this story? What theme does he seek to convey? (The Model maintains that Poe hoped to leave his readers anxious, excited, shaken, upset; that the story has left the reader with a lasting impression. One theme in the story is that the human heart cannot endure the burden of guilt, especially in the case of murder. The guilty must confess somehow or be consumed by his or her conscience. The narrator might not learn anything in the story, but the reader does.)	from "The Tell-Tale Heart" in their own conclusions when they write their narratives. If students come across words they have difficulty with while reading the Model, refer them to the Glossary on the Access 1, 2, and 4 handouts. **Advanced** **Identify the Parts.** Have students read the Model and answer the questions on the Access 3 handout. If students have difficulty during their reading of the Model, refer them to the glossary on the Access 3 handout to clarify the meaning of difficult or unfamiliar words. Once they've completed the questions, pair Advanced students with more proficient students to allow them to share their answers.
	Extend **Unscramble.** This will be a group activity. Before class, create printouts of three or four basic plot outlines (ensure you have a set for each group) including one or two sentences each for: an introduction, a climax/falling action, and a conclusion. Cut the conclusions away from the remainder of the outlines, place them in an envelope or bag, and mix them up. Then, have each group work to match the conclusions to the corresponding stories. Once all work is complete, review each story and conclusion as a class, discussing which elements led students to pair what conclusions with what stories, as well as how the conclusions resolved the plots, what elements were used, and how each conclusion made the students feel.

Copyright © BookheadEd Learning, LLC

Teacher's Edition

Core Path	Access Path

Core Path

Practice.

1. Ask students to complete a short writing assignment and apply the skills they have learned for writing narrative conclusions.

2. Students have had a chance to practice writing an introduction for their narrative, as well as a scene containing dialogue. Now have students explore the elements of a strong narrative conclusion by drafting a conclusion for the Student Model narrative. How will they use the previous events of the story to finally drive the suspense home? What details will they include to elicit an emotional reaction from their readers? How will they use pacing to create suspense? What is the final message they hope to leave their readers with?

3. Remind students that they will use the skills they practice here to draft a conclusion to their own Student Model narrative in response to the upcoming prompt.

4. Students can complete this draft of their narrative conclusion on paper, or you can create a Write Assignment on StudySync, and they can submit their drafts online for anonymous peer review.

Access Path

Beginner
Write Your Conclusion.

1. Prior to writing their conclusions, ask students to complete the sentence frames on the Access 1 handout.

2. After students have finished the sentence frames, ask them to discuss with a partner what they plan to write about, clarifying any language as needed before writing their conclusions.

3. Then students should write their own conclusions, being sure to include falling action that brings the story to a natural resolution. Encourage them to refer back to the Student Model if needed.

Intermediate
Finish Sentences. Have students fill in the sentence frames on the Access 2 handout. Review their answers with them, and after making any clarifications needed, allow them to use their answers to craft their conclusions. Then allow them to join Advanced students to discuss and edit their conclusions.

Advanced
Clarify and Edit. Have students refer to the Student Model narrative as they write their conclusions. Have them read their conclusions aloud to another Intermediate or Advanced student to check for language that needs to be clarified and to answer the following questions:

- Does the conclusion contain a falling action that brings the story to a natural resolution?

- Do the details used in the conclusion cause an emotional reaction from the reader?

- Does the conclusion provide a final message or lesson for the reader to take away? Does the resolution represent a definite ending to the story?

Allow students time to make edits to their scenes as necessary.

Approaching
Finish the Sentences.

1. Prior to writing their conclusions, ask students to complete the sentence frames on the Access 4 handout.

Please note that excerpts and passages in the StudySync® library, workbooks, and PDFs are intended as touchstones to generate interest in an author's work. The excerpts and passages do not substitute for the reading of entire texts, and StudySync® strongly recommends that teachers and students seek out and purchase the whole literary or informational work in order to experience it as the author intended. Links to online resellers are available in our digital library. In addition, complete works may be ordered through an authorized reseller by filling out and returning to StudySync® the order form enclosed in this workbook.

Teacher's Edition **429**

Core Path	Access Path
	2. Once they have completed the statements with the information they plan to write about, have them begin writing their conclusions. Remind students that they should use the skills they have learned in previous assignments to draft an effective conclusion, including pacing, dialogue, and descriptive language.
	Extend **Resolution Remix.** Working in pairs, have students swap their practice Student Model conclusions. Using their partners' conclusions, encourage students to practice writing a different version of their partners' conclusion using the basic, key elements of the conclusion; in other words, if their partners' conclusion is a narrative, have them rewrite it as a dialogue, or vice versa; if the conclusion incorporates both techniques, have them rewrite using the one that is least favored. Invite students to share their rewrites and reasoning with the class.

3. YOUR TURN

Core Path	Access Path
Assess and Explain. Have students answer the comprehension questions to test for understanding. Share the explanations for Parts A and B (located online) with your students.	
	Extend **Write.** Pair or group students and have them write two Your Turn questions about the conclusion of a different text from the unit, using the Your Turn questions from this lesson as a model. They should include multiple-choice answers to their questions. Once all groups are finished, have them trade and give their questions to other groups.

EXTENDED WRITING PROJECT:
Draft

OVERVIEW

This lesson asks students to write a draft of their suspenseful narrative. To do so, they will use relevant details about suspense collected from the texts, Blasts, and other work in this unit. Students are instructed to use their prewriting graphic organizer, plot diagrams, and any other planning materials to complete a draft of their suspenseful narrative. As students draft, they should focus on the exposition of their introduction, the logic behind and flow of their narrative technique and how it addresses their purpose and affects their audience, the relevance and impact of their descriptive details, their use of dialogue to reveal details of setting and character as well as drive the plot, and the strength of their conclusion. Before they submit their drafts, students should check to be sure they have fully addressed the writing prompt.

OBJECTIVES

1. Identify and discuss the features of narrative writing: organization, narrative introductions, narrative techniques and sequencing, descriptive details, dialogue, audience and purpose, and narrative conclusions.
2. Draft a narrative essay in response to a prompt.
3. Participate effectively in a range of conversations and collaborations to express ideas and build upon the ideas of others.

   ELA Common Core Standards:
   Writing - W.8.3.A, W.8.3.B, W.8.3.D, W.8.3.E, W.8.4, W.8.5, W.8.6, W.8.10
   Speaking & Listening - SL.8.1.A, SL.8.1.C
   Language - L.8.2.C, L.8.4.B

RESOURCES

Grammar Handout: Adjective Suffixes

Access 1 handout (Beginner)

Access 2 handout (Intermediate)

Access 3 handout (Advanced)

Access 4 handout (Approaching)

Please note that excerpts and passages in the StudySync® library, workbooks, and PDFs are intended as touchstones to generate interest in an author's work. The excerpts and passages do not substitute for the reading of entire texts, and StudySync® strongly recommends that teachers and students seek out and purchase the whole literary or informational work in order to experience it as the author intended. Links to online resellers are available in our digital library. In addition, complete works may be ordered through an authorized reseller by filling out and returning to StudySync® the order form enclosed in this workbook.

Teacher's Edition   431

1. WRITE

Core Path	Access Path

Discuss. Before students begin to write, review with the class the writing prompt/directions. Have a volunteer read them aloud. Ask whether students have any questions either about the prompt or the directions. Respond to their questions, and explain the importance of addressing the prompt fully and completely. Then read aloud the peer review criteria that students will use to comment on one another's work. Students will use the feedback to develop their writing in different stages of the writing process. Point out that understanding the peer review criteria can help students focus their writing on important features of narrative writing.

Here are the peer review criteria for this assignment:

- From which point of view is the story told? Is this an effective narrative choice?

- What do I know about the characters and setting after reading the story's introduction?

- What is the conflict in this story? Where does it first appear?

- Which details in the story help me visualize the characters and setting? Which areas of the story require more descriptive details to make the writing suspenseful and engaging?

- What suggestions can I make to help the writer improve the organization of the story?

- How effective is the pacing in the story? Where might the pace be quickened or slowed to have a better impact on readers?

- How does the dialogue in the story help develop the characters? Does it move the plot forward? If the dialogue isn't effective, what can I suggest to improve it?

- Does the conclusion present a reasonable resolution of the conflict? What suggestions can I offer to help the reader strengthen the resolution?

English Learners All Levels & Approaching
Review Writing Draft Checklist. Read aloud the Narrative Writing Draft Checklist on the Access 1, 2, 3, and 4 handouts with students. Encourage students to circle unfamiliar words and underline anything that is confusing or unclear. Then take a few minutes to clarify unknown vocabulary, answer questions, and provide examples for any items that students do not understand. Explain that they will need to include each of these items in their writing. For each checklist item, point out an example in the Student Model "The Silver Box" and read it aloud.

Beginner & Intermediate
Vocabulary. After discussing the assignment with the class, have students do the Match Definitions activity on the Access 1 and 2 handouts to review the vocabulary used in the checklist. Remind students to refer to the checklist as they draft their narrative.

Beyond
Critique. If students have extra time, give small groups photocopies of a writing sample to collaboratively evaluate. Have them identify the elements of writing that are strong, as well as those that are weak or in need of improvement. Then ask them to generate strategies students can use when they complete their peer reviews to ensure their critiques are substantive. Have them make a list of their strategies to share with the class.

Core Path	Access Path

Core Path

- How have the characters changed as a result of the action? Where do I see opportunities for further, meaningful change that will strengthen the story's impact?

- What impression am I left with after reading this story? What revisions can the writer make to strengthen the impact of the story's conclusion?

Remind students that a peer reviewer's comments are most useful when they are clear, constructive, and presented with a positive attitude. Make sure students understand your expectations for all aspects of the assignment before beginning their work.

(G) Grammar, Usage, and Mechanics. Review with students the spelling focus on words ending in the adjective suffixes *-ous*, which comes from the Latin meaning "full of," and *-ible* and *-able,* which come from the Latin meaning "able to be" or "in accordance with." Distribute the StudySync Grammar handout: Spelling Adjective Suffixes. Review with students the use of adjective suffixes as explained in the handout. Then have students complete the practice exercise. (Answers for the practice exercise appear online.) Finally, encourage students to apply what they have learned by analyzing the use of the adjective suffixes in the Student Model narrative "The Silver Box." Be sure students have access to a print or online dictionary. Ask students:

1. Can you identify any words ending in the suffixes *-ous, -ible,* or *-able* in the Student Model narrative? Where do they appear? (the words *audible* and *sensible,* which appear in the second half of the narrative)

2. What is the root of the word *audible*? (The root of *audible* is *aud-*.) Look up the Latin root. What does it mean? (The root *aud-* comes from the Latin meaning "hear" or "listen.")

3. Why do you think the writer has chosen to describe Mrs. Carey's giggle as "barely audible"? How does the use of this adjective help the writer develop Mrs. Carey's character? (This descriptor helps readers understand that

Access Path

Beginner & Intermediate

Mechanics. Provide students with more practice in recognizing and spelling words ending in the suffixes *-ible* and *-able* by having them complete the Mechanics activity on the Access 1 and 2 handouts.

Core Path	Access Path
Mrs. Carey is giggling unintentionally, because she is nervous. It shows readers that she sometimes fails to suppress her reactions in tense situations.)	

Core Path

4. What is the root of the word *sensible*? (The root of *sensible* is *sens-*.) Look up the Latin root. What does it mean? (The Latin root *sens-* means "feel," "perceive," or "think.")

5. Why do you think the writer has chosen to describe Mr. Carey's hope that he has made a "sensible" decision? How does the use of this adjective help the writer develop Mr. Carey's character? (This adjective helps readers understand that Mr. Carey hopes he has thought the decision through before putting his family in danger. His uncertainty about the sensible nature of the decision shows that he might sometimes make hasty decisions, or that he is not always sure he is making the right decision.)

6. How do you think choosing precise adjectives will improve your own narrative writing? (Choosing precise adjectives helps writers develop the characters and plot events and describe the setting. If I choose the right adjectives, I will communicate helpful information about the characters, setting, and plot to my readers.)

Organize. Remind students to refer to their prewriting graphic organizer, as well as the plot diagram they completed in the Plan lesson, before they begin writing.

Access Path

English Learners All Levels & Approaching Freewrite. After reviewing the prompt and revision criteria with the class, tell Approaching and ELA students that writers have many different ways of getting started on a draft. Suggest that the best method is to review lists, outlines, diagrams, and graphic organizers that the writer has prepared. Explain that some writers might also try to "freewrite" for a brief, timed period. Explain that a "freewrite" is just that—a few moments to write absolutely freely and as fast as possible on a topic, without thinking about correct grammar or precise language, or even making sense.

Discuss the approach with students and answer any questions they may have about it. Stress that a freewrite is different from a draft. Like a brainstormed list, it may produce an interesting thought or phrase. It

Core Path	Access Path
	can also be a spur to get a writer writing! If students want to try freewriting on their topic, allow them no more than two minutes for the exercise. Then suggest they reread their freewrite to see if it has produced any words or ideas they might want to include in their formal first draft. Sometimes a new approach can produce a surprising insight.
Write. Ask students to complete the writing assignment using narrative techniques such as sequencing, dialogue, and descriptive details to suit their audience and purpose. Remind them to spell words with adjective suffixes correctly. Once they have completed their writing, they should click "Submit."	**Beginner** **Write with Support.** Review the Narrative Writing Draft Checklist on the Access 1 handout with students before they write. Then have students use their Plot Diagrams to complete their draft with teacher support as needed. Before they write each step in the plot, ask students to state orally what they want to say. They can do this in small groups with support from the teacher or in pairs with an on-level partner who can provide quality feedback. Talking through their writing before they put pen to paper will help them clarify their ideas and their language and use of descriptive words. **Intermediate & Advanced** **Use Dialogue, Description, Sensory Details.** Have students use the Narrative Writing Draft Checklist on the Access 2 and 3 handouts as they write. Remind them to focus on using dialogue, description, and sensory details to help readers understand the events and to create a feeling of suspense. **Approaching** **Use the Road Map to Write a Draft.** Remind students to consult all the prewriting documents they have created — narrative prewrite graphic organizers and road map — to help them craft their narrative. It may be particularly useful for Approaching students to use their Narrative Road Map to structure their writing. Explain that they can follow the order of the outline they created, but in their draft they will need to add details and develop their writing. Have them use the Narrative Writing Draft Checklist in the Access 4 handout to make sure they include a strong introduction with details that describe the setting, the characters, the events, as well as a conclusion that provides a satisfying resolution to the story.

Please note that excerpts and passages in the StudySync® library, workbooks, and PDFs are intended as touchstones to generate interest in an author's work. The excerpts and passages do not substitute for the reading of entire texts, and StudySync® strongly recommends that teachers and students seek out and purchase the whole literary or informational work in order to experience it as the author intended. Links to online resellers are available in our digital library. In addition, complete works may be ordered through an authorized reseller by filling out and returning to StudySync® the order form enclosed in this workbook.

Teacher's Edition   435

Core Path	Access Path
Review. Once students complete their writing assignment, they should submit substantive feedback to two peers.	**Beginner** **Review the Checklist.** Help students to go through the Narrative Writing Draft Checklist item-by-item on the Access 1 handout to check their writing. Provide support to help them make changes as needed. **Intermediate & Advanced** **Use the Checklist.** Have mixed-proficiency partners read their completed drafts aloud to one another and use the Literary Analysis Draft Checklist on the Access 2 and 3 handouts to check their writing. Remind them to check that they used description, dialogue, and sensory details to help readers understand the events and to create a feeling of suspense and to make suggestions for how the sequence of events could be clarified.
	Extend **Capture an Audio Think Aloud.** An alternative to a traditional written freewrite is an audio Think Aloud. Tell students they can use a voice recording app, like Voice Memo (iPhone/iPad) or Smart Voice Recorder (Android), to capture their thoughts before they begin writing. Tell them it's okay if they ramble or if their recordings are not clearly organized. The objective is to record and capture as many thoughts as possible in 3 minutes. Then they can listen to their recordings to revisit their ideas.
	Extend **Critique.** Project a writing sample on the board and ask the class to identify the elements of writing that are strong, as well as those that are weak or in need of improvement. Alternatively, you can put students in small groups and give them photocopies of a writing sample to collaboratively evaluate. After students have had an opportunity to evaluate student samples, work as a class to generate strategies students can use when they complete their peer reviews to ensure that their critiques are substantive.

OVERVIEW

Students will learn how transitional words and phrases connect and clarify ideas and help readers understand the structure of events in a narrative. Students will examine an excerpt from "The Monkey's Paw" to learn how transitional devices help the reader identify changes in the setting as well as the sequence of events in the story. Students will then practice revising their drafts to strengthen transitions and clarify the order of events in their own suspenseful narratives.

OBJECTIVES

1. Discuss and demonstrate an understanding of the purpose and function of transitions in narrative writing.
2. Practice concrete strategies for identifying and using transitions in narrative writing.
3. Participate effectively in a range of conversations and collaborations to express ideas and build upon the ideas of others.

ELA Common Core Standards:
Reading: Literature - RL.8.1, RL.8.3
Writing - W.8.3.C, W.8.4, W.8.5, W.8.10
Speaking & Listening - SL.8.1.A, SL.8.1.B, SL.8.1.C, SL.8.1.D

RESOURCES

Access 1 handout (Beginner)

Access 2 handout (Intermediate)

Access 3 handout (Advanced)

Access 4 handout (Approaching)

Please note that excerpts and passages in the StudySync® library, workbooks, and PDFs are intended as touchstones to generate interest in an author's work. The excerpts and passages do not substitute for the reading of entire texts, and StudySync® strongly recommends that teachers and students seek out and purchase the whole literary or informational work in order to experience it as the author intended. Links to online resellers are available in our digital library. In addition, complete works may be ordered through an authorized reseller by filling out and returning to StudySync® the order form enclosed in this workbook.

Teacher's Edition   437

1. DEFINE

Core Path	Access Path

Core Path

Read and Discuss. Either individually or as a class, read the Define section of the lesson. In small groups or as a class use the following questions to spur discussion among your students about the purpose and function transitions in narrative writing. Remind students to follow the rules for collegial discussions.

1. According to the definition, what are transitions? How can specific transitional words and phrases help readers follow the events in a story? (Sample answer: Transitions are words or phrases that help carry a thought from one sentence to another, from one idea to another, or from one paragraph to another. Transitions between events in a plot can help readers understand how certain events are related and work together in a story, building toward a climax.)

2. Why do you think transitions are important in narrative writing? What would be the effect of omitting transitions in a written narrative? (Sample answer: Transitional devices link sentences and paragraphs together smoothly so that there are no sudden jumps or breaks between events or ideas. Without transitional phrases, readers would be confused if a block of time passes in a narrative, or the scene suddenly changes.)

3. How might a writer use transitions to heighten suspense in a narrative? Can you think of any transitions that are commonly used in suspenseful stories? (Answers will vary but should demonstrate an understanding of transitions and their purpose and effect.)

Access Path

Beginner
In Your Own Words. Have students read the definition and then use their Access 1 handouts to pause after each bullet point to rewrite the components of transitions in their own words. Once students have completed this activity, ask them to complete the fill-in-the-blank activity on the Access 1 handout.

Intermediate
In Your Own Words. Have students read the definition of transitions and then use their Access 2 handout to pause after each bullet point to rewrite the components of transitions in their own words. After they've rewritten each of the bullet points in their words, work with students to develop their own definitions of the term.

Advanced
In Your Own Words. Have Advanced students read and then discuss what they have learned about transitions with an English-proficient partner or in mixed-proficiency groups. After their conversation, have Advanced students write the definition of transitions on the Access 3 handout.

Approaching
Restate the Definition. Have students read the define section and then use their Access 4 handouts to restate the most important points in their own words. Clarify questions to aid students' comprehension as needed. Then have students participate in mixed-level groups with the class to discuss the purpose of transitions in narrative writing.

Core Path	Access Path
	Beyond **Jigsaw.** If students have extra time, put them in small groups and assign each group a different text from the unit (or a previous unit). Then challenge them to work together to identify the transitions used in that text. • What information do the transitions give the reader? Are the transitions connecting ideas, showing a change in the time order of events, or indicating a change in the setting? • Are there any places in the text where you feel a transition is needed or could be added to improve the clarity of the writing? If so, write sentences or phrases that include the transition needed. Allow each group time to share their findings with the class.
	Extend **Apply.** Group students and provide groups with a short list of transitions related to time and place, such as those listed here: Time: • later • earlier • now • soon • in the meantime • immediately • this time Place: • here • there • nearby • above • below • beyond

Core Path	Access Path
	Challenge each group to write a paragraph, with transitional words or phrases at the beginning of the second or third sentence. Instruct students that the paragraphs should contain an element of suspense to keep a reader entertained and engaged. Then invite groups to share their paragraphs with the class, and discuss which paragraphs had the strongest element of suspense.
	Extend **Tech Infusion** **Poll.** Ask groups to submit their paragraphs electronically and use them to create a class poll indicating which paragraphs contained the most effective elements of suspense. Have students complete the poll, and discuss the results as a class. Ask students if the effect of seeing and reading the written paragraphs was different from hearing them read aloud and why.

2. MODEL

Core Path	Access Path
Read and Discuss. As students read the Model text use these questions to help students understand the functions of transitions in narrative writing: 1. The Model explains that the transitions in the excerpt from "The Monkey's Paw" help the reader understand the setting and the sequence of events. What transition does the author use to help readers understand the setting? How does this transition help to convey information to readers? (The author uses the transition "In the huge new cemetery" to help readers understand that the setting of the story has changed, from the Whites' parlor to the cemetery where the couple is now burying their son.)	**Beginner, Intermediate, & Approaching** **Underline Transition Elements.** Have students look closely at the elements of transitions alongside the Model text from, "The Monkey's Paw" on the Access 1, 2, and 4 handouts. Then ask them to find and underline the elements of transitions they learned about in the Define section. Make sure students understand these elements. Explain that they can use elements of transitions similar to those found in the excerpt from "The Monkey's Paw" when they write their narratives. If students come across words they have difficulty with while reading the Model, refer them to the Glossary on the Access 1, 2, and 4 handouts.

Copyright © Bookheaded Learning, LLC

Core Path	Access Path

Core Path

2. What transition does the author use to help readers understand the sequence of events in "The Monkey's Paw" after the death of Herbert Walker? How does this transition help to convey information to readers? (The author uses the transition "But the days passed" to help readers understand the sequence of events in the story. This transition helps readers understand that some time has passed since the couple buried their son, and that the couple has passed from a feeling of expectation to one of hopeless despair.)

3. How do transitions in a story act as bridges? Explain your ideas based on what you've learned in the Model. (Good transitions can act as bridges, and turn disconnected, "choppy" writing into a unified whole that flows smoothly from one point or event to another.)

Practice.

1. Ask students to complete a short writing assignment and apply the skills they have learned for using transitions in narrative writing.

Access Path

Advanced

Identify the Parts. Have students read the Model and answer the questions on the Access 3 handout. If students have difficulty during their reading of the Model, refer them to the glossary on the Access 3 handout to clarify the meaning of difficult or unfamiliar words. Once they've completed the questions, pair Advanced students with more proficient students to allow them to share their answers.

Extend

Apply. Before students begin writing, lead the class in writing a paragraph that uses transitions. Begin the activity by writing on a whiteboard or an overhead projector. Introduce two characters and setting. Write a sentence on the board and then challenge students to suggest what kind of transition to use for the next sentence. Be sure to have students suggest the proper language for the kind of transition they are suggesting. Continue this process until the class has helped to craft an entire paragraph, about 4–5 sentences long. If there's time, review the paragraph, pointing out where transitions were used and how effective they were for the quality of the paragraph.

Beginner

Write Your Paragraph.

1. Prior to writing their paragraphs, ask students to complete the sentence frames on the Access 1 handout.

Core Path	Access Path
2. Students have had a chance to think about many aspects of their suspenseful narrative, from drafting an introduction and conclusion, to crafting descriptive details and dialogue, and writing with audience and purpose in mind. Now have them write one paragraph for their essay that uses transitions to indicate the passage of time or to show relationships among character experiences and story events.	2. After students have finished the sentence frames, ask them to discuss with a partner what they plan to write about, clarifying any language as needed before writing their paragraphs.
	3. Then students should write their own paragraphs being sure to use clear language that clues the reader that a transition is occurring in the story.
3. Remind students that they will be able to use either this paragraph or a revised version when they write their suspenseful narrative.	**Intermediate**
	Finish Sentences. Have students fill in the sentence frames on the Access 2 handout. Review their answers with them, and after making any clarifications needed, allow them to use their answers to craft their paragraphs. Then allow them to join Advanced students to discuss and edit their paragraphs.
4. Students can complete this paragraph draft on paper, or you can create a Write Assignment on StudySync, and they can submit their drafts online for anonymous peer review.	
	Advanced
	Clarify and Edit. Have students refer to their Prewrite Worksheet and as they write their paragraphs. Have them read their paragraphs aloud to another Intermediate or Advanced student to check for language that needs to be clarified and to answer the following questions:
	• Do the transitions effectively link sentences or ideas together?
	• What kind of changes in the story do your transitions indicate? Does time pass within the paragraph? Does the setting change? Is there a sequence of events being described?
	Allow students time to make edits to their scenes as necessary.
	Approaching
	Finish the Sentences.
	1. Prior to writing their paragraphs, ask students to complete the sentence frames on the Access 4 handout.
	2. Once they have completed the statements with the information they plan to write about, have them begin writing their paragraphs. Remind students that they can use transitions in a variety of ways. Challenge them to follow the sentence frames and include transitions that connect ideas, events, or signify changes in the passage of time or setting.

Core Path	Access Path
	Extend **Analyze and Annotate.** Ask students to reread Edgar Allan Poe's "The Tell-Tale Heart." Then group students and ask each group to identify the transitions in the story. Have each group annotate the text to explain the function of each transition Poe uses. Then project each group's annotated text onto the board or share your screen and discuss the annotations. Use the activity to gauge students' understanding of transitions in narrative writing and provide them, if necessary, with further guidance.

3. YOUR TURN

Core Path	Access Path
Assess and Explain. Have students answer the comprehension questions to test for understanding of transitions and their function. Share the explanations for Parts A and B (located online) with your students.	
	Extend **Tech Infusion** **Poll the Class.** Use Socrative (http://socrative.com) to quickly poll the class about their answer choices. Review the responses to determine if there are patterns in incorrect answers. If several students chose the same incorrect answer, expand on the rationales for why the answers are incorrect and provide and discuss examples in which the incorrect answers would be correct.

Please note that excerpts and passages in the StudySync® library, workbooks, and PDFs are intended as touchstones to generate interest in an author's work. The excerpts and passages do not substitute for the reading of entire texts, and StudySync® strongly recommends that teachers and students seek out and purchase the whole literary or informational work in order to experience it as the author intended. Links to online resellers are available in our digital library. In addition, complete works may be ordered through an authorized reseller by filling out and returning to StudySync® the order form enclosed in this workbook.

Teacher's Edition   443

EXTENDED WRITING PROJECT:
Revise

OVERVIEW

This lesson asks students to revise the draft of their suspenseful narrative. Students will also complete a mechanics review activity on spelling words that are often confused. Students will present their revised drafts for peer review and receive feedback on the effectiveness of their suspenseful narratives, including reader engagement, logical sequencing, and details used to develop plot, characters and setting.

OBJECTIVES

1. Identify and discuss elements of a narrative writing.
2. Revise a narrative to improve content and organization.
3. Participate effectively in a range of conversations and collaborations to express ideas and build upon the ideas of others.

ELA Common Core Standards:

Writing - W.8.3.A, W.8.3.B, W.8.3.C, W.8.3.D, W.8.3.E, W.8.4, W.8.5, W.8.6, W.8.10
Speaking & Listening - SL.8.1.A, SL.8.1.C
Language - L.8.2.C

RESOURCES

Grammar Handout: More Words Often Confused

Access 1 handout (Beginner)

Access 2 handout (Intermediate)

Access 3 handout (Advanced)

Access 4 handout (Approaching)

1. WRITE

Core Path	Access Path
Discuss. Before students begin to revise, review with the class the writing prompt/directions. Ask whether students have any questions either about the prompt or the revision process. Respond to their questions, and explain the importance of thoughtful, focused revisions. Then read aloud the peer review criteria that students will use to comment on one another's revision. Students will use the feedback to develop their writing in different stages of the writing process. The peer review criteria for this assignment are as follows:	**Beginner, Intermediate, & Approaching** **Review the Revision Checklist.** Read aloud the Narrative Writing Revision Checklist Access 1, 2, and 4 handouts with students. As the teacher reads each item on the checklist, students should read along. Encourage students to circle unfamiliar words and underline anything that is confusing or unclear. Then take a few minutes to clarify unknown vocabulary, answer questions, and provide examples for any items that students do not understand. Explain to students that they will need to check their own writing for each of these items.

Core Path (continued):

- What elements of the narrative are suspenseful and engaging?

- How effectively does the introduction establish a context and narrative point of view?

- Can you describe the conflict and resolution of this story? Does the resolution make sense?

- How well does the sequencing of events support the story's conclusion? Can you describe the story's beginning, middle, and end?

- What descriptive details has the writer included to help you visualize characters and setting? How does the writer develop the story's characters and setting?

- How does the dialogue help develop the characters? How does it advance the action of the story?

- Can you see any areas where the details or language can be strengthened or improved?

- How do you feel after reading the story's conclusion? How closely does the conclusion follow from and reflect on the events in the body of the narrative?

- Do you feel the writer created the story with a specific purpose or audience in mind? What elements of the story cause you to feel this way?

Access Path (continued):

Advanced

Read and Discuss. Pair Advanced students with an on-level partner and ask them to review the Narrative Writing Revision Checklist on Access handout 4. Allow time for them to discuss each item to ensure the students understand what they are being asked to do.

Please note that excerpts and passages in the StudySync® library, workbooks, and PDFs are intended as touchstones to generate interest in an author's work. The excerpts and passages do not substitute for the reading of entire texts, and StudySync® strongly recommends that teachers and students seek out and purchase the whole literary or informational work in order to experience it as the author intended. Links to online resellers are available in our digital library. In addition, complete works may be ordered through an authorized reseller by filling out and returning to StudySync® the order form enclosed in this workbook.

Teacher's Edition   **445**

Core Path	Access Path
Remind students that a peer reviewer's comments are most useful when they are clear, constructive, and presented with a positive attitude. Make sure students understand your expectations for all aspects of the assignment before beginning their revisions.	

Highlight. Each student should start this activity with a copy of his or her narrative draft either printed on paper or open in a word-processing program. Students will conduct three rereads of their own narratives, each with a different focus.

1. First, have students read through their drafts to be sure they have included previous peer suggestions, as needed.

2. Next, ask students to look for underdeveloped aspects of their narratives. Students should look for sentences that lack detail regarding appearances of characters and setting, or actions of characters. Ask students to highlight in blue any sentences needing expanded details.

3. Finally, instruct students to read through their drafts a third time. This time students should evaluate the elements of suspense in their stories, including order of events and clear transitions that build to the story's climax, as well as those that lead to the story's conclusion. Challenge them to find at least two places where they can build reader suspense, and then to highlight them in yellow.

English Learners All Levels & Approaching Mixed-Level Partner Editing. Have all students form mixed-level pairs in which partners vary one level up or down from one another. Then have them work together on their drafts to identify and highlight areas they need to improve when they edit their drafts.

Beginner & Intermediate
Highlight. It may be helpful for some Beginning and Intermediate students to first read their stories aloud to help them find places where they need to provide smoother transitions or clarify what is happening.

(G) Grammar, Usage, and Mechanics. Review with students the spelling focus on words that are often confused. Distribute the StudySync Grammar handout: More Words Often Confused. Review with students the uses of often-confused words as explained in the handout. Then have students complete the practice exercise. (Answers for the practice exercise appear online.) Finally, encourage students to examine the use of often-confused words in the Student Model narrative "The Silver Box." Be sure students have access to a print or online dictionary. Ask students:

Beginner
Complete the Sentences. To help students with spelling frequently confused words, have them use the Complete the Sentences exercise on the Access 1 handout. Discuss the exercise in small groups with students to confirm their understanding.

Intermediate
Complete the Sentences. To help students with spelling frequently confused words, have them use the Complete the Sentences exercise on the Access 2 handout. If time allows, have students practice spelling frequently confused words by writing their own sentences in their journals.

Core Path	Access Path
1. Based on what you learned earlier in the unit about words that are often confused, can you identify any often-confused words in the first half of the narrative? (The word *imminent* is an often-confused word used in the Student Model narrative.)	

1. Based on what you learned earlier in the unit about words that are often confused, can you identify any often-confused words in the first half of the narrative? (The word *imminent* is an often-confused word used in the Student Model narrative.)

2. What word is often confused with the word *imminent*? (the word *eminent*)

3. Look up the word *eminent* in the dictionary. What does it mean? ("conspicuous" or "prominent")

4. Now look up the word *imminent*. What does it mean? ("about to happen" or "happening soon")

5. Read the sentence from "The Silver Box" that uses the word *imminent*. Why is this the correct word choice for this sentence? (Because the mother is warning the family that something dangerous is about to happen when she states that "the sun will be coming up in just a few hours.")

6. Look at the second half of the narrative. Can you identify any other often-confused words? (the word *eluding*)

7. What word is often confused with the word *eluding*? (the word *alluding*)

8. Look up the verb *allude* in the dictionary. What does it mean? ("to indirectly refer to something")

9. Now look up the verb *elude*. What does it mean? ("to skillfully avoid or escape something")

10. Read the sentence from "The Silver Box" that uses the word *eluding*. Why is this the correct word choice for this sentence? (because Captain Burns is telling the family that no one has been able to use the silver box to successfully avoid the sun's rays entirely)

Then, ask students to reread their narratives to make sure they have chosen the correct words to support meaning in their stories. Encourage students to look up any words they may have used incorrectly to determine whether or not they have chosen words with the proper meaning to support their writing.

Core Path	Access Path
Write. Ask students to complete the revision based on the prompt and on the completed highlight activity. Remind them to look out for words whose meanings and spellings are often confused. Once they have completed their writing, they should click "Submit."	**Beginner, Intermediate & Advanced** **Use Checklist.** Have all English Learners use the Narrative Writing Revision Checklist to help guide their revisions. Provide additional differentiated support as indicated below. **Beginner** **Focus on Sensory Details.** Encourage students to use sensory details in their narratives. Remind students that sensory details add information about people, places and things, which makes a story more interesting. Write the following sentences on the board: • His eyes were green. • His eyes were greener than a field of summer grass. • She was strong. • She was strong, like a mighty warrior. • The apple pie smelled good. • The apple pie smelled like you were walking in the woods on a warm autumn day. Ask students to identify the sensory details. Encourage students to discuss how the sensory details add much more information to the original sentences. Have students review their own writing to find sensory details. Encourage students to revise some details to include more information. **Intermediate** **Focus on Transition Words.** Remind students to include a variety of transition words in their narratives. Write the following sentences on the board: *Finally, I got the courage to look under the couch. At that moment, the snake slithered out quickly.* Explain that the word "Finally" and the phrase "At that moment" show the timing of the events. Remind students that authors use transition words in narratives to link ideas as well as to give a sequential order to the narrative. Have students review their own writing to find transition words and phrases. Encourage students to revise their work to include more transition words and phrases.

Core Path	Access Path
	Advanced
	Use Precise Language. Ask students to work with an English-proficient partner to identify and underline places in their story where language could be made more clear or vivid.
	Then have them use the two-column Precise Words chart on the Access 3 handout to list words students underlined in their narrative that need revision and brainstorm a list of new words to replace these words.
	Give them time to discuss which words are strongest (creating a feeling of suspense, showing clear and vivid description) and choose the best to include in their story.
	Approaching
	Practice Editing. Have Approaching students use the Description exercise on the Access 4 handout to practice identifying instances of descriptions that could be replaced with more vivid or exact language. After they have written their revised example paragraph, allow them to work with an on-level partner to read through their own drafts. They should focus on identifying and underlining instances of words that could be replaced with more vivid or exact language. Then have them make their revisions independently. Have them check their revised essay against the Narrative Writing Revision Checklist before they submit their revision.
Review. After completing their writing assignment, students should submit substantive feedback to two peers.	**Beginner**
	Review with Teacher Support. As a small group, help students to go through the Narrative Writing Revision Checklist on the Access 1 handout item-by-item to review one another's writing. Provide individual support to help them make changes as needed.
	Intermediate & Advanced
	Use Checklist. Have mixed-proficiency partners read their completed drafts aloud to one another and use the Narrative Writing Revision Checklist on the Access 2 and 3 handouts to check that their writing includes all of the required revisions. With teacher guidance as necessary, encourage them to suggest ways their partner could make any needed changes.

Core Path	Access Path
	Approaching **Use Checklist.** Have partners use the Narrative Writing Revision Checklist on the Access 4 handout to make sure their completed revisions include all the necessary elements.
	Extend **Spotlight on Dialogue.** Select a narrative text from the Unit, such as *Lord of the Flies,* and project the text onto the board. Ask students to examine the use of dialogue in the selection, and present students with the following questions: 1. Does the author use direct or indirect dialogue? How can you tell? 2. Is it clear which characters are speaking? 3. Are there elements of the dialogue that are confusing to you? Which ones? What steps would you take to revise the dialogue and eliminate reader confusion? 4. Does the dialogue help drive the action of the story forward? How so? 5. Does the dialogue help develop the characters of the story? What do you learn about the characters by reading the dialogue? 6. Do you think the dialogue serves any other purpose in the story? Explain. Discuss the answers to these questions as a class. Ask students to think about how they can apply the results of the discussion to their own story revisions. **Extend** **Critique.** Project the Student Model narrative on the board and ask the class to identify the suspenseful elements of the narrative, including details and sequencing. After students have had an opportunity to evaluate this aspect of the Model, work as a class to generate strategies students can use to ensure that their peer reviews are focused and substantive.

EXTENDED WRITING PROJECT:
Edit/Proofread/Publish

OVERVIEW

This lesson asks students to edit, proofread, and publish the revised versions of their suspenseful narratives. Students are instructed to edit for final improvements in detail, dialogue, and organization, and to proofread for the correct use of grammar, spelling and punctuation. Finally, students are encouraged to explore different methods for sharing and publishing their work.

OBJECTIVES

1. Identify editing, proofreading, and publishing skills.
2. Edit and proofread text to finalize plot, dialogue, descriptions, and organization, and to eliminate errors in grammar, punctuation, and spelling.
3. Participate effectively in a range of conversations and collaborations to express ideas and build upon the ideas of others.

ELA Common Core Standards:
Reading: Literature - RL.8.7
Writing - W.8.3.A, W.8.3.B, W.8.3.C, W.8.3.D, W.8.3.E, W.8.4, W.8.5, W.8.6 W.8.10
Speaking & Listening - SL.8.1.A, SL.8.5, SL.8.6
Language - L.8.1.A, L.8.1.B, L.8.1.C, L.8.2.C

RESOURCES

Grammar handout: Verb Moods Review

Access 1 handout (Beginner)

Access 2 handout (Intermediate)

Access 3 handout (Advanced)

Access 4 handout (Approaching)

Please note that excerpts and passages in the StudySync® library, workbooks, and PDFs are intended as touchstones to generate interest in an author's work. The excerpts and passages do not substitute for the reading of entire texts, and StudySync® strongly recommends that teachers and students seek out and purchase the whole literary or informational work in order to experience it as the author intended. Links to online resellers are available in our digital library. In addition, complete works may be ordered through an authorized reseller by filling out and returning to StudySync® the order form enclosed in this workbook.

Teacher's Edition   451

1. WRITE

Core Path	Access Path
Discuss. Before students begin to edit, review with the class the writing prompt/directions. Have a volunteer read them aloud. Ask whether students have any questions either about the prompt or the process of editing and proofreading. Respond to their questions, and then review criteria that can help students make final adjustments and corrections in their texts. Remind students that: • The narrative should reflect skills in writing narratives, including the narrative techniques of dialogue, pacing, description, and sequencing of events. • The narrative should have a beginning (with an expository introduction and conflict), a middle (with rising action and a climax), and an end (with a conclusion and resolution of the conflict). It should also include transitions between events in the plot. • The narrative should have a suspenseful theme that is engaging to readers. • The narrative should show proper use of words that end in a suffix, commonly confused words, and verb moods. • The narrative should be free from other errors in grammar, punctuation, and spelling.	**Beginner** **Use Writing Support.** Walk Beginning students through the proofreading checklist on the Access 1 handout item-by-item. Help them to identify and underline the sections of their narrative they will need to edit. **Intermediate** **Use Checklist.** Have Intermediate students preview the Editing and Proofreading Checklist on the Access 2 handout before they begin their final editing process. Make sure they understand everything on the checklist. As needed, help individual students identify the items on the checklist that they need to pay special attention to as they edit their narrative. **Approaching** **Support Proofreading.** Walk students through each item on the Editing and Proofreading Checklist on the Access 4 handout. Encourage students to circle unfamiliar words and underline anything that is confusing or unclear. Then take a few minutes to clarify unknown vocabulary, answer questions, and provide examples for any items that students do not understand. If you have identified individual students' challenges, circle those items on the checklist that they need to pay special attention to and provide individual support, or pair them with an on- or beyond- level student to make their final edits.
	Extend **Tech Infusion** **Test.** Have students submit their paper to PaperRater (www.paperrater.com). This site checks for grammar and spelling errors. Students can also select from the dropdown menus to have the engine provide feedback for style, word choice, and citations.

Core Path	Access Path

Core Path

(G) Grammar, Usage, and Mechanics. Distribute the StudySync Grammar handout: Verb Moods Review. Review with students the use of verb moods as explained in the handout. Then have students complete the practice exercise. (Answers for the practice exercise appear online.) Finally, encourage students to examine the use of verb moods in the Student Model narrative "The Silver Box." Ask students:

1. When is a verb in the indicative mood? (when it is part of a simple statement or question)

2. What indicative verbs do you see in the Student Model narrative? Where do they appear? (in the first paragraph: "had replaced" and "had become"; in the third paragraph: "will be coming")

3. When is a verb in the subjunctive mood? (when it expresses an idea that is contrary to the fact, is doubtful or uncertain, or is an assumption or a wish)

4. What subjunctive verbs do you see in the Student Model narrative? Where do they appear? (in the first paragraph: "had been standing"; in the third paragraph: "should stop")

5. Look at the first paragraph of the Student Model. Why are the verbs "had replaced" and "had become" considered indicative rather than subjunctive, even though they contain the word "had"? (These verbs are each part of a simple statement and do not express an idea that is contrary to the fact, is doubtful or uncertain, or is an assumption or a wish.)

6. When is a verb in the imperative mood? (when it is part of a command or request)

7. What imperative verbs do you see in the Student Model narrative? Where do they appear? (in the ninth paragraph: "Tell")

Access Path

Beginner & Intermediate
Mechanics. Have students practice using the subjunctive mood, words such as *can, could, shall, should, will, would, may* or *might*, in the sentence frames activity on the Access 1 and 2 handouts.

Please note that excerpts and passages in the StudySync® library, workbooks, and PDFs are intended as touchstones to generate interest in an author's work. The excerpts and passages do not substitute for the reading of entire texts, and StudySync® strongly recommends that teachers and students seek out and purchase the whole literary or informational work in order to experience it as the author intended. Links to online resellers are available in our digital library. In addition, complete works may be ordered through an authorized reseller by filling out and returning to StudySync® the order form enclosed in this workbook.

Teacher's Edition   **453**

Core Path	Access Path
8. Look at the third paragraph of the Student Model. How could the writer rewrite the sentence "You should stop this silliness and get to bed" so that the verb is in the imperative mood rather than the subjunctive mood? ("Stop this silliness and get to bed.")	
Write. Ask students to complete the writing assignment. Suggest, if there's time, that they set their narrative aside for a few minutes, and that they then proofread it one more time. Remind them to check that words with affixes and words that are often confused are spelled correctly. Advise them to check that their verbs reflect the correct mood. Once they have completed their writing, they should click "Submit."	**Beginner & Intermediate** Before students begin to make their final edits, have them review the Editing and Proofreading Checklist in pairs. Refer pairs to the checklist on the Access 1 and 2 handouts. Encourage students to discuss the checklist and their narratives. When they begin editing their final drafts, remind students that they were supposed to incorporate sensory details. Explain that now they will check to make sure they have used enough sensory details in their narratives. Display and review the sensory details using the following sentences: • It was hot at the beach. • It was so hot at the beach that if felt like I was walking on lava. Guide students to underline all the sensory details in their essay. They can work with a teacher or English-proficient partner to check and confirm that they have used enough sensory details.

Core Path	Access Path
	Intermediate & Advanced **Read Aloud to Proofread.** Explain to students that reading their work aloud is a great way to check for errors they might have otherwise missed. After students have completed their editing using the Editing and Proofreading Checklist, have them read their story aloud to an English-proficient partner. Tell them that if they stumble in their reading it may indicate a place where they need to adjust punctuation or sentence structure. Have their partner listen for correct use of grammar and suggest corrections if needed. **Approaching** **Support Writing.** Have students check their final draft against the Editing and Proofreading Checklist on their Access 4 handout to make sure they made all the edits needed. Ask them if they have questions or found any part of the assignment challenging. If so, provide clarification and assistance so that they can make their final edits and proofread before submitting their work.

Present. Because they develop a compelling story through dialogue and action, narratives—and especially suspenseful ones!—offer a unique opportunity for students to practice their presentation and performance skills.

Have students form small groups of between three and five, read one another's narratives, and select a passage from one that they feel best lends itself to an oral performance.

Ask them to consider how they might transform the passage into a script to be read aloud and performed as a dramatic scene, in the style of Reader's Theater. As they prepare their scripts, advise students to ask themselves questions such as the following:

- How can we convey to the audience information about the characters, setting, or conflict that was provided by the narrator? For example, how might the dialogue in our chosen passage be enhanced to communicate necessary details?

Core Path	Access Path
<ul><li>What "stage directions" should we add to our script to help the actors perform the scene? For example, what cues will they need about how to deliver their lines?</li><li>How can we include visual displays and other "props" to enhance the audience's ability to visualize details about the characters and plot of our narrative scene?</li></ul>Suggest that group members assign roles and responsibilities, such as the following:<ul><li>Who will adapt the prose text to make it a dramatic script?</li><li>Who will perform the parts?</li><li>Who will provide props and/or scenery?</li><li>Who will "direct" the performance, providing feedback to the actors and adjusting the script as necessary?</li></ul>Have students consult the Narrative Checklist and the Narrative Presentation Rubric in the Speaking & Listening Handbook as they prepare for their presentations. Ask students to present their dramatic narrative scenes to the class. After each performance, audience members should ask questions and provide constructive feedback to their peers. What in the performance needed a little more work to keep the suspense going, and what tingled their spines or kept them on the edge of their seats?	
	Extend **Evaluate Plot Sequence.** Encourage students to evaluate their plot sequences one final time by dividing their narrative into scenes. Have students record each scene on a new page of a document and then read each scene, clicking on the "Next Page" feature to navigate to the next scene. Alternatively, students can print each scene page and create a flip booklet that allows students to navigate from one scene to the next. Have students review their scenes in order and evaluate the logical order of their plot events.

Core Path	Access Path
	Extend **Publish Online.** Suggest that students use Pen (http://tinyurl.com/3lsaa8u) to publish their narratives online instantly. Alternatively, or in addition, students can use a program such as Bookr (http://tinyurl.com/3by72c/) to add images to their stories and publish as an online photobook.

Research

Suspense!

TYPE

Research

TITLE

Grade 8 Unit 1: Suspense!

TIME

140 minutes (research and presentations)

OBJECTIVES

1. Engage students in reading, writing, and researching the topic of suspense in order to expand their content knowledge, improve their understanding of theme, and increase their familiarity with plot devices.
2. Participate in conversations and collaborations to express ideas and build upon the ideas of others.
3. Practice and apply research strategies to produce a presentation with multimedia features.
4. Practice, apply, and reinforce the following Grade 8 ELA Common Core Standards for reading literature and informational texts, writing narrative pieces, conducting research projects, and speaking and listening:

> Reading: Literature - RL.8.1, RL.8.2, RL.8.3, RL.8.4, RL.5, RL.8.6, RL.8.7, RL.8.10
> Reading Informational Text - RI.8.1, RI.8.2, RI.8.3, RI.8.4, RI.8.5, RI.8.6, RI.8.7, RI.8.8, RI.8.10
> Writing - W.8.3, W.8.4, W.8.5, W.8.6, W.8.7, W.8.8, W.8.9.A, W.8.9.B, W.8.10
> Speaking and Listening - SL.8.1, SL.8.2, SL.8.3, SL.8.5, SL.8.6
> Language - L.8.1, L.8.2, L.8.3, L.8.4, L.8.5, L.8.6

RESOURCES

Library, online resources, links to topics
StudySync Speaking & Listening Handbook

OVERVIEW

What attracts us to stories of suspense? In order to better understand why readers and audiences are attracted to stories of suspense, students will research examples and impacts of suspense in mediums such as radio stories, articles, films, and documentaries. If introduced in the first half of the unit, this research project will serve as a resource for the Extended Writing piece students will produce toward the unit's close.

To help students plan and conduct their research and prepare and deliver their presentations, refer them to the relevant lessons (noted below) in the Speaking and Listening Handbook.

As students work to complete their research projects, remind them of the skills they have practiced and applied during the unit. They should incorporate this knowledge into their work as they discuss, plan, research, and create the project, and as they deliver their presentations. Story elements and themes in literature and point of view in nonfiction, as well as the distinctions between formal and informal language in writing and speech, should be emphasized after the lessons for both fiction and informational texts have been taught, practiced, and applied.

Suggested topics for small-group research and presentations include:

- How do film, text, and radio versions of the same story treat the elements of suspense and horror in different ways? For example, what differences become clear after listening to the radio version of *Sorry, Wrong Number* and watching the film version? How does the medium affect the content and impact of the story?

- Why do we watch suspense and horror movies? Interview friends and family about what attracts them to such movies.

- What is the role of music in creating suspense in film or radio?

- How is suspense handled across different genres? How might the mystery genre employ suspense? Is suspense used differently in a tale of horror?

- How might a reporter utilize suspense in an article? Why?

- How might a writer manipulate characters' or readers' fears in order to achieve suspense?

Links to some of these topics can be found on the Unit Blast under Research Topics.

REVIEW AND DISCUSS (10 MINUTES)

1. **Revisit Unit Blast and Unit Preview** *(SL.8.1.A–D, SL.8.2)*. As a group, reread the Big Idea Blast and watch the Unit Preview again. Discuss the purpose of each, as well as how and why its information is presented in a certain way. Use the following questions to guide a discussion prior to research:

    a. What is the most interesting or surprising lesson this unit has taught you about suspense?
    b. What themes or plot devices are represented in the thrilling tales you have read in this unit?
    c. What topics from the reading are you most interested to learn more about?

CONDUCT THE RESEARCH (80 MINUTES)

To help students conduct their research and prepare their presentations, refer them to the Speaking and Listening Handbook lesson, "Using Various Media."

Copyright © BookheadEd Learning, LLC

2. **Break Students Into Small Groups. Assign Each Group a Topic, or Let Groups Self-Select. (40 Minutes)**

    a. **Make a Research Plan** *(W.8.7)*. Instruct students to formulate research questions for their topic. After students prepare questions, collaborate with them on the best places to search for information, the most useful keywords to use in their search, and the type of resources available to them during the research process. Remind students that their research should focus on the role suspense plays in different mediums and the different impacts it has in these mediums.

    b. **Gather Resources** *(W.8.8)*. Instruct students to gather a selection of the following: print and digital text resources, videos, audio recordings, graphics, and photos. Remind students to evaluate the validity of a source before using information from that source.

    c. **Review and Discuss** *(SL.8.1.A–D)*. Advise groups to assign each member a research task to complete on his or her own. Tasks should be completed and presented to the group by each member individually.

3. **Assemble the Research in Each Group (40 minutes)**

    a. **Share** *(RL.8.7, RI.8.7; SL.8.1.A–D, SL.8.2, SL.8.4)*. Instruct students in each group to share what they have learned about their individual research and why this information is important. They should discuss the purpose of each resource they explored and how and why the information is presented in a certain way. As students develop their research presentations, they should remember to include relevant evidence, sound reasoning, and well-chosen details, definitions, and concrete details.

    b. **Focus** *(W.8.7, W.8.8)*. Ask students to review the information they have gathered and to select the information that is most relevant. Encourage students to revise their research questions, as needed. Each group should then create a bibliography of their resources.

    c. **Write Explanations of Facts** *(W.8.8)*. Instruct group members to write brief explanations of any facts they uncovered during their research. Remind students to be careful to cite their sources properly, using the correct format for quoting or paraphrasing material drawn from research. This information can be included in the group presentation.

    d. **Plan a Short Presentation** *(SL.8.1.A–D)*. Ask groups to plan a short presentation of the information they compiled. Students should follow the format below:

        i. **Title:** The title of the presentation should provide information about the topic.

        ii. **Introduction:** *(W.8.7)* The introduction should include a general description of the topic and state the research questions.

        iii. **List of Top Facts:** *(W.8.9.B)* The list should include five to ten key facts about the subject derived from research.

        iv. **Multimedia Element** *(SL.8.5)*: Remind each group to integrate multimedia and visual displays into their presentations (video, graphic, photo, recording) to clarify information, to strengthen claims and evidence, and also to add interest.

        v. **Conclusion:** Explain how this topic is relevant today.

PRESENT THE RESEARCH (35 MINUTES)

To help students prepare and deliver their presentations, refer to Presentation Skills and the Informative Presentation Rubric in the Speaking and Listening Handbook.

4. **Group Multimedia Presentations (5-7 minutes per group)**

    a. **Present** *(SL.8.2, SL.8.4-6)*. Each group should take turns presenting their findings to the class, making use of digital media to enhance their presentations. Remind students that a good presentation involves speaking in a clear and professional manner. This includes organizing ideas to create a logical flow, reinforcing main points with relevant and valid details, and using appropriate grammar, direct eye contact, an adequate and effective volume, a proper style and tone, and meaningful gestures to keep the audience's attention and to emphasize key points. To introduce quoted material or specific facts, remind students that they can say, "According to," and follow this with the source of the information. Stress the importance of using both academic language and formal English correctly and citing textual evidence in their conversations to support their ideas.

    b. **Summarize** *(SL.8.4)*. Ask each group to briefly summarize their presentation.

    c. **Questions** *(SL.8.1.C)*. If time allows, students in the audience should ask relevant questions, to which group members should respond with relevant evidence.

EXTENSION: RESPOND TO AND POST THE PRESENTATIONS (10 MINUTES)

5. **Write** *(W.8.10; SL.8.3)*. Have students use the Informative Presentation Rubric to respond to the presentations. In addition, have students write about what they have learned from the presentations by:

    a. listing three things they know now that they didn't know before; and

    b. writing a paragraph explaining how the presentations informed their understanding of suspense.

POST THE RESEARCH (10 MINUTES)

Set up an area in the room for students to review the research of other groups.

Post information about students' findings on a class website or blog.

Ask student groups to briefly present their research at an open house or other school event.

Full-text Study

Suspense!

Lord of the Flies

William Golding

INTRODUCTION

Lord of the Flies is William Golding's hauntingly dystopian 1954 novel about a group of young boys stranded on a deserted island during a nuclear war, their attempts at maintaining self-order and finding a way off the island gradually devolving into savagery. In the beginning, the boys devise plans for survival and elect a leader, Ralph, who uses a conch shell to gather the group, and whose friend, Piggy, possesses their only means of making fire: his eyeglasses. Soon thereafter, Ralph becomes increasingly at odds with a rival, Jack, who wants power and has become increasingly enamored with the act of hunting. As the group splits into different factions, the boys will come to learn that the biggest threat to their collective survival lies within.

William Golding (1911–1993) was an English author who won the 1983 Nobel Prize in Literature for his novels, which frequently depict mankind's duality of nature as an eternal struggle between civilization and savagery, most famously in *Lord of the Flies*. He was knighted by Queen Elizabeth in 1988, and he is commonly listed among the most admired British authors of the 20th century.

As students read *Lord of the Flies*, ask them to think about the implications of the boys' actions, especially regarding mankind's capacity for civilization and order. Why does the situation on the island descend so quickly into chaos and disorder, and what larger lessons or observations can we draw from this descent?

USING THIS READING GUIDE

This reading guide presents lessons to support the teaching of William Golding's *Lord of the Flies*. Organized by sections of grouped chapters, the lessons preview key vocabulary words and include close reading questions tied to the Common Core State Standards. The lessons identify a key passage in each section that will help you guide students through an exploration of the essential ideas and events in *Lord of the Flies*. This passage will also serve as the jumping-off point from which students will engage in their own SyncTV-style group discussion.

Each section of the reading guide also includes a list of comparative texts—provided in *Lord of the Flies* Full-text Unit on StudySync—that go along with that section. For each comparative text, the reading guide includes important contextual notes and ideas for relating the text to *Lord of the Flies*.

LORD OF THE FLIES

CHAPTERS 1–2: Stranded on an Island

After their plane crashes on a deserted island during a nuclear war, Ralph and Piggy use a conch shell to summon the other survivors, all of whom are young boys. To the chagrin of Jack, a rival, the majority of the boys appoint Ralph as leader. Ralph forms an expedition, along with Jack and Simon, to explore the island, and he proposes they build a fire to signal for help.

CHAPTERS 3–4: Going Native

Tensions emerge between Ralph and Jack over Jack and the hunters' failures to catch any food. Some time passes, and the boys are beginning to enter into a routine on the island. Jack becomes more and more obsessed with killing a pig and is finally successful, returning from a brutal expedition in a frenzy.

CHAPTERS 5–7: The Beast on the Mountain

Ralph calls a meeting and admonishes the boys for their lack of order. The boys' fear of ferocious beasts on the island has them in a panic. When a dead parachutist who has landed on the island is mistaken for a monster, Jack, Ralph, and a group of hunters head out to find this "monster" and are terrified by their discovery.

CHAPTERS 8–9: The Beast Inside

Jack splits with Ralph to form his own faction, and most of the other boys join him. Ralph and Piggy discuss building another signal fire on the shore, but Jack's tribe raids their camp. Simon encounters a demonic apparition in the woods, and when he returns to camp, the boys attack and kill him, thinking he's the monster.

CHAPTERS 10–12: Castle Rock

Jack has become an increasingly deranged and savage leader, and he sends two boys to Ralph's camp to attack them and steal Piggy's glasses. Ralph and Piggy travel to Castle Rock to confront Jack and his tribe, resulting in a violent and deadly confrontation.

CHAPTERS 1–2: Stranded on an Island

KEY PASSAGE | Chapter 1, Paragraphs 229–234

In this passage, the boys are in the middle of a meeting, trying to decide how to proceed now that they are stranded on a strange island without means of escape. After long last, the "dark boy" Roger puts forth an idea of his own: to elect a chief of the group. The candidates are few and far between, and before a formal vote is cast, the group already seems to have rallied around Ralph. The qualities that define Ralph as a leader are perhaps more subtle: Piggy is the smartest of the group, and Jack is the most natural leader, but Ralph possesses a quiet poise—not to mention his stature, his good looks, and the mysterious conch shell he possesses that had summoned them all together in the first place. Holding it in his hands, Ralph assumes a mysterious, barely understood power over the boys.

WHY IT'S KEY

Characters: Although the boys are stranded and entirely on their own, they do still exhibit a capacity, if not a propensity, for organization and rules. Among them, natural or obvious leaders have already begun to emerge, before any formal voting or recognition of a leader. Ralph, Jack, and Piggy are similar in that they all exhibit certain qualities of leadership. Jack shows hubris, Piggy shows intelligence, and Ralph has something more intangible: his size and attractive appearance, his stillness, and a conch shell that can be used as a horn and confers an air of authority and worthiness.

Theme: Even in the story's earliest moments, it's possible to infer that a certain power struggle is going to occur between the boys. The character details we're given about Jack, Ralph, and Piggy are all different attributes that will help or hurt them in the process. Thematically, *Lord of the Flies* is a story about the nature of power and how the struggle for power emerges in this new, uncivilized state. Who will end up with the upper hand? Which kinds of people are drawn to having power, and what does it take to keep it? Already, the novel suggests these questions as thematic concerns.

Symbol: The text focuses specifically on the conch shell that Ralph possesses, "most obscurely, yet most powerfully . . ." The fact that the narrator gives such direct, explicit attention to an item or object is a good clue of its importance, literally and/or symbolically, to the narrative. Here, the conch shell represents power in the hands of Ralph. It takes on an almost mystical level of significance to the boys on the island.

YOUR STUDYSYNC® TV

Discussion Prompt: Several of the boys exhibit natural leadership qualities, but Ralph (at least in the beginning) emerges as their choice for chief. What makes a good leader? What are some different leadership qualities, and which ones are most important? Discuss the idea of leadership, referring to the different leadership traits exhibited by Ralph, Piggy, Jack, and Simon in this passage and others.

Standards: RL.8.1, RL.8.2, RL.8.3; SL.8.1.A, SL.8.1.C, SL.8.1.D

VOCABULARY

decorous
dec•or•ous *adjective*
Polite or proper; in good taste
Athletes are expected to show decorous behavior during post-game interviews, keeping their appearance and their language clean.

contemptuously
con•temp•tu•ous•ly *adverb*
In a manner showing strong dislike or disdain towards something
The critic spoke contemptuously about the new film, calling it "a complete waste of time."

hindering
hin•der•ing *verb*
Obstructing; impeding
Partisan politics and character attacks have been hindering Congress's ability to accomplish anything.

ebullience
e•bul•li•ence *noun*
The quality of showing enthusiasm and exuberance
He grinned and threw open his arms in ebullience as his wife ran to him after a year's absence.

recrimination
re•crim•i•na•tion *noun*
The act of making a counter-accusation against an accuser
The journalist wrote a scathing editorial in bitter recrimination against those who dared to criticize him.

indignantly
in•dig•nant•ly *adverb*
In a manner showing anger towards someone because of a perceived wrong
After sitting in the lobby for two hours, Patricia indignantly asked the receptionist how much longer she'd have to wait.

Copyright © BookheadEd Learning, LLC

CLOSE READ

QUESTION 1: What is the significance of the "man with the megaphone"? What do this and other details tell you about the setting of the novel?

Sample Answer: The "man with the megaphone" is not identified, but we can infer that he was someone at an airport, probably during an evacuation. The megaphone is also important because it echoes the authority of Ralph's similarly amplifying conch. This tells us, in the midst of the unspecified nuclear war and the bombs being detonated, that the story takes place in an apocalyptic future or alternate reality.

Standards: RL.8.1

QUESTION 2: Which "leadership" role on the island does Jack settle into, and what does this indicate about his character?

Sample Answer: Jack decides that his group—the choir boys—will be in charge of hunting. His eagerness for hunting shows a certain proclivity towards violence and aggression.

Standards: RL.8.1

QUESTION 3: Why is Jack unable to kill the piglet in the curtain of creepers, and what does he resolve to do about it?

Sample Answer: Jack hesitates when he is about to bring the knife down on the pig, and the pig gets away. He denies it, but the others know that it is "the unbearable blood" that made him pause. He resolves not to make the same mistake again.

Standards: RL.8.1

QUESTION 4: At the meeting, what do Ralph, Simon, and Jack report back about the island? What famous books do they reference in describing it, and why?

Sample Answer: Ralph says it's "a good island" and they mention the presence of rocks and plants, as well as food and drink. They also compare it to books they've read, like Treasure Island and Coral Island. This is the boys' frame of reference for their situation. For the author, literary allusions are one way to add meaning to a story.

Standards: RL.8.1

QUESTION 5: Why are Piggy's eyeglasses important? How does Piggy respond to his glasses being used for this purpose?

Sample Answer: Piggy's glasses are important because they are the means of making fire. He is angry about Jack and the others pushing him around, but he doesn't show the strength to stand up to them.

Standards: RL.8.1

 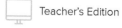

COMPARATIVE TEXTS

Text: *The Coral Island: A Tale of the Pacific Ocean* by R. M. Ballantyne

Compare to: Chapter 1 of *Lord of the Flies*

Connection: Three times in *Lord of the Flies*, in Chapters 1, 2, and 12, references are made to another book, *The Coral Island*. Published seventy years before *Lord of the Flies, The Coral Island* was a popular boys' adventure book by R. M. Ballantyne about three British boys showing their superior survival skills while marooned on an island. William Golding turned that stereotype on its head in his novel, ironically naming his two main characters after Ralph and Jack in *The Coral Island*.

Text: *Book of Genesis* from Revised Standard Version Bible

Compare to: Chapter 2 of *Lord of the Flies*

Connection: The third chapter of the Book of Genesis presents man and woman with their first moral test: whether to obey God's order to avoid the fruit of the tree of knowledge, or to give in to the persuasion of the serpent. Their choice—to disobey God—is considered by some to be the Original Sin that all humans are born with. In the Eden-like island of *Lord of the Flies*, there are biblical echoes—the rumored snake, Ralph's rule to never let the fire go out, and fear and law competing with the freedom to be independent. As you read both texts, think about the roles the serpent and the snake play in Chapter 3 of the Book of Genesis and in Chapter 2 of *Lord of the Flies*.

CHAPTERS 3–4: Going Native

This passage begins with Jack's inner thoughts following his group's return from their first successful hunting expedition. Carrying a dead pig on a stake, Jack and the boys are in a frenzied state when they encounter Ralph, Simon, and Piggy, fresh from a swim in the lagoon. Jack first notices Ralph's "scarred nakedness" and the awkward silence of the encounter; it occurs to Jack that Ralph, Piggy and Simon weren't present for the hunt, and aren't feeling the same rapturous excitement. Unable to contain his emotions, Jack fantasizes to himself once more about the precise moment of the kill and the primal rush when they took the pig's life.

WHY IT'S KEY

Plot: Jack, obsessed with the idea of killing a pig, goes into a frenzy once the deed is done. Returning from the jungle with his hunters, they are covered in blood and chanting a bizarre incantation. Ralph and the others are deeply unsettled by their return and by the eagerness they demonstrate for violence and savagery.

Character: Jack, already one of the latent antagonists of the story, undergoes a disturbing development in this passage and scene. From the beginning, he has clearly exhibited a desire for power and control—and Ralph, the novel's main protagonist, is the one who stands in his way. In hindsight, Jack's interest in hunting seems even more like bloodlust, because once "freed" from the propriety of civilization, he has embraced the lust to kill and grown more wild and barbaric.

Language: An important turning point in Jack's ascendancy to the novel's antagonist occurs here. He is drunk on the power of killing another living thing. Pay careful attention to the language Golding uses in the description of this turning point: Jack and the other hunters enjoy the "knowledge that they had outwitted a living thing, imposed their will upon it, [and] taken away its life like a long satisfying drink." In their more savage state, the act of killing and the power that comes with it bestows knowledge and satisfaction on the killers.

Point of View: Golding employs a close third-person perspective here and in other key passages in *Lord of the Flies*. The narrator is an external observer of the action but also possesses insight into what certain characters, including Jack, are thinking. Jack's mind is "crowded with memories," and without close third-person insight, we wouldn't know what any of these memories were.

YOUR STUDYSYNC® TV

Discussion Prompt: At this point in the story, do you think Jack and the hunters are going crazy? Or are they merely embracing their savage, animalistic state? Discuss the effects of island life on Jack and the other hunters, versus how it has affected Ralph, Piggy, and Simon. Do you think Jack and the hunters are *evil*, or do you think this is just a normal reaction to life in a more uncivilized state? Explain.

Standards: RL.8.1, RL.8.3; SL.8.1.A, SL.8.1.C, SL.8.1.D

VOCABULARY

incredulous
in•cred•u•lous *adjective*
Showing strong disbelief or skepticism
She had an incredulous look on her face when I told her that her car had been stolen.

tacit
ta•cit *adjective*
Implicit or clear without being stated
The roommates had a tacit agreement that they would keep the common areas clean and keep noise to a minimum.

clamorously
clam•or•ous•ly *adverb*
In a loud or rowdy manner
The crowd pushed clamorously into the store on the morning of the grand opening.

procession
pro•ces•sion *noun*
An organized group traveling together, especially in a formal or ceremonial manner
The funeral procession traveled two miles from the church to the cemetery.

implications
im•pli•ca•tions *noun*
The possible results or effects of something, often suggested or not directly obvious
The tragedies of September 11th had massive implications in the legislation and enforcement of national security matters.

malevolently
ma•lev•o•lent•ly *adverb*
With maliciousness and hostility
Many fairy tales depict a conflict between a brave hero and a malevolently powerful villain.

CLOSE READ

QUESTION 1: How is Jack different in Chapter 3 from how he was before? What caused the change?

Sample Answer: Possibly fueled in part by his inability to kill the pig in Chapter 1, Jack has become obsessed with hunting down a pig. He tracks pig droppings and sniffs the air, having evolved (or devolved) into a much more primitive state.

Standards: RL.8.1

QUESTION 2: How is Simon's behavior different from that of the others? What kinds of conclusions or observations about Simon can we draw from his actions at the end of Chapter 3?

Sample Answer: Simon is good-natured, helpful, and fairly reserved, and seems to possess a wisdom greater than the others. When he walks into the jungle at the end of Chapter 3, he shows his individualistic nature to think and act apart from the "crowd."

Standards: RL.8.1

QUESTION 3: Based on what traits or characteristics do the boys on the island divide and organize themselves?

Sample Answer: The primary division is between biguns and littluns, or the older boys and the younger ones. There are distinctions within each, and even though Ralph is chief, the choirboys have as strong an allegiance to Jack, if not stronger.

Standards: RL.8.1

QUESTION 4: Does Jack accept any responsibility for letting the signal fire die out? What are the boys' various reactions to his admission of guilt, or lack of guilt?

Sample Answer: Jack ultimately apologizes for his irresponsibility, but it takes a while, and it's only after he bullies Piggy and punches him in the face. The choirboys all support Jack and his apology, but Ralph is a little less forgiving and asserts his dominance over Jack once again.

Standards: RL.8.1

QUESTION 5: Why doesn't Ralph want to eat the meat Jack is roasting? What is the eventual result of this, and what does it suggest about Ralph?

Sample Answer: Ralph wants to show his disapproval of Jack and his actions, and doesn't want to be seen as a hypocrite for enjoying the pig that Jack and the hunters caught. However, he is ultimately unable to resist the craving of meat. Although Ralph is not like the others, this suggests that he is not as "above it" as he might have thought.

Standards: RL.8.1

COMPARATIVE TEXTS

Text: *Robinson Crusoe* by Daniel Defoe

Compare to: Chapter 3 of *Lord of the Flies*

Connection: Robinson Crusoe, perhaps the best-known castaway in English literature, shows that he is an organized man, both in the practical matter of taking inventory of his possessions and in the mental sorting of the good and bad points of his predicament. Faced with a similar dilemma, Ralph and Jack's moods begin to diverge: Ralph despairing at the failure of building shelter and Jack excited by the prospect of hunting pigs. Meanwhile, Simon finds comfort in solitude.

Teacher's Edition

Text: *African Genesis* by Robert Ardrey

Compare to: Chapter 4 of *Lord of the Flies*

Connection: In *African Genesis*, author Robert Ardrey finds patterns of behavior in the animal world that are mirrored in the behavior of humans, particularly acts of aggression—from road rage to war. Recalling biologist Konrad Lorenz's study of jackdaws, Ardrey shows how the pecking order in jackdaw society adjusts to changes. What conclusions can be drawn about the "pecking order" between Ralph, Jack, Piggy, and other characters in Chapter 4 of *Lord of the Flies*?

CHAPTERS 5–7: The Beast on the Mountain

In this passage, Piggy confides in Ralph and Simon that his fears of Jack Merridew have begun to dominate his thoughts. Piggy fears Jack's thirst for power, and explains to Ralph that Jack hates him too, jealous as Jack is of Ralph's status as chief. Jack would never hurt Ralph directly, Piggy explains, but he might try to hurt Ralph by lashing out at those close to him, such as Piggy himself. Simon urges Jack not to falter in his confidence as chief, because Ralph is the only one who can control Jack Merridew. The passage concludes as the boys reflect on how their newfound independence, once a source of excitement, has begun to turn rotten as the pressures of self-governance take their toll.

WHY IT'S KEY

Plot: With Jack and the hunters in a barbaric frenzy—and the littluns' fear of beasts and monsters stalking their every move—order on the island is beginning to break down. After Jack and the others run off, only Ralph, Simon, and Piggy remain. They encourage Ralph to hang in as chief, even though he feels his control of the group gradually slipping away.

Character: Although he isn't present, Jack Merridew is the subject of this passage. Jack's intimidation is affecting Piggy and threatening whatever semblance of order Ralph and the others have. In a few lines, this passage exemplifies the different characters' personalities and their dynamics with each other: Piggy is clever but weak (his asthma is a small but telling detail); Simon is sensitive and passive, and Ralph, as their friend, represents their best hope on the island. Ralph and Jack have emerged as the two "natural" leaders among the group, but the differences between them are vast.

Dialogue: This scene relies upon dialogue to provide exposition and reveal aspects of character. Ralph has been having his doubts about his role as chief, but Piggy and Simon are both insistent that he should remain. Piggy seems to be motivated primarily by his own fear of Jack Merridew, thinking that Jack might try to hurt Ralph through him. Piggy is the most vocal and alarmed of the three boys; his breathless passages of dialogue demonstrate this, especially in contrast to the shorter and more measured statements of Ralph and Simon.

Setting: A note about the setting, because as a determinant in any story it is just as important as the plot and characters—and especially so in *Lord of the Flies*. Naturally, the deserted island where they now live allows them the ability to behave in a way they wouldn't where they're from. It provides both opportunities and setbacks, as the final statement in this passage demonstrates: "At home there was always a grownup. Please, sir; please, miss; and then you got an answer. How I wish!" Although the boys have more freedom and responsibility on their own, they also don't have any parents or authority figures to help them when they need it, assuming the responsibility for rules, structure, and moral guidance.

YOUR STUDYSYNC® TV

Discussion Prompt: Based on this passage, how has the glamor of the boys' freedom from authority given way to some hard truths? Discuss how the boys' view of island life has changed, and any potential lessons or messages that can be drawn from their shift in understanding. Why do you think *Lord of the Flies* has been interpreted as a criticism of adventure stories like *Treasure Island, The Coral Island*, and so forth? Explain.

Standards: RL.8.1, RL.8.2, RL.8.3, RL.8.9; SL.8.1.A, SL.8.1.C, SL.8.1.D

VOCABULARY

perpetually
per•pet•u•al•ly *adverb*
In a ceaseless or never-ending manner
Nature is perpetually in motion, teeming with vast ecosystems of life.

intimidation
in•tim•i•da•tion *noun*
The act of trying to control or influence someone's behavior by using force or causing fear
Intimidation was a huge factor in his game, bullying the smaller players with his seven-foot three-hundred-pound frame.

emphatic
em•phat•ic *adjective*
Said or done forcefully
When her crush finally asked her to the prom, she responded with an emphatic yes.

diffidently
dif•fi•dent•ly *adverb*
In a manner showing a lack of confidence
He sat diffidently in class, too shy around the other students to answer questions or express his opinion.

daunting
daunt•ing *adjective*
Causing feelings of apprehension; difficult or frightening
Hiking the entire Inca Trail seems a little daunting, but I think we're all up for the challenge.

impervious
im•per•vi•ous *adjective*
Unable to be affected; impenetrable
Iris was so confident of her popularity, she was impervious to criticism from her rivals.

CLOSE READ

QUESTION 1: Why does Ralph call a meeting in Chapter 5? What are Jack's and Piggy's contributions to the meeting?

Sample Answer: Ralph calls a meeting to establish order and reinforce several rules of the island, including always keeping the signal fire lit. Jack and Piggy both try to calm down the littluns and tell them there's no beast, but Jack eventually incites them to run off in search of it.

Standards: RL.8.1

QUESTION 2: What is Simon's opinion of the "beast" inhabiting the island? How do the others react to his opinion?

Sample Answer: Simon states that maybe there is a beast, after all, but he wonders if "it's only us"—meaning that the boys themselves are the beasts. The others are immediately dismissive of his wisdom, and he is unable to express what he's truly trying to say.

Standards: RL.8.1

QUESTION 3: Why doesn't Ralph blow the conch shell to summon Jack and the others to return? Explain his hesitation and what it suggests about the symbolic power of the shell.

Sample Answer: Ralph decides not to blow the conch shell because he's afraid they won't listen to him, and if that happens, the shell will have lost its power. The shell has been the one thing they all listen to and respect, and he fears that once that respect is lost, they'll be like animals.

Standards: RL.8.1

QUESTION 4: What is the true nature of the "beast" they're seeking? What different factors do you think have enabled this misapprehension to spread?

Sample Answer: The beast on the mountain is a dead parachutist, but Sam and Eric think it is a monster because they are afraid of beasts, and already on the lookout. Any bizarre or unusual-looking thing, at this point, would probably be mistaken for a "beast."

Standards: RL.8.1

QUESTION 5: How does Ralph react to his first "hunting" experience? What can we infer from this?

Sample Answer: During his first hunting experience, Ralph is proud that he hits a boar with his spear (even though he doesn't kill it), and he wonders if maybe hunting is an enjoyable activity after all. This, coupled with his participation in the violent "game" later, shows that Ralph is tempted by barbarism and savagery just the same.

Standards: RL.8.1

COMPARATIVE TEXTS

Text: "Superstition" by Emmet D. Owens

Compare to: Chapter 5 of *Lord of the Flies*

Connection: What is it that compels the "littluns" and some of the bigger boys in *Lord of the Flies* to believe in beasts and ghosts? Is it irrational, supernatural threats that quickly become contagious through their fearful imaginations? Is it the bogeyman, the fear of the unknown, a primitive instinct that kicks in, or all of these? A passage about superstitions provides some context for discussing the tense assembly in Chapter 5.

Text: "The Tyger" by William Blake

Compare to: Chapter 6 of *Lord of the Flies*

Connection: In Chapter 6 of *Lord of the Flies*, a glimpse of a dead paratrooper translates into a newly credible beast, and a search party of Jack, Ralph, Simon, and others goes to an unexplored part of the island. Another beast achieves larger-than-life dimensions in William Blake's poem "The Tyger." How do the two beasts compare? How does the poet's awe compare with the boys' responses?

Text: "If" by Rudyard Kipling

Compare to: Chapter 7 of *Lord of the Flies*

Connection: In Chapter 7 of *Lord of the Flies*, Ralph feels helpless against the vastness of the ocean and the remoteness of his memories of home. Baited by Jack in a reluctant pursuit of the beast, Ralph might well be the intended audience for Rudyard Kipling's poem "If," a kind of campaign poster for staying cool in a crisis and not getting too carried away by success or failure.

Please note that excerpts and passages in the StudySync® library, workbooks, and PDFs are intended as touchstones to generate interest in an author's work. The excerpts and passages do not substitute for the reading of entire texts, and StudySync® strongly recommends that teachers and students seek out and purchase the whole literary or informational work in order to experience it as the author intended. Links to online resellers are available in our digital library. In addition, complete works may be ordered through an authorized reseller by filling out and returning to StudySync® the order form enclosed in this workbook.

Teacher's Edition   **481**

CHAPTERS 8–9: The Beast Inside

KEY PASSAGE | Chapter 8, Paragraphs 340–342

In this passage, the evil apparition called the "Lord of the Flies" speaks to Simon one-on-one in the forest and reveals to him the true nature of the supposed "Beast" on the island. Speaking through the impaled head of the pig the boys hunted and killed, the Lord of the Flies offers his ominous explanation to Simon: that the Beast is not a literal, external threat, but something more elusive that dwells within the souls of each and every one of the boys on the island. After a chilling laugh, the Lord of the Flies tells Simon to return to the other boys and forget their entire encounter.

WHY IT'S KEY

Simon's encounter with the titular *"Lord of the Flies"* is woven into the narrative of Chapter 8, as he leaves the group for a supernatural encounter of sorts in the forest. The *"Lord of the Flies,"* as it were, is the impaled head of a sow that speaks to Simon and delivers to us the most direct explanation of the lesson or moral of the novel—albeit still somewhat obliquely.

Tone: The novel has been building its ominous tone for some time now, but with this scene, it reaches the occult with its most disturbing and frightening image yet: an impaled pig's head, swarming with flies, animated and come to life before Simon. This is the first time in the novel where the narrative has truly entered the paranormal, but it should be noted that there is reason to believe that Simon is hallucinating (his nosebleed seems to suggest that he is epileptic). But the novel's ominous and frightening tone has certainly prepared us for this disturbing episode.

Title: Finally, we understand the significance of the book's title, as *"Lord of the Flies"* refers to this supernatural apparition that Simon sees in the forest. The fact that this is the title is a pretty solid clue that this scene is important. It should also be noted that *"Lord of the Flies"* is the literal translation of the name Beelzebub—in classical mythology, Beelzebub is either a demon or the head demon himself.

Central Idea: "Fancy thinking the Beast was something you could hunt and kill!" the *Lord of the Flies* tells Simon. With this, the lesson or moral of the novel—and its significance as an allegory about civilization and savagery—comes into focus. As the boys have been seized by fear of a "beast" on the island, here comes the *Lord of the Flies* to reveal that this beast is not a literal one but the "beast" that lies inside the hearts of men. There is no actual monster on the island: the boys' capacity for brutality and savagery is what's really haunting the place.

YOUR STUDYSYNC® TV

Discussion Prompt: "Fancy thinking the Beast was something you could hunt and kill!" Simon hears the *Lord of the Flies* say this, implying that the real "Beast" is the evil and savagery inside the hearts of the boys on the island. Do you agree with this diagnosis of the problem? Why or why not? Discuss whether you think the primary threats on the island are "internal" or "external" threats. What part does fear or hysteria play in the origin of the Beast?

Standards: RL.8.1, RL.8.3; SL.8.1.A, SL.8.1.C, SL.8.1.D

VOCABULARY

fervor
fer•vor *noun*
Passion or intensity of feeling
At the political rally for the candidate, her supporters chanted her name with deep fervor.

indignity
in•dig•ni•ty *noun*
Humiliation or shame
Rather than suffer the public indignity of an impeachment trial, Richard Nixon chose to resign from the presidency.

corpulent
cor•pu•lent *adjective*
Overweight or obese
Your dog will soon be corpulent if you keep feeding it table scraps.

derision
de•ri•sion *noun*
Mockery; ridicule; jeers
Most of the fans' derision was directed at the coach for calling the wrong play at the end of the game.

superficial
su•per•fi•cial *adjective*
Affecting or existing at the surface level and no deeper
Eva was relieved that the cut was only superficial, and wouldn't require stitches.

CLOSE READ

QUESTION 1: What does the pig's head—the "Lord of the Flies"—tell Simon? Do its prophecies come true, and if so, how?

Sample Answer: The Lord of the Flies tells Simon that the "Beast" on the island is not what they think it is; rather, it is inside of them. It also tells Simon that the boys are going to "do" him. Both of these prophecies come true. Simon finds that the "Beast" is only the body of a parachutist, and when he returns to the beach, the boys descend upon him and kill him.

Standards: RL.8.1

QUESTION 2: What does Jack tell the boys about Ralph, and why? What are his arguments in opposition of Ralph as chief?

Sample Answer: Jack tells the boys that Ralph insulted the other hunters, is just like Piggy, and was a coward up on the mountain. He says that they shouldn't follow Ralph because he can't hunt and that they don't owe him any allegiance.

Standards: RL.8.1

QUESTION 3: How do the boys respond to Jack's initial calls for Ralph's removal as chief? When does the power shift in Jack's direction, and why?

Sample Answer: No one is willing to raise a hand in favor of Ralph's removal, at first. However, the power begins to shift when Jack and his hunters kill a huge pig and roast it for everyone on the island. Jack has also begun calling himself chief.

Standards: RL.8.1

QUESTION 4: Who is responsible for Simon's death?

Sample Answer: The entire group is responsible, as they take turns attacking him when he appears during their wild dance.

Standards: RL.8.1

COMPARATIVE TEXTS

Text: *The Call of the Wild* by Jack London

Compare to: Chapter 8 of *Lord of the Flies*

Connection: In Jack London's novel *The Call of the Wild*, the sled dog Buck assumes leadership of the pack and stirs up a mood of rebellion. In this lawless atmosphere, wolfish instincts take over in his pursuit of a rabbit. London compares Buck's ecstasy to the elation of the artist and of the soldier in battle. How does it compare with the intense feelings of Jack or Simon in Chapter 8? (Note: See additional Lesson Plan for this text in the StudySync library.)

Text: "The Song of Hiawatha" by Henry Wadsworth Longfellow

Compare to: Chapter 9 of *Lord of the Flies*

Connection: Chapter 9 of *Lord of the Flies* brings the two tribes together after Jack's secession. A feast, which Ralph and Piggy attend, is followed by a frenzied dance, which is followed by the killing of Simon, mistaken for the beast. How does this savage behavior compare with the actions of people who were popularly called "savages"? Published a century before Golding's novel, the poem "The Song of Hiawatha" represents a new view of the "noble savage," seeing in native people an unspoiled model of humanity, more in touch with nature, more dignified, and willing to "bury the hatchet" and make peace.

Please note that excerpts and passages in the StudySync® library, workbooks, and PDFs are intended as touchstones to generate interest in an author's work. The excerpts and passages do not substitute for the reading of entire texts, and StudySync® strongly recommends that teachers and students seek out and purchase the whole literary or informational work in order to experience it as the author intended. Links to online resellers are available in our digital library. In addition, complete works may be ordered through an authorized reseller by filling out and returning to StudySync® the order form enclosed in this workbook.

Teacher's Edition   **485**

CHAPTERS 10–12: Castle Rock

KEY PASSAGE | Chapter 11, Paragraphs 201–209

In this passage, coming moments before the novel's climax, Piggy makes his last effort to quell Jack Merridew and his wild crowd of boys at Castle Rock. He reprimands them and tells them that their behavior is childish, and he lifts the white conch shell, hoping that the power it once held will remind the boys of order and the rule of law. Speaking rhetorically, Piggy presents to the boys the question at the heart of the story: is it better to act like savages, or civilized members of society? He urges them all to return to reason and order—but, against Piggy's protestations, the tribe drowns him out with shouts and clamor. Meanwhile, standing high overhead, Roger leans his weight on a lever, preparing to send a massive boulder plummeting below.

WHY IT'S KEY

Context: This passage from Chapter 11 comes immediately before the story's climactic moment at Castle Rock. Most of the boys on the island have pledged their allegiance to Jack's savage "tribe," and only Ralph and Piggy protest. When Jack and his "hunters" steal Piggy's glasses to make fire, Ralph and Piggy go to confront him armed only with reason and the once-mystical conch shell.

Climax: The entire plot of *Lord of the Flies* has led us to this moment. Soon, something must happen that will have dramatic ramifications among remaining protagonists and antagonists of the story. A novel's climactic moment is the apotheosis, or highest point, of the rising tension and action in the narrative. It is the scene or moment in the story—whether a battle, a revelation, a decision, etc.—whose outcome has the highest stakes for the characters and their situation(s).

Character: Piggy and Ralph emerge as the last voices of reason between the boys and barbaric savagery; Piggy holds the the white conch shell, which returns as a symbol of order and cohesion, although its significance at this point in the narrative is much different. At the beginning of the story, the boys were all in it together. There had been disagreements, but they all shared a common goal. But the setting has done its damage, and by now, the characters have either attempted to resist the impulses for violence and savagery or embraced them entirely.

Structure: In this passage, Piggy presents the central choice at the heart of the narrative: "Which is better—to have rules and reach a consensus, or to hunt and kill?" However, the implicit answer to his question, based on the events that have transpired, is not a positive one. In this manner, *Lord of the Flies* is constructed as an *allegory*—a narrative that serves to express a lesson or message—about man's inherent nature. The novel asks: what choices would a group of young boys make if freed from the "constraints" of civilization and authority? Through the use of allegory, the boys' individual experiences express larger truths about society.

YOUR STUDYSYNC® TV

Discussion Prompt: Piggy presents their dilemma in this passage as a conflict between two moral sides: "To have rules and agree, or to hunt and kill?" Looking back on the novel, do you think this divided outcome was inevitable? If this were to happen on a different island with a different group of characters, do you think the situation would turn out the same? Debate whether *Lord of the Flies* is an illustration of man's inescapable thirst for violence and barbarism—or if the breakdown that occurred was more specific to their circumstances. Be sure to cite examples from this passage and others.

Standards: RL.8.1, RL.8.3; SL.8.1.A, SL.8.1.C, SL.8.1.D

VOCABULARY

conviction
con•vic•tion *noun*
Confidence or certainty in something
The dismissal of all charges against the senator did not shake her conviction that he was somehow involved in the scandal and the subsequent coverup.

luminous
lu•mi•nous *adjective*
Very bright or shining
The surface of the lake appeared luminous as the bright full moon shone down.

truculently
truc•u•lent•ly *adverb*
In a manner demonstrating anger and readiness to pick a fight
He was glad to discuss his latest project, but he scowled truculently when the reporter asked about his personal life.

cessation
ces•sa•tion *noun*
The official or formal ending of something
The signing of the peace agreement led to an immediate cessation of hostilities on both sides.

quiver
quiv•er *verb*
To shiver or tremble
Many guests would quiver in fear as they walked through the dense fog of the haunted corn maze.

tentatively
ten•ta•tive•ly *adverb*
Hesitatingly; apprehensively
I tentatively agreed to go to the party with Marcela, but I was secretly hoping I'd get the measles.

CLOSE READ

QUESTION 1: How do Ralph and Piggy feel about their role in Simon's death? What does this say about their respective states at this point in the story?

Sample Answer: Ralph feels intense guilt about his involvement in Simon's death, whereas Piggy equivocates about the circumstances of the murder and wonders if Simon could still be alive after all. As clever as Piggy is, he is much more in denial than Ralph.

Standards: RL.8.1

QUESTION 2: How is Piggy killed, and whose responsibility is it? What "dies" along with Piggy, and why is this a turning point on the island?

Sample Answer: While Piggy is speaking and imploring the boys to listen to reason and order, Roger pushes on a lever that sends a boulder crashing down, knocking Piggy off the mountain and killing him. With the conch also destroyed, Jack announces that he is now the unquestioned chief.

Standards: RL.8.1

QUESTION 3: How do Sam and Eric treat Ralph when he shows up at Castle Rock? Whose side are they on, and what is the shocking news that they deliver to Ralph?

Sample Answer: Sam and Eric don't tell anyone that Ralph is there, but they urge him to leave at once. They do smuggle him some meat as he leaves, so they are clearly sympathetic to Ralph, but they're unwilling and unable to stand up to the power of Jack and Roger. The shocking news they deliver to Ralph is the news that the hunters are going to come looking for him tomorrow, and that Roger has sharpened a stick at both ends.

Standards: RL.8.1

QUESTION 4: Based on textual evidence in Chapters 11 and 12, how are Jack and Roger similar? How are they different?

Sample Answer: They are both antagonists in the story, but Jack seems to desire power above all, whereas Roger derives more of a delirious joy from violence. Roger activates the lever that kills Piggy, and Sam and Eric believe that Roger is the worse of the two.

Standards: RL.8.1

QUESTION 5: Why do you think the description of the officer "allowing his eyes to rest on the trim cruiser in the distance" serves as the final line of the novel? Explain the potential significance of this image of a military cruiser in the narrative's final resolution.

Sample Answer: Answers may include the irony of the naval officer's disappointment at the boys' savagery contrasted with the image of a military cruiser—a sleeker, more structured delivery of violence. Goldman likely ends his novel with this detail to make a point of how mankind—amidst both civilization and savagery—has an appetite for violence.

Standards: RL.8.1

COMPARATIVE TEXTS

Text: *Leviathan* by Thomas Hobbes

Compare to: Chapters 10–11 of *Lord of the Flies*

Connection: Thomas Hobbes did not have a hopeful view of human relations in his book *Leviathan*. With the dryness of a scientist, he explains how two people with the same desire—and unwilling to share—become enemies. Fueled by competition, self-defense, and dreams of glory, hostility becomes a state of war, in which "every man is enemy to every man" and life is "nasty, brutish, and short." It might well be a blueprint for the eruption of violence between camps in Chapters 10 and 11 of *Lord of the Flies*.

Text: *First Contact: New Guinea's Highlanders Encounter the Outside World* by Bob Connolly and Robin Anderson

Compare to: Chapter 12 of *Lord of the Flies*

Connection: Hunted by savages, Ralph abruptly encounters a visitor from the civilized world he once belonged to, but which now seems surreally out of context. A different clash of cultures—described in *First Contact*— occurred in the unexplored highlands of the island of New Guinea in 1930, when gold prospectors from Australia encountered native New Guineans who had never before made contact with the outside world.

Text: *A Long Way Gone: Memoirs of a Boy Soldier* by Ishmael Beah

Compare to: Chapter 12 of *Lord of the Flies*

Connection: In the passage from *A Long Way Gone: Memoirs of a Boy Soldier,* Ishmael Beah recalls the end of one stage of his life and the beginning of another. War is in the background, still far enough removed to allow him time with his grandmother, time to buy groundnuts from a street vendor, time to have a push-up competition with his friends. Then the rebels close in, school is canceled, people panic, friends separate, and Ishmael sees murder up close: the war is about to steal his childhood. Similarly, the boys in *Lord of the Flies* go through a loss of innocence in the stress of survival and the environment of savagery and war.

WRITE TO REVISIT

CREATIVE WRITING

Prompt: Put yourself in the place of the naval officer who arrives in the midst of the brutal pursuit of Ralph. Knowing what he knows about the global war, the downed plane, and now the boys' descent into chaos and violence, write a 400- to 500-word reaction of the officer in the form of *one* of the following: a letter to a friend; a journal entry; a newspaper interview; or an official report to his commanding officer. The extent of his emotional response or his philosophical conclusions is up to you. The composition should represent the officer's character and should cover the content of what he knows.

Standards: RL.8.1; W.8.3.A, W.8.3.B, W.8.3.C, W.8.3.D, W.8.3.E, W.8.4, W.8.5

PERSUASIVE WRITING

Prompt: Many characters play a vital role in *Lord of the Flies*. Write a persuasive essay, making a case for the character or characters who have the biggest impact on the novel. Your essay should consider many options leading up to your final decision and should bring in as many themes from supplementary readings as seem relevant. For example, which character or characters are connected to the theme of the beast? The theme of aggression? The "ecstasy" of the artist and soldier? Keeping your head about you while others are losing theirs? Surviving? Your final decision may be a single character, or it may be a pair of equal importance in their interaction. The choice must be supported with ample evidence from a minimum of four texts in addition to *Lord of the Flies*. So—get ready for your closeups, Jack, Ralph, Simon, Roger, and Piggy! You too, littluns!

Standards: RL.8.1, RL.8.2, RL.8.3; RI.8.1, RI.8.2, RI.8.3; W.8.1.A, W.8.1.B, W.8.1.C, W.8.1.E, W.8.4, W.8.5, W.8.9.A

PHOTO/IMAGE CREDITS:

Cover, ©iStock.com/CostinT, ©iStock.com/alexsl, ©iStock.com/GiuseppeParisi
p. iii, ©iStock.com/GiuseppeParisi, ©iStock.com/zabelin, ©iStock.com/Pgiam, ©iStock.com/gkuchera
p. v, Apic/contributor/Getty Images, ©iStock.com/gaiamoments, ©iStock.com/kertlis, ©iStock.com/ABDESIGN,
©iStock.com/technotr, ©iStock.com/poco_bw, ©iStock.com/Leonsbox, ©iStock.com/alexey_boldin
p. vi, ©iStock.com/skegbydave, ©iStock.com/alexey_boldin, ©iStock.com, ©iStock.com/Massonstock,
©iStock.com/RMAX, ©iStock.comprudkov, fair use, ©iStock.com/szefei, ©iStock.com/ gaiamoments,
©iStock.com/technotr ©iStock.com/Marilyn Nieves, ©iStock.com/welcome-to-carol-world,
©iStock.com/adisa, Yale Joel/Yale Joel/Getty Images, ©iStock.com/StephenSewell, Archive Photos/Archive
Photos, ©iStock.com/DNY59, ©iStock.com/dblight
p. vii, Hero Images/Getty Images
p. ix, Apic/contributor/Getty Images
p. x, ©iStock.com/alexey_boldin, ©iStock.com
p. xii, ©iStock.com/simarik, ©iStock.com/mrcmos, ©iStock.com/ Vimvertigo ©iStock.com/blackred, ©iStock.
com/Brainsil, ©iStock.com/Delpixart, ©iStock.com/SaraWinter
p. xiii, ©iStock.com/MoreISO, ©iStock.com/bizoo_n, ©iStock.com/dtokar, ©iStock.com/gkuchera
p. xv, ©iStock.com/gkuchera
p. xvii, ©iStock.com/dtokar, ©iStock.com/Bunyos, ©iStock.com/ThomasVogel
p. xviii, ©iStock.com/Kamchatka, ©iStock.com/moevin
p. xix, ©iStock.com/bizoo_n
p. xxi, ©iStock.com/DNY59
p. xxiii, ©iStock.com/kemie, ©iStock.com/belchonock, ©iStock.com/melissasanger, ©iStock.com/ErikaMitchell
p. xxiv, ©iStock.com/Toa55, ©iStock.com/sturti, ©iStock.com/IzabelaHabur, Stephen F. Somerstein/Getty
Images
p. xxv, ©iStock.com/TuomasKujansuu
p. xxvi, ©iStock.com/Caval, ©iStock.com/kamonlai, ©iStock.com/ImagineGolf
p. xxvii, ©iStock.com/GeorgePeters, ©iStock.com/Aleksander, ©iStock.com/duncan1890,
©iStock.com/aniszewski, ©iStock.com/ExcellentPhoto, WIN MCNAMEE/Getty Images
p. xxviii, ©iStock.com/PhotoZidaric, ©iStock.com/neoblues, ©iStock.com/DaveAlan,
©iStock.com/stockstudioX
p. xxix, ©iStock.com/makosh, ©iStock.com/m-imagephotography, ©iStock.com/sam74100
p. 1, ©iStock.com/MoreISO, ©iStock.com/GiuseppeParisi, ©iStock.com/alexey_boldin,
©iStock.com/ skegbydave
p. 2, ©iStock.com/MoreISO

Text Fulfillment
Through StudySync

If you are interested in specific titles, please fill out the for
below and we will check availability through our partner

ORDER DETAILS

Date:

TITLE	AUTHOR	Paperback/ Hardcover	Specific Edition *If Applicable*	Quantity

SHIPPING INFORMATION

Contact:

Title:

School/District:

Address Line 1:

Address Line 2:

Zip or Postal Code:

Phone:

Mobile:

Email:

BILLING INFORMATION ☐ *SAME AS SHIPPING*

Contact:

Title:

School/District:

Address Line 1:

Address Line 2:

Zip or Postal Code:

Phone:

Mobile:

Email:

PAYMENT INFORMATION

☐ CREDIT CARD

Name on Card:

Card Number: Expiration Date: Security Code:

☐ PO

Purchase Order Number:

StudySync Text Fulfillment, BookheadEd Learning, LLC
610 Daniel Young Drive | Sonoma, CA 95476